当代国外语言学与应用语言学文库（升级版）

语用学引论

第二版

Pragmatics: An Introduction (Second Edition)

［丹麦］Jacob L. Mey 著

徐盛桓 导读

外语教学与研究出版社
FOREIGN LANGUAGE TEACHING AND RESEARCH PRESS
北京 BEIJING

WILEY

京权图字：01-2023-0304

图书在版编目 (CIP) 数据

语用学引论：第二版 = Pragmatics: An Introduction (Second Edition)：英文 / （丹）雅各布·L. 梅伊（Jacob L. Mey）著；徐盛桓导读. -- 北京：外语教学与研究出版社，2023.3
（当代国外语言学与应用语言学文库：升级版）
ISBN 978-7-5213-4321-2

I. ①语… II. ①雅… ②徐… III. ①语用学 - 研究 - 英文 IV. ①H030

中国国家版本馆 CIP 数据核字 (2023) 第 041940 号

出 版 人　王　芳
项目负责　姚　虹　李亚琦
责任编辑　徐　宁
责任校对　宋锦霞
装帧设计　李　高
出版发行　外语教学与研究出版社
社　　址　北京市西三环北路 19 号（100089）
网　　址　https://www.fltrp.com
印　　刷　唐山市润丰印务有限公司
开　　本　650×980　1/16
印　　张　27
版　　次　2023 年 3 月第 1 版　2023 年 3 月第 1 次印刷
书　　号　ISBN 978-7-5213-4321-2
定　　价　67.00 元

如有图书采购需求，图书内容或印刷装订等问题，侵权、盗版书籍等线索，请拨打以下电话或关注官方服务号：
客服电话：400 898 7008
官方服务号：微信搜索并关注公众号"外研社官方服务号"
外研社购书网址：https://fltrp.tmall.com

物料号：343210001

记载人类文明
沟通世界文化
www.fltrp.com

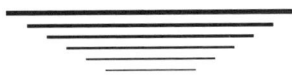

当代国外语言学与应用语言学文库

（升级版）

学术委员会

（按姓氏拼音排列）

出版前言

"当代国外语言学与应用语言学文库"（以下简称"文库"）从2000年至今已出版近200个品种，深受语言学与应用语言学专业师生和研究者的欢迎，大家既把"文库"视为进入语言学与应用语言学百花园的引路人，又把"文库"视为知识更新的源泉，还把"文库"当成点亮科研之路的明灯。

为了追踪相关领域的研究进程，并满足广大读者的需求，外语教学与研究出版社从2020年开始启动了"文库"的更新升级工作，与牛津大学出版社、剑桥大学出版社、劳特利奇出版社等世界知名出版机构合作，推出"文库"（升级版）。

"文库"升级的原则如下：

1. 对原有经典图书，若无新版，则予以保留，并予以必要修订；若有新版，则以新版代替旧版，并请相关领域学者撰写新版中文导读。

2. 引进语言学与应用语言学领域的新锐力作，进一步拓展学科领域。

3. 用二维码代替CD-ROM，帮助读者更加快捷地获取内容。

"文库"（升级版）定位为一套大型的、开放性的系列丛书，希望它能对我国语言学教学与研究和外语教学与研究起到积极的推动作用。外语教学与研究出版社亦将继续努力，力争把国外最新、最具影响力的语言学与应用语言学著作奉献给广大读者。

外语教学与研究出版社

2021年8月

导 读^①

徐盛桓

1. 引言：欧洲大陆的语用学研究

本书作者梅伊（Jacob L. Mey），丹麦人。他的这本语用学著作较多地反映了欧洲大陆语用学研究不同于英美研究的传统。

二十世纪六七十年代，英美语言哲学家、语言学家筚路蓝缕，开启了"语用学"这块语言学研究的"山林"，以言语行为理论和会话含意理论为两大理论支柱，终于将语用学从概念发展为语言学的一个分支学科。八十年代，C. C. Levinson和G. Leech的《语用学》和《语用学原理》分别出版，使语用学的学科理论体系得以确立。

几乎与此同时，欧洲大陆的语言学家在欧洲大陆语言学研究传统的基础上，也为语用学的建立和发展作出了贡献。1977年，本书作者梅伊同H. Haberland一道在丹麦创办了《语用学杂志》

---

① 牛保义、王振华、李淑静为本文的撰写与修订提出过不少有益的意见、建议和问题，谨表谢忱。

（*Journal of Pragmatics*），这多少传递了欧洲大陆语用学研究活跃程度的一些信息。1988年，在各国语用学家的推动下，"国际语用学会"（International Pragmatics Association）成立，总部设在比利时。一般认为，《语用学杂志》的创办、Levinson的《语用学》的出版、"国际语用学会"的成立，是标志着语用学已成为语言学研究的一个分支学科的三个主要事件。在这三个事件中，两件大事发生在欧洲大陆。七次国际语用学大会中有五次是在欧洲大陆各国举行的：1985年在意大利的维亚雷焦；1987年在比利时的安特卫普；1990年在西班牙的巴塞罗那；1998年在法国的兰斯；2000年在匈牙利的布达佩斯（另两次分别是在日本和墨西哥）。1991年国际语用学会在比利时创办了学术季刊《语用学》（*Pragmatics*）。这些都显示了欧洲大陆语用学研究的活力和实力。欧洲大陆语用学研究建基于欧洲大陆语言学研究的传统之上，形成了自己语用学研究的路向；出版的一些论著，常常给人以耳目一新的感觉。其中，梅伊的这本《语用学引论》和J. Verschueren的《语用学探究》（*Understanding Pragmatics*）产生了较大的学术影响。

2. 本书的写作、出版

梅伊，南丹麦大学（奥登塞校区）语言学终身名誉教授，现仍任他参与创办的《语用学杂志》主编。他编辑出版的《语用学简明百科》（*Concise Encyclopedia of Pragmatics*）是语用学研究的一本重要工具书。

本书初版于1993年，后经六次重印。现我国获得版权出版的是作者于2001年经大幅修订后推出的第二版。

梅伊在初版的"前言"中谈到了本书的写作经过。1989年，他在丹麦的大学给一年级研究生开设"语用学"课。这些研究生修的专业分别是哲学、历史学、经济学和现代语言课程，原来不一定了解很多语言学的基础理论和基本知识。梅伊感到，当时能得到的教材内容太多，不大合适他们教学的需要，于是决定边教边编写教材，即写出每周上课的讲课撮要。以后在反复使用中不断修订、充实，成为本书的初版。本书最初的使用对象是人文科学和社会科学多学科的学生，这一点对本书的结构和内容不无影响。同时，由于本书在很大程度上是由课堂讲课的讲稿加工而来，行文风格有点像饱学的智者对学生娓娓而谈，旁征博引、细细分析，以引导思考，而少作结论；不像有些教科书以严谨的论证结构来强化教材的观点。此外，不少章节最后会提出思考性的问题以同新的章节联系，就像教师讲课在下课前会留下一些问题以便引起对下一节课内容的期待与思考一样。这些都请读者在阅读本书时多加注意。从1989年起，经过多次使用——在这期间作者还到过多个国家的大学进行研究、教学和交流——考虑了同行、学生的反馈意见和批评建议，作者对本书作了大量的修订。据梅伊说，第二版同第一版相比，有一半是新写的，其余部分大都作了修改。

3. 本书的结构特点

本书的结构和内容明显地表现了梅伊不同于英美语用学研究传统的思路和取向。

语用学研究，如果不算C. Morris在二十世纪三十年代将"语用学"作为一个概念提出来，最初是由英国日常语言学派学者从关于日常语言的使用是否只关注语言的真值的研究发展起来的。当时，这些学者花了很大的气力来研究说话者的"意图"（intention）和自然意义与非自然意义的区分（Grice，1957），着手推翻真值条件是语言理解的核心这一逻辑实证主义的观点（Levinson，1983）。这样开始的语用学研究，很自然就会专注于语言运用者是如何表达或领会在言谈中的"意图"的。因此，传统的语用学研究将指示语、言语行为、会话含意理论、预设以及会话结构等作为语用学研究的基本内容毫不奇怪，因为这些方面的研究都直接或间接地同话语意图的推导有关。这几个专题，就构成了Levinson的《语用学》及其后相当一部分语用学教科书的基本内容，并成为受这一传统影响的语用学研究的主要课题。

欧洲大陆的语言学研究有深厚的根基和鲜明的特色，近几十年就先后出现过对语言学研究有深远影响的法兰西学派、布拉格学派、哥本哈根学派等，这些学派的代表人物如A. Meillet、J. Vendryes、R. Jakobson、L. Hjeimslev等都十分强调语言的社会功能，认为语言同社会、文化、环境等密不可分，形成了语言学研究的"社会学学派"、"功能学派"等。梅伊作为欧洲大陆的语言学家，在语用学研究中传承了这一传统，表现出他的广义的语用学意识。他的语用学研究包括微观语用学、宏观语用学、元语用学。对于什么是微观/宏观/元语用学，并没有一个统一的定论。从书中安排的内容来看，梅伊所指的微观语用学，是围绕着对语言符号在言谈交际中的指称和意义中的"意图"的理解而展开的语用学课题的讨论，例如语境、含意、言语行为、指称和指示语等，另外还包括了会话结构的分析，这大体是从话语运用的层次来研究。宏观语用学讨论的是社会−文化层面对语言运用者言语运用的宏观调控中所体现的语用问题。元语用学是对语用学研究自身的考察、审视和反思，它是对语用学研究中方法论和理论体系建构问题的思考，如对语用学理论、语用规则、语用原则、语用限制等作理论上的反思。

根据这样广义的语用学意识，作者为本书安排了一个"总−分"的结构：第一部分讨论"基本概念"，特别是对"语用学"作出界定，为全书各专题的讨论从语用观的角度提供一个认识框架，这是"总"。以下是"分"：第二部分关于"微观语用学"，共四章（第三章至第六章），分别讨论含意和同含意有关的"语用原则"、言语行为理论和会话结构；第三部分考察语用学在宏观层次上的研究。在讨论宏观语用学的一些具体课题之前，作者安排了一章专门阐释"元语用学"所涉及的问题（第七章），作为对宏观语用学问题展开研究时的方法论观点。这一点值得注意。当我们进行宏观语用学的研究时，要注意对研究进行审察和反思，使研究不致太泛化，失去语用学的品格、特性和自身价值。"宏观语用学"的讨论包括：语用行为；文学作品所涉及的语用学问题；跨文化活动所涉及的语用学问题；同社会生活密切相关的某些方面如教育、传媒、性别、医患关系、权势等甚至"社会斗争"所涉及的语用学问题。

　　全书开头有"前言"，说明了再版修订的过程；书末有参考文献、注释、主题和人名索引。"注释"常常是作者用以澄清某些含混、误解或用以对某些相关的地方作出的说明，国外学者写论著时对这方面十分注意，建议读者不要忽略。还要特别一提的是本书每一章后面都有"复习和讨论"，少的有三四页，多的有八到十页，值得本书的使用者好好运用。本书初版时，这部分称作"练习与复习问题"。再版时不称作"练习"，也许是作者想强调读者的灵活思考和处理，因为作者认为，为语用学的问题提供一个简单的答案对教与学都没有好处，而且往往不会有一个标准答案。作者为每一个问题都提供详细的语境和背景的说明；为许多问题提供了"提示"；有时还为问题提供一个"解决参照"（model solution），让读者看到其中一种可能的解决办法。总的精神是：不无方法，不求定法。全书有不少有趣而又有启发性的例子，读者可细细玩味。

4. "基本概念"和"微观语用学"

　　第一部分的第一、二章阐释一些基本概念，如定义、语言运用者等。

梅伊认为，二十世纪六七十年代之交，G. Lakoff 和 J. Ross 等从生成语言学分离出来，N. Chomsky 的"唯句法研究"（syntax-only approach）"分崩离析"（collapse），这促成了早期对语言进行语用学研究的最初尝试。Chomsky 的学派是否已"分崩离析"，读者从当代语言学研究的发展不难自行作出判断；但从那时起，研究句法外的因素在"语言规则"方面起的作用，的确吸引了越来越多的研究者，语言学家越来越深刻地认识到，语境和语言使用者对话语意义的确定起决定性作用。语言研究的"转向语用学"（pragmatic turn）是从语法理论，特别是句法理论研究范式转向研究语言运用者的范式。"语言运用者视点"是确立语用学研究取向的最为重要的一点。作者在这一讨论的基础上提出了他所界定的较为宽泛的语用学定义："语用学研究由社会各种条件所决定的人类交际中的语言使用"。作者还说明，这里的"社会条件"主要指社会制度性的内容（society's institutions），而不光是指社会环境，这一点请读者给予注意。

关于语用学的用处，梅伊列了许多语用学可以派上用场的场合后指出：我们之所以需要语用学，从理论上说，是因为它可以对人类的言语行为提供更充分、更深刻、更合理的解释；从实用上说，有些语言现象只有通过语用学的分析才能说明问题。

在第二章第一节，作者以语用学家的睿智与宽容，将对语用学的揶揄之词"废纸箱"，化解为对语用学研究的包容性与辐射性的说明。在以后的几个小节，梅伊从语言学研究存在的一些"灰色地带"、句子的真值判断在日常语言中所遇到的困难、句法规则有时在日常语言中的窘境、语言运用者所处的不同"世界"（worlds of users）等方面，进一步说明了什么是语用学和语用学在语言学研究中的学术品格。

第二部分具体讨论"微观语用学"，共四章（第三、四、五、六章），讨论日常交际言语所涉及的一些重要的语用学问题。作者强调，语境是一个动态的概念，是交际者在言谈交际时不断变动着的环境；交际者在这样的环境里进行言谈交际，并在这样的环境中获得对交际言语的理解。同时，语境是以语言使用者为指向的，不同的人对同样的语境感受会不同。语言是规约性的，语言是在社会语境中形成的。语言运用者运用的是具有社会规约的语言表达形式，语境决定了语言的运用。作者认为：会话含意是隐含在会话里的意思。语用学之所以对含意研究有兴趣，那是因为这种语言现象是句法或语义的"规则"所无法应付，而专门要由语用原则来解释的。"含意"译自 implicature。Implicature 和 implication 均来自动词 imply，但在逻辑学里 implication 是一个专门术语，意为"蕴涵"；而 implicature 表示言语运用中语用推理所得到的含意，二者不是一回事。话语表达通常体现为会话；在会话中进行语用推理得到的含意叫会话含意。会话含意的推导要依赖语境。此外还有"规约含意"；规约含意的推导不必依赖独特语境。

梅伊在第四章里讨论和比较了几个语用原则。首先，梅伊提出一个"交际原则"："人们交谈的目的是要向对方传递一定的内容"。他认为这一原则是人们在交际中必定要遵循的，是一切言谈交际默认的前提。梅伊正是以此作为语用行为研究的前提。

许多语用学教科书对"合作原则"的论述通常是讨论会话含意的分类、性质，对四项准则的遵守或违反会得出什么含意等等，以此作为对含意理解机制的解释。本书则从"交际原则"所阐述的言谈交际的根本要求出发，对"合作原则"的"合作"作出阐释。他认为，会话的目的是要实现交际，要尽量被正确理解，不被误解。这样，交际就要在交际双方共同认定的语境下进行，谈什么决定于在一定的语境下可以说什么和根据对方的期望必须说什么，这就是"合作"。不合作，"交际将非常困难，甚至失败"。学术论战、家庭争吵，甚至说羞辱他人的话，都需要对方一点点的"合作"，因为至少对方要明白说话人为什么说这样的话语。据此，梅伊认为"合作"是一条具有独立地位的语用原则。梅伊还对荷恩（L. R. Horn）的两原则（Q（量）原则和R（关系）原则）和D. Sperber、D. Wilson提出的"关联原则"进行了评论。荷恩的"两原则"作为新格赖斯语用推导机制，梅伊认为包括了格赖斯"合作原则"的量原则下的两分则，并涉及格氏的方式准则和关系准则，可简明地解释一系列的言语现象，是对简化语用原则的有价值的尝试。梅伊认为"关联原则"是"交际原则"的变体，也是"合作原则"的专门化（specification）；交际者之间能合作，"就能知道在话语里隐含了什么、没有隐含什么，从而知道在什么时候和如何从中作出正确的推导"。"关联原则"又是交际理论的最简理论，因为这里只有一条原则，而且这一原则并不要求人们刻意"遵循"，甚至想违反也违反不了，应用（apply）这一原则是没有例外的，这一原则可用于解释一切过去归于其他原（准）则解释的现象。但是，梅伊认为，"关联"成为一个如此无所不包（all-encompassing）的概念，会因而失去它的解释力。梅伊同时还批评了"关联理论"没有考虑语言运用的社会维度。

第五章讨论言语行为理论。梅伊将言语行为放在语用行为的层面来讨论。梅伊首先系统地说明了J. Austin和J. K. Searle提出、发展和完善言语行为理论的过程，分析了Austin对施为句（performatives）和陈述句（constatives）的区分，并较详细地叙述了Searle间接言语行为的观点和五种言外行为的分类。梅伊认为，尽管我们可以发现言语行为理论特别是Austin前期的研究有不少不足之处，如Austin关于言语行为的界定太泛、他们两人的研究基本上局限在一个例句一个案例的做法上等，但Austin关于"言"可以"有所为"这一发现的意义是不会随时间的消逝而消逝的。还有一点值得注意的是，梅伊为间接言语行为列举了两种理论的解释：推理说和语用行为说。"推理说"认为，间接言语行为包括两个行为：次要的言语行为——作出一个言语表达和基本的言语行为——表示实际的言外之力，而基本的言语行为要通过次要的言语行为实施类似于含意的推导来实现。"语用行为说"则认为，在一定语境下被运用的所谓"间接"言语行为，在该语境下其实是最"直接"的表达方式，因为社会生活的诸方面都会在语言中得到反映，即人们的信念、共识、习惯等会通过语言实现"编码"，成为"社会事实的语言结构式"（linguistic construction of social facts），成为该语境下最恰当的语用行为；这"间接"的言语行为要比"直接"的言语行为有效得多，这是间接言语行为运用的深层原因。

第六章研究会话分析。梅伊指出，语用学研究会话分析，是因为会话是语言运用的"原型"。人们运用语言不是用一个单词、一个句子，最常见的方式是若干人一起说话，这就是"会话"。会话体现了多种多样的言语行为，包括大量的间接言语行为。梅伊介绍了 H. Sacks、G. Jefferson、E. Schegloff 等所提出的会话分析的基本构架和方法。梅伊认为，会话分析包括形式和内容两方面。从形式来分析，梅伊介绍了诸如话轮、轮接、过渡关联处等概念。从内容来分析，梅伊着重讨论了相邻对、偏好话语组织结构等的作用。此外，作者还分析了衔接与连贯在会话中的表现。梅伊认为，对相邻对类型的判断并不容易，要结合语境来判断。

5. 关于"元语用学"和"宏观语用学"

本书用一半的篇幅对宏观语用学进行论述，这是梅伊这本语用学专著的一大特色。

第七章讨论元语用学。在科学研究中，"元××学"指的是对"××学"进行反思、分析、研究之"学"。"元语言学"是对对象语言学作出分析、研究之"学"；同样，"元语用学"是对语用学的研究进行审视、反思、研究之"学"，通俗地说，就是对语用学研究的研究。一个学科的"元"研究的建立，既是这一学科成熟的标志，也是这一学科成熟后期待进一步发展的需要。元语用学的研究也是这样。元语用学要反思语用学研究的范围、对象、目标、任务、方法、理论框架、观点等，正如梅伊所说，"在高一级的层面对对象语用学进行研究"，分析我们界定和研究语用学的思路、讨论为什么这一定义优于另一定义、甚至研究该不该把诸如"会话分析"之类的课题纳入语用学等等，审视既往、发展未来。任何人进行语用学的创新研究都必然自觉或不自觉、有形或无形地先进行元语用学思考，对上面提到的诸方面进行审视，作出扬弃。梅伊在这里对元语用学作出专论，就是要提醒研究者提高自觉意识，并为这种反思研究建立可取的研究框架，使元语用学研究更为规范化。梅伊叙述了元语用研究的三种取向：（一）建构语用学的元理论，使语用学研究在研究范畴和方法论上得到理论上的指导，不致泯灭自身的学科地位和学科品格；（二）研究各种语用限制使用的条件；（三）"指示语式"的研究。指示语的运用可以使我们得以确定话语中的所指，"指示语式"的研究就是将话语看成是隐藏着一些看不见的"指示语"的，即话语有可能隐性地透露出说话者是什么人、是在什么环境下说的等等。

第八章研究语用行为。梅伊将语用行为定义为语境化的适应性交际活动，认为言语行为以及一切使自己适应语境或使语境适应自己的交际性活动，都可概括为语用行为。这些活动包括言语行为、间接言语行为、会话行为、表征感情的外露行为等，甚至"静默"也可以是一种语用行为。言语行为总是发生在一定的情景之中，通常表现为某一类制度化了的社会活动，如教学、邀请、看医生、参加茶会等，这些场合可称为言语事件。在言语事件里，言语的运用是预先已有设定的。因此，梅伊认为个别言语行为只有在言语事件里才有意义。每个这样的具体场合，梅伊称为"具体的语用行为"。把言语行为以及一切语境化了的交际活动概括为语用行为，可能具有值得重视的理论蕴涵，它将语用学对人们的言语行为以及其他言语交际活动的考察纳入人类的社会行为之中来考察，使语用学对言语活动的研究具有更加深刻的社会性。

第九章、第十一章将语用学的研究扩展到文学活动以及社会各方面，即研究"文学语用学"和研究"语用学在社会各方面的运用"。这是"语用行为"理论的必然延伸。在第八章讨论"语用行为"时，梅伊曾提到像教学、看病等情景下的言语活动都是语用行为；在第九章谈到文学作品时也明确认定，文学作品的阅读也是一种语用行为。可以说，"语用行为"理论是梅伊的宏观语用学的理论基础。

梅伊认为，在文学作品阅读中，读者、作者以及可能包含在作品中显性或隐性存在的叙述者，都是语言运用者。文学活动的语用学研究的重点，是研究文学作品意义产生的辩证过程：文学作品是读者同作者共同创造的，作品文本既是作者取向（author-oriented）的，同时也要以读者为取向（reader-oriented），只不过是由作者作指引（author-guided），而由读者驱动（reader-activated）的。读者通过填充文本留下的空白，参与作者对故事的创造；读者对文本的理解并不完全依赖于文本说了多少，而是主要依赖文本所提供的语境。梅伊还移植了叙事学的一些分析手段来构建文学作品文本分析的机制。

在谈到语用学在社会各方面的运用时，梅伊首先说明，语用学理论同对语用敏感的语言现象的关系，就像"纯"语言学同应用语言学的关系。正如要消除"纯"语言学同应用语言学的分离现象一样，研究语用学在社会各方面的运用就是要消除语用学理论自身同这一学科的理论在社会各方面运用之间的隔阂。为什么需要语用学？梅伊认为，这是因为语用学表现了社会对语言需要的程度和语言与社会的相互作用。研究语用学在社会各方面的运用，必须把握住"语言运用者"这一基本概念，如在这一语境中的语言运用者是谁、语言运用者所面临的语言运用条件是什么，以及语言运用者所获得的语言运用条件对语言运用者的影响又是什么等。梅伊具体讨论了教育考试（如 GRE）的语言、传媒语言、医患语言、性别语言、语言歧视等。他从"语言运用者"这一角度出发分析了西方国家在这些方面的语言运用情况，认为存在着语言运用的权力不平衡现象。梅伊还进一步谈到"语用学与社会斗争"问题，认为语用学在社会各方面的运用虽然可以表现为多方面的问题，但有一点是共同的，即都集中在"是谁的语言"这个问题上。语用学要帮助人们认识语言运用权力不平衡现象，认识"语言歧视"现象，并努力去结束这种状况。梅伊认为，在语言运用权力不平衡的情况下，人们在会话中的自由度是不大的；语用学研究就是要争取加大这一自由度。所以，在梅伊看来，言语行为的研究不能满足于研究其分类及各种合适条件，而是要进一步研究在这样的条件下可以怎样做和如何做得更好。

第十章讨论跨文化中的语用学问题。梅伊强调，一定的表达形式的社会合适性总是密切结合特定语境的；文化不同、语言不同，语境也会不同。因此，言语行为总是依赖于一定文化的。不同文化所提供的语用预设（"文化预设"）常会造成理解失误。作者举了这方面的许多现象，包括"默言不语"的运用。但这一问题的讨论似乎缺少理论形态的说明。

总的来说，本书的宏观语用学研究给我们勾勒了该类研究的广阔领域和诱人前景。梅伊着重讨论了宏观语用研究的重要性、必要性和重大价值以及研究可涉及的方面。在讨论中，梅伊总是不忘将宏观语用学的研究回归到他给语用学下的定义，使读者信服这里所讨论的宏观语用学的确应该是语用学研究的一部分。但同微观语用学的讨论相比，似乎缺少像微观语用学研究那样的理论体系和具体的分析框架。这可能是因为书中微观语用学所谈论的问题都是近三四十年来几代语用学家深入探讨过的。唯其是这样，梅伊所讨论的宏观语用学仍然给我们开辟了理论发展的巨大空间并提供了深入研究的重大课题。

参考文献

Austin, John L., 1962. *How To Do Things With Word* [M]. Oxford: Oxford University Press.

Caffi, C., 1994. Metapragmatics (A). In *Encyclopedia of Language and Literature*. Oxford: Pergamon.

Grice, Paul H., 1975. Logic and conversation (A). In Peter Cole and Jerry Morgan (eds.), *Syntax and Semantics*, Vol. 3: *Speech Acts*. New York: Academic Press.

Haberland, H. and J. L. Mey, 1977. Editorial: Pragmatics and linguistics (A). *Journal of Pragmatics*. Vol. 1, 1.

Horn, L. R., 1984. Toward a new taxonomy for pragmatic inference: Q-based and R-based implicative (A). In Deborah Schiffrin (ed.), *Georgetown Round Table on Language and Linguistics*. Washington D. C.: Georgetown University Press.

Levinson, S. C., 1983. *Pragmatics* (M). Cambridge: Cambridge University Press.

Sacks, H., E. Schegloff and G. Jefferson, 1974. A simplest systematics for the organization of turn-taking in conversation (A). *Language*, Vol. 50, 4.

Searle, J. R., 1975. Indirect speech acts (A). In Peter Cole and Jerry Morgan (eds.), *Syntax and Semantics*, Vol. 3: *Speech Acts*. New York: Academic Press.

Searle, J. R., 1979. The classification of illocutionary acts (A). *Language in Society*, 8.

Sperber, D. and D. Wilson, 1995. *Relevance: Communication and cognition* (2nd ed.) (M). Cambridge, MA: Harvard University Press.

Verschueren, Jef, 1999. *Understanding Pragmatics* (M). London: Arnold.

Contents

Contents

Preface

to the second, entirely revised and greatly enlarged edition

The past few years have seen a proliferation of textbooks in pragmatics: four or five have come out, and more are waiting in the wings. Hence, doing a second edition of a book that first appeared more than seven years ago places a clear demand on the author to convince the readership of the necessity of such a new edition.

This new edition differs in substantial ways from the first. For one thing, roughly half of the book is entirely new, while the rest has been thoroughly revised; not a sentence or paragraph has been spared. Some of my critics had half-jokingly accused me of bringing 'skeletons out of the closet' that better would have been left inside. This was said to be especially the case for the three chapters (6, 7 and 8) on speech acts, which now have been shortened and consolidated into one substantial chapter (5), in which all the various facets of speech acting are highlighted. Similarly, with regard to conversation analysis, others had remarked that with the wealth of literature on CA that is readily available, there was no need for a pragmatics textbook to delve into too many technical details. Consequently, the new chapter 6 replaces the former chapters 10, 11 and 12 and concentrates on the basic notions of conversation analysis; for the finer points, the readers are referred to other sources.

As to the new material that has been brought in, this is mainly to be found in chapters 7 through 11 (plus in a number of major and minor rewritings throughout the book). Chapter 7 extends the discussion of metapragmatic phenomena to the phenomena often referred to, in the US anthropological-pragmatic tradition, by the term 'indexing'. In chapter 8, the theory of pragmatic acts (which had been embryonically present throughout the earlier edition) now has been given a full-fledged treatment. The new chapter 9 on literary pragmatics incorporates, in condensed form, insights that have been developed more fully in my 1999 book *When Voices Clash*, whereas chapter 10 (which also is entirely new) treats of the intercultural differences that make pragmatics at the same time interesting and intractable. Finally, chapter 11, now called 'Social Aspects of Pragmatics', is double the size of the old chapter 14, and (among other things) covers recent research in the rapidly evolving 'critical' orientation. To this, let me add the following comment.

A number of users of the book had expressed their disappointment at what they experienced as the rather meager contents of the earlier chapter on 'Societal Pragmatics'. One critic explicitly stated that, since I was known as a proponent of the societal importance of linguistics, one would expect a more outspoken stance when it came to discussing 'real' issues and the importance of putting pragmatics to work in 'real-life' contexts. Upon reading this, I couldn't help being reminded of the words of the American critic Richard Schickel, who once remarked (in his review of the 1971 book by David Cooper, *The Death of the Family*, where he also indirectly criticized the work of the famous British anti-psychiatrist R.D. Laing) that:

> the weakest part of any social criticism is likely to be that thin last chapter in which the author finally addresses himself to proposals for reformation of the present practices he has just finished brilliantly devastating. As a rule, this material tends to be something of a letdown – either pragmatically paltry or improbably visionary, and so it has become the custom among our grander gurus to go gnomic (if not positively Delphic) at this moment of truth. (Schickel 1971:104)

Even without counting myself among the gurus (let alone the grander ones), I think that Schickel's caustic innuendoes may have some bearing on the way I treated societal pragmatic matters in the first edition of my book. This second edition has furnished me with a welcome opportunity to be explicit, rather than 'gnomic' or 'Delphic', and thus work in a visionary perspective without being 'improbable', as well as strive for a pragmatic realization that is not 'paltry'.

In this connection, I have paid a fair amount of attention to work done by people in the 'critical linguistic' tradition, a direction of research which I consider eminently pragmatic, inasmuch as it incorporates an explicit stance towards the users of language and their resources as members of the language community. Norman Fairclough and his 'Lancaster School' loom large here; I could also (and indeed, have occasionally) refer(red) to my own earlier work in this area, especially the themes I elaborated in my 1985 book, *Whose Language?*, where explicit mention is made of the pragmatics of everyday life and the needs of the everyday user in discovering and unveiling all sorts of linguistic manipulation.

A frequent criticism of the first edition had to do with the exercises at the end of each chapter. Many colleagues and their students objected to the degree of difficulty of the exercises and to the amount of knowledge these presupposed; some went even so far as to suggest that 'solutions' be provided for all of the exercises and problems. As to the latter suggestion, I decided to follow it, but not indiscriminately: partly because I felt that providing and receiving simple solutions to sometimes difficult problems is a bad way of teaching and learning, but also because many of the problems could not be pinned down to one standard, pat (type of) answer.

What I have done instead is to provide detailed commentaries on the individual problems, such that their background and context could become clearer. In addition, I have in many cases provided 'hints' as to how the problem could be attacked (and perhaps solved); a couple of times, I have offered a 'model solution', illustrating one way of dealing with the problem. I hope that in this way, the book has become more useful and easier to use. As to the individual exercises themselves, these have been revamped and rewritten, and the questions reformulated with a 'user-friendly' touch. Similarly, about half of the old notes have disappeared, as have many of the digressions that (according to some of my readers) tended to slow down the flow of argument; some of the latter have been relegated to the sections at the end of each chapter now called 'Review and Discussion' (replacing the earlier 'Exercises and Review Questions').

In a field like pragmatics, which is progressing at the speed of lightning, it is of course impossible to keep track of all the new developments and bright ideas that come to us almost every day via the different media: journals, books, now even the Internet. Bringing the book completely up to date would have been a Herculean, not to say a Sisyphean task. All the more grateful am I to the people who alerted me to omissions and misunderstandings, and who took the trouble of reading parts of the book in manuscript, or even commented on earlier editions.

I am deeply obliged to Alan Firth, who intervened at a critical stage of the second edition and acted as a go-between, eliminating a number of misunderstandings and snags on the editorial level. At one point, Alan and I even considered doing the new edition together; alas, at that time, the circumstances of our lives (with him in Australia, me in Brazil) and our commitments to other tasks ruled out this project. Still, Alan's input was crucial at the time, and he is at least in part responsible for the reorganization of the book (abridging the CA portion was his idea); he was also one of the first to comment on what he called my 'chattiness', an expression which at the time didn't make too much sense to me. Later, while rewriting the book, I found out that what he had really meant to criticize was my 'wordiness' – but being a nice guy, he didn't quite want to put it like that. In any case, if the present edition is less 'chatty', it is not least Alan's merit.

Andreas Jucker generously shared the comments that he and his students had prepared during a two-semester use of the first edition as a textbook in his *Hauptseminar* (a graduate course) at Giessen University. These comments were especially useful as they represented, so to speak, the 'voice of the people', a pragmatic user feedback from the floor that I couldn't have obtained in any other way.

Ken Turner, at Brighton University, took the trouble to write four densely covered pages of comments on the first edition, after I'd prodded him to expand an obscure half-sentence teaser in his review of another pragmatics textbook (Jenny Thomas's *Meaning in Interaction*, a book that also has been very useful during the rewriting process). Ken's input came from a radically different orientation than mine, and thus was extremely helpful, even though I still have a hard time admitting (with Ken) Frege as the True Founding Father of Pragmatics!

The University of Texas and its host city, Austin, where I have spent so many delightful and rewarding years, again were a pleasant backdrop for much of the current revision. I am particularly grateful to a number of people associated with that university. Elizabeth Keating read several chapters of the revision in pre-proof version, and not only provided great moral support, but in addition gave much useful feedback on matters of practical and theoretical import, mostly in the areas of conversation analysis and speech acts. Inger Mey, in addition to being a full-time graduate student in anthropology, took out time to discuss and criticize the revised chapters as they rolled off my laptop, never forgetting to remind me how she, the anthropologist, first 'discovered' pragmatics in the seventies, while I, the linguist, initially resisted her overtures as not being 'linguistic' enough. Alexandra Mey, though overly busy researching viruses and other beastly species, and her husband Ygnacio (a.k.a. Jimmy) were always there when it came to rescuing a father in distress or an unhappy cat, and to keeping away unwelcome visitors. Finally, Avram Zilkha kept my spirits up and my Hebrew alive through his well-taught and inspiring classes. To all of them my heartfelt thanks.

My old friends and collaborators Claudia Caffi, Hartmut Haberland and Dick Janney came up with a number of suggestions for improving the book, as did many of my students and colleagues at the various universities I was teaching at during the rewriting process: Odense, Frankfurt, Campinas and – last but not least – Haifa, where a providential 44-days' strike in the autumn of 1998 not only provided me with an opportunity of getting ahead with my long-forgotten Hebrew, but also made me take some important steps towards the completion of the revision. The fact that I could test out the new ideas as I went, so to speak, on my students and colleagues at that beautiful town's two institutions of higher learning, Haifa Technion and the University of Haifa, was instrumental in making the rewriting a very pleasurable experience, in more than one way. A special thanks goes to Dennis Kurzon, who took time out of his busy life to read the whole MS and suggest some useful improvements.

In addition to the above-mentioned, Blackwell's seven-odd anonymous readers need to be acknowledged with gratitude (some of these I could easily spot and have included in my thanks above, while others I couldn't pinpoint and thus have to thank publicly in this fell sweep). Harumi Sawada, the translator of the first Japanese edition, provided a very helpful correction of a Searle (mis)quotation on 'directives' that I had been guilty of in the old chapter 8. A further set of (two) referees commented extensively on the revised version which I submitted to Blackwell in January of 1998. Their comments, too, were worth waiting for; even so, the final rewriting and revising had to be delayed until the summer/fall of 1999, when I found a congenial working environment at the new university college of Södertörn, Stockholm, Sweden. Thanks to my colleagues there for providing much-needed moral and material support for the work!

The illustrations in Chapter 8 are reproduced from *RASK, International Journal of Language and Communication*, by kind permission of the authors and editors.

Last but not least, my thanks go – again – to Philip Carpenter and Bridget Jennings, who helped stabilize this second edition whenever it seemed to wander off the track and who, by their never-failing support and unwavering encouragement, made it possible to continue the work in the face of numerous overt and hidden threats. Fiona Sewell, my indefatigable copy editor, did a great job spotting a number of infelicities while reading the manuscript in preparation to typesetting.

It is my hope that this second edition will find its place alongside other recent efforts to carry the pragmatic message across the linguistic community, in the spirit of complementarity and collaboration, rather than of sectarianism and competition.

Austin, Texas, and Odense, Denmark
12 December 1998

PART I
Basic Notions

CHAPTER ONE
Defining Pragmatics

1.1 Preliminaries

1.1.1 A look at history

The past twenty-odd years have witnessed an ever-growing interest in pragmatics and pragmatic problems. There have been seven international conferences (Viareggio 1985, Antwerp 1987, Barcelona 1990, Kobe 1993, Mexico 1996, Reims 1998, Budapest 2000). The International Pragmatics Association, IPrA, has been in existence for more than fifteen years; two international journals (the *Journal of Pragmatics* since 1977; *Pragmatics* since 1991) are currently publishing, between the two of them, close to 3,000 yearly pages (in thirteen, respectively four issues). Many other (official and unofficial) publications, newsletters and so on have seen the light (some of which have survived, some not); add to this an unestablished number of working papers, theses, dissertations, book series and books on pragmatic topics (among the latter, at least six major reference works and textbooks as well as a *Concise Encyclopedia of Pragmatics*; 1998), and the picture is complete. Pragmatics has come into its own, and it is here to stay.

But even allowing that this is a spectacular development, it still is the case that pragmatics didn't just 'happen' by itself, appearing out of nowhere. We must ask ourselves: how could pragmatics expand so fast and become such a popular trend in such a relatively short time?

The answer to this question is important, as it may give us a first approximation to a better understanding of what pragmatics *is*, and thus lead us to a tentative definition – a definition that will have to be supplemented with a description of what pragmatics *does*, even though it is notoriously difficult to limit the field in such a way that we can say where pragmatics stops, and the 'beyond' begins.[1]

The first efforts at establishing something like a pragmatic approach to linguistics date back to the late sixties and early seventies (as evidenced in work by Ross, Lakoff and others). What we see there is the collapse of earlier theories and hypotheses (in particular, of the 'syntax-only' approach of Chomsky and his followers). Slowly and with intermittent success, a new model emerged: pragmatics was in the making, even though initially its practitioners were not aware of this themselves. (Some would even say that we are dealing with a 'paradigm shift' in the sense defined by Kuhn 1964.)

Naturally, a necessary development such as this one can only be established in a historical hindsight that allows us to observe how the old paradigm came under attack, and how the contours of a new one gradually took shape. All one could see at the time was a growing number of unexplained (and, in fact, unexplainable) observations, giving rise to numerous theoretical paradoxes. Many of these were first noticed, not by linguists, but by philosophers working in the gray zone where philosophy and linguistics share a border. Others came to the attention of linguists trying to overstep the narrow boundaries of syntax and (later also) semantics.[2]

To name but a few of these phenomena: there was the troubled relationship of language with logic, as originally evidenced in the realm of syntax, but subsequently also in that of semantics; I will come back to these problems in section 2.3. Then there were the closely related linguistic problems that arose from the prestigious, but forever hidden, tenet that a linguistic description had to be syntax-based or at least syntax-oriented to be valid. It turned out that extrasyntactic, indeed extralinguistic factors played a major role in what was called the 'rules of the language'. Furthermore, there were difficulties of how to interpret and treat certain assumptions (called 'presuppositions') that somehow guided our understanding of language, yet could not be easily formulated in any of the available frameworks (see further section 2.5). And finally, the whole gamut of problems having to do with users and contexts turned out to be a decisive factor in determining the meaning of what is being uttered at any given time, at any given place (see further the next section and section 2.6).

The 'pragmatic turn' in linguistics can thus be described as a shift from the paradigm of theoretical grammar (in particular, syntax) to the paradigm of the language user. The latter notion is of particular importance for defining pragmatics, since it brings a number of observations to the same practical denominator, as we will see in the following.

1.1.2 The importance of being a user

Most definitions of pragmatics pay lip service to Charles Morris's famous definition of pragmatics as "the study of the relation of signs to interpreters" (1938:6). In a modern, communication-oriented terminology, we prefer to talk about 'messages' and 'language users'; in contrast to traditional linguistics, which first and foremost concentrates on the elements and structures (such as sounds and sentences) that the language users produce, pragmatics focuses on the language-using humans. Put differently, pragmatics is interested in the process of producing language and in its *producers*, not just in the end-*product*, language.

If pragmatics, as suggested in the previous section, indeed is a new paradigm (or program) of research, it is obliged to come up with a new definition of the object of that research. What would such a new definition imply with regard to the research object in question, language, in its 'old' vs. its 'new' interpretation: language as a human product vs. language in its human use? One could, of course, simply divide the study of language into two, pretty much independent, parts: one, a description of its structure (as dealt with by the traditional methods of grammars), the other, a description of its use (to be taken care of by pragmatics).

The proper domain of pragmatics would then be what Chomsky has called *performance*, that is to say, the way the individual goes about using language. This concrete linguistic practice would be distinguished from an abstract *competence*, understood as the user's knowledge of the language and its rules. This viewpoint is neatly captured by Katz, who says: "Grammars are theories about the structure of sentence types . . . Pragmatic theories, in contrast, . . . explicate the reasoning of speakers and hearers" (1977:19).

However, some major questions remain: how to delimit pragmatics vis-à-vis syntax and semantics (let alone phonology)? What is the role of pragmatics in the so-called 'hyphenated areas' of research (psycho-, neuro-, socio-, ethno-, . . . etc. linguistics)? How about newer research areas such as mathematical and computational linguistics, discourse linguistics, not to forget the vast field covered by the term 'applied linguistics'? Whatever the outcome of our quest for a definition and delimitation, the language user is in the center of attention in pragmatics. Thus, we can talk about the 'user's point of view' as a common orienting feature for pragmatic research.

Still, for a number of reasons, this does not give us a satisfactory definition. For one thing, there are the various pragmaticians' varying interpretations of the term 'use of language', as well as of what is implied by the role of the language user. For instance, one can either consider 'language use' to be whatever happens when users are 'doing things with words'; or, following a more restrictive procedure, one can demand that pragmatics refer *explicitly* to a user, whenever language is discussed.[3] I will discuss the latter viewpoint first.

Levinson demands that "explicit reference [be] made to the speaker, or to put it in more general terms, to the user of the language" (1983:2–3). Accordingly, having discussed and rejected a number of definitions, Levinson's own suggestion is to consider pragmatics as being . . . "the study of those relations between language and context that are *grammaticalized*, or encoded in the structure of a language" (p. 9; emphasis in original).

This definition accepts only those uses of language as pragmatically relevant that have a distinct grammatical expression, i.e., that operate with phonological,

morphological and syntactic elements under the direction of grammatical rules;
this is what Levinson means by 'grammaticalized'. He does not tell us, however,
how we may connect user and grammar, or how language and context relate,
with or without grammar's helping hand (the problem of 'contextualization'; see
section 3.1).

The other point of view takes language use to be whatever happens when users
are 'doing things' in and with language; pragmatics comprises everything that
characterizes people as users of language. Some (like Levinson) have called this
a "very broad usage of the term [pragmatics]"; in fact, it is but a natural extension of the notion of pragmatics as a theory of use. Also, it "still [is] the one generally used on the Continent", as Levinson further comments, somewhat
regretfully, it might seem (1983:2). It rests on the assumption that the language
users, being members of society, depend on the rules and norms that are valid at
any time, in any place, in the community they belong to.[4]

The next section will expand on this societal character of pragmatics in order
to arrive at a definition and clear up some of the 'boundary problems' that we
have encountered.

1.2 Pragmatics: definition and delimitation

1.2.1 A definition

As we have seen in the previous section, restricting pragmatics to purely linguistic matters is not an acceptable point of view for those who want to include the
whole of human language use (even though such a restriction may strengthen the
definition as such; Levinson 1983:11). So-called 'extralinguistic' factors can only
be excluded from a pragmatic evaluation on the penalty of neglecting the user.
A truly pragmatic consideration has to deal with the users in their *social context*;
it cannot limit itself to the grammatically encoded aspects of contexts, as the
'grammaticalization requirement' seems to imply.

Communication in society happens chiefly by means of language. However,
the users of language, as social beings, communicate and use language on society's
premises; society controls their access to the linguistic and communicative means.
Pragmatics, as the study of the way humans use their language in communication, bases itself on a study of those premises and determines how they affect,
and effectualize, human language use. Hence:

> *Pragmatics studies the use of language in human communication as deter-
> mined by the conditions of society.*[5]

Having propounded this definition, our next task will be to look into what
characterizes pragmatics in relation to its closest neighbors. 'To define' means:

to impose an end or a boundary (cf. the Latin word *finis* 'end'; plural *fines* 'frontier'). 'Defining pragmatics' thus implies determining its frontiers with other, adjoining fields of research within (and possibly also outside) linguistics.

Unfortunately, the definitions that have been offered (including the one suggested above) do not delimit pragmatics either clearly and neatly, or to everybody's satisfaction. Many authors confine themselves to a strictly linguistically oriented definition (like the one I criticized in the preceding section); alternatively, they resort to a definition that, while incorporating as much societal context as possible, necessarily remains vague as regards the relation between pragmatics and the other areas of linguistics (even leaving aside the problem of these areas' autonomy vis-à-vis linguistics proper).

But why do we need clear, sharply demarcated boundaries at all, when pragmatics is in constant development, so that boundary markers, once placed, will have to be moved all the time? Maybe a 'pragmatic' definition of pragmatics could be found that avoids both the Scylla and Charybdis of the above alternative?

In the literature, such an idea seems to have been received with some enthusiasm. The most prominent representative of this 'pragmatic eclecticism' is Geoffrey Leech, who advocates *complementarity* as his solution to the dilemma. This is what he says about the relation between pragmatics and its nearest linguistic neighbor, semantics: "The view that semantics and pragmatics are distinct, though complementary and interrelated fields of study, is easy to appreciate subjectively, but is more difficult to justify in an objective way. It is best supported negatively, by pointing out the failures or weaknesses of alternative views" (1983:6).

Leech distinguishes between three possible ways of structuring this relationship: semanticism (pragmatics inside semantics), pragmaticism (semantics inside pragmatics) and complementarism (semantics and pragmatics complement each other, but are otherwise independent areas of research).

As an instance of *semanticism*, one can mention the way people such as Searle originally were dealing with the problem of *speech acts*. For instance, when I utter a promise, do I then 'make' a promise because of the semantics of the verb 'to promise', or because of its 'active', pragmatic character? Clearly, the former solution forces the problem onto the Procrustean bed of what could be called 'pragmantics', a true pragma–semantic chimera.[6]

In contrast to this, consider the way Austin dealt with this problem. For him, the only real issue at stake was the effect that our words have when uttered, and the 'things' we can 'do' with them. In Leech's terminology, this means that the pragmatic aspect of language is the only really interesting one: clearly a case of *pragmaticism*.[7]

Finally, it seems plausible to assume that the main reason why Austin's work stayed unknown territory for so many linguists for such a long time was precisely the same anxiety that innovative views traditionally inspire in those that are concerned about territorial rights and privileges, and hence worry about

boundaries. Professionally established syntacticians or semanticists want to continue doing their work in their own, accustomed ways; the moment some people
start telling them how to do linguistics, their territorial integrity is in danger. So,
in order not to rock the boat, most traditionally oriented linguists prefer to assign
pragmatics to a quiet corner, preferably a little bit outside of linguistics proper;
here, pragmaticists can do their own thing, in a complementary relationship with
the rest, but still clearly distinguished from it. This is how *complementarism*
solves the delimitation problem.

This last alternative seems still to be the preferred solution to the boundary
problem. Levinson, discussing the relationship between semantics and pragmatics, remarks: "From what we now know about the nature of meaning, a hybrid
or modular account seems inescapable; there remains the hope that with two
components, a semantics and a pragmatics working in tandem, each can be built
on relatively homogeneous and systematic lines" (1983:15).

An alternative solution to the problem of delimiting pragmatics will be discussed in the next sections.

1.2.2   Component, perspective or function?

1.2.2.1   *Component vs. perspective*

The question raised in the preceding section was basically how to divide the
linguistic pie, and where, once cut up, the individual pieces should go. The discussion was entirely framed in what one could call the 'component view' of linguistics. This view, popular ever since Chomsky's early works (1957, 1965) and
maintained faithfully by his followers despite their internal differences, assumes
that the grammar of a language consists of several 'components' (a phonological one, a syntactic one, and a semantic one, to name the most important). The
components correspond to different human abilities, and can be differentiated,
for instance, in the case of brain damage (e.g., syntactic or so-called Broca's
aphasia is very different from Wernicke's aphasia, which mainly affects the
semantics of language).

The component view is essentially based on a 'modular' conception of the
human mind. In this conception (which remains quite popular among today's
cognitive scientists and computer-oriented psychologists), the human faculties are
thought of as independent but cooperating units. In contrast, a 'perspective' view
of human language activity, as the name indicates, 'perspectivizes', focuses on,
that activity in its various aspects. Cf. "Linguistic pragmatics . . . can be said to
characterize a new way of looking at things linguistic [i.e., a 'perspective'], rather
than marking off clear borderlines to other disciplines" (Haberland and Mey
1977:5).

Thus, a *pragmatic* perspective will focus on the societal factors that make a
certain language use more or less acceptable, in contrast to other, perhaps
abstractly equivalent, but pragmatically radically different (because mostly unac-

ceptable) uses. Theoretically speaking, a Black inner-city dialect of English may be just as good as any other English dialect (Labov 1966), but in a pragmatic perspective, such a statement makes little sense: one simply cannot do the same things with Black as with Standard English in most societal surroundings. Here, the 'inner city' (or the 'urban' environment, as it is now somewhat euphemistically called) is the exception that confirms the rule: in order to pursue any sort of career in 'mainstream' society, knowledge, and use, of the standard language is *de rigueur*.

In the spirit of our "new way of looking at things linguistic", Verschueren has recently characterized *pragmatics* as "*a general cognitive, social, and cultural perspective on linguistic phenomena in relation to their usage in forms of behaviour*" (Verschueren 1999:7; italics in original). According to Verschueren, "pragmatics does not constitute an additional component of a theory of language, but it offers a different *perspective*" (ibid.:2), a perspective, moreover, which constitutes "a radical departure from the established component view which tries to assign to pragmatics its own set of linguistic features in contradistinction with phonology, morphology, syntax and semantics" (Verschueren 1987:36).

But what difference does such a 'radical departure' make? In the component view of linguistics, each 'module' works within a properly delimited domain, with well-defined objects and properly established, specific methods. Thus, phonetics and phonology busy themselves with speech sounds and phonemes, and leave syntactic objects such as sentences to the syntacticians. Similarly, the syntactic component does not interfere in the workings of semantics except in a sideways fashion. Neither does the semantic component meddle in pragmatic affairs, except when some philosopher forces it to (the case of 'pragmatics', referred to earlier).

In contrast, a perspectivist view emphasizes the pragmatic aspects of all parts of linguistics, including psycholinguistics, sociolinguistics, and other 'hyphenated' areas. On this view, the variables of sociology (such as income, housing, degree of education etc.) and psychology (such as IQ, character traits, sexual orientation etc.) would then be integrated in a pragmatics of the 'languaging' human as a social being. Thus, the pragmatic perspective could serve as an 'umbrella' for the various components and areas of linguistics; in accordance with a suggestion made by Östman (1988b:28), one could have the 'component' and the 'perspective' views existing side by side, so as to expand, rather than narrow, our epistemological horizon.

Thus, we could have a pragmatic component, understood as the set of whatever pragmatic functions can be assigned to language, along with a pragmatic perspective, i.e., the way these functions operate. We could either ask how users 'mean what they say', that is, how they communicate, using language, or how they 'say what they mean', employing the linguistic devices at their disposal to express themselves.

All this is nicely summarized by Östman as follows: "[if] the unit of analysis in semantics simply [is] *meaning*: the meanings of words, phrases, larger constructions, prosody, and so on, . . . then by the same token, the 'unit' of analysis for pragmatics could be said to be the *functioning of language*" (1988b:28; emphasis in original).

1.2.2.2 Function

The use of the term 'functioning' in the above quotation does by no means represent a recent development in linguistic thinking. As early as the mid-thirties, the German psychologist Karl Bühler elaborated his famous functional triangle of *Ausdruck, Appell* and *Darstellung* (roughly, 'expression' or 'manifestation', (speech) 'appeal' and 'representation') as characteristic of language (1934:29);[8] and in the sixties, Roman Jakobson elaborated on the Bühlerian model by adding three more functions: code, channel and poetic quality (1960:350ff).

Underlying these models of human language is a common sense of the importance of the user in the communicative process. Messages are not just 'signals', relayed through impersonal channels; the human expression functions as an appeal to other users and as a means of social togetherness.

One advantage of looking at linguistic phenomena this way is that it allows us to consolidate the different agendas of the 'componentialists' and the 'perspectivists'. Whereas the former mainly are interested in technical matters such as presuppositions, implicatures, deixis and so on (see further chapters 3 and 7), a typical perspectivist wants to deal with concepts such as "negotiability, adaptability and variability, motivations, effects, etc." (Östman 1988b:29). Both viewpoints can be brought together by considering the communicative function of language against the background of the available linguistic techniques, while conversely placing these techniques in a functional-communicative perspective.

Linguistic functions of use are best studied in situations where people interact normally, using language face to face, as in everyday conversation. There are basically two ways of studying this fundamental linguistic interaction: one, we can observe what's going on and try to describe, as exactly as possible, the participants' choices of expressing themselves to their own and others' satisfaction, as well as their options to join in at any given point of the conversation. This approach is taken in conversational analysis (see further chapter 6).[9]

Another approach goes 'behind' the conversation, as it were, establishing the minimal conditions for successful interaction both on the linguistic level and (maybe even more importantly) on the hidden levels of societal equality or inequality, of prejudice and class feeling, education and culture. Such an approach represents the linguistic dimension of social interaction; it is essentially a *pragmatic* one. Without this background information, successful conversation, "the sustained production of chains of mutually-dependent acts, constructed by two or more agents each monitoring and building on the actions of the other" (Levinson 1983:44), is both impossible in itself and impossible to understand.

In order to better realize what is involved here, let's do a thought experiment. Suppose we had to instruct two extraterrestrial beings in conversational techniques, what would we have to teach them? This problem is astonishingly similar to that of figuring out what it would take to teach a computer to understand human language, or even speak 'as' a human (Schank 1984:91–2). For one, we would have to teach our Elizas or 'ETs' the language itself: grammar, dictionary, pronunciation etc. But besides, we would have to specify, for each situation, what kind of language functions best.

Following Goffman, the constraints that operate in these cases can be separated into constraints belonging to the system (the grammar) and constraints of a ritual nature (the function), "where the first label[s] the ingredients essential to sustaining any kind of systematic interweaving of actions by more than one party, and the second those ingredients that, while not essential to the maintaining of the interaction, are nevertheless typical of it – they are, if one likes, the social dimensions of interaction" (1976:266–7). The latter constraints belong properly in the realm of 'metapragmatics', as we will see in chapter 7.

1.3 What use is pragmatics?

1.3.1 Theory and practice

The use of pragmatics can be characterized in different ways, depending on how we view linguistics and how we place pragmatics within it.

An *abstract* characterization will place emphasis on pragmatics either as a 'component' of linguistics (like phonology, syntax and semantics) or as a 'perspective' pervading the components and giving them a pragmatic 'accent'.

A *practical* characterization of the tasks and functions of pragmatics takes its point of departure in the traditional problems that linguistic research has grappled with over the years, and for which pragmatics provides a novel solution. Among these are the numerous practical problems that we meet in the exercise of our linguistic functions. Many of these problem areas have been opened up to pragmatics from the 'outside': problems of conversation and turn-control (ethnomethodology; see chapter 6); problems of argumentation (philosophy; see section 2.3); problems of language use in educational settings (applied linguistics; see chapter 11); problems of interaction between humans and computers (computer software and design; see Gorayska and Mey 1996; Mey 2000b); and in general, all sorts of communication problems in anthropology, ethnography, psychiatry and psychology, the public language inside and outside of social institutions, rhetoric, the media sciences, educational sciences, and so on and so forth. Other clusters of problems are more in the traditional vein: ambiguity of utterances, 'lazy' reference of pronouns, 'voice' in narrative and other texts and so on. The next section will give some examples; other problems will be discussed throughout the book.

A further question, of course, is what we need pragmatics for, and what its goals are; this also will be the subject of the following sections.

1.3.2   Uses and aims

1.3.2.1   *Why do we need pragmatics?*

What does pragmatics have to offer that cannot be found in good old-fashioned linguistics? What do pragmatic methods give us in the way of greater under-standing of how the human mind works, how humans communicate, how they manipulate one another, and in general, how they use language?

The general answer is: pragmatics is needed if we want a fuller, deeper and generally more reasonable account of human language behavior.

A more practical answer would be: outside of pragmatics, no understanding; sometimes, a pragmatic account is the only one that makes sense, as in the fol-lowing example, borrowed from David Lodge's *Paradise News*:

'I just met the old Irishman and his son, coming out of the toilet.'
'I wouldn't have thought there was room for the two of them.'
'No silly, I mean *I* was coming out of the toilet. They were waiting.' (1992:65)

How do we know what the first speaker meant? Linguists usually say that the first sentence is ambiguous, and they excel at producing such sentences as:

Flying planes can be dangerous

or:

The missionaries are ready to eat

in order to show what is meant by 'ambiguous': a word, phrase, or sentence that can mean either one or the other of two (or even several) things.

For a pragmatician, this is, of course, glorious nonsense. In real life, that is, among real language users, there is no such thing as ambiguity – excepting certain, rather special occasions, on which one tries to deceive one's partner, or 'keep a door open'. A famous example is the answer that the ancient oracle in Delphi gave the king of Epirus, Pyrrhus, when he asked what would happen if he attacked the Romans. The answer was that the king would destroy a great empire; whereupon he set out to win the battle, but lose the war, thus ultimately fulfilling the prophecy and destroying his own empire.[10]

In the dialogue from *Paradise News* cited above, the first speaker knows what she means; the misunderstanding is on the part of the hearer, but there is strictly speaking no ambiguity. The misunderstanding is furthermore cleared up in the next round; but notice that this can only happen in real dialogue: if we don't have a user to tell us what she or he means, we may speculate until the end of our days on the hidden meaning of utterances that are never brought to bear on a concrete situation, with real language users involved.[11] Ambiguity only exists outside of the actual speaking situation; abstract sentences can be ambiguous, real speakers are not (unless they want to – as, e.g., in telling a joke, where the ambiguity is intended; see Kittay 1987:80; Nerlich and Clarke 2000 in press).

Often, it is said that we must invoke the context to determine what an ambiguous sentence means. This may be OK, if by 'context' we understand all the factors that play a role in producing and understanding utterances. But 'context' is a notoriously hard concept to deal with (I shall have more to say on this later; see section 3.1); in particular, it is often restricted to a kind of 'prehistory' of a particular utterance, the sum and result of what has been said and done up to now.

The concept of context that is invoked here is a purely static one; it bears a certain likeness to the thinking of classical physics, where the conditions preceding a particular state of affairs in the physical world are thought of as completely determining the next development. However, language is not a controlled experiment in the physics classroom or in the laboratory. Whoever says: 'Give me all the information, and I'll predict what is going to happen, what this or that utterance is supposed to mean' is at best a would-be pragmatician. In such a conceptual framework, no matter how hard we 'milk' the context, we will never arrive at a pragmatic understanding.

Consider the following dialogue:

(*Two linguists, call them Jacob and Mark, are coming out of a lecture hall at a university which is neither's home territory, but where Jacob has been before; so he thinks he knows the campus, more or less*)

JACOB: "Do you know the way back to the dining hall? We can go in my car."

(*Mark gets into the car; after the first turn, he starts giving directions, which greatly amazes Jacob, and irritates him a little; he was under the impression that he needed to guide the other, not the other way round. After several more turns – which Jacob is taking at greater and greater speeds, so the other doesn't get a chance to interfere – Mark says:*)

MARK: "Oh, I thought you *didn't* know the way to the campus."

(*To which Jacob replies:*)

JACOB: "I thought *you* didn't know!"
(*whereupon they both start laughing*).

In a case like this, the classical concept of 'context' as 'that which has been the case up to and including the present moment' makes no sense. There is no way in which the original utterance 'Do you know the way back to the dining hall?' can be interpreted correctly. Clearly, Mark takes Jacob's utterance not as a 'real' question, but as a 'pre-request' for information (see section 6.3.2).

Jacob, on the other hand, assumed that Mark was not familiar with the campus, and so wanted to give him a ride. This is why he was surprised at Mark giving him directions: that activity only makes sense if you know where you're going.

The moment the situation is resolved, we can look back and understand what has happened: but the correct 'illocutionary force' (see section 5.1.3) of the first utterance could not have been 'predicted' on the basis of the context, understood as: what had happened before. Such a concept of context is established independently of the ongoing interaction between the interlocutors, and for this reason is completely useless. The *dynamic* development of the conversation, that which gives us the clue to an understanding, cannot be predicted, as it depends entirely on the individuals and their individual choices at every moment.

We are all familiar with these phenomena from our daily lives. Take the case of family fights and other arguments. As our mother used to say, 'One word takes the other, and you never know where you're ending up.' Afterwards, one looks back and is unable to understand how all this happened, and how things came to be said "which are not easily forgotten" (Robert L. Stevenson, *Kidnapped*), with sometimes terrible consequences for one's relationships with other persons.

A dynamic context is an environment that is in steady development, prompted by the continuous interaction of the people engaged in language use. Context is the quintessential pragmatic concept; it is by definition *proactive*, just as people are. By contrast, a pure linguistic description is retroactive and static: it takes a snapshot of what is the case at any particular moment, and tries to freeze that picture. Pure descriptions have no dynamics; they can never capture the richness of the developments that take place between people using language; the synchronic snapshot of the 'here and now', the classical *hic et nunc*, is a philosophical abstraction.

This brings me to a final point. If pragmatic linguistics defines itself as opposed to descriptive linguistics, what are its declared aims?

1.3.2.2   The aims of pragmatics

In linguistics, it has long been an article of faith that the science of language has to be practiced for its own sake. Linguists have talked about the 'immanence' of linguistic theory, by which they mean that linguistics is accountable only to itself as to its methods and objectives. Historically, this has been understandable in a relatively young science such as linguistics: it needed to become independent of the surrounding sciences, and to carve out its own domain, so to speak. But for a developed science, the desire for immanence is not a sign of maturity; on the contrary. The immanent approach to the study of language has tended to isolate its different aspects, and in many cases the practitioners of linguistics have not been able to talk to each other except in very general terms. When it comes to doing things for a purpose, such as describing languages, often thought of as the prime practical endeavor of linguists, the consensus remains largely theoretical. Here is an example.

In the course of the past decades, it has become increasingly clear that the descriptive endeavor of linguistics is in great danger of being irrevocably thwarted. All description is strictly a terminal process, that is, a process with a built-in *terminus ad quem*: when everything has been described that there is to describe, description has to come to an end.

In the heydays of description, this never used to be a real concern: there were always enough languages to describe. The times when every Ph.D. candidate in linguistics could travel to the 'field' and pick himself or herself a language to work on are not so long past, after all.

However, with the ever-increasing westernization and industrialization of the Third and Fourth Worlds, many languages of those worlds have begun to disappear at an ever-more rapid speed. According to fact-based projections, we are looking at a loss of languages in the order of several thousand in the next fifty years or so. Linguists speak of 'endangered languages', and vote on resolutions about what to do to 'save' those languages.

For the describer, it is clearly a loss to have one's potential object of description vanish from under one's eyes. And as long as the purpose of descriptive linguistics is to go 'out there' and collect as many as possible of the vanishing species of languages, it is clearly a catastrophe when those species start disappearing on a grand scale. The linguistic remedy for this evil is to save the languages by accelerating and perfecting the descriptive process, through better targeted and more generous funding, through the training of native linguists, through providing teachers and other personnel that can help in 'alphabetizing' those mostly unwritten and unrecorded languages, so that we at least may have some documentation to show our successors in the trade, and can parry the reproach of having squandered away the linguistic patrimony of generations to come, by saying: 'Here's what we've done – it may not be perfect, but we did our best.'

However, the best in this case isn't good enough. Description, as the ultimate aim of linguistic science, digs its own grave; but when all is said and done, describing the language that has disappeared has not done a thing for the people that went with it. The question "why do languages disappear, and what can we do about the causes of this linguistic decay" is seldom raised. In other words, saving languages is thought of as a process of putting away, cataloguing, describing; not as a process that saves the languages by saving their *users*, providing the latter with living conditions that allow them to continue using their languages. A pragmatic look at the problems of endangered languages tells us not just to go out there and describe, but to fight what has been called 'linguistic genocide', or 'linguicide', for short (Skutnabb-Kangas and Phillipson, 1994). The next chapter will go into more detail as to what such a 'pragmatic look' is all about.

Review and discussion

1. One of the tasks of pragmatics is to explain how the same content is expressed differently in different (cultural, religious, professional etc.) contexts. Often, such contexts will be linguistically different, as is the case from language community to language community. The following is an example of this.

In the US, whenever an interstate highway starts climbing a hill, you will find that a new, 'slow' lane is added to the right of the (usually) two already existing ones. This lane is destined for trucks and other slower vehicles, to prevent them from clogging up the traffic in the faster lanes. On a sign posted well in advance of the widened pavement, you will read the following text:

SLOWER TRAFFIC KEEP RIGHT

However, in Canada the same situation may be 'worded' differently:

KEEP RIGHT EXCEPT TO PASS

In terms of our discussion above, we may say that the semantic content of the two expressions is partly the same ('Keep right'), partly different (a reference to 'slower traffic' as compared with 'to pass') – yet the signs seem to *function* in more or less the same way.

Questions:
Using Östman's definition at the end of section 1.2.2.1, would you say the expressions are pragmatically different?

Is there another difference that could be called 'pragmatic', taking the 'user aspect' into consideration? Would there be a possible difference in effect?

2. (Due to Alvaro G. Meseguer) During a strike among the crew personnel of the Spanish airline Iberia in 1990, the following bilingual document was presented to the travelers. Read the text, paying special attention to the first sentence in each version.

Estimado cliente:

Debido a la huelga de nuestros Tripulantes de Cabina de Pasajeros, Vd. recibirá a bordo un servicio distinto al habitual.

IBERIA está haciendo todo lo posible para reducir su incidencia en nuestros clientes . . .

Muchas gracias. Recibe un cordial saludo.

Dear Customer,

The industrial action being taken by our cabin crew means that the on-board services you receive will not be those which we normally offer our passengers.

IBERIA is doing everything possible to minimize the inconvenience to our clients. . . .

Thank you very much. Sincerely yours,

(sign.) Pilar Villanueva

Explanatory commentary and questions:
The above notice, by its bilingual nature, aims at an audience in which there are speakers of English as well as of Spanish. *A priori*, one would assume that the contents of the message to both classes of readers would be identical (no semantic difference).

Do you think this is the case? (For those not familiar with Spanish, it should be pointed out that the word *huelga* means 'strike'.)

Why do you think the Spanish text uses the word 'strike', whereas its English counterpart has 'industrial action'?

Is there a difference of content (a semantic difference) between the two messages?

Is there any reason for the English text to avoid using the word 'strike' in this context?

In terms of a 'fuller, deeper and generally more reasonable account of human language behavior' (cf. section 1.3.2.1), which of the two versions is, in your opinion, the best qualified, pragmatically speaking?

3. The following cases all have to do with ambiguity (cf. section 1.3.2.1).
   (a) Consider the following excerpt:

'What are we going to do about Baba', she asked.
'What do you mean?'
'She can't remember anything.'
'Did she ask you whether she was taking medicine?'
→'No.'
'No she's not or no she didn't ask?'
'She didn't ask.'
'She was supposed to,' I said.
'Well, she didn't.' (Don Delillo, *White Noise*. New York: Viking/Penguin, 1986. p. 61)

In the above excerpt, the arrow (→) indicates an ambiguous utterance: 'No.' In the next reply, the interlocutor tries to find out what the 'No' is supposed to negate: the main clause 'Did she ask you' or the dependent clause 'whether she was taking medicine'.

From a strictly grammatical (syntactic) viewpoint, the 'No' should not be taken to refer to a clause within a clause: 'No' negates the main verb in the receding sentence 'Did' ('No, she didn't'). The fact, however, that the interlocutor is prompted to ask for an explanation shows that pragmatically, a negation can have another 'scope' than strictly syntactical.

(b) Consider now the following examples, all containing a negation ('No') along with a noun. Usually, this kind of construction is not difficult to handle; it is often used in connection with some prohibition, injunction, etc. ('No Smoking', 'No Pets' etc.). However, the three examples below exhibit some apparent irregularities. Try to identify what they negate, and how this can be explained from a pragmatic point of view. (Hint: when in doubt try to construct a suitable context in which the 'No's make sense.)

(1) 'No Parking Violators Will Be Towed Away' (sign in San Juan, Pwerto Rico; example due to Bruce Fraser)

(2) 'No Shoes, No Shirt, No Service' (sign on door of the Bevo Shop on 'The Drag', the university portion of Guadalupe Street in Austin, Tex.)

(3) 'No Checks, No Exceptions' (hand-lettered notice on the cashier's counter in the cafeteria of the University of Chicago 59th Street campus)

(c) In the dialogue in (a) above, you will find nine occurrences of the pronoun 'she'. Reading the dialogue, you should have little difficulty in establishing the identity of the various persons referred to.

Questions:

Is there an occurrence that causes you some trouble? Which? How do you explain it (away)?

How does this example compare to the one quoted in 1.3.2.1 about the old Irishman and his son? (Hint: syntactic vs. pragmatic ambiguity.)

What is 'she was supposed to' (last turn but one) referring to? How do you know?

Do you think the last reply is ambiguous? Why (not)?

CHAPTER TWO
Some Issues in Pragmatics

2.1 The pragmatic waste-basket

Pragmatics is often called the 'waste-basket' of linguistics. Despite its negative connotations (a waste-basket is usually for things that we don't want any longer), this way of speaking acquired a certain status, especially in the early years of pragmatics. How did this come about, and how can it be reconciled with the view on pragmatics that I have been pleading for in the preceding chapter (1.2.3.1): as indispensable to any sound linguistic treatment of people's ways with words?

The notion of waste-basket goes back to the Israeli logician-philosopher and linguist Yehoshua Bar-Hillel (1915–75), who called semantics the 'waste-basket' of syntax (1971). To see what he meant by this, we have to consider the ambitions of linguistics as a science in the late fifties and early sixties, with its emphasis on formal reasoning and abstract symbolism. Linguistics was ideally conceived of as an 'algebra' of language; the expression was first used (following Leibniz's earlier notion of a 'conceptual calculus') by Hjelmslev in 1943, but has been borrowed by many.

Usually, when we try to apply formal (e.g., mathematical) methods to our daily life, we realize that life is more than a mathematical abstraction. The phenomena of real life cannot be exhaustively accounted for by the idealizations that are typical of mathematical methods and which, strictly speaking, do not exist. For example, in mathematics even such a simple thing as a line is not a line in reality, but only a well-defined concept, to which the line I draw on the ground or on paper is but a poor approximation.

In the mid-fifties, when Noam Chomsky developed his famous theory of 'generative-transformational grammar', he was aware that much of what he said the grammar could do was valid only for a limited subset of the language, with all the fringes cut off. In his earliest attempts, Chomsky made syntax into the main component of the grammar, completely divorced from the semantics, the meaning of the language, and postulated that sentences could be described perfectly well on the syntactic level without ever having to 'mean' anything – just like algebraic formulas, which, taken by themselves, don't mean anything until we assign values to the variables, but still can be quite easily tested for correctness.

Consider Chomsky's notorious example (1957):

Colorless green ideas sleep furiously.

From a syntactic point of view, Chomsky points out, this sentence is perfectly correct; however, it is strictly 'meaning-less', since the meaning of, e.g., 'green', a color, is canceled out by 'colorless', and so on. Since syntax has nothing to do with meaning, such considerations are strictly meaning-less, too, and should be left to the people dealing with meaning, the semanticists. In this way, semantics came to be called the 'waste-basket' of syntax.

In the philosophy of the fifties, people didn't think too much about their trash; it was not until several decades later that waste disposal got to be a major worry in the world at large. And as the world changed, so did human science. Many philosophers and linguists began to speculate about what went into the semantic waste-basket and why. Chomsky himself came up with a suggestion for trash-disposal some years later: he explained the fact that certain sentences didn't make sense, even though they were perfectly good constructions, by saying that when combining words into sentences, you had to take certain precautions. Words should be picked according to their 'selection features', traits that would guarantee their possible coexistence with other words. And since the selection process was entirely governed by the syntax, it could be formally explained by its (quasi-)mathematical rules.

As long as semantics remained an abstract science whose main concern was the conditions under which a sentence could be true or false, it was unable to explain certain phenomena that transcended (or sometimes even voided) those conditions. For instance, how to explain that certain parts of a sentence remain true, regardless of whether the entire sentence is true or false? For example, if I say:

Fats regretted that he had to pay alimony to Bessie,

I presuppose that Fats indeed paid what he owed Bessie; but when I negate that same sentence:

Fats did not regret that he had to pay alimony to Bessie,

I presuppose likewise that Fats was not misbehaving, but actually paid his dues.[12]

Considerations such as these led pragmaticians to the conviction that there were more things happening between people than were dreamt of by the philosophers. The semantics basket being filled to the brim, another waste-basket had to be created to catch the overflow. As time went by, the linguists dropped more and more of their unresolved questions into this new, pragmatic basket, which became a not-too-tidy collection of rather heterogeneous problems, many of which kept bothering the linguists, in particular those defending a pragmatic approach.

In contrast to the linguistic philosophers, for pragmaticians the truth value of a sentence, taken in its abstract form, is of little interest. People rarely utter something in order to be proven true or false. We want to know *why* people say something; whether what they say is true or false is only interesting in special surroundings, such as the philosophical debate or the courtroom. The truth, or full meaning, of an utterance may not even be accessible to the users at the time of speaking or hearing, as long as they do not know what motivates the other's use of language, as shown by the story of the two befuddled linguists in section 1.3.2.1. Ascertaining the truth of an utterance is not enough; pragmatics rests on the *cooperation* between language users (as we will see in section 4.2.2, where I discuss the 'Cooperative Principle').

Far from being a receptacle for discardables, the pragmatic waste-basket is more like a can of worms: the problems that the basket contains tend to spill over into all the domains of linguistic thinking. Instead of making linguistics neat and clean, in the best logical or mathematical style, the waste-basket imposes its unruly order on our explanations. The following sections will go into some detail as to how this happens.

2.2 Linguists without borders

The British pragmatician Geoffrey Leech has compared the development of modern pragmatics to a process of colonization, by which some brave settlers tried to expand their horizons by venturing into hitherto uncharted (or so they thought) territory: "[this] colonization was only the last stage of a wave-by-wave expansion of linguistics from a narrow discipline dealing with the physical data of speech, to a broad discipline taking in form, meaning and context" (1983:2).

The notion of 'colonization' as invoked here by Leech comprises two elements: first, there must have been some conflicts back home that forced the settlers into exile (just as the Founding Fathers left their native England because of its oppressive religious policies); furthermore, there are the natives, the people who were there originally, and to whom, in the historical parallel, not much respect was paid.

But were there conflicts on the home front, and if yes, what were they like? One possible candidate is the opposition between a theoretical and a practical

approach to the study of language, between the 'theoretical' and the 'applied' linguists, as we have seen earlier. However, not everybody agrees as to the nature
or the reality of this conflict. The eminent British linguist Sir John Lyons goes to
great lengths to argue that there was no 'real' conflict between the 'abstract' and
the 'practical': "[there is] no conflict between the peculiarly abstract approach to
the study of language which is characteristic of modern, 'structural' linguistics[,]
and more 'practical approaches'" (1968:50–1).

Lyons does indicate the existence of certain 'practical' and 'realistic'
tendencies which, however, are not opposed to real linguistics, except in
the minds of people who (for whatever reason) insist on creating such an opposition: "However abstract, or formal, modern linguistic theory might be, it
has been developed to account for the way people actually use language"
(1968:50–1).

Whatever the case may have been for Lyons in 1968, in hindsight one wonders:
if there wasn't any conflict, why did a number of people apparently (and as it
turned out later, not without reason) think there was?

Another, more 'internal' conflict had its origin in the 'syntacticism' of the
Chomskyan school of linguistics, whereby all of linguistic science (inclusive
phonology and semantics) was supposed to fit into the syntactic framework.
Linguists such as John Robert ('Háj') Ross and George Lakoff were the first to
protest against this syntactic straitjacket; an alternative framework, 'generative
semantics', was proposed by Lakoff in the late sixties (see the next section). But
it was only after the publication of John R. Searle's landmark work *Speech Acts*
(1969) that Chomsky's rebellious students found the courage to make the first,
timid inroads into what later became known as pragmatic territory. But, to their
great surprise, these Lord Marchers of the Language Realm found the invaded
region already populated, and even partly cultivated, by various tribes of
philosophers:

> [w]hen linguistic pioneers such as Ross and Lakoff staked a claim in prag-
> matics in the late 1960s, they encountered there an indigenous breed of
> philosophers of language who had been quietly cultivating the territory for
> some time. In fact, the more lasting influences on modern pragmatics have
> been those of philosophers; notably, in recent years, Austin (1962), Searle
> (1969), and Grice (1975). (Leech 1983:2)

What these philosophers cultivated had essentially been semantic virgin land;
and the visions that struck the early colonizers there must have been quite refreshing after the old country's emphasis on strict structure and syntax. Especially
interesting in this connection is the fact that it was not the linguists who were
the first to discover and explore the *terra incognita* of pragmatics, but the philosophers, whose reflections on language had a significant and lasting impact on the
development of modern linguistics, especially pragmatics. But what had these
philosophers been doing?

2.3 Philosophers, ordinary people and ordinary language

Traditionally, philosophers busying themselves with problems of language have concentrated on the relationships between logically defined expressions and sentences in natural languages. This tradition goes back all the way to the ancient philosophers such as Plato, St Augustine and the medieval nominalists; among modern philosophers, we have names such as Russell, Wittgenstein, Carnap, Ryle, Quine, Strawson and many others.

As to ordinary people discussing problems of language, one of the most inveterate and hard-to-change ideas that go the rounds is the notion that language is a matter of logic, to mean: a correct use of language presupposes the use of logic; any other use of language is either metaphysical (read: non-accountable), emotional or simply bad. Our everyday language is a bastardized and illegitimate variant of the pure language of logic, as it materializes in mathematics, formal logic (and maybe even abstract music). If logic is the 'handmaid of philosophy', then language certainly is the handmaid of logic.

For many philosophers and lay people alike, logic is thus prior to language. In contrast to this view, the school usually referred to as 'ordinary language philosophy' puts strong emphasis on the way people *use* their language. Its most famous protagonist, John L. Austin, the 'father of speech act theory' (on which more in chapter 5), was also the author of *How To Do Things With Words* (1962), a work which had an enormous influence on the development of pragmatics.

The title of Austin's book contains an implicit (indirect) question, the answer to which is that people communicate by means of language, not necessarily defined as the ensemble of correct sentences or logically valid propositions. And one of the most effective incitements for the development of modern pragmatics has precisely been a growing irritation among many of the younger, 'nonaligned' linguists with the lack of interest on the part of established linguists and logicians in what really goes on in language, in what people actually 'do with words'.

Many of the early discussions on the foundation of pragmatics have been on the possibility and desirability of letting pragmatic conditions govern the correct use of logical propositions, when disguised as 'ordinary language' utterances. Unfortunately, logic and language do not travel too well together, and the amount of ground they cover between them is rather small. Let us consider a well-known case.

According to a familiar rule of logic, when conjoining two propositions (let us call them p and q, and symbolize their conjunction by the formula $p \,\&\, q$), it is not important in which order the two constituents of the formula appear: $p \,\&\, q$ is logically equivalent to $q \,\&\, p$.

Now consider the following example, due to Levinson (1983:35). Somebody utters the sentence:

Getting married and having a child is better than having a child and getting married.

Supposing we can identify our everyday language conjunction *and* with the logical conjunction '&', we would be looking at a logical proposition of the form *p* ('getting married') & *q* ('having a child'), expressed in everyday language by means of a sentence like the above. Such an utterance should then, by the laws of logic, be equivalent to the proposition *q* ('having a child') & *p* ('getting married'). Hence, the above utterance would be logically equivalent to the one below:

Having a child and getting married is better than getting married and having a child.

But although these two sentences have the same 'truth conditions' (which is the same as saying that they are logically equivalent), the two sentences clearly do not have the same meaning, in everyday life as in everyday language use; far from it. Which of the two is true as actually uttered, can be inferred from the general observation that people usually let the order of their words follow the order of their actions in accordance with a general 'principle of orderliness' (Grice 1981:186; see further chapter 4). However, as Bruce Fraser has remarked (in personal communication), this 'iconicity', as it is often called, is not the rule, as seen from the following example, in which *and* does not necessarily imply an ordering:[13]

I both crashed my car and got drunk.

A further, even more profound difficulty lies in the fact that there is no *a priori* guarantee that any logical symbols (such as *and* or its logical 'sister' *or*) can be faithfully represented by the words of a natural language (such as *and*, *or* in English). Conversely, each word of the language does not uniquely correspond to one particular logical entity; the conjunction *but* is very different from *and* in daily use, yet it normally does not have a separate logical symbol. In the case of the following two sentences:

Mary is a nice girl *and* she takes swimming lessons

Mary is a nice girl *but* she is poor at tennis,

many logicians would argue that both *and* and *but* have to be rendered by the same logical conjunction *and*, symbolized by '&'; the difference is that *but* carries a 'conventional implicature' of 'adversativity' (Grice 1978:117; see further section 3.2.4).

Logic is in essence an abstraction from language and should never be made into its dominant perspective; this holds in matters of both syntax and semantics. The semanticists' efforts to save "the entire body of logical machinery built up over two millennia of thought about linguistic and philosophical problems" (Levinson 1983:145) by inserting some special rules concerning, e.g., implicatures may well founder on the rocks of ordinary language use; in the words of a well-known philosopher and logician, "ordinary language has no exact logic" (Strawson 1950:344; cf. Levinson 1983:175). The following section will deal with some problems in syntax that arise from the use of the logic-inspired rewrite rules that were devised by Chomsky and his school (cf. also our earlier discussion of 'selection features').

2.4   Of cats and ducks

In 1968, George Lakoff published an article, entitled 'Presupposition and relative well-formedness' (reprinted as G. Lakoff 1971b), which perhaps documents the earliest outbreak of the anti-Chomsky rebellion.[14] It is in this article that Lakoff for the first time, publicly and in writing, rejects the formal-logic criterion of syntactic 'well-formedness', imposed by Chomsky as the ultimate standard by which to judge a linguistic production.

In the Chomskyan linguistic tradition, well-formedness plays the role of the decision-maker in questions of linguistic 'belonging': a language consists of a set of well-formed sentences, and it is these that 'belong' in the language; no others do. This definition – explicitly invoked or assumed implicitly – has been the pillar of the Chomskyan system for forty years; it is also the definition that, from the earliest times, has come most often under attack from the quarters of the 'Ordinary Working Linguists' (also called 'OWLs'), and the one that makes least sense if we for a moment consider what it is that people *really* say, and how they judge well-formedness in relation to their own language's 'correctness'.

This latter notion has a lot to do with what speakers know about themselves, about their conversational partners (the 'interlocutors'), about the topic of the conversation; especially important is how the participants feel about the progress they're making in conversation as opposed to 'not getting anywhere'.[15] Moreover, what *we* perceive as correct often collides with correctness as prescribed by some grammarians. As an example, take the *constructio ad sensum*, by which a singular noun denoting a collective body takes a plural verb form, since we perceive the plurality of the 'sense' as more important than the grammatical rule that prescribes the singular in connection with a singular noun (as in 'The board of directors have decided not to pay dividends this year', and similar constructions). The following is another case in point.

The grammar of English tells us to use the relative pronoun *who* when we are dealing with a noun which is human (and naturally animate), whereas we use *which* for a non-human (possibly also non-animate) referent. Thus, we have:

The man *who* kissed my daughter ran away (human subject)

The car *which* hit John's bicycle disappeared around the corner (non-animate, non-human subject)

The bird *which* shat on my nose flew away (non-human, animate subject).

Such are the rules. But are they always maintained? Or are there cases where strict rule observation is less 'correct' than breaking the rule? Consider one of Lakoff's additional examples:

My cat, *who* believes that I'm a fool, enjoys tormenting me.

This sentence is not all, or always bad, depending on the cat, the speaker, and their relationship. Given a special, intimate connection between human and pet ("if I happen to have such a cunning feline", G. Lakoff 1971b:330), it may even be the case that *which*, for a cat of a certain quality and lineage, is totally inappropriate, even unthinkable.

The same is the case in the following extract, describing a program (called 'CREANIMATE') that will allow children to create animals of their choice, using the computer:

In a typical interaction, a student may indicate that he wants to create a bird that swims. The system may respond by discussing some existing aquatic birds such as ducks and penguins. It could display video sequences demonstrating how these birds use the ability to swim to help them survive in the wild. The tutor would try to get the student to refine his design by asking whether the bird will use *his* wings to swim, the way a penguin does, or *its* feet, the way a duck does. (Schank and Edelson 1990:9; my emphasis)

Strictly speaking, the above is not only ungrammatical: reference ('anaphora') is made to a non-human being (a penguin) by the human pronoun *his*, but, moreover, inconsistent. Both penguins and ducks are non-human, yet only the latter are referred to by *its*. So why is a duck 'it', a penguin 'he'?

The question is not just about human-likeness (penguins 'dressed up' in black ties, like noble corporate gentlemen at a social occasion). The different conceptualizations relate to the total context in which we see penguins, ducks and humans; here, visually and conceptually, the arms are somehow characteristic of human swimming. While 'hand-swimming' is typically human, 'doggie-style swimming' (with all four feet) is more animal-like. Penguins swim with their 'hands', practicing 'human-swim'; ducks swim with their feet, like dogs: they 'animal-swim'.[16]

We are dealing here with an instance of a more general case, in which "extralinguistic factors very often enter in judgments of well-formedness", as

Lakoff remarks (G. Lakoff 1971b:330). It is precisely those 'extralinguistic factors' that open the door for apparently ungrammatical behavior.[17]

The next section will examine the case of these extralinguistic factors more closely.

2.5 Linguistics and reality: presupposition

Many linguists used to believe that meaning is something that should be dealt with outside of linguistics. The very term 'extralinguistic' carried with it the connotation of 'unscientific', and suggested that the linguist relying on outside information somehow was cheating on method. Leonard Bloomfield, the father of American structuralist linguistics and author of the classic work *Language*, expressed the opinion (in his chapter 9, 'Meaning') that since linguistic meaning only could be studied through speakers' utterances in situations, we shouldn't be worried about 'real', independent meaning (1950:143ff). Charles Hockett, author of a widely used textbook in the strict Bloomfieldian tradition (*A Course in Modern Linguistics*; 1959) doesn't even offer a chapter on semantics. The same aversion to dealing with matters of meaning can be found in authors as different as Louis Hjelmslev and Noam Chomsky. Still, the problem of 'real' meaning is here to stay; to a pragmatician, the very idea of 'extralinguistic' meaning, as if belonging to another, forbidden 'real' world, is suspect.

Suppose I utter the following:

John managed to sell his shares before the market crashed,

to which a bystander remarks:

No, he didn't.

The reply (whose full, non-ellipted form would be 'No, John didn't manage to sell his shares before the market crashed') contradicts the first utterance and denies its truth: both utterances cannot be true at the same time (they have different truth conditions). Even so, in both cases, we understand that John seriously tried to sell his shares. This remains true, even though the utterances have opposite meanings: according to the first speaker, John was successful and sold his shares, whereas the second maintained that he was not and had to take a financial beating.

A possible explanation would be that both utterances contain an underlying element (a 'proposition' of the form 'John tried to sell his shares') which remains constant, whether or not it is true that John actually sold those shares. Such an element is often called a *presupposition*. In our case, the presupposition that 'John tried to sell' survives his failure to do so, the negation contained in 'He didn't'. (More on presuppositions in section 7.2.3.2.)

According to some linguists, the 'survival' property of a presupposition is built into the very semantics of a particular lexical item, a word. For instance, Karttunen (1971) believed that a verb such as *to manage* conventionally implies 'trying seriously' (on implicature, see section 3.2). For others, presuppositions are inextricably tied to a particular lexical item, as when the checker in an American supermarket tells you to "Hurry back [to the store]." Here, the use of the word 'back' logically presupposes that you've been to the store before: otherwise, you couldn't come 'back'.

However, most cases are not such clear-cut instances of semantic or logical presupposition.[18] Most of the time, neither a purely logical account, based solely on the truth or falsity of sentences in isolation, nor an exclusively semantic account, based on the value of individual lexical items, will be satisfactory; we must appeal to a *pragmatic* explanation, based on the particular context of a particular utterer. Consider the following pair:

John regrets that he failed the exam.

John doesn't regret that he failed the exam.

Both sentences rest on the presupposition that John has failed his exam – and that there in fact has been an exam.[19]

But compare now a composed sentence such as:

John doesn't regret having failed, because in fact he passed. (Levinson 1983:201)

The second half of the above sentence ('because in fact he passed') presupposes (in fact, logically reduces to) 'John passed'; in contrast, the first part presupposes that he failed. Hence, we have a logical contradiction: the conjunction of the two sentences involves conflicting truth values.

The reason that the above sentence does not strike us as illogical is that we can easily conjure up a situation where a person would say exactly that. Imagine, e.g., that the utterer has trapped somebody into believing that John had failed the exam, whereupon this latter person might say something to the effect that s/he is sure that John regrets his having failed. Then, the former speaker might swoop down on the unsuspecting victim and utter the above sentence in a triumphant tone of voice.

A further point is that in real interaction (as Talbot has pointed out; 1987:183), the presupposition implied in the 'regretting' is the *one* speaker's only: since the other speaker knows that John has failed, he or she doesn't have to 'undo' (or 'cancel') the presupposition. That is, presupposing is more than just a matter of implying and inferring abstract conditions on speaking: what I can imply or infer, given a presupposition, depends on an active choice made in the face-to-face confrontation with my interlocutor – that is, in the last instance, on the Cooperative Principle (see section 4.2.2) and its active management. Put in another way, for a presupposition to be realized in conversation, we have to execute some kind of *pragmatic act* (more on this in chapter 8).

We conclude that, since presuppositions like the ones discussed here rest entirely on the user context, they are *pragmatic*, rather than semantic: their "only plausible use [is] in interaction" (Talbot, ibid.)[20] Moreover, since all (linguistic or other) interaction is impossible without the presence of 'interactants', that is, of persons who engage in interaction, the ultimate 'real-world' presupposition is the pragmatic 'actant', the *language user*. Thus, the stage is set for examining the role that this user plays in scenarios such as the ones we've been looking at so far.

2.6   A world of users

The renewed interest in the users of language, as compared to an earlier focus on language as an abstract system, is among the main factors that have made pragmatics possible. But registering the fact that pragmatics now is a fully accepted part of linguistics shouldn't prevent us from asking questions such as: how can we explain this interest, and where did it come from?

Levinson (1983:35ff) notes several 'convergent reasons'. First of all, there are the historical reasons: mainly, the earlier-mentioned discontent with Chomsky's aseptic and abstract model of a grammar. Along with this external factor, there are the internal linguistic problems, stemming from the grammar's inability to deal with language as it is being used. Since users and their language are at the core of all things pragmatic (cf. the Haberland and Mey quotation in section 1.2.2.1), the 'world of users' is the very condition for doing any pragmatics: a truly *existential* condition.

Consider once more the example given above:

Getting married and having a child is better than having a child and getting married.

Our understanding of utterances like these depends crucially on the worlds in which their speakers live, both in general with regard to the conditions of their (married) lives, and in particular as to matters and manners of child-begetting and -rearing. These 'worlds of users' cannot be predicted from the language viewed as a logical system, but can only be discovered by looking at the way language is used in those worlds. Suppose I discovered (to continue a thought experiment suggested by Gazdar 1979:115) a copy of the papal encyclical *Humanae Vitae* on the utterer's night-table – that would no doubt have a big impact on my efforts to make sense of the above statement, which then could be attributed either to the utterer's wish to identify with an adage of age-old wisdom, or to his or her total ignorance of the facts of life: it all depends on the user's world, the speaker's linguistic, social, cultural and general life context. An utterance such as the one cited above does not make any sense until we place it in its human context.

This context is not just 'more of the same', a widening of the sentential perspective to encompass more words and phrases. As Bilmes has perspicuously remarked, the context is the total social setting in which the speech event takes place: "the meaning of an utterance is determined in large part by how it responds and how it is responded to, by its place in an interactional sequence" (1986:127), that is, a context of use.

Historically, the importance of this point of view has been most forcefully advocated in non-traditional linguistic work, such as that by Boas, Malinowski, Firth and others, not to forget the anthropologically and sociologically inspired language studies by people like Goffman, Fishman, Halliday, Hymes (just to name a few).

But also more traditional linguists have recognized the need to incorporate the context into their explanations. Pragmatics specifies this context as one in which the users are of paramount interest, inasmuch as they represent the driving force behind the linguistic enterprise, both in its theoretical (grammar-oriented) and its practical (usage-bound) aspect.

In this user context, one operates with notions such as the 'register' (is an utterance formal or relaxed; does it connote social prestige; and so on); the modal aspects of the utterance (having to do with language users' attitudes); questions of rhetoric (e.g., 'how to get one's point across'); and so on. These and similar issues have been almost totally neglected by linguistics (as they had been, until recently, by mainstream philosophy ever since the demise of the Sophists).

Now, if we confront this world of users and usage with the universe of *rules*, so characteristic for traditional linguistics, we cannot but marvel at the chasm separating the two domains. Even stranger is the fact that the practitioners of traditional linguistics did not seem to worry too much about a situation which nevertheless affects not only the syntax (as the case of 'who' vs. 'which' has shown), but also the semantic rules, discussed above in connection with presuppositions. A further area of common linguistic neglect used to be that of *speech acts* (to be discussed in chapter 5), and its expansion into *pragmatic acts* (chapter 8).

All these phenomena (along with many others, sometimes called 'extralinguistic') can be brought together under the umbrella of *context*, basically the linguistic version of the 'human condition'. In the chapter that follows, we will examine this contextual condition with the aid of the various linguistic and pragmatic notions and devices that we have at our disposal.

Review and discussion

1. In section 2.3, I criticized the idea that language has to obey the laws of logic. If you agree, then what to make of the following cases?

(a) Here is an anecdote, told about the famous inventor Thomas Alva Edison:

After Edison had tried, for the longest time, to construct a dry cell battery that would generate as much current as the unwieldy wet cell ones, somebody asked him if he wasn't discouraged by the fact that he had had no results. To which Edison is said to have replied:

"No results? I now know of 963 things that don't work!"

In normal language use, 'result' means: 'a result that satisfies my expectations', and hence, a negative result is 'no result'. Logically, one could argue that any result, even a negative one, is some result; which was what Edison pretended to maintain in the face of his critic.

Question:
What does Edison's remark show about the relationship of language and logic?

(b) Similarly, doubts occur to Alice, when she is told by the White Queen to try and believe that she, the queen, is:

"just one hundred and one, five months and one day."
"I ca'n't believe *that*!" said Alice.
"Ca'n't you?" the Queen said in a pitying tone. "Try again . . ."
Alice laughed. "There's no use trying," she said: "one ca'n't believe impossible things."
"I daresay you haven't had much practice," said the Queen. "When I was your age, I always did it for half-an-hour a day. Why, sometimes I've believed as many as six impossible things before breakfast." (Lewis Carroll, *Through the Looking-Glass*, in: *More Annotated Alice*, Martin Gardner, ed., New York: Random House, 1990, p. 237)

The question raised here by the White Queen is one of the oldest problems in philosophy, and one for which there is no true linguistic solution. Doing an impossible thing is, on strict logical terms, impossible. As the late Thomas Ballmer once ironically remarked (pers. comm.): "Impossible worlds? No way!" What he meant was that there is no way that we could rule out something as impossible, and at the same time believe it, or do it (a proposition that goes under the name of 'Moore's Paradox'). In the Scholastic debates of the sixteenth century, the question of whether God knows things that could have happened, but were never realized because something else happened that made them impossible, attracted great attention among philosophers, the Dominicans maintaining that God, since he knows everything, also must know this kind of 'non-happening' or 'futurable'; whereas the Jesuits affirmed that God, being the ultimate in rational thought, wouldn't waste his time thinking about non-things (or non-sense).

Question:
How could the White Queen assert that she had believed ". . . six impossible things before breakfast", and how would you counter such a postulate?

(c) Finally, what to say about the following, uttered by a mother cooking spaghetti for her family, who are impatiently waiting for their dinner:

They are done whether they are or not? (Rundquist 1992:443)

'Logically' speaking, this makes no sense: spaghetti are done when they are done, and not done when they are not. In this sense, the utterance carries no 'information': it is an 'empty utterance', semantically speaking. So what is the point of the mother saying this? What sense does it make, and how is this possible?

2. On October 4, 1992, an El Al cargo plane lost control and plummeted into an apartment complex in the southwestern part of the city of Amsterdam, The Netherlands. More than 75 apartments were razed, and an unknown number of people killed; the official estimates ran as high as 250, but were later downscaled, as fewer bodies were found than expected. The day after the crash, the mayor of Amsterdam, Ed van Thijn, was on Dutch radio, where he was asked how many people he estimated had been killed in the accident. The mayor replied:

"We expect 250 persons to be killed".

Now, if you were a teacher of English, your first reaction would be that the mayor, not being a native speaker of English, in reality meant to say that he expected 250 people to have perished in the crash – an estimate which later on, and fortunately, turned out to have been too high. However, suppose the mayor had been one of these stubborn Dutchmen who always think they are right, he might have countered with the following reasoning:

"Since 'to be killed', practically as well as logically, means the same as 'to be dead', when I say the sentence 'I expect 250 persons to be killed', what I'm saying is logically equivalent to 'I expect 250 persons to be dead', and therefore there is absolutely no reason to correct me."

Question:
Would you agree with Mayor van Thijn? If not, how would you argue against such a view, using syntactic, semantic or pragmatic arguments (or maybe all three kinds)?

3. In many philosophical schools, the basic logical unit is the 'proposition' (also called 'judgement', in deference to Aristotle and the School). The classic example is 'Socrates is mortal', a type of proposition that conjoins a subject and a predicate by means of a copula (*is* in English). While the logicians may insist that no proposition is complete without this copula, natural languages take a different view. Compare the following original Spanish email conversation, in which the sender asks the receiver 'How are you?', and immediately continues, without waiting for the other's reply, with 'I'm OK':

> [Alma to Robin:] ¿Hola Robin que tal? Yo bien, aunque con el sindrome de la computadora.
> ("Hi Robin, how are you? I'm OK, except for my computer syndrome.")
> (Alma Bolón to Robin Cheesman, 9 May, 1991; pers. comm.)

On closer examination, neither of the Spanish expressions *¿que tal?* and *yo bien* strictly corresponds to its translation, containing some form of the copula 'to be'. Some would, of course, argue that what Alma is saying is logically the same as *Yo estoy bien*, or even that she should really have uttered that phrase (literally: 'I am well'; from the Spanish verb 'to be': *estar*); however, that is not what she does. Similarly, in the second half of Alma's 'reply' to Robin's unuttered answer, we have to intrapolate a form of 'to be' in the literal translation 'even though [I am] with the syndrome of the computer'. Again, although this may be a logical necessity, the language with sovereignty disdains such user-unfriendly pretensions.

Questions:
How does this phenomenon relate to the 'duck-penguin' case in section 2.4?
Does it strengthen or weaken the demand for a 'logical structuring of language', as it was advocated by philosophers like Russell and Carnap?
How would a pragmaticist argue about such apparent 'anomalies' (of which the world of languages is full, by the way)?

4. *Euphemism*
The emphasis on logic, syntax and truth-functional conditions which is characteristic of much of modern linguistic thinking hampers our understanding of the use of human language when it is perceived as non-permitted, being either 'illogical', 'incorrect' or even content-less or 'false'. Yet, many of the ways in which people use their language rest precisely on such 'illicit' operations; one of them is called 'euphemism', an act of language by which I assert something else than (sometimes even the opposite of) what I really want to say. According to classical rhetoric, 'euphemistic' language allows us to talk about negative-laden subjects in terms that deliberately try to pre-empt any negative reaction on the part of our interlocutors. This is why euphemism is rampant in areas that are (in large

parts of Western society) subject to cultural taboos, such as sex, death, sickness, money, religion, politics, bodily functions etc.

Question:
Can you give one example of a euphemism in each of the areas referred to above?

Next, consider the following:

In the movie *The Panama Deception*, the excerpt below of a National Public Television transmission was shown after a screening of actual movie and video clips of the US military going into a poor section of Panama City and methodically destroying street after street by throwing hand grenades and incendiary bombs into each house, as they went along. In the excerpt, US Army Speaker Peter Williams was interviewed about the role of the US military in the invasion of Panama, and said the following ('a thing like that' refers to previous accusations by journalists of willful killing of civilians and destruction of their property by the American invasion forces):

> No, the military folks wouldn't do a thing like that . . . I cannot recall having seen any evidence of military folks being engaged in operations like burning down houses. (*The Panama Deception*, Barbara Trent, dir., David Kasper, ed., Empowerment Project, 1992)

Questions:
Identify the euphemisms in the above passage.

What does the expression 'military folks' suggest to you? (Hint: during Hurricane Georges in September of 1998, a speaker on KUT (the University of Texas Broadcasting System) admonished the listeners to solidarity with "the coastal folks" in Florida and Louisiana).

As we will see later, there is a fourfold condition on human communication, expressed in the short formula 'want, can, do, must': "Given that I *want* to communicate, what I *do* communicate depends on what I *can* communicate, given my circumstances, and on what I *must* communicate, given my partner's expectations"; section 4.2.1). Using this formula, show how the condition operates in speaker Williams's communicative efforts. In particular, ask yourself the following questions:

Does Williams communicate successfully?
   If not, why not?

Then, turning the tables, ask yourself how the movie-makers use the formula given above. (Hint: consider how they exploit the contrast between the speaker's words and the actual footage of the invasion.)

If 'credibility' is the name of the game in the (especially visual) media, how would you say Williams comes through as a credible communicator, as compared to the movie-makers? (Hint: one could define 'credibility' as 'being able, actively or passively, to make people believe not only what you *must* communicate, but what you *can* communicate'.)

PART II
Micropragmatics

CHAPTER THREE

Context, Implicature and Reference

3.1 Context

From what has been said in the previous chapter, it has become clear that pragmatics is definitely more than just a linguistic waste-basket, an extension of linguistics on its own terms. Rather, linguistics will have to be extended on 'extralinguistic' terms by breaking away from the strict, local paradigm of grammar; this is where the notion of *context* comes in. The present chapter will elaborate on this.

3.1.1 The dynamic context

In section 1.3.2.1, I noted the importance of the context in figuring out ambiguities in spoken or written language. Context is a *dynamic*, not a static concept: it is to be understood as the continually changing surroundings, in the widest sense, that enable the participants in the communication process to interact, and in which the linguistic expressions of their interaction become intelligible.

I also mentioned the difference between a 'grammatical' and a 'user-oriented' view of language: on the former view, the linguistic elements are described in isolation, as syntactic structures or parts of a grammatical paradigm, such as case, tense etc., whereas on the latter, one asks how these linguistic elements are used in the context of interaction.

A view of pragmatics that limits the context to what is grammatically expressed, to the exclusion of any wider, 'extralinguistic' contexts, has, of course, a big advantage: it eliminates a number of potentially irrelevant factors from the scope of our investigation. For instance (to take a well-known example from

Chomsky 1957), the presence of food in the mouth while speaking may be part of *some* context, yet it is not a linguistic factor, and maybe not even a pragmatic one.

Consider also the ways in which we refer to persons or things: using proper names, pronouns, articles and so on. A person named 'John' is referred to as 'John' only in his own, known context; a person named 'the policeman' is an officer we know (or are supposed to know). Saying 'John is the policeman' makes sense only in a context where there is a person John whom I know by name and who happens to be the policeman (or is assigned that role in a play).

Being user-oriented, contexts can be expected to differ from user to user, from user group to user group, and hence also from language to language. Take the case of household appliances, where the same instructions appear side by side in different languages, depending on the user groups one wants to target. The differences are often remarkable, both in the choice of wording and in the length of the message. Consider the following text in English and Spanish, found on a towel dispenser in a restaurant in Cadillac, Michigan:

↑	9″	DEJAR QUE
	MAXIMUM	CUELGE UN
	LOOP	MAXIMO DE
↓		9 PULGADAS

(The Spanish text translates literally as: 'Allow [it, viz. the towel] to hang a maximum of 9 inches').

Our first reaction, upon noticing this different way of expressing the same thing, could be that Spanish is more verbose, or more elegant, than English. Alternatively, one could assume that Spanish-speaking people know little about modern restaurant gadgetry, and therefore have to be instructed more explicitly. This explanation, even though it smacks of racial or ethnic superiority, nevertheless contains a grain of truth, and leads us on to the different *contexts* that surround this message and determine its encoding: a North American context, using English, vs. other environments, where mainly Spanish is spoken.

Without necessarily subscribing to racial prejudice, one may safely assume that more Spanish speakers than speakers of English will be unfamiliar with such gadgets as towel dispensers in restaurants. Among the personnel who maintain washroom facilities, there may likewise be a number of people who have not been exposed to the blessings of American civilization long enough to appreciate towel dispensers, seat protectors and other salubrious devices found in American toilets. For such people, explicit instructions for installing and maintaining a towel dispenser may be necessary and helpful. Even for English-speaking users, this type of instruction on packages or wrappings for tools can be notoriously hard to follow; for one who is not familiar with the hardware, the laconic language of the English instructions ('nine inch maximum loop') may create a problem. Only when we see the gadget, read the explicit instructions and place the words in their proper context does the text begin to make sense.

Context is more than just reference. Context is action. Context is about understanding what things are for; it is also what gives our utterances their true pragmatic meaning and allows them to be counted as true pragmatic acts, as we will see later (chapter 8). As a case in point, consider the following utterance:

It's a long time since we visited your mother.

This sentence, when uttered at the coffee table after dinner in a married couple's living room, has a totally different pragmatic meaning than the same sentence, uttered by a husband to his wife while they are standing in front of the hippopotamus enclosure at the local zoo.[21] It is this latter context which allows an innocent remark (a seemingly neutral speech act of asserting) to be transmogrified into a pragmatic act of 'mother-in-law bashing'.

Context is vitally important not only in assigning the proper values to reference and implicature (about which more in the following sections), but also in dealing with other pragmatic issues, both those to be discussed later (such as the pragmatic act) and those mentioned in the previous chapter (such as presupposition). Other context-related features were also briefly touched upon there, among them the phenomenon of 'register'.

By *register*, one understands the linguistic resources that speakers have at their disposal to mark their attitude towards their interlocutors. Thus, we have the formal vs. the informal register, often expressed by different forms of address, as in the so-called 'T/V system' (Brown and Gilman 1961) of languages like French, where the familiar *tu* alternates with the formal *vous*. Other languages may use different verbs: for the informal 'to be', Japanese has -*da*, which alternates with the more formal -*desu*, and the highly formal *gozaimasu*. Such alternations may contrast in pretty similar, yet subtly different contexts; thus, the engineers operating the city loop in Tokyo, the formerly state-owned Yamanote Line, routinely announced the upcoming station using -*desu* (pronounced [das], with something like the Midwestern American sound in 'West'), whereas their colleagues on the private railways were under orders to use only the highly polite *gozaimasu*.[22]

Another example occurred on German television's Program 2 (*ZDF*) on March 26 of 1992. The famous East German poet and singer Wolf Biermann, whose escape to the West and subsequent 'denaturalization' (he was deprived of his East German citizenship as a punitive measure) created quite a stir in the mid-eighties, was on a panel with his former friend and impresario Sasha Andersen, who still lived in the East, even after the Berlin Wall had come down.

In the course of the conversation, the discussion touched upon such delicate matters as Andersen's relationship with the *Stasi*, the German secret police. Biermann maintained that he had information showing that his friend had been an informer for the police, which Andersen denied. The latter also reminded Biermann of how he (Biermann) only had been able to work in the East thanks to Sasha Andersen's intercession and support, among other things, as a publisher and printer of Biermann's songs.

In a pragmatic perspective, the most interesting feature of this conversation was that at a given point, the two friends started addressing each other by the formal *Sie* for 'you', whereas they before had used the familiar *du* (as they probably had been doing all their lives). This sudden and total change of register was due to the fact that the *context* had changed: from a relaxed one, in which the two friends indulged in camaraderie and good-natured banter, to a matter of (literally) life and death. Much to the discomfort of whoever happened to watch the scene, accusations and invectives were hurled across the table; one could literally observe how beyond a certain, 'critical' point the familiar form *du* no longer could be tolerated, in the same way as water cannot exist as a liquid above a certain, critical temperature. This critical point, however, was only implied in the context, never exactly specified; still, both interlocutors spontaneously obeyed its unwritten law. In the changed context, certain forms of speaking were simply 'canceled' and the 'nicer' speech acts were made pragmatically impossible.

It is characteristic of a pragmatic view of contextual problems to acknowledge, and to want to explain, this tension between the interactants' spontaneous and allowed ways of expressing themselves. Pragmatics does this by appealing to the use of language (among other things, in speech acting and in choice of register) as not only prescribed grammatically, 'grammaticalized', but mainly affordable pragmatically, 'pragmaticalized', so to speak. The next section will give some particulars.

3.1.2 Context and convention

No matter how natural our language facilities or how convention-bound their use, as language users, we always operate in contexts. Therefore, the context looms large, and has to be taken into account whenever we formulate our thoughts about language.

There is a built-in contradiction between the conventionalized and more or less rigid forms that the language puts at our disposal, and the spontaneous, individual expression of our thoughts that we all strive to realize. This is true not only of the more technical rules of the grammar (especially those governing the inflection of words and the structure of sentences), but also of what is usually discussed under the general heading of 'meaning represented in propositions'. As the Danish linguist Johan Nicolai Madvig expressed it one and a half centuries ago, "Humans want to speak, not just name isolated representations. Language begins with the sentence" (1843:31). In other words, humans are made for 'speaking' (that is, communicating in spoken sentences or utterances), rather than for carrying on abstract discourses about the meaning of things, in "isolated representations".

Meaning can be natural, as expressed in the old Scholastic saying *Urina est signum sanitatis* ('Urine is a sign of health'); that is, from a person's urine it is possible to conclude about the person's health; and this conclusion is immediate, natural and, in most cases, non-controversial.

In contrast to such a natural sign, language is *conventional*: that is, there is no immediate, natural connection between a word and what it expresses.[23] If we had to rely exclusively on 'natural signs', our communication would be rendered extremely restricted and difficult, if not impossible and indeed paradoxical, as we will see.

The *general* paradox of language is that it is natural only inasmuch the desire to communicate, and the need to express themselves, are natural for all humans. But we cannot 'read off' this 'speaker meaning' of an utterance in the same way, and as directly, as a physician is able to interpret the 'natural meaning' of the color and other significant properties of a person's urine.

In contrast, linguistic meaning (also called 'sentence meaning') is purely conventional (or 'non-natural'), inasmuch as it operates only within the rules of the grammar and the context of a given society. Acquiring the linguistic and social communicative conventions is a task that language users acquire gradually, and many of them only imperfectly. The *specific* paradox of pragmatics is, then, that language users must employ socially conventional, linguistic means to express their individual intentions. The invisible workings of their minds cannot be immediately expressed, in a natural way, but must be coded in non-natural, conventional and contextual, carriers.

The paradox of conventionality vs. spontaneity is undone by the fact that the mediating carriers (the 'media', one might say, in the proper sense of the word) are conventionalized through human use. In fact, we get so used to the medium of language that it becomes our second nature. Speech becomes so natural to us that in order to characterize our language in contrast to 'artificial' (logical or computer) language, we use the adjective 'natural' – despite the fact that, strictly speaking, all languages have been developed among users and for users, as social artifacts. There strictly are no such things as 'natural' languages.

This leads us to an important conclusion as regards pragmatics. Since language is developed in a social context, its use is governed by society rather than by the individual speakers. Language users do not decide, on the spur of the moment, which medium to choose in order to get their ideas or feelings across; they use the *artificial* signs that *natural* language provides them with, given the affordances of their actual, historical context. The context determines both what one can say and what one cannot say: only the pragmatics of the situation can give meaning to one's words.

Thus, one and the same utterance can obtain completely different, even diametrically opposed effects, depending on convention and context. Well-known phenomena such as irony, sarcasm, metaphor, hyperbole and so on show us the richness and diversity of the life behind the linguistic scene, as compared to what transpires on stage through the official roles and costumes. For instance, if I say 'Great!' to the airline agent who just has told me that – due to double booking – I cannot get a seat on my plane, and will have to spend the night in the airport, I am using this 'sentence meaning' in a quite novel way to express my 'speaker meaning': what I'm really saying is something like "This is the worst thing that could happen to me right now."

However, this is not tantamount to a linguistic variant of 'anything goes'. Even if linguistic forms, by themselves, do not limit, or exhaust, the uses a speaker may make of them, they are still among the most important elements of human communication, and have to be respected as such. But how do we go about recognizing what Levinson has called the "full communicative intention" of a speaker (1983:18)? Levinson answers his own question as follows: "By taking into account, not only the meaning of [an utterance] U, but also the precise mechanisms [such as irony etc.] which may cause a divergence between the meaning of U and what is communicated by the utterance of U in a *particular context*" (1983:18; my emphasis).

The following conversation offers some striking examples of the context's importance in understanding utterances:

(*A and B are on the telephone, talking over arrangements for the next couple of days*).

A: So can you please come over here again right now.
B: Well, I have to go to Edinburgh today sir.
A: Hmm. How about this Thursday? (Levinson 1983:48–9)

It does not take us long to realize how many presuppositions, implicatures, references and other factual and contextual conditions have to be drawn upon in this exchange in order for it to make sense. All of this cannot be accounted for by semantics or syntax, let alone by reference to 'bare facts'. For instance, the time of the conversation ('today') is understood as being different from 'this Thursday' (time reference: see section 3.3.2), but not only that: 'this Thursday' only makes sense if uttered on a day between 'last Thursday' and the Tuesday preceding 'this Thursday' – otherwise the speaker would probably have said 'tomorrow' or 'the day after tomorrow' (conversational implicature: see the next section). Further, the place from which A is speaking is obviously not Edinburgh, but neither is it a place that is too far removed from either Edinburgh or the speaker's location (presupposition: see section 2.5). In addition, A (being addressed as 'sir') seems to be in a position that allows him to give orders to B (presupposition and implicature). And so on. All these facts are dealt with not as 'bare facts', on their face value, but as elements forming part of a context that they pragmatically determine and presuppose, and which 'reflect our ability to compute out of utterances in sequence the contextual assumptions they imply:

...the spatial, temporal and social relationships between participants, and their requisite beliefs and intentions in undertaking certain verbal exchanges' (Levinson 1983:49).

Pragmatically speaking, the decisive importance of context is that it allows us to use our linguistic resources to the utmost, without having to spell out all the tedious details every time we use a particular construction. However, the observation that language operates in force of contextually implied conditions and assumptions is by no means restricted to the above case. In the following sections, we will look into cases where the very existence of such implicit relationships has given rise to an important, independently motivated concept in philosophy and linguistics: that of implication, and its pragmatic variant, *implicature*.

3.2   Implicature

3.2.1   What is an implicature?

The word 'implicature' is derived from the verb 'to imply', as is its cognate 'implication'. Originally, 'to imply' means 'to fold something into something else' (from the Latin verb *plicare* 'to fold'); hence, that which is implied is 'folded in', and has to be 'unfolded' in order to be understood.[24] A conversational implicature is, therefore, something which is implied in conversation, that is, something which is left implicit in actual language use. The reason that pragmatics is interested in this phenomenon is that we seem to be dealing here with a regularity that cannot be captured in a simple syntactic or semantic 'rule', but has to be accounted for in other ways. As Bilmes has expressed it, "In everyday talk, we often convey propositions that are not explicit in our utterances but are merely implied by them. Sometimes we are able to draw such inferences only by referring what has been explicitly said to some conversational principle. In certain of these cases, we are dealing with 'conversational implicature' " (Bilmes 1986:27).

To obtain a satisfactory account of implicature, we appeal not just to some general 'conversational principles', but to specific, *pragmatic* ones. The following is a first approach; on pragmatic principles, see further the next chapter.

3.2.2   Implications and implicatures

The term 'implication', as distinguished from 'implicature', defines a logical relationship between two propositions. Let these propositions be symbolized as p and q; then the logical implication is the relation 'if p, then q', or:

$$p \rightarrow q.$$

If-then relationships are well known also in daily life, and can be expressed in everyday language. Suppose I have a hedge that needs cutting, and a son who might do the job, given the necessary inducements. Let the 'proposition':

you cut my hedge

be symbolized by p, and:

I'll take you out to dinner

by q. Then the logical expression $p \rightarrow q$ will stand for:

If you cut my hedge, I'll take you out to dinner.

Suppose I say this to my son, he will have a rightful grudge against me if he cuts the hedge, yet I refuse to make good on what he considers to be a promise. And his grudge is not only rightful; it is also logical: $p \rightarrow q$, or: p implies q, as one could also say. So far, so good.

But what if my son does not cut the hedge? Then, it will be OK for me not to take him out for dinner, and he will have no claim on me. However, logically speaking, I *could* still take him out to his favorite hamburger joint: from the non-truth of the first proposition (p), I cannot conclude to the non-truth of the second (q). Logically, non-p does not imply non-q.[25]

As we see from the above example, a logical implication does not have to correspond to what in everyday life we understand by 'implies'. In the above case, we would say that my son's not cutting the hedge 'implied' his not getting a dinner, just like his cutting 'implied' his being taken out. However, logic and everyday life do not always look at things the same way. This is why we need another term: in addition to the logical implications, we will speak of *conversational implicatures*. They will be discussed in the next section.

3.2.3   Conversational implicature

In a first approximation (a more precise definition will be given below), one could say that 'conversational implicature' concerns the way we understand an utterance in conversation in accordance with what we expect to hear. Thus, if we ask a question, a response which on the face of it doesn't make 'sense' can very well be an adequate answer. For instance, if a person asks me:

What time is it?

it makes perfectly good sense for me to answer:

The bus just went by,

in a particular context of conversation. This context should include the fact that there is only one bus a day, that it passes by our house at 7:45 a.m. each morning, and furthermore, that my interlocutor is aware of this and takes my answer in the spirit in which it was given, viz., as a hopefully relevant answer. Notice also that if we limit pragmatic explanation to the strictly grammatical (cf. Levinson 1983:98), we would have to exclude such relevant answers, since there are no grammatical items in this interchange that carry the required information about the users and their contexts.

To know what people mean, you have to interpret what they say. But interpretation is a tricky affair; misunderstandings are always possible, and sometimes seem to be the rule rather than the exception. As Leech remarks, "[i]nterpreting an utterance is ultimately a matter of guesswork, or (to use a more dignified term) hypothesis formation" (1983:30–1). We can show this, using Leech's own example.

Suppose one of my aunts has a birthday, but I don't remember the exact date. I can ask another member of the family, e.g., by saying:

When's Aunt Rose's birthday?

and the person I'm asking may answer:

It's sometime in April.

'Sometime in April' means, strictly speaking, that it could be any day in April, between, and including, the 1st and the 30th. However, in real life, such an answer means a whole lot more: on hearing that it's 'sometime in April', we understand that it probably is not on the first or the last day, or even on one of the first or last days of the month. People born on April 1 usually are remembered for that particular lack of luck, and in general, when it comes to remembering birthdays, we seem to be able to do better than just an unspecified 'sometime' in a month; we would say, for instance, 'sometime in early April', 'in the middle of April' or 'at the end of April'.

All these possibilities logically imply 'sometime in April'. But (although logically, it's OK to say 'sometime in April', even though the actual birthday is on the 1st, around the middle, or perhaps on the 30th of the month), *if* our conversational partner knows the date, and does *not* offer this information, the answer 'sometime in April' will strike us as somewhat bizarre. We may even suspect the speaker of bad faith or of withholding essential information: if he or she knew the exact date, why did he or she choose such a vague expression?

Supposing that our partner is not liable to allegations of ill will, conversational (as opposed to logical) implication tells us that the only thing the speaker remem-

bered in answering our question about auntie's birthday was the month in which
it occurred. But how does this conversational implication, or 'implicature', come
about?

We have already seen that strict semantic or logical criteria will not help;
neither will just guessing, unless qualified in relation to the particular circumstances of the question, the persons involved in the situation, their background
and so on. The more we know about this context, the more qualified our guesswork is going to be. The reason that people normally do qualify as guessers has
a lot to do with the fact that their interlocutors are 'guessable', and that their
common context, including their language, predisposes them for certain guesses.
But there is more.

As Thomas puts it, "in conversational interaction, people work on the assumption that a certain set of rules is in operation, unless they receive indications to
the contrary" (1996:62). Normally, what we expect when asking a question is
that people *cooperate* by giving us an answer; and whatever comes our way, following a question, will normally be taken for an answer. Such cooperative mechanisms have very little to do with logic and semantics, but are grounded in the
pragmatics of conversation, in particular the 'Cooperative Principle'; this will be
discussed in more detail in section 4.2.2. For now, let's focus on another property that separates conversational from logical implication: the fact that the
former can be undone (or 'canceled'). The following example is adapted from
Leech (1983:85).

If I want to express the fact that one of my children has had her hand in the
raisin box, by uttering:

Alexandra ate some of the raisins,

then my allegation has a well-defined conversational scope: Alexandra ate some,
but not all of the raisins. Now, if in the course of the (presumably somewhat
heated) interchange that follows, I inadvertently were to say to my daughter
something like:

But why did you have to eat all those raisins?

she will rightfully accuse me of conniving or manipulating, and she may point
out that logically and conversationally, 'some' and 'all' are not the same.

While it is true that, on a strictly logical interpretation, 'some' does not
always have to exclude 'all' (there is a sense in which 'all' can be said to be a
very special case of 'some'),[26] this does not help us to interpret the 'raisin
case' in accordance with the intention of the speaker and the understanding of
the hearer: that some, but not all of the raisins were eaten (presumably by Alex).
The solution to this dilemma is, again, that there is a conversational implicature
at work here, telling us that if a speaker says 'some', she or he does not mean
'all', because in that case, she or he would have said so. Saying 'some' conver-

sationally implies that I do not mean 'all', because if I did mean 'all', I would have said 'all'.[27]

This view squares well with the observation that conversational implicatures, once established and accepted, have nothing of the 'eternal', durable quality of logical implications. Conversational implicatures can always be 'untied', canceled, in the course of further conversation: being 'implicated' by a particular conversational context, another conversational context can 'ex-plicate' them again.[28]

In the case at hand, I can abrogate the implicature by adding more context, as when, having uttered:

Alex ate some of the raisins,

I add, as an afterthought:

– in fact she ate *all* of them.

Here, the added context undoes, 'cancels', the first utterance's implicature: 'some' turns out to be 'all', after all.

The context is the 'universe' of everyday language use, the sum total of what people do with each other in conversation. Hence, in a case like the above, it is the current conversational context and its conversational implicatures that decide whether the contradiction between the quantifiers 'all' and 'some' is a logical or a pragmatic one. Consequently, for my reaction to be adequate, I will have to adapt it to the particular context of utterance. What is contextually formed as a logical implicature will not tolerate a pragmatic answer, and conversely, a pragmatic implicature will make no sense in a purely logical or formal-grammatical environment. The ultimate reason for this, as we will see later, is that in the final analysis, both logical and conversational implicatures, in order to play a role in human interaction as pragmatic acts, must conform to their pragmatic contexts of use.

Not all implicatures, however, are either logical or conversational; there is another, so-called 'conventional', kind, which will be the topic of the next section.

3.2.4   Conventional implicature

The use of conversational implicatures to plug the holes left by our not-too-careful use of truth conditions and logical terms may for some logicians and philosophers invoke the proverbial pragmatic waste-basket. Fortunately for them, there are other implicatures around that are not subject to the fickle finger of conversational fate, and do not depend on a particular context of language use: the 'conventional' implicatures.

Certain expressions in language implicate by themselves, or 'conventionally', a certain state of the world, regardless of their use. Such implications cannot be attributed to our use of language in conversation, on the contrary: they become manifest through (sometimes despite) such use. For instance, the word 'last' always denotes (by conventional implicature) 'the ultimate item in a sequence', as in 'the last page of a book or manuscript'; in contrast, in conversation it might imply: 'that which came before the time of speaking', as when a speaker refers to 'last winter'.

Consider also the case of 'speaking with an accent' – be it a provincial or rural twang or burr, or a more exotic, foreign intonation. An accent is like the 'natural sign' of the Scholastic philosophers: if my urine is a 'sign of health', it is because it shows something about my health, whether I want it to or not (as we have seen in section 3.1.2). Similarly, my dialect tells people where I am from, independently of my will.[29]

However, accents may also indicate social inferiority (which is true, in general, of 'oppressed' language forms and languages: see section 11.3.2; cf. also Mey 1985:25–6). This 'inferiority' has nothing to do with the language as such; one generation's dialect may become the speech of the ruling classes in the next, as history has demonstrated over and over again. Rather, the problem (as with all deviant language) is in what dialects imply: namely, that speakers with an accent do not belong in the socially 'received' world of language use.[30] Speaking a non-standard variety of the language usually connotes a socially lower standing, a lack of culture and education, and in general a lot of negative features. Such implicatures are standardized by convention, and cannot be changed even if we invoke another context; hence they are called 'conventional'.

One may wonder whether conventional implicatures have anything to do with pragmatics; some authors seem to be of the opinion that they do not, since they are, so to speak, 'automatic' and therefore non-cancelable: once a Galilean, always a Galilean (*pace* Professor Higgins's Eliza, the exception confirming the rule). Cf. 'Conventional implicatures are non-truth-conditional inferences that are *not* derived from superordinate pragmatic principles like the [Gricean] maxims, but are simply attached by convention to particular lexical items' (Levinson 1983:127). This 'attachment' may take the form of unavoidable, almost logical conclusions, such as when Leech remarks that on hearing a sentence like:

Sally is the secretary,

we automatically conclude that:

Sally is a secretary (1983:90).[31]

On this view, a conventional implicature is automatic and non-cancelable. Such a view is open to criticism, however. First of all, one should resist the temptation to believe that anything in pragmatics can be explained by 'laws'. No matter how conventional the implicature, the very conventions which govern its use are historically developed, culture-specific and class-related: conventional *implicatures* may clash with conventional *uses*.

As an example, take the well-known case of the 'polite' vs. 'impolite' forms of address, as they are realized in French in the form of the contrasting pair *vous* and *tu*. Using an example originally due to Edward Keenan (1971:52; Levinson 1983:177), if I utter:

Tu es Napoléon,

the conventional implicature is that the addressee is either familiar with me or located below me on the social scale. In contrast, saying:

Vous êtes Napoléon

would be appropriate in case I was addressing the first consul himself, or anybody else with that name who commanded my respect.

However, such conventional implicatures are well defined in their proper contexts of language use only; when these contexts change, the 'conventionality' of the implicatures will change as well. As a result, one may be confronted (both historically and locally) with a 'gliding scale' of in principle non-cancelable, or conventional, implicatures and implicatures that are cancelable or 'non-uptakeable' (as in conversation). For instance, two or three generations ago, French children would mark their respect for their parents by addressing them with the pronoun *vous*; today, such a use is virtually non-existent in French society. Or, to take another example, it is quite all right to use the 'non-polite' form (*tu*) when asking for a drink in a Québec bar, whereas no one would ever do so in France: the conventional implicature of 'familiarity' is in this case cancelled out by the language use of the Québecois pub culture. Neither is it possible in such a context to 'exploit' the implicature to obtain a special effect (e.g., of being impolite in a surrounding where politeness is required, or vice versa).[32]

Second, even straightforward conventional implicatures are not always exploited in a uniform fashion. The most frequently quoted instance of such a 'graded' exploitation is the English word *but*. On a strictly truth conditional view (as we have seen in section 2.3), the value of *but*, when conjoining two phrases or sentences, is the same as that of *and* (that is, sentences conjoined with *but* are true in exactly the same cases as the identical sentences conjoined with *and*). When the conventional implicature is exploited, it normally creates a contrast: what follows *but* is perceived as being opposed to what precedes, whereas in the case of *and*, no such implicatures are generated.

However, there is no strict, universally valid rule that would impose *but* rather than *and* in any particular context; in many cases, the two are almost interchangeable, as in the Bible, where Hebrew *wa* 'and' often functions like a 'but', and vice versa; cf. Genesis 14:21–2: "And the king of Sodom said to Abram

...", "But Abram said to the king of Sodom ...."; 15:2–3: "But Abram said ...",
"And Abram said ...", and so on.

While the Hebrew particle *wa* fulfills both functions ('and' and 'but'), other
languages, such as Latin, may conjoin phrases and sentences without any formal
conjunction at all, as in the 'asyndeton' or 'conjunctionless conjunct' (a well-
known example is Caesar's *Veni, vidi, vici*, 'I came, I saw, I vanquished'). In other
cases, we use pauses or (in writing) a semicolon or colon, rather than 'and' or
'but', leaving the choice of interpretation to our listeners or readers.[33]

I conclude, with Bilmes, that as far as implicatures go, "the rules are not
analogous to scientific laws. The laws of physics are never violated, ...
[c]onversational rules are usually obeyed, and when they are broken, the
breach is 'observable', 'noticeable' (Sacks)" (Bilmes 1986:50; see further
chapter 6).

3.3 Reference and anaphora

3.3.1 On referring

Let's suppose I'm in a foreign country, sitting in my hotel room at night. There
is a knock on the door. I don't open the door, but ask: "Who's there?" The
stranger answers: "It's me." Now, what do I do?

Basically, there are two possibilities. Either I recognize the visitor's voice, and
then I can decide whether or not to open the door. Or I don't, and then I'm in
a quandary. What can I do with a voice that refers to a 'me', when I don't know
who that 'me' is? Since a 'me' always refers to an 'I', and every 'I' is a 'speaking
me', the utterance 'It's me' is always and necessarily true, and hence totally uninformative, when it comes to establishing a speaker's identity. In more technical
terms, there is no known referent for 'me' exclusively by virtue of the linguistic
expression *me*; the reference of a word such as 'me' changes with the person
uttering it.

The philosophical problem of 'referring' has serious consequences not only for
theoretical linguistics, but also for our use of the language; reference is not least
a *pragmatic* problem. We use language to refer to persons and things, directly or
indirectly. In the case of direct reference, we have names available that will lead
us to persons and things: we know who 'John' is, we understand the meaning of
'tax return', and so on. But when reference is made indirectly, as in the case of
the person talking through my hotel door, we need to have recourse to other
strategies, linguistic as well as non-linguistic, in order to establish the correct
reference.

For instance, when the other person says "It's me", I can retort "Me WHO?",
or "Who's talking?", or simply repeat my first utterance ("Who's there?"), maybe
in an irritated tone, or with increased volume. Depending on the answer I get, I

then decide what to do. If the other person says: "It's a friend", I probably will want to know more, as the reference of the indefinite article ("a") is, by definition, undetermined. If the person says: "It's Natasha's mother", and Natasha happens to be the name of one of my important contacts, I probably will open the door, especially if I have the additional information available that comes from recognizing Natasha's mother by her voice.

In extreme cases, I will need substantially more reference-establishing documentation, as when the voice outside starts the conversation by pronouncing: "Police. Open the door!" In such a case, I will at least try to have my interlocutor show me a piece of identification, such as a plastic card or a tag, in order for me to be quite sure of the correct reference.

As the German psychologist-philosopher of language, Karl Bühler, expressed it more than sixty years ago,

> Everybody can say *I*, and whoever says it, points to another object than everybody else; one needs as many proper names as there are speakers, in order to map (in the same way as in the case of the nouns) the intersubjective ambiguity of this one word into the unambiguous reference of linguistic symbols. (1934:103; my translation)

According to Bühler (and in the spirit of the times), 'unambiguous reference' is what is demanded of language by the logicians. In the same spirit, some of the latter in all sincerity proposed that we should abolish words with 'unclear reference' as 'I' or 'you', because there is no way of checking whether they correspond to something 'out there': their reference is always shifting.[34]

3.3.2   Reference, indexicals and deictics

Proper nouns (from Latin *nomen proprium*, 'a name that belongs [to somebody or something]') are the prime examples of linguistic expressions with 'proper' reference: names name persons, institutions and in general, objects whose reference is clear. It is possible to make reference to a certain person or object without using such a 'proper' expression; the classic examples include Sir Walter Scott, referred to either by the expression 'Sir Walter (Scott)', or by any of his attributes, such as 'the author of *Waverley*' (Rudolf Carnap's example; 1956:39ff). Similarly, one can refer to Napoleon as either 'the victor of Jena' or 'the loser of Waterloo' (Edmund Husserl's example).

In contrast to proper nouns, 'regular nouns' (as one might call them), despite their etymological affinity with the word for 'name' (*nomen* in Latin), have a certain indefiniteness in their naming: the word *cow* names any female representative of the *genus bovinum*, and doesn't tell us anything about what a particular cow is called, what it might look like, where it might be in the pen, how many gallons of milk it yields per year, and so on and so forth. To refer to a particular cow, we need something indicating what to look for, and where: an *in-dexical* expression, in short.

Indexical expressions are a particular kind of referential expression which, in addition to the semantics of their 'naming', their *sense*, include a *reference* to the particular context in which that sense is put to work. Suppose somebody utters:

I am six feet tall. (Levinson 1983:58)

The meaning of 'six feet tall' is given by what the individual words mean, and any competent user of English will understand them, in the context of the utterance, as indicating a certain height (in this case, of the person uttering the words). The problem is in the 'I am': how do we understand that the asserted height is indeed that of this particular speaker? That can only be decided by looking at the contextual 'coordinates' of the utterance; only after establishing them can we decide whether or not the utterance makes sense. In order to fix those coordinates, we resort to 'indexicals', as they are called; they include pronouns (especially personal pronouns), local and temporal adverbs, verb tenses, and so on. (Other functions of indexicals will be discussed in section 7.2.4.)

Indexical expressions are *pragmatically* determined, that is, they depend for their reference on the persons who use them. The chief linguistic means of expressing an indexical relationship are called *deictic* elements;[35] we can think of such expressions as 'pointers', telling us where to look for the particular item that is referred to. But if we do not know who is pointing, using an indexical expression, our system of coordinates will be hanging in mid-air. Since all 'indexing' or 'pointing' is done by human beings, and therefore all pointing expressions have to be related to the uttering person, pointing in a particular place and at a particular time involves the traditional philosophic and linguistic categories of person, place and time.

Karl Bühler, whom I have mentioned earlier, has gathered these notions in the term 'index field' (German *Zeigfeld*), centered on an 'origin', i.e., the point of intersection of the main coordinates of the 'here-now-I' system (1934:149). This origin is the base line of the system; it gives any speaker utterance its proper pragmatic meaning in a referential context of person, place and time: *who* is the 'I' that is speaking, *where* does he or she speak from, and *when*, at what point of time?

A word of caution is appropriate here: it seems natural to assume that speaker and 'I' are identical (the 'I' as 'speaking me'). Such an ego-centered organization of deixis, however, is not always and necessarily the case, even though it may be, at least in our culture, the 'default' alternative. But one can imagine other possibilities, as the case of the so-called 'honorifics' shows.[36]

In many Far Eastern languages (such as classical Chinese, Japanese, Korean, Javanese etc.), the base line for determining the honorific use of a particular expression is not necessarily and always located in the speaker's 'origin'. Speakers may downgrade themselves by using less honorific expressions about their possessions, relationships, capacities etc., taking their own origin as the point from which these possessions etc. are looked at and linguistically evaluated, using 'negative honorifics'. But when they speak about other persons' attributes and possessions, the origin shifts: now, it is placed in the intersection of the other person's coordinates. For instance, in Japanese I may refer to my daughter as *musume*, literally '[my] girl'; another person's daughter is called *o-joo-san*, literally '[your] honorable Miss daughter'; similarly, we have several sets of pronouns for person index, all measured against the varying scales of social prestige and (positive) 'face', as it is often called (see further sections 4.2.2.2 and 10.2.3).

Such a change in perspective is sometimes referred to as a shift in 'point of view', an important notion also in other pragmatic contexts such as narrative theory, where the question of whose 'voice' is being heard in narration is one of the major problem areas (this will be discussed at length in chapter 9). Here, let me recount an anecdote to make my point clear:

> A melamed [Hebrew teacher], discovering that he had left his comfortable slippers back in the house, sent a student after them with a note for his wife. The note read: "Send me your slippers with this boy." When the student asked why he had written "your" slippers, the melamed answered: "Yold! [Fool!] If I wrote 'my' slippers, she would read 'my' slippers and would send her slippers. What could I do with her slippers? So I wrote 'your' slippers, she'll read 'your' slippers and send me mine." (Rosten 1968:4; quoted Levinson 1983:68)

This story illustrates the importance of anticipating the way other people construe the world, and of being able to adopt *their* point of view, in addition to our own. Normally, when there is any doubt as to whose point of view is currently being taken, we will add something to clarify the situation: for instance, when I utter: 'To the left!', I can either specify it as 'To *your* left!', or leave the point of view implicit in the context, as happens at army training camp, when the sergeant gives orders to his recruits and shouts "EEEYZZZ LEFT!" – which of course is understood as 'to their left', not his. Similarly, the Yiddish story's *melamed* would have been in trouble had he followed 'normal procedure': he had to use the equivalent of a military drill routine in order to get what he wanted from his wife – a true eye-opener on 'point of view', one might say.[37]

All indexical expressions refer to certain world conditions, either subjective or objective in nature. Consider the case of 'time'. If I say: 'I saw him last week', my 'point of time', viz. 'last week', depends on the point of time I'm at now: that is, the time of my uttering 'I saw him last week.' Now, last week is, of course, the week that came before the current week, the week that is my point of time. I cannot use 'last week' for any old week that has come before some other week; it has to be the week that is 'last' from my current point of view. For a week that precedes (an)other week(s), in general, we use 'the preceding week' or 'the week before'.

The same happens with 'next', as in 'next week'. If we simply want to express the idea of 'following', we say 'the following week'; however, if this following week does indeed follow the present week from the point of view where I am situated, then, and only then, can (and must) I use 'next week'.

Some languages codify these 'points of view' regarding time by giving them specific, lexicalized expressions. For instance, French has lexical pairs for days that follow, and precede, the current day, as well as for days that are not defined with respect to the current 'point of time': while *demain* means 'tomorrow', for 'the day after', the French use *le lendemain*. Similarly, *hier* is 'yesterday' in French, but 'the day before' is elegantly rendered by *la veille* (which is the same word, originally, as English 'vigil').

Problems may arise when we try to connect such 'points of view' across the hemispheres. If I write to Allan, my colleague in Brisbane, Queensland, that I would like to teach at his university during the summer quarter, chances are that he will not know when to arrange my stay. Am I writing from my point of view (my 'summer'), or am I adopting Allan's 'I-origin' for the time coordinates, in Bühler's terminology? And what does my friend Denise from Campinas, Brazil, mean, who (while on a sabbatical in Europe) is telling me a story that is supposed to have happened to her 'last summer'?

In such cases, the context can be made more explicit by adding some further deictic coordinates. I could say, e.g., 'the summer quarter in Australia', to eliminate all ambiguity. Alternatively, I could put myself in the others' perspective by adopting their time line ('your summer'); a similar practice was common for letter-writers in ancient Rome, who deferred to their correspondents by using a past tense when dating their letters: *Scribebam Romae Idibus Martiis*, literally: 'I was writing [this] in Rome, March 15.' (On 'point of view' in a literary connection, see further chapter 9 and Mey 1999.)

Similarly, speakers can use their 'own' past tense for present happenings, if such a happening is seen as the result of a past process, from their point of view. In Japan, on finding the house-key that you had been looking for frantically for the past half hour, you would exclaim: *Ah – arimashita!*, literally: 'Oh – [there it] was'; not: 'There it is', as one does in English. Likewise, when something good has happened, especially in cases where a bad thing had been expected, one says *yokatta* (literally: '[it] was good'), rather than (as in English) 'That's splendid.' Danish has similar usages: *Dér var det* (literally: 'There it was'); *Det var godt* (literally 'That was good', in the sense of 'Good for you' or 'Good for him/her/me/us'), much like the Japanese *arimashita, yokatta*.

3.3.3 From deixis to anaphora

As the cases discussed at the end of the previous section illustrate, we need to refer to the context, not only in order to establish the proper reference for deictic terms such as 'next' or 'last', but also in the case of other deictic expressions whose referents cannot be identified outside of their proper (spoken or written) context. When I use the pronoun *this*, as in:

I need a box *this* big,

I make reference to a certain desired size of box; in the spoken context, I will moreover move my hands and arms to indicate exactly how big the box should be, which normally presupposes that my partner can see me (but see section 7.2.3.1).

But what about:

I met *this* girl the other day;

do I really wish to 'index' this particular person, or am I using 'this' simply to refer to a certain young female who needs no further introduction? In this particular case, her identity might of little interest; alternatively, it could be already sufficiently established in other ways – the case of so-called 'reminder deixis' (Gundel et al. 1993:302). Cf. the well-known refrain 'Gimme *that* old time religion', or the following extract from a 'shadow' traffic report: "the Tri-State very slow, there is *that* overturned car at Touhy" (radio station WBEZ, Chicago, November 13, 1992).

The demonstrative pronouns of Latin show similar indexical traits. Not only do they serve to indicate the dimensions and distances of speaker space but in addition, they may indicate speaker evaluations. Here's how Nathan the prophet spoke to King David, after he had told him the fable about the rich, greedy landowner who virtually had stolen his poor neighbor's only possession, the ewe lamb that was "unto him like a daughter", ate from his plate and "lay in his bosom": *Tu es ille vir*, 'Thou art that [very] man' (2 Samuel 12:3–7). Here, we have a very strong deictic reference, both of pointing and truly 'in-d[e]icting': '*You* are precisely the man I was talking about: *you* stole your neighbor's wife.' (David had in fact 'stolen' Bathsheba, Uriah the Hittite's wife, having placed him in a combat zone where there was not much hope of survival, and marrying her upon the general's death in action.) Compare this strong deixis with the use of 'this', 'that', in the earlier examples of 'reminder deixis', or of *ille* in the title of A. A. Milne's well-known children's book: *Winnie Ille Pu* ('Winnie the Pooh', in its Latin translation), and one notices the difference: here, we have almost no deictic indexicality, but must depend on (implicit) contextual elements.

As we see from the above example, a deictic element often indicates other things than the original spatial or temporal relationships. The Latin pronoun *ille* belongs to a deictic triad consisting of: *hic* (close to the speaker), *iste* (close to the addressee), and *ille* (away at some distance from speaker and addressee); at the same time, *ille* and *iste* connote positive or negative evaluations, respectively. Thus, *ille* connotes 'famous', 'superior', 'important' (as in the above example);

iste 'contemptible', 'miserable' etc., as when Cicero accuses M. Antonius of being the cause of all the Republic's misfortunes, just as the beautiful Helena was of Troy's: *iste huic rei publicae . . . causa pestis atque exitii*, 'this creature . . . who has brought plague and ruin on our Republic' (*In M. Antonium* II:22; Cicero 1856:90).

Over time, such deictics may lose their specific referential powers altogether, as in the case of *ille*, which survives in the Romance languages as the definite article (cf. French *le*). What is left of deixis in such expressions is the pure function of referring to earlier mentions of the noun that the definite article in question identifies. It is precisely this referring function (in a sentence or discourse context) that is called *anaphora*.

Typical anaphoric referrers are the *pronouns*, whose very name suggests that they refer to, 'stand in' for, something else, the 'referent'. In a sentence or discourse context, such pronominal referents are identified by their anaphoric relations. In the following, simple example (*avec hommage à* Teddy Roosevelt):

The man was walking softly; he carried a big stick,

the marks 'the man' as a known referent (he has been spoken of earlier, or is identified in other ways); *he* refers anaphorically to 'the man'. It is a matter of debate how much 'earlier' such a referent is allowed to occur while still claiming a valid anaphoric relationship with its deictic 'stand-in'. And when it comes to the *direction* of referring, in addition to anaphora, where the referent comes before the pronoun, we have 'cataphora', where the referent occurs 'later' in the text.

Another point to observe here is that anaphora does not always obey the strict referential rules of grammar, as in the case of the so-called 'lazy pronouns' (Partee 1972) and other elements with ambiguous 'local reference' that everybody accepts and understands correctly because, in a given context, they are unambiguous. The classic example (due to Lauri Karttunen 1969) is:

He's been to Italy many times but he still doesn't speak *the* language.

Cf. Partee's example:

The man who gave his paycheck to his wife was wiser than the man who gave *it* to his mistress. (1972:434)

In cases like these, we understand the anaphora to cover references that strictly do not have a referent in the text, or have the 'wrong' referent: *the* language does not refer to any language that has been mentioned previously; however, we understand it immediately as 'the language of Italy', since Italy has been mentioned. Similarly, in the other example, despite the fact that *it* grammatically refers to the paycheck the man did not give to his mistress, but to his wife, pragmatically we understand it to refer to the paycheck the man gave his mistress, not his wife.

What interests us most in this connection is not the technicalities of anaphoric reference as such, but its *pragmatic* aspects. A pragmatic approach to anaphora tries to take into account not only what the anaphorical pronoun is referring to, the 'antecedent' (i.e., that which precedes the pronoun and to which the pronoun refers), which can be a noun or noun phrase, a piece of (con)text, but also the whole situation. Over and beyond that, the question is what 'hidden dimensions' there are in anaphorical reference, in particular, what kind of values are implicit in the way we use anaphoric expressions.[38]

A case in point is the reference that holds between gender-marked articles and pronouns and their corresponding nouns. Under the influence of the feminist movement, the controversy about the 'generic masculine' has been reactualized in the past decades; the question is whether it is acceptable to refer to female persons and to 'mixed' sets of humans by the masculine, used 'generically'. In English, there are some quick-and-easy solutions to this problem (using the 'generic plural' *they*, or 'combined pronouns' such as *s/he*, or the more awkward *he or she*); however, not all languages have these options.

For instance, in Spanish (as in other Romance languages), every noun has its specific grammatical gender. As a consequence, most professional appellations come in gendered varieties, one for the male, one for the female practitioner; moreover, referential expressions must agree in gender with the anaphorized ones. In a situation where there are both male and female teachers present, referring to them by saying *los profesores* ('the male teachers') is making a choice. Theoretically, I could also have said *las profesoras* ('the female teachers'); or I could have chosen to spell out the gender distinctions (*los/las profesores/as*), or used the heavier technique of repetition (*los profesores y las profesoras*). Even so, I still encounter the generic reference problem in the corresponding anaphoric pronouns: do I say *ellos* or *ellas*, masculine, feminine, or maybe both?

Consider also the following Spanish examples:

la catedrático 'the female (university) professor'

un modelo morena 'a (female) brunette model'.

Here, we have a real-world reference to women (manifested by the feminine article *la*, respectively the female adjectival ending *-a*); as such, it conflicts with the masculine gender of the head nouns *catedrático* and *modelo*. Rather than characterizing this violation of the grammatical rules as "an insufferable syntactic clash", as is done by the Spanish academician Julio Casares (1947:303) *à propos* these suggested 'feminized titles' (type *la catedrático*; cf. Nissen 1990:14), the pragmatically oriented linguists turn their attention to the real-world reasons for such a 'clash'. The true concern of pragmatics is not to what extent the rules of grammar have been observed, but whether the rules serve to veil, or reveal, the conditions that govern their use, and whether they conceal, as in the case at hand, the existence of a linguistically underprivileged segment of the population, the 'invisible professional women', who grammar-wise have to borrow their titles from their male colleagues.

Such concerns are not just a matter of grammar; they identify a *pragmatic* problem. What is at stake is not simply correctness in observing the grammar rules, but the ways these rules reflect the patterns of domination that are at work in our society. Whereas the grammarian only tells us to avoid *syntactic* clashes, pragmatics informs us about the clashes of interest between social groups, and specifically about how these clashes are expressed (or not, as the case may be) in the language, including the syntax. (See further chapter 11 and Mey 1985.)

Review and discussion

1. The following text was found on the back wall of an airline toilet (in an American Airlines Boeing 757) on 5 April 1995:

> PLEASE USE THE TRASH CONTAINER
> FOR ANYTHING OTHER THAN
> TOILET PAPER

Taken by itself, this instruction could mean that it would be OK to deposit all sorts of rubbish in the trash container; in the narrow context of the airline toilet, this could even be read as inviting people to use the trash as a toilet. In order to understand this notice properly, one has to be familiar with airline mores (and preferably with the background for a request such as this: namely, to avoid blocking the toilet and causing an environmental and physical hazard).

Now consider the following notice found on the back wall of the men's toilets in the Universidade Federal de Brasília, Brasília D.F., on March 25, 2000:

> SEA EDUCADO
> JOGUE O PAPEL NO LIXO

('Be Educated
Throw the Paper in the Waste Basket')

Questions:
Based on your general 'education' in matters of toilets and proper sanitary behavior, would you say this notice is ambiguous?

Would a person from Mars be able to understand it without further explanation?

How to account for these diametrically opposite 'proper behaviors' in American airplanes and Brazilian university toilets?

How is understanding of these contradictory messages dependent on the context?

How do they both make sense, even if objectively contradictory, when we put them in their proper context?

What do the words 'anything other' in the above American instructions mean?

What is the 'paper' referred to in the Brazilian notice?

How do we know this?

2. Study the following sign, appearing at selected private parking sites throughout the Greater Chicago, Ill., area:

> ALL UNAUTHORIZED VEHICLES
> WILL BE TOWED BY LINCOLN
> TOWING SERVICE TO 4884 N. CLARK
> *FEE $80.00   CASH, VISA &*
> *MASTER CHARGE ACCEPTED*
> PHONE 561-4433

Signs such as these are quite common in modern cities, where parking is at a premium and people always try to sneak into spaces that do not belong to them, in order to avoid paying the costly parking fees. Towing wrongly parked cars thus has become quite a profitable business. In New Haven, Conn., a private wrecker service made it a point to stay close to vehicles parked illegally in areas signed 'Absolutely No Parking 4–8 p.m.', in order to be able to pounce on them as soon as the clock struck four, even in the presence of the dismayed owners who might already have their keys in the lock.

On the background of this contextual knowledge, try to answer the following questions.

About the message as such:
Is this an official message, and is there anything strange in its wording, if you consider the message as threatening or implying a punishment for violating the official parking regulations issued by the Police Department?

Who is addressed by whom? Who do you think is the sender of the message: the owner of the parking space, the owner of the phone number or the police?

About the hidden message-within-the-message:
While the sign tells you explicitly something about what might (have) happen(ed) to your car, there is also a strong implicit message. To find out what that is, try

to concentrate on what the sign says about methods of paying the fine. How important is this aspect compared to the 'law-breaking' aspect that is also (or even primarily) involved in parking illegally? Try also to think of other ways of dealing with this kind of violation (in other cities, other countries).

How would you "compute out of [the] utterances [i.e., of this sign] the contextual assumptions they imply" (Levinson, as quoted at the end of section 3.1.2)?

Judging from the text of the message, would you say that illegal parking is a criminal act in Chicago? Also compared to other experiences, elsewhere?

3. In many cases, the immediate context does not by itself furnish all the clues to understanding an utterance pragmatically. Especially in the case of jokes, we rely heavily on the 'non-said', that is, the common understanding that we have of certain things in a cultural environment such as our own. For this reason, it's almost impossible to understand a joke that originates as little as a couple of hundred miles away from one's own location (thus, the inhabitants of the capital of Norway, Oslo, allegedly cannot understand jokes from the city of Trondheim, 250 miles to the north).

With this in mind, consider now the following interchanges:

(a) From a movie script:

> A. 'Your name isn't really Misty Beethoven, is it?'
> B. 'You're right – it's Teresa Beethoven'.

The above interchange is a funny one, because we do not expect people in our day and age to go around and be called 'Beethoven' or 'Mozart' (or, for that matter, 'Quisling' or 'Hitler') – numerous jokes have been built around this common knowledge of our recent political and cultural history. So, if we ask a girl whether her name really is 'Misty Beethoven', we want to make sure that she is no direct descendant of the great composer, but instead, has taken that name as a stage name, for instance. Her answer throws us, because we don't feel 'Misty' to be as 'loaded' as 'Beethoven' – we probably assume it's a nickname, or short for something else. It is this context, with its built-in presuppositions (on which see more in chapter 7) that makes the unexpected reply humorous, because it in reality doesn't remove the 'strangeness' of the name: 'Teresa Beethoven' is every bit as bizarre as 'Misty Beethoven', even in the context of the movie from which this interchange is culled.

Armed with this knowledge, consider the next two examples, and try to establish a contextual condition for their being funny, or unexpected.

(b)

> A. 'What's your name?'
> B. 'Betty Skymitch.'
> A. 'Spell it, please.'
> B. 'B - E - T - T - Y.' (Bruce Fraser)

Given that 'it' in the above interchange is ambiguous, we are led down a so-called 'garden path' (see further section 4.2.2.3), expecting to receive a spelling of the unfamiliar name 'Skymitch' – only to be thrown off abruptly in the last reply.

Question:
How would you describe this effect, using the model give in (a)?
(c) Here's a joke that was told during World War II in the occupied countries of Europe:

> A German peasant comes to the Office of Vital Statistics (a.k.a. the birth registry) in his hometown, and inquires about the possibility of having a name change.
>
> The official on duty asks him what his current name is, and when he hears that it is 'Adolf Scheisse', he immediately understands the farmer's predicament and starts pulling out forms for him to fill in.
>
> Being a bit curious, the official cannot refrain from asking the peasant what he would like be called instead.
>
> The answer, 'Johann Scheisse', is as baffling as it is unexpected. (For those not familiar with German, the word *Scheiße* means 'shit'.)

Questions:
What's funny about this story?

And how much context (world or personal) is needed to make this joke understandable?

How come that a joke probably becomes less funny once you have to make all the hidden presuppositions clear; for example, that Hitler's first name was Adolf (in case you didn't know) and so on?

Given that all jokes are built up towards a punch line, could you give a definition of the punch line in pragmatic terms?

What should such a definition minimally include?

4. Cultural contexts can be very different from country to country, even though on the surface the members of those cultures do and say the same things. The

Japanese imbibe as much Coca Cola and beer as do people in a Western country such as Denmark; and they profess the same interest in fitness and golf as their American counterparts. Yet, the way they go about these things is always slightly different and sometimes quite unexpected. With this in mind, read the following advertisement, and characterize it in terms of a pragmatic understanding of its context, thinking especially of the senders and potential receivers of this message (its 'users', in pragmatic terms).

The text below appears in a shop window on Aoyama-dori in Tokyo, close to the Aoyama Gakuin University underpass. The shop in question deals in high-class sporting goods, and is proud of having been in the business for at least thirty years, witness its name, 'Sweat Studio 1978'. Their flagship sales articles are 'Authentic Color Sweat Shirts by IFCO Corporation', as a note in the window informs us. This note is flanked by a calligraphed text on a 12-by-18-inch laminated plaque, on prominent display among the goods, which reads as follows:

Here, healthy people who drain refreshing sweat gather.
Here, people who know the pleasure of creation gather.
Here, people who find the pleasure of designing one's life plentifully gather.
People with sound body and mind who will endeavor, will all win eternal glory and utmost satisfaction.
So, let's live the limited life utmost!

January 1974

Questions:
What do you think is the pragmatic function of this text?

As an advertisement, do you think it is effective?

What is minimally needed for a person to be an effective sender, respectively a happy receiver of this message?

5. Conversational implicatures are often discovered as a result of a 'clash' in meaning: between what is expected, normal, and what is actually received. For example, when I ask: 'What time is it?', I don't expect an answer like: 'You just stepped on my toe'; however, if that *is* the answer, I will try to make sense of it (maybe in some surrealistic, Beckett-like scene, where the protagonists practice bizarre rituals such as stepping on each other's toes at certain times of the day).
    The cases below all rely on an implied understanding of the total context in which they are produced; the immediately surrounding environment (the 'co-text', as it is often called) not being sufficient.

(a)

A: Let's go to the movies.
B: I'll bring the Kleenex. (Bruce Fraser)

In this example, the context will for some be immediately recognizable as the showing of a particular cult film (*The Rocky Horror Picture Show*); but even if that environment is not available, the implicature may be read off as: 'going to a tear-jerker of a show', or something other in that vein.

For the following examples, try and assign similar implicatures to the uttered or written words:

(b)

A: [*in store*] Good morning. Do you have anything to treat complete loss of voice?
B: Good morning sir. What can I do for you today? (Bruce Fraser)

This one should be self-explanatory!

(c)

A: Did you get to look at those dresses?
B: No, I didn't come that way. (Amy B. Tsui)

The implicature is that 'that way' has something to do with 'those dresses' – but what? (See section 3.3.3.)

(d)

"Road Legally Closed. Proceed At Your Own Risk" (Former Connecticut road sign)

Since one cannot normally 'proceed' on a 'closed road', we must look for other explanations.

(e)

"Frida is a real Friskies cat. She can't wait to come home and have a bowl." (Advertisement for Friskies cat food)

Even if I don't specify the content of the 'bowl' that Frida is looking forward to, there is a clear implicature here.

(f)

> "A Meal To Remember" (road sign for the 'Golden Rooster' restaurant on US Route 3A in Scituate, Mass.)

'Remember' – but for what? (A rather tricky way of advertising, one could say.)

(g)

> "We don't make compromises, we make Saabs" (radio spot on station WBFT, Chicago, August 26, 1992)

Here, the implied meaning must be something that unites the 'making compromises' with car-making – but exactly how?

6. Consider the following father–daughter interchange (Rundquist 1992:433):

> [*A child walks into the kitchen and takes some popcorn*]
> FATHER: I thought you were practicing your violin.
> CHILD: I need to get the [violin] stand.
> FATHER: Is it under the popcorn?

Questions:

What conversational implicatures are generated in this interchange? (Hint: What is the father really telling his daughter? In this interchange, the father, while trying to be humorous, clearly has another agenda: he thinks his daughter should practice, not sneak out into the kitchen after popcorn. His very first reply is taken by the child as an expression of that fatherly feeling; her answer is a defense. Clearly, the father's remark 'Is it under the popcorn?' makes no true sense: everybody knows that violin stands are not normally hiding under popcorn. So there must be a conversational implicature at work. Try to work out this implicature; see also section 3.2.3.)

Are any conventional implicatures present? (Hint: what is the connection between 'practicing' and '[violin] stand'? Cf. section 3.2.4.)

CHAPTER FOUR
Pragmatic Principles

4.1 Principles and rules

The concept of 'principle' is a familiar one in linguistics (as in other branches of science). One encounters the term in many standard titles of linguistics, old and new, and of widely varying content: from Hermann Paul's older work *Prinzipien der Sprachgeschichte* (1874; English translation 1891), through Louis Hjelmslev's theoretical exposition *Principes de grammaire générale* (1929) to contemporary dissertations in the Chomskyan tradition, such as Eric Reuland's *Principles of Subordination and Construal* (1979).

Scientists often use the word 'principle' as having to do with (elementary) understanding, as in Euclid's famous treatise *Principles of Geometry* (410 BC). Principles can be not only 'elements of understanding' but even 'prerequisites to understanding', going all the way from elementary knowledge to high-level, theoretical and metatheoretical speculation. A related use of the term is found in another important work by Hjelmslev, *Prolegomena to a Theory of Language* (1943), in which he lays down three methodological principles for linguistics: *simplicity*, *non-contradiction* and *exhaustivity* (1953:15). These principles are simply conditions for a sound description of a language, and should not be confused with the rules of description themselves, as often happens in modern uses of the word. Thus, Reuland takes 'principle' as being equivalent to 'proposal for description' (1979:2); in the parlance of Chomskyan grammatical writing, 'principled' usually is a mere synonym for 'reasoned', or simply 'justified' (Chomsky 1965:27).[39]

Another term that is frequently encountered in modern, grammatical writing is that of *rule*. Even before Chomsky arrived on the scene, people knew that they had to look in the grammar to find the rules of the language; but it is only in the

wake of the 'Chomskyan revolution' that grammars are thought of as simply consisting of rules. The rules *are* the grammar, not to say: the language.

However, since the Chomskyan rules were purely syntactic, the need arose to
have another term for phenomena of a semantic or pragmatic nature; a term,
moreover, that would create a contrast to the transformational model of language
description (Mey 1991a). We can bring out the need for such a contrasting terminology by asking ourselves what a Chomskyan 'rule' possibly could do outside
of the domain of syntax. Is there any sense at all in talking about rules in semantics, or even pragmatics? What would a semantic or pragmatic rule have to look
like, and what use would it be?

To answer these questions, consider the chief property of a grammatical rule:
its ability to *predict*. The rules of the grammar contain all the information needed
to establish ('generate') the entire set of correct ('well-formed') sentences of a language, and only these; as far as syntax is concerned, language is rule-generated.

But how could this set of well-formed sentences (Chomsky's 'language') ever
be predicted by rules in cases where semantics (or *a fortiori* pragmatics) is
involved? In semantics, the concept of well-formedness is controversial, to say
the least. What a person is saying, and what this person *means* by what he or
she says, are clearly an exclusive concern, not to say privilege, of that person;
hence semantic 'rules' only make sense outside of actual language use (such as
in a dictionary, or in constructed examples). On the other hand, it remains true
that as a rule, the person who moves too far away from the normal meaning of
the words will have difficulties in being understood; but this semantic 'rule' is
one of *usage*, not of prediction.

As I said, the above applies *a fortiori* to pragmatics, where the point of view
of the user is paramount. There, if anywhere, the user 'rules the waves' (and, as
the case may be, waives the rules). Thus, it seems reasonable, as Leech has suggested (1983:5), that we restrict the use of rules primarily to syntax; in pragmatics, we prefer to work with principles. The next sections will examine some
of these.

4.2   Some principles discussed

4.2.1   The Communicative Principle

There is more to the question of rules vs. principles than a mere squabble about
terminology. All-important is the fact that people engage in communicative activity whenever they use language; whether or not they observe a particular syntactic rule is not too important. People talk with the intention to communicate
something to somebody; this is the foundation of all linguistic behavior. I call
this the *Communicative Principle*; even though this principle is not mentioned in
the pragmatic literature (at least not under this name – a variant, the 'Principle

of Relevance', will be discussed later in this chapter), it is nevertheless the hidden condition for all human pragmatic activity, and the silently agreed-on premise of our investigation into such activity. As the US psychiatrist Watzlawick and his co-workers expressed it more than a generation ago, in a book that unfortunately never attracted the attention it deserved among linguists, it is impossible not to communicate: "no matter how one may try, one cannot *not* communicate" (1967:49).

The above, of course, is not to say that users actually always communicate what they set out to do, or what they think they do. However, this problem has nothing to do with the question of whether or not the users observe any rules of grammar. As Leech puts it, speakers often "mean more than they say" (1983:9); compare the cases of conversational implicature, discussed in section 3.2.3. At other times, speakers un- or subconsciously express thoughts or feelings that they consciously would have liked to suppress – something which must be explained in the wider framework of the psychological (and sometimes even pathological) aspects of language use.[40]

As an example, consider the 'scalar implicatures' discussed by Gazdar (1979:56–8). Suppose I utter the following:

Many of the delegates opposed the motion.

On a normal reading, such a sentence would convey the impression that although many delegates voted for the motion, there were a number of them that were against, and voted accordingly. The sentence would thus not be taken to mean that all of the delegates voted against the motion, even though, strictly speaking ('many' doesn't say how many), such a reading would be consistent with the normal reading – especially if I complete my utterance (as in the 'raisin' example of section 3.2.3) by adding something like:

In fact, all of them did.

The question is why anybody would say 'many', if in actual fact there were no others? If I could have used the stronger expression ('all'), why didn't I?

There seems to be a general understanding that people, when they give out information, prefer to do so with a certain parsimoniousness (the 'maxim of quantity', discussed below). But what we're confronted with here is, rather, an instance of the Communicative Principle: when communicating, speakers try to be understood correctly, and avoid giving false impressions. No matter how logically correct and true (according to some abstract semantic 'rule') my speech is, if it confuses or misleads my hearer, then my utterance will not have its proper effect: I will not have communicated what I had in mind.

In Gazdar's terminology, we can talk about a 'strength' scale of expressions, ranging from stronger to weaker; an example is the following scale (adapted from Levinson 1983:134):

all, most, many, some, few, none,

where the strongest 'scalar' expression occurs to the left, with strength decreasing as one moves right. Normally, by using a weaker expression, we exclude the stronger ones; the use of 'many' implies that 'all' cannot be used. The use of a vague expression such as 'some' or 'many' tells our interlocutors that (all other things being equal) we *want* to be vague; and we want them to (correctly) assume that we would have used a more rigorous expression (such as 'all', 'none') if, and only if, there was indeed a need for it. In accordance with the Communicative Principle, we avoid giving our interlocutors either an over- or an underdose of information. (The Communicative Principle, as we will see in section 4.2.1, relies on another principle, that of cooperation, and in particular on the maxim of 'quantity', by which we are supposed to always provide the suitable amount of information.)[41]

Consider now the following. Since, in accordance with what was said above, the occurrence of 'many' implies that 'all' is out of the question, instead of the original:

Many of the delegates opposed the motion,

I could have uttered:

Not all delegates opposed the motion.

This sentence is both more 'rigorous' and easier to verify than the original one; besides, as we have seen, it is implied in it (by conversational, and perhaps even scalar implicature), so why don't I just say this and avoid all misunderstandings?[42]

Again, the answer to this question is given by the Communicative Principle. Given that I *want* to communicate, what I *do* communicate depends on what I *can* communicate, given my circumstances, and on what I *must* communicate, given my partner's expectations. Communication is not a matter of logic or truth, but of cooperation. In the case at hand, it is more cooperative to use the vaguer expression 'many', even though in theory, I could have chosen the more stringent 'not all'. To see this, consider the following example (adapted from Leech 1983:9).

The scene is a political meeting; a motion is proposed and carried by a show of hands. Under normal circumstances, it is more important that the motion is carried than to know whether all of the delegates actually voted in its favor; the question of unanimity is irrelevant to the motion's fate. In fact, as long nobody asks for a vote count or a written ballot, and the secretary of the meeting has enough evidence for a majority vote, it is safer to record in the minutes of the meeting that 'a majority of the delegates' voted for the motion than to qualify the vote as 'unanimous'; even though there may have been a unanimous vote, such a vote is impossible to establish by a show of hands.

Alternatively, imagine that I am the party whip, and that it is my responsibility to ensure that all the party members toe the party line and vote to *oppose* the motion. Suppose further that I'm less than successful in keeping my voters in line; then I might want to de-emphasize this fact, e.g., by stating, in my report to party headquarters, that:

when the question was asked, many of our people voted against.

In a situation like this, the party's executive secretary, criticizing me for my failure to enforce party discipline, might say something like:

but you didn't do your job properly: after all, not all of our people voted against, so

Although from the point of view of strict logic, the second sentence ('not all of our people voted against') is more rigorous than the first ('many of our people voted against'), it does not contain more information. Its effect in the context, however, is strikingly different, as it depends on what the user wants to communicate, in accordance with the Communicative Principle. From my point of view, it is important to emphasize that 'many' people voted against, so that I can pride myself on a job well done. From the secretary's point of view, I did a lousy job; hence it is important to stress that 'not all' voted as required by the party line. This difference is essentially *pragmatic*, since what these utterances emphasize is the user's point of view, as given and limited by the circumstances of context and speech.

To conclude this imagined interchange, I may choose to counter the secretary's remark by saying:

Well, but even so, many of them *did* oppose the motion,

again emphasizing the positive aspects of my behavior, seen from my point of view.

What this example shows is how the Communicative Principle, unlike a grammatical rule, operates in a concrete context, rather than in the abstract space of linguistic speculation. The next sections will go into more detail as to how this principle is interpreted in the pragmatic literature by various authors in different ways.

4.2.2 The Cooperative Principle

In the preceding section, I introduced the Communicative Principle, by which it is understood that people, when communicating, have something to tell each other. Communication, furthermore, requires people to cooperate; the 'bare facts' of conversation come alive only in a mutually accepted, pragmatically determined context.

Cooperation has itself been elevated to the status of an independent principle in the works of the late British/American philosopher H. Paul Grice (1975, 1989), whose *Cooperative Principle* (abbreviated: CP) consists of four pragmatic sub-principles, or 'maxims', to wit:

The maxim of *quantity*:
1 Make your contribution as informative as required;
2 Do not make your contribution more informative than required.

The maxim of *quality*:
1 Do not say what you believe to be false;
2 Do not say that for which you lack adequate evidence.

The maxim of *relation*:
Make your contribution relevant.

The maxim of *manner*:
Be perspicuous, and specifically:
1 avoid obscurity
2 avoid ambiguity
3 be brief
4 be orderly.

These four maxims can be seen as instances of one superordinate (as Grice calls it) Cooperative Principle:

> Make your contribution such as is required, at the stage at which it occurs, by the accepted purpose of the talk exchange in which you are engaged. (Grice 1975:47)

To begin with, let's ask how the CP works, not in the abstract world of principles, but in actual language use. When do we use the maxims, respectively when do we fail to use them, and why are they necessary in the first place?

The answer to the last question is: because otherwise communication would be very difficult, and perhaps break down altogether. The first two questions may be illustrated anecdotally by the following story, showing the usefulness and necessity of some of the maxims in everyday conversation.

4.2.2.1 Dostoyevski and the rubber ball

When my daughter Sara was about six years old, we stayed for a couple of days at some friends' house. These people were lovers of books, and their whole living room was filled with them: there were bookshelves all around and all the way up to the ceiling.

While Sara was playing, somehow her little bouncing ball managed to get itself lost behind a row of books on one of the lower shelves; but since she hadn't seen it disappear, she didn't know where to look for it. Meanwhile, the owner of the books, who was reading his newspaper in an armchair nearby, had observed the ball's wayward course. So, when Sara asked him if he had seen her ball, he replied:

Why don't you look behind Volume 6 of Dostoyevski's Collected Works?

Why is such an answer a non-cooperative one?

First of all, because it violates the maxim of *manner* by offering information in a way which is not 'perspicuous'. For a six-year-old, the name 'Dostoyevski' doesn't have any meaning; at that, this particular collection of Dostoyevski's writings happened to be in Russian, so she couldn't even have obtained the necessary information by going to the shelves and trying to read the author's name and the titles off the backs of the books.

Furthermore, the answer sinned against the maxim of *quantity* by containing, at the same time, too much and too little information:

- too *much* information for one who doesn't know anything about Dostoyevski, and for whom a book still is just a material object of a particular shape and color, but not much more. An answer such as "behind one of those fat brown books in the middle of the bottom shelf" would have been more informative, although it gives less information, 'says less'.
- too *little* information, because what is proffered is not enough to assist the little girl in retrieving her lost toy.

On both counts, the adult interlocutor failed to observe the principal demand set up by Grice in the CP: namely, to cooperate with your conversational partner. In this case, that would have meant to be forthcoming with one's knowledge, rather than squirreling away and niggardly handing out small nuggets of information in a manner that may have impressed some of his adult audience, but certainly alienated the young person considerably (and her parents as well; in fact, when the owner of the Dostoyevski collection had to get up from his chair and get the ball for Sara, we all thought: 'Serves him right').

4.2.2.2　Cooperation and 'face'

When people discuss the CP, two views often clash. One is that of cooperative behavior as a kind of abstract, philosophical *rationality*; the notion of cooperation reduces to what is minimally necessary to explain people's actual use of language (if A says such-and-such, then B is supposed to react in a specific way; more technically: A's saying such-and-such implies conversationally that certain things will be assumed to be the case by B, who will then act in accordance with that assumption).

The second view raises problems of moral philosophy and practical ethics ('without cooperation, communication wouldn't be possible, hence we had better cooperate').[43] Applied to politics, it questions whether the Communicative Principle is robust enough to make people with conflicting interests, and who sometimes in fact are battling with one another (such as Palestinians and Israelis, Iraqis and Americans, Serbs and Albanians and so on), adopt cooperation as the basis for their communicative behavior.[44]

As to the question of rationality, let me quote what Levinson has to say on the subject:

> Are they [the maxims of conversational behavior] conventional rules that we learn as we learn, say, table manners? Grice suggests that the maxims are in fact not arbitrary conventions, but rather describe rational means for conducting co-operative exchanges. If this is so, we would expect them to govern aspects of non-linguistic behaviour too, and indeed they seem to do so. [A number of illustrative cases from daily life follow here, such as: When asked to pass the brake fluid, you don't pass the oil, and so on.]
>
> In each of these cases the [non-cooperative] behaviour falls short of some natural notion of full co-operation, because it violates one or another of the non-verbal analogues of the maxims of conversation. This suggests that the maxims do indeed derive from *general considerations of rationality* applying to all kinds of co-operative exchanges, and if so they ought in addition to have universal application, at least to the extent that other, culture-specific, constraints on interaction allow. Broadly, this too seems to be so. (1983:103; my emphasis)

In the next section, I will draw attention to certain problems that are posed by Levinson's notion of 'full co-operation', and show that this notion is a utopian one, inasmuch as our pragmatic world does not operate on fictions such as a 'general . . . rationality', especially where culture-specific considerations enter the picture. Here, I want to say a few words about a concept that has attracted considerable attention in recent years, especially among people studying cooperation phenomena from a practical point of view (such as the 'ethnomethodologists'; see section 6.3.1.1), namely, the notion of *face*.

'Face', as an explanatory concept in human interaction, was originally introduced by Goffman (1967). It is believed to derive from common Far Eastern notions of deference and politeness (Scollon and Scollon 1995:34), as expressed in the familiar locution 'to lose face'. In its usual interpretation (established by Brown and Levinson, 1978), 'face' has two aspects: a *positive* one, by which a person's status as an autonomous, independent, free agent is affirmed; and a *negative* one, which stresses a person's immunity from outside interference and undue external pressure. Analogously, we could define positive freedom as the freedom to express oneself, to vote, to travel, to choose one's own company; negative freedom would mean being free from oppression, from threats to one's safety, from political persecution, police harassment, importuning sales people, and so forth.[45]

Acting cooperatively, people try to build up their interlocutors' 'positive faces', while trying to avoid posing threats to their 'negative faces'. This is especially important in linguistic interaction, since every engagement in conversation opens up the possibility of 'losing face': I may either be 'drawn out', and say something I didn't really mean to say, or didn't have the intention of sharing with my interlocutor (as often happens in 'open-microphone' interviews), or I may be subjected to bullying treatment by someone who doesn't like me, who thinks my presence is unwelcome, or who wants to exploit me for her or his own profits.

When face is being threatened in interaction, both faces, the positive and the negative one, come under attack. A request to help someone may, for instance, constitute a threat to my positive face ('What kind of crazy person is this who thinks I'm here to help her?' – actually a variant on the old theme of 'Am I my brother's (sister's) keeper?'; Genesis 4:9), as well as to my negative face ('I don't want to be bothered'). My interlocutor can (especially if she knows me) think of how to minimize these face-threats, either by building up my positive face ('You're actually the only person in the world who could help me') or by catering to my negative face ('I know this is an imposition, but could you please help me?').

In the first case, my partner tries to make me feel appreciated, loved, indispensable; in the second, she shows me due respect by stating that she realizes she is intruding on my privacy, and that she is sorry for that.

There is, however, a third possibility, depending on how well I know the person, and how much social distance there is between me and my interlocutor. This strategy is called 'to go bald on record' (as having requested help, information or whatever, as in the example above). The circumstances may force me to use a 'bald' imperative, as when I discover there is a bomb in the car, and I yell at my passengers: 'Get out of here, quick!' In a family situation, bald imperatives are frequent ('Pass the salt'); also, when the request is to the addressee's benefit, we are more likely to go bald on record (as Kunst-Gnamuš has remarked; 1991): 'Have a good morning', 'Help yourself to some more bourbon' and so on.

Expressions that take the edge off face-threats are often called 'mitigation devices' (see, e.g., Fraser 1980); here, one also could include the techniques that we will study later on, when we talk about 'indirect speech acts' (section 5.4), 'pre-sequences' (section 6.3.2) and 'pragmatic acts' (chapter 8). In this connection, one such class of cases especially deserves to be mentioned: the 'forgettable' requests, named thus by me for a frequent 'opting-out' expression: 'Forget it.'[46]

If somebody asks me for a favor without really making a formal request, for example, by 'dropping a hint' ('Gee, that ice cream looks really good' –

implying: 'Can I have a taste?'), the 'request' is made 'off record', as Brown and Levinson call it; hence I, the addressee, do not have to go 'on record', either, as acknowledging it and reacting to it. An appropriate off-record reply (amounting to a more or less polite refusal) would be: 'Yes, aren't they clever, those Swenson people?' ('Swenson' being the name of the ice-cream makers). Since my face was never officially threatened by this request, I don't have to deal with any implicit 'threat' to my face: the reply is just as much 'off record' as the request.

Alternatively, I could react by saying: 'Yes, why don't you get yourself one, too?' Here, the implicit request is more explicitly denied, and I go on record as having detected the real reason for the other's remark. In this case, I may officially pretend not to have registered a request for ice-cream sharing; but the mitigating effect of my answer is not as complete as in the first case, though a lesser threat to my interlocutor's face is posed than by the use of abrasive, face-threatening replies such as 'Get lost', 'You're wasting your time', 'Leave me alone' or indeed 'Forget it!'

We see how cooperation is a complex concept, involving many layers of interactive behavior, including politeness and 'face'. By being polite, we conserve our integrity as interlocutors while being considerate of our partners' faces – in one fell sweep. Politeness is our strategy for conversational cooperation with least cost and maximum benefit to all interlocutors; see further section 4.2.3, where the 'Politeness Principle' is discussed.

4.2.2.3   Cooperation and 'flouting'

People like Levinson, who deduce the notion of cooperation from 'general considerations of rationality', tend to overlook a number of problems that actually occur between cooperating humans. In the following, I will identify three important areas where such problems may arise.

First, there is cooperation itself, taken as a general, inviolable and indisputable rule of behavior. As has been pointed out by many authors (see, e.g., Leech and Thomas 1988:15 for some references), this assumption is simply too broad and sweeping. I will not go into any detailed treatment of this question here, but refer to what I have written on the subject elsewhere from a societal point of view (Mey 1985).

Second, there are significant intercultural differences in cooperative behavior. Among the Malagasy (as studied by Elinor Ochs Keenan 1976), conversational cooperation seems to consist in making one's contribution as opaque, convoluted and non-perspicuous as possible, in apparent flagrant violation of the CP. In fact, however, we're looking at ways of exercising the virtues of conversational cooperation which are normal, and even highly valued, in this particular community.

Some linguists (e.g., Gazdar 1979:54–5) have understood these findings as implying that cooperation, interpreted as strict adherence to the Gricean principles ('Be brief', 'Be perspicuous' etc.), is always defined relative to a particular culture. Others (e.g., Green 1989) have pointed out that the Malagasy's 'opaque-ness' is not simply a withholding of information, but a culture-specific way of dealing with sensitive issues ('information provided strictly on a need-to-know basis', as they say in the military); compare that "information [which] does not threaten the speaker's position in the community [or violates a taboo] . . . is not withheld" (Green 1989:96). Green concludes that Malagasy speakers abide by the CP, even if they sometimes need to let the maxim of quantity play second fiddle to that of quality.

The third issue is rather different, even though it has a superficial similarity to the first two. One cannot help noticing that certain forms of social (including language) behavior are preferred (and hence rewarded), while others are subject to sanction; as the Bible says: "Or what man of you, if his son asks him for bread, will give him a stone?" (Matthew 7:9). (On preference in conversation, see section 6.3.2.3.) Or, to take Levinson's (1983:103) example: if a car-owner tells a passer-by that he is out of gas, the cooperative conversationalist assumes that the purpose of the remark is to inquire about the possibility of obtaining gasoline somewhere near. The reply:

Oh; there's a garage just around the corner,

is considered, in normal conversation, to mean that the car-owner will be able to obtain gas there.

Conversely, if such expected cooperative behavior is not forthcoming, we do not necessarily assume that some kind of general 'exception' to the rule of con-versational cooperation is in effect; rather, we infer, by conversational implica-ture, that something else is going on.

When people "blatantly fail to observe one or several maxims" (Thomas 1996:65), we speak of 'flouting' a maxim, either semantically or pragmatically. The first happens when I use a word in a sense that is contrary to what is com-monly accepted, and I know that my interlocutor is not aware of this. Smither-man quotes the case of Muhammad Ali, who caused a great international commotion by publicly pronouncing that "there are two bad men in the world. The Russian white man and the American white man. They are the two baddest men in the history of the world" (Smitherman 1984:103). Here, the semantic content of 'bad' is in blatant contradiction of its 'official' content (which is usually the case in American Black English cf. "he baaad, man", uttered as a compli-ment); but Muhammad Ali's international, mostly non-Black audience could not be expected to know this.

As to the second, pragmatic kind of flouting a maxim, we must consider the effects people want to obtain by their linguistic behavior. Recall the case of Sara's rubber ball, discussed in section 4.2.2.1: here, the violation of the Gricean maxims may have been motivated by a desire to impress the girl's parents, or maybe even – who knows? – to introduce a six-year-old to Dostoyevski. Whatever effect was intended, and even if we may safely assume that any utterance potentially has an 'indirect' address to what is sometimes called the 'innocent by-stander', Leech and Thomas's (1988:15–16) general observation remains valid: "we can make a blatant show of breaking one of the maxims . . . in order to lead the addressee to look for a covert, implied meaning", thus gently nudging the listener or reader to the assumption of one or more conversational implicatures. Consider the following incident and accompanying dialogue.

In 1969, my wife Inger and I were attending a conference in New Orleans, Louisiana. On the first evening, after the talks, we decided to go to a discotheque with friends. My wife was stopped at the door, and the guard asked her to produce an ID. Here's an extract of the conversation that followed:

> DOORMAN: I need to see your ID, it's the rule.
> INGER: But I left it back at the hotel.
> DOORMAN: Sorry ma'am, then I can't let you in.
> INGER: But I'm twenty-nine and the mother of four!
> DOORMAN: Yes, and I'm the pope's grandfather and have six kids.

By way of response to Inger's (direct and indirect) reference to her age, the doorman gives out a blatantly false piece of information concerning his own age (he could not have been a day over twenty-five). By flouting the maxim of quality, he thus intends to convey a message: viz., that he considers my wife's explanation and justification as untruthful. He could have told her directly: 'I don't believe you', or: 'That's clearly false', but instead, he chose to convey his message in a more elegant, and just as effective, way. Needless to say that, even if we had to go back to the hotel to get Inger's driver's license, in the end, she was not altogether unhappy about the incident: at the time, the drinking age in Louisiana was 18! Thus, one could say that the flout had the pragmatic effect of a compliment, although it most likely was not intended as such. (See further chapter 8 on this kind of 'pragmatic act'.)

In special cases, the pragmatic effects intended by the flouting may not be immediately available for inspection, as they are postponed for better results; cases in point are jokes and stories. Suppose that, when telling a joke, I start out by revealing the punch line. That won't do me any good, nor will my audience appreciate my observation of the maxim of quantity ('Be as informative as possible'). I'm simply being a bad joke-teller. A similar misunderstanding happens in the case of the author who, when telling a story, puts all his or her cards on the table. We do get the information, and it is as complete as can be – but do we like to be treated that way? Certainly not; as readers, we want to be fooled, at least up to a certain point (Mey 1994d). The author who plays it sincere cannot expect to be taken seriously: good authors have always something up their sleeves, and may allow themselves deliberate omissions, misleading statements, uninformative or disinformative remarks and all sorts of narrative tricks in order to better develop the plot.

The late Argentine writer Julio Cortázar was a past master of this gentle art of deception; in one of his novellas, 'Clone' (1982), he leads us down a 'garden path' of musical narrative, only to reveal, at the very end, that he all the time had been playing with a double deck of cards; in other words: that he had been deliberately flouting most of Grice's maxims. What happens in the novella is a contemporary re-enactment of an historical tragedy: the double murder of the Prince of Venosa, Gesualdo's wife and her lover at the hands of the crazed, cuckolded husband. Cortázar executes this re-enactment by assigning his protagonists the parts of the piece of music they are performing: they are clad, as it were, in the voices of a Gesualdo madrigal – except that this crucial musicological information is withheld from us until we have finished our first reading; whereupon the author takes us through a second reading, 'if we wish', where we are given all the necessary information.

On another occasion, in an uncanny 'spider story' ('Historia con migalas'; 1985), Cortázar plays an ingenious cat-and-mouse game with his readership, entrapping them in a web of morphological subtlety, based on the Spanish language's uninformativeness as to the gender of non-compounded plural verb forms. Only in the last two lines is it revealed that the persons we had been thinking of as a 'normal' couple are in reality two 'black widows', who devour the men they come in touch with. (An analysis of this narrative masterpiece is provided in Mey 1992b.)

In the final analysis, since 'flouting the maxims' can be many things, there is no way of prescribing or proscribing a particular violation as useful or detrimental. Here, as in all other matters of linguistic consumption, the producer is judged by the willingness of his or her clientele to buy into the violated maxims: the proof of the pudding is, as always, in the eating.

4.2.3 Politeness and other virtues

A criticism that is often offered of Grice's maxims is that they can be interpreted as a *moral* code of behavior: 'How to be a good conversationalist' ('good' in both senses of the word: 'expert' and 'virtuous'). And it is easy to understand why: obeying the rules of any game both marks you as a decent kind of person (one who doesn't cheat) and may even give you a chance of coming out ahead of the others.

However, the moral aspect of the matter is not what has kept philosophers and linguists busiest. The former's avowed aim (adopted by many of the latter as well) is to construct a *rational* philosophy of language use, to "describe rational means for conducting co-operative exchanges" (Levinson 1983:103). The underlying assumption here is that of a rational language user; I will have more to say on this later on, in chapter 7, when discussing metapragmatic principles. For the moment, let's concentrate on another principle (or rather, set of principles): *politeness*, as mainly advocated by Leech (1983).

First, one has to know what being 'polite' means. According to Leech, "[s]ome illocutions (e.g., orders) are inherently impolite, and others (e.g., offers) are inherently polite" (1983:83). This view assumes politeness to be an abstract quality, residing in individual expressions, lexical items or morphemes, without regard for the particular circumstances that govern their use. Being 'inherently' polite implies being *always* polite, without regard for the contextual factors that define what is polite in a given situation.

Such a view is wrong on two counts. First, the social position of the speakers may indicate different politeness values for individual cases. The existence of a social hierarchy (as in institutionalized contexts such as the schools, the military, religious communities etc.) often pre-empts the use of politeness altogether. Rather than claiming that an order in the military is polite whenever the command structure is right, I prefer to say that an order is vindicated in its own right, if it conforms to the demands of the military hierarchy; commands are neither polite nor impolite. The same goes for official exchanges between participants in institutionalized situations: the priest imposing a penance after hearing one's confession is neither polite nor impolite when he issues the order *Ter Ave* (meaning: "I order you to say three times the 'Hail Mary' as a penance for your sins").

Second, the politeness of the order also depends on the positive or negative effects it has on the person who is given the order. Olga Kunst-Gnamuš (1991) has shown that this 'cost–benefit scale' is decisive in assigning politeness values even to 'bald' imperatives. Her statistics show that "the evaluation of the politeness of a request expressed in the imperative form depends on the evaluation on the cost and benefit scale stemming from the required act" (1991:59). In other words, I can use a 'bald' imperative if the order is beneficial to my addressee ('Have another sandwich'), as opposed to an order which imposes a hardship on the hearer ('Peel the potatoes'); in Kunst-Gnamuš's words, "requests to the hearer may be expressed directly in the imperative form without being considered impolite" (1991:60).

Another problem has to do with what is called 'mitigation'. The principle of politeness tells us to minimize (or 'mitigate') the effects of impolite statements or expressions ('negative politeness') and to maximize the politeness of polite illocutions ('positive politeness'); all the time, of course, respecting the intentions that direct the ongoing conversation. Leech provides some examples (1983:80):

PARENT: Someone's eaten the icing off the cake.
CHILD: It wasn't ME. (*with rising-falling intonation on the emphasized ME*)

In this case, according to Leech, a parent relying on a conversational implicature to generate an insinuation of a possible misdemeanor is considered more polite than a parent uttering a direct accusation, such as:

You have eaten the icing off the cake.

In the latter case, the child would have been insulted, especially if the accusation in fact was incorrect. By contrast, the first utterance, although it is not as informative as possible, or maybe not even relevant at all, and thus violates the maxims of quantity and/or relation, still obeys the Politeness Principle, and thus is able to rescue the Cooperative Principle "from serious trouble", as Leech remarks.

Similarly, in the following example:

A: We'll all miss Bill and Agatha, won't we?
B: Well, we'll all miss BILL. (*intonation pattern as in the above example*),

the principle invoked by Leech is, again, politeness, not cooperation. By not mentioning Agatha, when you don't agree about her being missed, you're being more polite than by saying outright that you don't miss her.[47] Here, too, cooperation takes a back seat to politeness: B, in not offering any comment on a part of A's utterance, knowingly and willfully sins against the maxim of quantity, but does so for reasons of politeness.

Notice that in this case, flouting the CP does not necessarily imply that B is being 'nicer' in dealing with unpopular people like Agatha: politeness and being nice are not necessarily connected. One could arguably maintain that the way the speaker in the above example treats Agatha in her absence is a lot *less* nice than baldly mentioning her as a *persona non grata* would have been – if for no other reasons, then because Agatha's possible cooperation in the exchange is *a priori* and summarily excluded: she is not even mentioned in B's reply, but made 'invisible', as so often happens to women in our society.

One of the functions of politeness is to create (or manifest) a distance between the interlocutors, as in the case of social-hierarchical placements that have to be maintained through language use. Distance, in most cases, reduces the need for expressed verbal collaboration: yet another case of cooperation yielding to politeness. The standardized replies in the military ('Sir! Yes Sir!') offer one example among many.

Leech's Politeness Principle is supposed to collaborate with, and even 'rescue', the Cooperative Principle and its associated maxims. However, it is not at all clear, as we have seen, that the CP is in need of being rescued. It is even less clear that a principle of politeness indeed would be able to do so; at the least, such an ability is not borne out by Leech's examples.

Still, the observations that Leech offers on his various maxims, such as those of 'tact', 'generosity', 'approbation' etc. (1983:131ff), have a certain descriptive value; the same holds for his other principles (such as that of 'irony'). While these principles are neither theoretically nor practically on the same level as the CP, one could make a point of subsuming them under the latter principle in some form or other, once one agrees on the need for cooperation, as expressed in the four Gricean maxims. The next sections will discuss some proposals that want to do away with (some or all of) the maxims, yet retain the notion of cooperation as the basis of conversation.

4.3   Rethinking Grice

Grice's four maxims and the associated principle of cooperation have been under attack almost from the very beginning. On the one hand, the critique has focused on the values attached to the maxims; for instance, there is a greater value attached to the maxim of quality than to the others: "violating it amounts to a moral offense, whereas violating the others is at worst inconsiderate or rude" (Green 1989:89). Clearly, the maxims have various weightings in people's minds.

A further question here is whether the maxims have the same weight, and are used in approximately the same manner, in different situations. For instance, it seems likely that one is more polite in a business exchange than, say, in an academic or domestic fight; still, the cooperation that Grice talks about cannot be excluded even in the latter case on the grounds that the partners to the interaction either hate each other, or do not want to cooperate in other ways. Normally, too, I cannot verbally insult an institution, or a dead body, or an animal (in most cases); even an insult requires a modicum of cooperation on the part of the insultee, if only insofar as the other needs to have a minimal understanding of what I'm trying to do with my words.

On the other hand, one may also question the necessity of having all of the maxims around: couldn't they be simplified somewhat? Green mentions her doubts about the maxim of quantity, second part ('Do not make your contribution more informative than required'), and considers the possibility of letting it be included in the maxim's first half ('Make your contribution as informative as required'); alternatively, she suggests (with Grice) to let it be included under the maxim of relation ('Be relevant').

Similarly, in the case of the maxim of quality, one could argue that the second half of the maxim ('Do not say that for which you lack adequate evidence') logically implies ('entails') the first ('Do not say what you believe to be false'): if I never say anything which I have only inadequate grounds to believe, then I necessarily never will say anything which I believe to be false.

As to the maxim of relevance itself, this has been the subject of two major efforts at rethinking Grice. The first is due to Horn (1984); the other to Sperber and Wilson (1986). The two proposals are a bit alike in that they both concentrate on relevance; they are different in that Horn's model keeps relevance within the general framework of Gricean theory, whereas Sperber and Wilson make the maxim of relevance the cornerstone of their own approach to 'communication and cognition', aptly described as Relevance Theory (RT).

The two proposals are also different as to the amount of attention they have attracted. When Sperber and Wilson published their book, *Relevance: Communication and Cognition*, over ten years ago, it generated a lot of interest; a second edition, with a number of additions and clarifications, appeared in 1995. (For a comparative review, see Jucker 1997.) In the wake of this interest, a strong RT movement has arisen (by some even called a school: 'the London School of Pragmatics'). In the framework of this school (so far mostly concentrated in Britain), RT is discussed and used as a model for further theorizing (see, e.g., Blakemore 1992, as well as the numerous theoretical and descriptive articles and monographs by younger authors, listed in the vastly expanded bibliography of Sperber and Wilson's second edition).

Horn's neo-Gricean theory, on the other hand, has remained a more isolated effort, which has never attained a similar status; yet, Horn's article (originally published in 1984, reprinted 1998) still deserves close attention for its painstaking analysis and elegant formulation of some rather original thoughts on the Gricean maxims.

I will treat the two proposals separately below.

4.3.1   Horn's two principles

Horn focuses on a central problem in conversational cooperation: some utterances, on a certain reading, have a clear and unambiguous meaning, while other interpretations require a special effort on the part of the listener.

Thus, for example, if I say:

I cut a finger yesterday (Horn 1984:15; example slightly adapted),

the normal reading is that the cut finger is mine, and it takes some stretch of imagination to read 'a finger' as one that belongs to someone else.

By contrast, some seemingly very similar utterances require an extra effort in order to be interpreted along the lines of the 'normal' reading of the utterance above, whereas no effort is required to obtain the alternative interpretation. Thus, when I say:

I'm meeting a woman tonight,

the woman is not 'mine' (whatever that implies); every other interpretation is just a joke, and is frequently exploited as such. Here is an example:

STEVEN: Wilfred is meeting a woman for dinner tonight.
SUSAN: Does his wife know about it?
STEVEN: Of COURSE she does. The woman he is meeting IS his wife. (Leech 1983:91)

To explain the humorous 'force' of this joke (actually a kind of 'garden path' construction of the kind we have seen in section 4.2.2.3), it won't do to make *ad hoc* adjustments to the original, 'finger' case, such as stipulating that the part involved in the cutting must be a member of a set of body parts. For example,

replacing 'finger' with 'nose' in Horn's example would not give the same result
(as pointed out by Grice): 'I cut a nose yesterday' will always be understood (if
at all) as referring to somebody else's nose. The problem lies deeper, and it is
Horn's merit to have suggested a plausible interpretation, based on the selected
conversational maxims of quantity and relation, of this curious phenomenon:
that two utterances which are remarkably alike in structure can still have diametrically opposed meanings.

The two principles that Horn introduces are: the *Q-principle* ('Q' for 'quantity'), telling us to 'say as much as we can'; and the *R-principle* ('R' for 'relation'), which says that we should 'say no more than we must'. If I state that I
cut a finger yesterday, I invoke the R-principle to establish the fact that the finger
is mine (I needn't say more; if I do say more, people will think I'm a member of
the *yakuza*). In the case of Wilfred meeting a woman, we invoke the Q-principle
in order to establish the fact that it is not his wife or regular girlfriend he's seeing
(if it had been either of them, my spokesperson wouldn't have said what she or
he actually did say).

The differences become a bit clearer when we think of possible replies to both
sentences. Normally, when somebody tells me about a mishap like the finger case,
my reaction will be one of commiseration; I might utter something like:

That's too bad,

and not much more can be said on the subject (a friend who were to retort:
'Whose finger?' would at the least deserve an inquisitive look).

However, in the case where my interlocutor uses the second utterance above
misleadingly, in order to make me believe that Wilfred is having an extramarital
affair, I probably will say something in the line of:

Really? And who is she?

the inference being that there is a lot more to tell (and that my partner wants me
to know all the gory details). Contrariwise, if I non-committally answer something like: 'Good for him', the intended joke will fall flat on its face, and my
interlocutor will be rightfully disappointed at my lack of cooperation.

Using Horn's terminology, in the Q-case, I have provided as much information as I have to, or can, given the circumstances; in the R-case, I let the circumstances speak, and give out only the relevant information. In his system, the
Q-principle covers the Gricean maxim of quantity$_1$ (being the first half of the
maxim), whereas the R-principle contains within it the second half of the quantity maxim (quantity$_2$) plus the maxims of manner and relation. As to the maxim
of quality, Horn leaves it alone, since, as he says, we need that in any case unless
we want to see "the entire conversational . . . apparatus collapse"; 1984:12).

Horn's two principles explain a variety of phenomena in the realm of politeness, negation, the lexicon and so on, in an elegant and economical manner; they

stand out as a worthwhile attempt to simplify the matter of pragmatic principles, bringing them to some common denominators.

4.3.2 Relevance and 'conspicuity'

According to Sperber and Wilson, pragmatics needs only one principle, that of *relevance*. The assumption, or principle, underlying relevance theory is that in any given context, what people say is relevant. This 'Principle of Relevance' can be seen as a further specification of the Gricean notion of cooperation; moreover, since "the principle of relevance is much more explicit than Grice's co-operative principle and maxims", as Sperber and Wilson say (1986:161), it also carries less of a functional burden.

Earlier in this chapter, I defined the Communicative Principle as the need for people to communicate; in fact, communication was said to be unavoidable. In particular, as language users, our intention is to communicate some meaning to somebody; the way we are able, and enabled, to go about this business is what is properly studied in pragmatics (in particular the part that deals with 'pragmatic acts'; see chapter 8). It follows that (since what is communicated supposedly is of importance to both the speaker and the hearer) communicating something meaningful may be supposed to be relevant to the partners in communication. In this sense, the Principle of Relevance is a variant of the Communicative Principle.

According to many (including Sperber and Wilson, as well as the present writer), Grice's Cooperative Principle, especially when taken literally, puts too much of a strain on our linguistic interaction. By contrast, the Principle of Relevance does not make the claims on successful communication known from Gricean theory, such as: "common purposes or set of purposes" (1975:45), mutual knowledge, implied or shared presuppositions and so on. For Relevance Theory, in accordance with the Communicative Principle, achieving successful communication by way of the relevance of what is being said is a sufficient aim in conversation or other verbal interaction. RT is thus a minimalist theory of communication; relevance is all we need.

But how to characterize a 'successful communication'? This notion is taken here in the sense that the speaker, the would-be communicator, is recognized by the interlocutor(s) as one who has something to say that matters, is relevant. The successful communicator is one who makes his or her intention to convey information, to persuade, to make believe etc. 'manifest' to both himself or herself and his or her partners. As Sperber and Wilson remark, "the realization that a trustworthy communicator intends to make you believe something is an excellent reason for believing it" (1986:163). The 'mutually manifest assumption' of an informative intention is at the core of Sperber and Wilson's thinking.

This assumption, moreover, is a central trait of human communicative behavior, even to the point that one cannot properly maintain (say Sperber and Wilson) that one 'follows' the Principle of Relevance: "Communicators do not 'follow' the principle of relevance; and they could not violate it even if they wanted to. The principle of relevance applies without exceptions" (1986:162). Sperber and Wilson's approach is thus useful in many ways because it forces us to rethink a number of central questions in linguistics, especially in semantics and pragmatics. The purpose of communication, according to RT, is not to "duplicate thoughts", but to "enlarge mutual cognitive environments" (Sperber and Wilson 1986:193).

In communicative modeling, in both its computerized and 'manual' varieties, the main obstacle is said to be the ambiguity of natural language expressions. Such an ambiguity is often thought of as a purely semantic affair; for example, in programs for automatic translation of text, we have to 'disambiguate' the expressions that have an unclear meaning, and do contextual guesses in a sort of bottom-to-top procedure. For Sperber and Wilson, by contrast, everything is ambiguous, as long as it is taken by itself, while nothing is strictly ambiguous if we look at it top-down, placing it in its proper, cognitive environment (cf. 1986:205).[48]

A pragmatic view of human language processing assesses the situation differently. Ambiguities are not just there to be resolved at the first possible occasion. Human communicators are prone to play on words, and often try to keep things fluid as long as possible. Thus, in Japanese business talks, with their notorious and to Westerners quite insufferable ambiguity, the point of leaving things undecided could be to have the other party reveal their intentions before one is drawn out oneself. And in a recent article, Nerlich and Clarke (2000 in press) argue that "we are not so much interested in 'disambiguation in context' but instead in what one might call 'ambiguation in context'" (2000 in press: 7). In such a view, the prime purpose of communication might well be in many cases to achieve 'conspicuity' rather than 'perspicuity'; the famous 'garden path' situation (see section 4.2.2.3) and activities such as punning and word-play turn essentially on this assumption (which goes directly against Grice's maxim of manner: 'Be perspicuous'; see section 4.2.2 and Nerlich and Clarke 2000 in press: 6).

According to Sperber and Wilson's presumption of relevance, we are ready for something that will make sense ('is relevant'), and we will build our understanding around that assumption. The utterance we're hearing or reading is 'accessible' as part of our mutually recognized, common cognitive environment or context; as such, the utterance is relevant. By contrast, we are not equally ready for something that would not be easily accessible, because it does not belong in such a common, cognitive environment. Take Sperber and Wilson's example (1986:168):

George has a big cat.

Here, the most common assumption is that we are talking about an animal such as a Norwegian Forest cat, a Maine Coon cat, or any other oversized (19–24 lb) species of the genus *Felis domestica*; in order to arrive at the interpretation 'lion, tiger, puma, cougar' etc., we must add something to that common environment, making it more specific (e.g., by building on the contextual information that George delivers wild animals to zoos and circuses). This latter interpretation would be less relevant, because under normal circumstances, it is less accessible. (On 'accessibility', see Ariel 1991; Gundel et al. 1993:276ff; one criticism that has been leveled at this notion is that it basically is a static one, and does not allow for the dynamics of text production. See Hajičová 1997; Mey 2001 in press.)

RT is said to be able to account for all the phenomena that earlier had been assigned to the other maxims for their explanation. Actually, this may seem rather a tall order for any theory; but as if this were not enough, Sperber and Wilson also assume their principle to operate without exception, being, indeed, irrefutable. In the end, either something relevant may be obvious and hence not interesting, or the notion of relevance itself may become so all-encompassing as to lose its explanatory force.[49]

Another serious problem lies in the fact that RT, despite its pronounced commitment to communication, says very little about real communicative interaction as it happens in our society. Like most of traditional linguistics and linguistic philosophy, RT does not include, let alone focus on, the *social* dimensions of language, as I have argued elsewhere (Mey and Talbot, 1989). Add to this that the conceptual backdrop of Sperber and Wilson's theory is the familiar current orientation toward the computer as a metaphor for human thinking processes, coupled with a pervasive tendency to see human mental processes as instances of economically rational behavior. Thus, much of their thinking on human cognitive activities relies heavily on the metaphor of information processing by computer (as admirably shown by Hinkelman in her comment on what she styles the 'relevance computer'; 1987:721). When they explain their theory, Sperber and Wilson draw on language borrowed from monetary economics ('cost–benefit relations'); alternatively, they mix 'computerese' and 'economese' (Mey 1994d), as when they say (e.g., on p. 204) that increased 'processing time' hampers understanding and puts obstacles in the way of communication. As Talbot remarks:

> people are depicted as individuals who confront unique problems in communication. In the real world, however, people are social beings who are working within pre-existing conventions. . . .
>
> In Sperber and Wilson's model, differences between people are depicted solely as differences between individuals' cognitive environments. These differences are assumed to stem from variations in physical environment and cognitive ability between people. Considerations of culture and society are notably absent in the characterization of individuals' cognitive environments. (1994:3526)

It is essentially under this latter, pragmatic aspect that RT, despite its many useful insights, falls somewhat short of the expectations raised by its program of research, and fails to honor all of its promises. In the end, it remains discon-

nected from the problems of everyday communication as these are brought to
the fore, e.g., in the theory of discourse (see sections 7.2.3.3 and 9.3.3) or when
discussing the concept of 'pragmatic acts' (chapter 8).

To conclude the present section and chapter, let me quote a story from the earliest efforts of constructing artificial intelligence (AI), which may show how what
we glibly call 'cooperation' is by no means a foregone conclusion. To see this, it
is useful to consider what happens in computer experiments simulating human
linguistic capabilities. One such experiment is called 'Tale-Spin' (Meehan 1981);
it consists of a program that understands the elements of a story, and continuously creates new stories on the basis of the original one.

Tale-Spin's characters live in an animal world, but are endowed with certain
human abilities (such as being able to speak) and have certain other human-like
properties (as in Aesop's fables). Here are Joe Bear and Irving Bird acting out a
very simple scenario: finding food:

> One day Joe Bear was hungry. He asked his friend Irving Bird where
> some honey was. Irving told him there was a beehive in the oak tree. Joe
> threatened to hit Irving if he didn't tell him where some honey was. (Meehan
> 1981:217)

Clearly, Joe Bear has missed the point of Irving Bird's reply. He didn't understand
the 'implicature' of the answer: that what he got, indeed, was an answer to his
question about the availability of honey.[50]

Notice that the inferences we're making in hearing stories like this one are
implied in normal conversation; they don't have to be told explicitly. The trouble
with Tale-Spin was that the program, not being human, should have been
instructed to make those 'explicatures' (which was only done by trial and error,
in subsequent versions). By contrast, a human, being a cooperative conversationalist, knows how and when to make the right inferences about what is implied
and what not, as we have seen in the preceding.

The next chapters will have a look at the linguistic means that are available
to us for this purpose.

Review and discussion

1. The Communicative Principle tells us that people want to communicate, while
the Cooperative Principle tells us something about how they go about communicating what they want to communicate. Sticking strictly to the maxim of quantity (section 4.2.2), they may decide to give out exactly what is needed, and no
more. Such 'parsimoniousness' (see section 4.2.1) can have undesired side-effects,
as when my interlocutors misunderstand my true intention, and conversationally
imply that I don't want to give out information (or tea, as the case may be).

Compare the following interchange from Lewis Carroll's well-known book *Alice in Wonderland*, a work much loved by children, logicians and linguists alike (among the last, Bruce Fraser, who brought the quotation to my attention):

"Take some more tea," the March Hare said to Alice, very earnestly.

"I've had nothing yet," Alice replied in an offended tone: "so I ca'n't take more."

"You mean you ca'n't take *less*," said the Hatter: "it's very easy to take *more* than nothing."

(In *More Annotated Alice*, Martin Gardner, ed., New York: Random House, 1990, p. 89)

Questions:
How would you evaluate the Hatter's cooperativeness in this interchange?

What effect does one, in general, obtain by 'sticking to the logic' of language (cf. also section 2.3)?

In the story, Alice gets confused (and no tea); was anything at all communicated? How could Alice properly have answered the Hatter?

2. The following sentence was found inside a North American (AMTRAK, USA) railway carriage (example due to Bruce Fraser):

All of the doors won't close.

Clearly, the intended message is that not all of the doors will close, rather than that none of them will (although logically, that possibility cannot be denied).

Question:
How does the principle of scalarity (section 4.2.1) apply here?

3. Consider again the father–daughter interchange in exercise 6 of chapter 3.

Questions:
In terms of the Cooperative Principle, how would you characterize the daughter's answer?

Is it 'really' an answer? (Then what was the question?)

Which maxim is violated by the father in the last reply?

4. The following two cases have to do with the well-established North American tradition of tipping for services rendered.

(a) A sign detailing the rights and duties of employees and customers, on display in Edward's Shoe Shop on Sherman Ave. in Evanston, Ill., tells us as item #5:

EMPLOYEES ARE ALLOWED TO ACCEPT UP TO U.S. $50.00 AS A TIP

(b) One miserable Sunday afternoon in downtown Toronto in January of 1993, having first missed the VIA/AMTRAK train back to Chicago, and in addition just having missed the Clark Airport Coach by a split second, I am approached by the driver of a livery car, who offers to take me to the airport for the modest fare of $30 (Canadian funds). Since it is cold, and I'm worried about not finding a plane (I have an early meeting on Monday) and besides, the next bus won't leave until an hour later, I accept. Upon arriving at the Lester Pearson International Airport, I tender the driver $40 (Canadian), whereupon he says,

"How much change do you want back on this, sir?"

Questions:
Referring to section 3.2.2, which presuppositions can you identify in these two sentences? (Hint: look for a common presupposition in both cases.)

And how about implicatures? (Hint: think of the possible size of the tip.)

What can we infer from the first sentence? And what from the second? (Hint: an inference has to be 'drawn out' of the text; it is something we establish, based on the available facts as contained in the text. A conversational implicature is something which arises among interlocutors as a result of their conversational activities; it is not as 'factual' and not as rigidly definable as an inference or, for that matter, a presupposition. For further details, cf. Thomas 1996:58–61.)

In terms of perlocutionary effect, which of the two sentences would be the most effective? Or would you say they are not comparable?

Thinking about tipping, list some of the expressions that come to mind in this connection. What do they reflect about 'tipping' as a social institution? (Hint: you certainly have come across 'No tipping, please' notices in restaurants, shops etc. How do people react to them?)

Can you suggest alternative (better or worse) expressions that could be used in the two cases above, seen from the point of view of:
the store owner
the taxi driver,
the customers,
the passengers?

5. The US linguist Suellen Rundquist (1992:447) has raised the question of whether "conversational inference [and by extension, such matters as relevance, politeness etc.] is based entirely on a cognitive foundation", or if we should rec-

ognize a "social component" as well. This view opens up the possibility of an interpretation of implicatures as based in the language user's social and cultural background, and hence being not strictly transferable across cultures. In light of these remarks, read the following newspaper report, on a visit by Pope John Paul II to Chile in 1987, as an illustration of a 'misfiring' implicature, due to different pragmatic presuppositions of a social and cultural kind (the report is entitled: 'The Papal Puzzle'):

> After appearing on the balcony with General Augusto Pinochet, the pope visited the slums of Santiago, where he embraced 19-year-old Carmen Quintero, still bearing the scars of the burning she received at the hands of Chilean security forces. Her companion, 19-year-old Rodriguez Rojas, died of burns in the torching.
>
> "Holy Father," said Carmen Quintero, "the military did this to me."
>
> "I know, my child," the pontiff replied. This assuaged the persecuted, for whom it is comfort to know that the pope is aware of their sufferings. (*Washington Post*, 2 July, 1987, p. A2)

Questions:
How cooperative would you say that the pope's reply to Carmen was? (Hint: Carmen's implicit question, posing as a statement, was: 'Why did this happen?' Was the pope's answer an answer to this question?)

The pope's reply 'I know' could of course mean: 'I just discussed this with General Pinochet while standing on the balcony', or something like that. Do you think that was what the Holy Father meant?

Turning the question around: what *could* John Paul II have answered, had he wished to be truly cooperative?

The journalist's final comment is remarkable in that it somehow forecloses any discussion of the whys and hows of this strange interchange and its background. What is the implicature that this remark about popes being aware of human suffering generates, or is supposed to generate?

Finally, give a suggestion as to why the original article was called 'The Papal Puzzle'.

CHAPTER FIVE
Speech Acts

5.1 History and introduction

5.1.1 Why speech acts?

The impressive success of certain theoretical developments in linguistics in the sixties (mainly within the framework of transformational grammar, following Chomsky's classic works: the 1957 *Syntactic Structures* and its 1965 companion *Aspects of the Theory of Syntax*) made it difficult for other workers in linguistics and the related sciences to have their voices heard. This was in particular the case with the philosophers of language, whose interests always had been more directed toward the semantic rather than the exclusively syntactic aspects of language.[51]

Much of the semantic work done by philosophers of language during the sixties and early seventies rested upon the 'truth-functional' definitions of semantics in the Carnapian tradition and continued by philosophers such as David Lewis (e.g., 1969). Other semantically oriented philosophers eventually joined hands with the formal syntactics tradition; Richard Montague and his school are the prime exponents of this development (called 'intensional semantics').

None of these directions of research will be dealt with here, as they are not directly relevant to pragmatics. Rather, I'll focus on what happened in another branch of philosophy, with origins in a British tradition of thinking about language, often referred to as 'Ordinary Language Philosophy', whose principal exponent was the Oxford philosopher John L. Austin. His posthumous work *How to Do Things with Words* (1962) had an enormous impact on linguistic philosophy, and thereby on linguistics, especially in its pragmatic variant. Austin's thinking (which in the course of time came to be known as 'speech act theory') was further developed and codified by the American philosopher John R. Searle, who had studied under Austin in the fifties, and subsequently became the main proponent and defender of the former's ideas.

A serious problem that the fledgling pragmatic tradition had to face was that of the limitations imposed on linguistic thinking by a semantics based on truth conditions. Philosophers working in the truth-functional tradition restrict themselves to 'propositions' representing one particular class of sentences, the so-called *declaratives*, which, in order to be true or false, must contain some testable proposition. If somebody tells us that:

It's cold outside,

we can go outside, if we wish, and test the truth or falsity of the 'declaration'. However, if I say to somebody:

Happy Birthday,

I can only talk about the truth of my feelings, or about the truth of the fact that I actually did pronounce those words, but not about the truth of this, or any other wish (e.g., 'Good luck', 'Congratulations', 'Well done' and so on). The reason is that wishes are not propositions: they are 'words with which to do things', to paraphrase Austin. In brief, they are *speech acts*.

The present chapter explores which criteria (different from the truth-functional ones) we need for dealing with those other (and, incidentally, most frequently occurring) human utterances.

5.1.2 Language in use

Many linguistic theories take their premises in some rather simple-minded assumptions about human language: that it is nothing but a combination of 'sound and meaning' (thus in most descriptive grammars), or that language can be defined as a set of correct sentences (thus in most generative-transformational thinking). The basic flaw in such thinking is that it does not pay attention to language as an activity which produces *speech acts*, defined as "the basic or minimal units of linguistic communication" (Searle 1969:16). As Searle puts it, "The unit of linguistic communication is not, as has generally been supposed, the symbol, word or sentence, . . . but rather the production of the symbol or word or sentence in the *performance of the speech act*" (1969:16; my italics).

Furthermore, speech acts are produced not in the solitary philosopher's think-tank, but in actual situations of language use, by people having something 'in mind'. Such a production naturally presupposes a 'producer' and a 'consumer', human agents, whose *intentions* are relevant and indispensable to the correct understanding and description of their utterances, quite contrary to the constructed, non-use-oriented examples of most grammarians and philosophers. To quote Searle once more:

> When I take a noise or a mark on a piece of paper to be an instance of lin-guistic communication, as a message, one of the things I must assume is that the noise or mark was produced by a being or beings more or less like myself and produced with certain kinds of *intentions*. (Searle 1969:16)

As we will see below, this intentional character of speech acts is among their most distinctive classificatory features. At the same time, we should not forget that intentionality is not just a matter of intentions ascribable to a particular speaker. For Searle, the main issue is how to establish the conditions (of sincer-ity, felicity etc.; see further section 5.2.1.2) that make communication possible. In a wider perspective, however, one should ask how a speech act functions in society, or even whether it functions there at all.

Asking how a particular communicative act functions in a particular society presupposes that we examine the conditions that hold for communication in that society. The language we use, and in particular the speech acts we utter, are entirely dependent on the context of the situation in which such acts are pro-duced. All speech is situated speech; a speech act is never just an 'act of speech', but should be considered in the total situation of activity of which it is a part (cf. Levinson 1979), and therefore, as we will see in chapter 8, it is always a *prag-matic act*, rather than a mere speech act.

This implies, moreover, not only that we must take the circumstances of the individual utterance into account (as does Searle), but that we cast our net wider, by incorporating the general conditions which allow, and afford, a particular act of speaking. Thus, while certain kinds of speech acts are forbidden in certain (e.g., tabooed) situations, others are *de rigueur*, sometimes even to the point where they are entirely predictable. To take an example due to Verschueren (1999:93): in a Dutch university, whenever the official university representative, the chief beadle, enters the locality where a doctoral defense has been in progress for the prescribed 45 minutes, nobody is in doubt about the utterance which will accompany his ritual stamping of the staff. Conversely, his uttering of the pre-scribed Latin formula *Hora est* ('Time's up') without the accompanying act would be a meaningless, isolated speech act and not have any pragmatic effect.

As a further illustration, consider the act of *promising* as it is practiced in soci-eties that are rather unlike our own. For anthropologists like Michelle Rosaldo (1980, 1982), a speech act such as a promise is dependent for its success not first of all on conditions of sincerity, felicity and so on, but on the ways it is supposed to sustain and confirm the existing order of things. In certain cultures, such as those of the Philippines people of the Ilongot or the Micronesian people of Pohnpei, it is dubious whether the concept of 'promising' and its concomitant notion of 'sincerity', viewed as a condition located in a particular individual, have any societal value at all (Duranti 1996:228, 230; Keating 1998 and pers. comm.).

As to the question of intentions, any discussion of intentionality should be aware of the relationships that exist among the individuals to whom the intentions are ascribed, and of the ways they perceive the others as 'intentional' beings in a greater, societal context. It is not primarily what I say, or intend to say, that determines my speech act, but the way it fits into the entire pattern of acting as a social being that is typical for my culture. Even though speech is a constitutive component of human individual and social life (as is language in general), it is still part of a larger context, of an even more encompassing activity. In the final analysis, we will have to ask ourselves how speech acts relate to our human activity as a whole: thinking 'globally' while acting 'locally', as the saying goes. It is for this ecological view of human acting, to which the societal and global environment provides the adequate (necessary and sufficient) backdrop, that I have devised the term 'pragmatic act'. (For further details, see chapter 8.)

5.1.3   How speech acts function

Speech acts are verbal actions happening in the world. Uttering a speech act, I do something with my words: I perform an *activity* that (at least intentionally) brings about a change in the existing state of affairs (hence the label, 'performative utterances', that originally was attached to speech acts).[52] For instance, if I say to a newborn human: "I baptize thee 'in the name of the Father, and of the Son, and of the Holy Ghost'" (cf. Matthew 28:19), then this human being is from now on and forever a Christian – provided I took care to let my words be accompanied by the flowing of water on the infant's head (or some other body part, in case of necessity). And if I belong to those who believe in the power of baptism, the world as a whole will now have changed as well: there will be one more Christian among the living.

This insight, viz., that words can change the world, is not only of importance in a religious context (where such changes may be subject to one's beliefs or may depend, as in the case of miracles, on the strength of one's faith); it is an essential part of speech act thinking as well. And as such, it has become an important linguistic discovery.

The original distinction between the different aspects of speech acting is due to Austin (1962). First, we have the *locutionary* aspect: this is simply the activity we engage in when we say something, e.g.:

It's cold in here.

Under normal circumstances, by uttering the above words, I am making a statement (not a wish, promise, threat, judgment or what have you). This particular aspect of the speech act is its *illocutionary* 'force' or 'point';[53] for many pragmaticians, this illocutionary force is intimately related to the very form the utterance may have: stating, wishing, promising etc. I will come back to this below.

However, if by saying:

It's cold in here

I obtain that, e.g., the person I'm addressing closes the door, or turns on the radiator, we are talking about the *perlocutionary* effect of my utterance. Such further effects depend, of course, on the particular circumstances of the utterance, and are by no means always predictable. (See Levinson 1983:236; Kurzon 1998.)

Even though, from a pragmatic point of view, the perlocutionary effect perhaps is the most interesting aspect of speech acting (since it may tell us something about people's motivation for using a particular speech act), illocutionary force is what has occupied speech act theorists most. In this connection, the conditions that must obtain before a speech act can be said to have a particular illocutionary force (or 'count as' a particular speech act) have been the object of much discussion. These are often called 'felicity conditions', since they have to be met for a speech act to happen 'felicitously' or 'happily', and to prevent it from 'misfiring', as Austin called it.

As an example, consider the following case. I utter the words:

I hereby pronounce this person dead.

What kind of conditions have to be fulfilled for this to be a valid speech act of 'pronouncing'? First of all, we have to be certain that the person enunciating these words actually has the power to do so, and second, we have to have the right circumstances for the uttering. For example, it won't do to 'pronounce' my neighbor 'dead' in a dispute over garden boundaries. I can *wish* people dead, but I cannot *pronounce* them dead (except in an imaginary world, where my words have this kind of magic effect, as when children at play say 'Poof – you're dead').

The correct circumstances (or 'appropriate', as Austin called them) are, in this particular case, that I am a doctor, and that somebody has been brought in to the hospital after a traffic accident, and that I, as a doctor, have to determine whether the person in case is alive or dead. I am given this authority and duty by my being on call at the emergency unit, and having been requested to produce such an official utterance, which then is entered into the official report as: 'The victim was pronounced dead on arrival [at the hospital].' In any other circumstances, the would-be speech act 'misfires'.

Or take the following case, where the 'misfiring' happens at the other end, so to speak. If I say to a friend:

I'll bet you ten dollars that the buses won't run on Thanksgiving, then (in case my prediction was correct) I can only claim my money if my friend has 'taken on' the bet. For her to do so, she has to perform a corresponding speech act expressing 'uptake' (in this case, of a bet), such as:

You're on.

Without this uptake, there is no felicitous act of betting: some (or all) of the parties involved will not have had the right intentions and/or conduct.[54]

What are, then, the appropriate circumstances for a particular speech act to be correctly performed? For various reasons, some of them historical, certain speech acts have always been favorites in this kind of discussion; among them is the speech act of 'promising'. The next section will be devoted in its entirety to a discussion of this act.

5.2 Promises

One general problem with speech acts is that the very wording of the act (e.g., 'I promise') can lead to misunderstandings. For instance, is the word *promise* a necessary element in the speech act 'promise'? Or, more generally: do I always have to use a so-called 'speech act verb' to perform a speech act? And, more practically: can one trust people to keep a promise even when they haven't used the word *promise*?

We are all familiar with the problem in everyday life. Going to a restaurant, we assume that our friends will have made the reservations, because that's what they promised (or so we believe). However, when we get to the restaurant, there is no table; and our friends maintain that they never said they were going to make a reservation, or if they had said so, they didn't think it was so important, and so on and so forth.

Consider how for young children, the only promise is one that has the word *promise* in it; and even adults are prone to 'fortifying' their promises, when needed, by using all kinds of 'super-promissory' devices (references to one's own, one's father's or even the Prophet's beard; moving a finger across one's throat, and so on). For others, a person's 'word' is good enough, and they will shun anything that goes beyond a simple 'Yes' or 'No'.[55]

Again, all depends on the circumstances of the promise: in some cases, we pay attention to the people who promise, rather than to their exact words, while in other contexts, we focus on the social frame in which the promise is given; after all, some of our socially most binding promises are given without the verb *to promise* ever being used. In the standard Christian marriage ritual, if I were to say 'I promise' in answer to the question: 'Wilt thou have this woman for thy wife?', I would *not* meet the felicity conditions for this kind of promise, and fail to execute the procedure completely and correctly.

What is it that 'counts as' a promise, to use Searle's expression (1969:36)? Something counts as something only within a specified set of rules. Thus, physically overthrowing the king in a game of chess only counts as 'admitting defeat' if it has been preceded by a situation of (actual or impending) checkmate. In general, it is the kind of activity in which people are engaged that makes us count certain utterances as promises, warnings, requests and so on. Thus, if I utter:

There is a policeman at the corner,

that will only and truly count as a warning if I utter it in a context where somebody is committing a burglary or is engaged in some other criminal activity. In another context, that same utterance could count as an assurance, a dare, a hint as to where to ask for directions, a reminder not to put that car in the space for the handicapped in front of the shop, and so on.

As to promises, there are dozens of ways to make a promise in any particular language, and it is only the context which can determine whether a particular expression counts as a promise (Searle 1969:52). If I say to a good friend, when making plans to go to a concert together, 'I'll be there at seven', that may, in the context of our friendship, count as a perfectly good promise, even if I am using a way of speaking that does not exactly correspond to the speech act's 'canonical' expression, the 'speech act verb' *to promise*. And, as we will see below (chapter 8), what constitutes the *pragmatic act* of promising is by no means limited to, or conditioned by, the words uttered: other words may be used, or even none at all.

The next section will illustrate some of the problems mentioned above by discussing the speech act of 'promising' in more detail. (On 'speech act verbs', see further section 5.3.)

5.2.1   A speech act's physiognomy: promising

5.2.1.1   Introduction: the problem

Talking about speech acts, we run into a problem of a rather general character, having to do with the way different languages deal with speech acting. Typical questions are:

- How can we determine a speech act?
- How many speech acts are there, and how are they expressed in language?
- What is the relationship between a speech act and a pragmatic act?
- Are there speech acts (or pragmatic acts) that are found across languages, or even in all languages? (The problem of the so-called 'universal speech acts'.)

The first of these questions will be dealt with exemplarily in the present section by choosing a model speech act, the 'promise', and exploring the conditions and rules governing its use. The exposition below (section 5.2.1.2) is based on Searle (1969:57ff), with the addition of a critical commentary (section 5.2.1.3).

The second question will be discussed in sections 5.3 through 5.5. As to the third and fourth questions, they will be dealt with in chapters 8 and 10, respectively.

5.2.1.2   Promises: conditions and rules

The first problem is: what are the conditions for a speech act to 'count as' a promise? Second, we have to know what rules govern a successful use of this speech act. Below, I will first list the nine conditions that Searle (1969:57ff) enumerates for successful promising; following that, I will examine his five rules.

Condition 1   Normal conditions must obtain for uttering and receiving a promise. Speakers must know how to deal with their language and they must not have any special handicaps (deafness etc.); furthermore, they must abstain from what Searle calls 'parasitic use of language' such as jokes and acting.[56]

Condition 2   The promise must have a content. Thus, in:

I promise I'll be there tomorrow,

the content is for me to be there tomorrow (or more precisely, the day after today).

Condition 3   At the moment of uttering, the content of a promise must have to do with a future, possible action of the speaker. Clearly, one cannot promise something that has happened in the past; neither can anybody promise anything in another person's stead (which of course is not the same as promising to try and *make* somebody else do something).

Condition 4   Clearly, what is being promised must be to the advantage of the 'promisee'. The difference between a promise and a threat, according to Searle, is that "a promise is a pledge to do something for you, not to you, . . . a threat is a pledge to do something to you, not for you" (1969:58).

Hence, even though the promiser uses the *words* 'I promise', there is no promise unless it is to the advantage of the promisee; a threat remains a threat, in accordance with the above, even though its wording is that of a promise:

If you don't behave, I promise you there's going to be trouble.

Condition 5   The content of the promise must not be something which clearly is going to happen anyway; I can't promise anybody that the sun will rise tomorrow. As Searle rightly remarks, "A happily married man who promises his wife he will not desert her in the next week is likely to provide more anxiety than comfort" (1969:59).

Conditions 4 and 5 are often called (in accordance with Searle's terminology) *preparatory* conditions, that is, conditions that must have been met before we can begin to talk about promises.

Condition 6 This condition has to do with the sincerity of the promiser in carrying out the act of promising; without that intention, we have no sincere promise.[57]

The condition we are dealing with here is appropriately called the *sincerity* condition.

Condition 7 This condition can be said to be the cornerstone of Searle's philosophy of promises: a promiser intends to put himself or herself under the obligation of carrying out the promised act. This is more than just intending to carry out the act: only if the intention is accompanied by the speaker's recognition of an inevitable obligation can one properly speak of a promise. Conversely, "if a speaker can demonstrate that he did not have this intention in a given utterance[,] he can prove that the utterance was not a promise" (Searle 1969:60; cf. also n. 54).

This condition, being essential to any promising, is aptly called the *essential* condition.

Conditions 8 and 9 These conditions emphasize that the language used in promising must be the normal one, that is to say, it obeys "the semantical rules of the language" (Searle 1969:61); furthermore, the conventions for using that language must likewise be the normal, that is to say, pragmatically correct, ones.

For instance, if in a certain linguistic or cultural environment (maybe even in a particular situation in our own culture), the word *promise* cannot be uttered successfully, then we wouldn't have a true promise, no matter how much we 'promised'. Compare that people who by their religion are forbidden to take oaths (such as the Pennsylvanian Amish) cannot technically pronounce the words *I swear* with the proper, speech-act-related effects. Similarly, Searle's husband-and-wife example cited above could be an example of a 'misfiring' promise; or one can think of promises made under 'duress' or in a socially recognized state of non-responsibility (in drunkenness, to children etc.). Common wisdom captures such situations by saying 'Never trust a drunk's promises', or (as many parents undoubtedly would agree) 'Promises to and by children don't count.'

Again, this is not a matter of semantics, or of semantics alone: what the words *I promise* mean is determined by the pragmatic conditions governing the use of the language in the particular context of, say, a certain family. In the final analysis, it is society that determines the validity of (or 'what counts as') a particular speech act. (See also chapter 10.)

Having established the conditions for proper speech act performance, we now turn to the question of what rules govern such acting; again, our 'showcase' will be promises. Before we start focusing on the specific conditions for this speech act, however, a general characteristic of the linguistic tools enabling such use is in order. This characterization is given by Searle under the name of 'illocutionary force indicating device' (henceforth for short called 'IFID'); generally speaking, conditions 1, 8 and 9 hold for all speech acts and their IFIDs. The specific conditions on promising are 2 through 7; from these, the following five rules governing the use of promissory IFIDs can be extracted:

Rule 1   Only use a promissory IFID when the content of the utterance is about something which is to happen in the future.
> This rule captures conditions 2 and 3, above; it is called the *content* rule.

Rule 2   Only use the promissory IFID when the promise contains something that the promisee actually wants to happen to him or her.

Rule 3   Only use an IFID for promising when the content of the promise does not concern the occurrence of an already scheduled, self-justifying or natural happening.
> Rules 2 and 3 are called the *preparatory* rules, in analogy with the preparatory conditions (4 and 5) above.

Rule 4   Only use a promissory IFID if you intend to carry out your promise.
> This is clearly the *sincerity* rule, corresponding to the sincerity condition (6) above.

These four rules together make up the 'regulations' for promising. But what is it that makes a promise a promise? That is done by the fifth rule:

Rule 5   Only use a promissory IFID on condition that the promise is uttered and recognized (accepted) as creating an obligation from the promiser to the promisee.
> This, finally, is the 'count as', or *essential*, rule, corresponding to the essential condition (7) above. This rule, in a way, has a higher status than the other four, since it has to do with the very essence of the speech act. I'll have more to say on this in the next section.

5.2.1.3   The pragmatics of rules

The five rules given above are not on the same level: while the first four can be called 'regulative', the fifth one is usually termed a 'constitutive' rule. What is the importance of this difference? An analogy taken from the game of chess may be helpful.

A *constitutive* rule, in the case of chess, is one that makes up, 'constitutes' the game of chess as that particular game and no other. Without the chess game's constitutive rules, the very game, as we know it, becomes impossible. *Regulative* rules, by contrast, regulate the behavior of the players in the game; such rules may be changed at will, and by mutual agreement, but those changes do not alter the nature of the game.

The constitutive rules of chess determine what counts as a move for the individual chess pieces: thus, pawns move one square except for the first time, when they can move over two; the knights 'jump' across the board, whereas the bishops move diagonally etc. Other constitutive rules define the number of chess pieces, the number of squares on the board etc. Changing these rules would define different kinds of chess, some of which are, or have been, recognized in other cultures and times as legitimate variants of the game.

Examples of regulative rules of chess could be that players are not allowed to 'undo' a move, that they can only use a limited amount of time for a certain number (e.g., 40) of moves (this is a common rule at chess tournaments), or that they are not allowed to touch the chess pieces unless they intend to make a move; and so on.

Let's now apply this to the particular speech act that we have been considering in the previous sections: 'promising'. Recall Searle's 'husband-and-wife' example: the constitutive rule (5) of promising is one according to which a "promise is uttered and accepted as creating an obligation from the promiser to the promisee". The rule says nothing about having to repeat that promise every time one goes on a trip; on the contrary, we have a regulative rule (3), telling us that we shouldn't utter a promise when its content is already scheduled to happen (husbands are supposed to be faithful on trips). The promise of fidelity (as enshrined in the marital vows) is therefore something that should not have to be reiterated every time one goes off on a journey; if one does utter such an inappropriate IFID, the implicature (see section 3.2) is that something else is afoot. Searle is right that in such cases, the promisee may indeed have cause for concern.

However, rules are no magic wands: although promises, once given, should not need to be renewed, they *are* sometimes broken (even if renewed). A pragmatic view on promising accepts this fact of life and makes us focus on the promiser and promisee, rather than on the promise itself. Such a view touches upon both aspects of promising: the constitutive one ('What is a promise, pragmatically speaking?') and the regulative one ('How are promises dealt with in an actual social context?'). Analogously in chess, if you play chess according to the rules, you have a valid chess game. But chess is not the same for everybody: the champion plays a very different game than the amateur; the rank beginner, who has just internalized the rules, has no clue as to how to actually win, even though she or he remembers everything that she or he was taught about the game.

In Austin's terms, the IFIDs of speech act theory only *indicate* illocutionary force; they don't put that force to work. To do that, we need to lift the speech act out of the domain of abstract description into that of concrete action: speech act becomes *pragmatic act*. (See further chapter 8.)

In my book *Whose Language?*, I have argued for a context-oriented, pragmatic view of language, as used by humans and for humans (Mey 1985:40ff). This pragmatic aspect should not be 'walled off' from the rest of linguistics or treated as a separate component, to be added on to truth-conditional semantics, propositional logic or 'classical' speech act theory. Rather, we should use a perspective in which the role of the interactive user is no longer external to our theorizing, but forms an integrated part of it. With respect to the contextual conditions for using promises, including the general conditions of 'setting up' a promisee, along with the specific ones for securing a particular 'uptake', such a role may be captured within the framework of the 'pragmatic act', as I will show in detail in section 8.3.2. Applied to the case of promising, this implies that we cannot, in all decency, talk about promising in the abstract: every promise is a promiser's promise, made to a real-life promisee. The pragmatic conditions of use for promises should, therefore, include these users, the promisers and promisees, as well as their conditions of interaction.

Similar things can be said about other speech acts. For example, the speech act of requesting has in its constitutive rule a stipulation that the requester wants the requestee to do something for him or her. But that doesn't mean that we, at all times and places, can or may request anything at all, as long as it's good for us (or we think it is). The sanctions embodied in the regulative rules ('What is an allowable request?'; cf. 'What is a correct way of playing chess?') derive from the fact that we, in our daily lives, want people to do things for us that are both possible for them, and necessary and beneficial to us. We do not want to, and cannot, request things that are blatantly unreasonable and out of the question (even though we may daydream about going to our boss and requesting that she or he double our salary).

There are some absurd cases around of requests that are not really about the thing they request, or even about anything at all, but are to be counted as expressions of a certain pragmatic necessity; for instance, that the requester recognize his lowly status, as in the military: 'Request permission to address my captain' (where the permission strictly is taken for granted, otherwise the request couldn't even be uttered), or in certain religious orders, where one must request permission to take an afternoon snack (called *potus*, literally 'a drink', but in reality two hefty sandwiches), even if one doesn't feel like having anything (and least of all two big chunks of white bread). Such a request in reality boils down to a 'pragmatic act' (see chapter 8) of recognizing the fact that as a member of the order (being duty-bound by a holy vow of obedience), one cannot do anything at all except in subordination, i.e., per request and by permission (*venia*).

The reason that a particular request cannot be put into action is not contained in its constitutive rule as such; yet, it derives from it, just like the sanctions that derive from the Fifth Commandment ('Thou shalt not kill') derive from the constitutive character of the Ten Commandments (whether they are seen as the embodiment of divine law, or as the expression of a basic respect for human life, property, truth etc.). Which shows that the regulative and the constitutive rules perhaps are not as easily separable as was implied earlier: the regulative rules define what the constitutive rules say they do; but the constitutive rules determine the weight that is given those rules in the daily exercise of them. As Anthony Giddens has remarked, "all social rules have both constitutive and regulative (sanctioning) aspects to them" (1979:66). Since in the above cases, the constitutive element of the speech act is almost totally subsumed under the regulative element, one understands why people like Giddens may want to abolish the distinction altogether.

The difficulties of sharply distinguishing between constitutive and regulative rules have their roots in the often-observed fact that speech act theory, even though in name and pretension a theory of *action*, in reality is a philosophical theory of, or about, *propositions*. Bickhard and Campbell express this concisely and to the point: "Speech act theory focuses on the 'action' inherent in an utterance (e.g., Austin 1962; Searle 1969), but it is still an action (a message transmission, not an *inter*action) based on an encoded [abstract] proposition" (1992:428). The illocutionary devices that Searle recognizes as carrying the 'force' of the speech act are not strictly pragmatic in nature, as they are exclusively speaker-oriented and tie in with an abstract content; it is only this (propositional) content of the speaker's act that is subject to the constitutive and regulative rules. Searle's IFIDs become thus purely abstract devices or "very general rules", not proper to any type of speech act, or to any concrete act of promising, requesting and so on:

> ... some of these rules seem to be just particular manifestations as regards promising of very general underlying rules for illocutionary acts; and ultimately we should be able, as it were, to *factor them out*, so that they are not finally to be construed as rules exclusively for the illocutionary force indicating device for promising as opposed to other types of illocutionary force indicating devices. (Searle 1969:63; my emphasis)

In contrast to this abstract, exclusive perspective, a pragmatic view emphasizes that the nature of speech acting always varies according to various linguistic uses, not only cross-language-wise, but also, and not least interestingly, within a single language. As we have seen above, the study of the existing speech acts of English (or any other language) is only useful as an approximation. The general problems raised by speech act theory, especially the difficult question of cross-language equivalencies and universal, interlanguage inventories, cannot be solved within such a framework, but require that we widen our perspective and consider speech acts under the angle that they rightly deserve: as pragmatic devices for human activity, or *pragmatic acts*. The following section will consider one aspect of this problematic: the so-called 'speech act verbs'. (I will come back to pragmatic acts in chapter 8; the cross-cultural diversity of speech acting will be taken up in chapter 10.)

5.3 Speech act verbs

5.3.1 The number of speech acts

In section 5.2.1.1, I brought up four questions, the first of which was answered in the preceding section. As to the second question:

• How many speech acts are there, and how are they expressed in language?

This has to do with the problem of the so-called 'speech act verbs', which is the name linguists have given to those verbs that somehow or other seem to be the natural way of expressing a particular speech act.

Many suggestions have been offered as to the number of (principal) speech acts that any particular language has to offer. The differences in opinion have to do with, among other things, the demands placed upon one's classificatory criteria.

Some linguists require the presence of some recognizable syntactic-morphological or semantic features that will tell us whether or not we are dealing with a 'real' speech act. One may obtain a rough-and-ready typology of speech acts by either following the traditional syntactic classification of verbal 'mood' rather closely (indicative, subjunctive, imperative, optative etc., are thus all typical expressions of some speech act); or, alternatively, by choosing to rely on broad, semantic distinctions. An example of the latter kind is the five-part classification offered by Searle (1979) into representatives, directives, commissives, expressives and declarations. Although this classification mainly rests on features of 'meaning', some of these are rather close to what traditional syntax would refer to as 'moods', such as 'indicatives' (Searle's 'representatives') or 'imperatives' (Searle's 'directives').[58]

Classifiers such as Searle belong to the category of what Verschueren (1979) has called the 'lumpers': those that lump together their speech acts in a few, large categories. Opposite them, we have the 'splitters', that is to say those who split up their speech acts in a great number of classes; the actual number may be "between five hundred and six hundred" (Verschueren 1979:10). The individual speech act realizations may range from 1,000 to 9,999 (as Austin has suggested), or even go up to the tens of thousands, all depending on our patience and acumen in making the necessary distinctions.[59]

Whatever the number of hypothetical speech acts, languages have historically shown their preferences for certain, well-defined exemplars of the species, and expressed this preference by bestowing the honors of specific, linguistic expressions on such acts; such expressions go by the name of *speech act verbs* (henceforth SAV).

5.3.2   Speech acts, speech act verbs and performativity

Traditionally, a number of languages associate some kind of activity with the word for 'verb' itself. Thus, Danish has, in its traditionally purist grammatical nomenclature, an autochthonous term for the morphological category 'verb': *udsagnsord*, literally: 'word for predicating [understood: about the subject]' – a term that clearly harkens back to the traditional grammar term 'predicate', denoting the role of the verb in the sentence. Another Germanic language that has fallen prey to the pranks of the purist grammarians is Dutch; here, a verb is called *werkwoord*, literally 'work word', as if it were the verb that was doing whatever work had to be performed in the context of the sentence – and all by itself. A similar 'dynamic metaphor' is encountered in the Japanese term for 'verb': *dooshi*, literally 'move-word'.

It thus seems natural to look for expressions of linguistic activity ('work') among the members of the category 'verb', and to call those that are found to denote speech acts (SA) 'speech act verbs' (SAV). Also historically, this makes sense: Austin's first discovery of the phenomena of speech acts happened in a strictly 'working' environment, the classic examples being institutionalized speech act verbs such as 'to baptize', 'to invest', 'to dub', 'to sentence' and so on. By contrast, other verbs were seen as merely describing situations; they were used to produce true or false 'statements' about those situations. Such 'stating' verbs were called by Austin (always "a man with an ear for a neologism", as Taylor and Cooren aptly remark; 1997:412) 'constatives'. Since the verbs denoting 'real' speech acts seemed to *do* something, rather than merely producing candidates for 'truth' or 'falsehood', Austin consequently called them 'performatives' (in his famous William James lectures at Harvard University in 1955; Austin 1962).[60]

There is, however, and has always been, a certain asymmetry in the relationship between speech act verbs (SAVs) and speech acts (SAs) proper. First of all, not all SAs are represented by a specific SAV; they may be represented by several (the sole exceptions being the 'pure', strictly institutionalized SAs, such as 'to baptize'). Thus, the SA of 'ordering' may be expressed in various, often indirect ways (see section 5.4) – by a direct 'ordering' verb, or by a 'normal' verb in the imperative, or even by a circumlocution:

I order you to shut the door
Shut the door!
You will shut that door,

where all three utterances express the same order.

Second, and conversely, not every SA has a corresponding, custom-made SAV of its own. The act of pronouncing a jury's finding is called 'to render a verdict'; however (in English at least), there is no SAV 'to *verdict'.[61] Apparently, not all SAs are on a par with regard to SAV status.

To see this more clearly, consider the case of the so-called 'performative verbs' (often called 'explicit performatives', since most verbs perform something anyway, but presumably implicitly; cf. section 5.1.3). The uttering of a sentence of the type:

I promise to come

carries out two separate functions: on the one hand, it tells the world that the speaker, in this case 'I', has performed something, namely, a promise of 'coming'; on the other, it binds me, the speaker, to my promise: the utterance 'I promise to come', when uttered by a speaker, *explicitly* establishes this "binding obligation" for the speaker (Searle's essential condition).

Now consider the same sentence in the past tense:

I promised to come.

Here, the second function, the 'explicit performative', is absent. What this sentence does is describe a state of affairs that has happened once upon a time; it is not a promising utterance, hence not an SA of promising, despite the use of the word 'promise'. Similarly, when I say:

He promised to come,

I have not in any way performed a promise for the person referred to by 'he' (cf. section 5.2.1.2, where it was stated that no promise could be given in another person's stead).

The above must not be interpreted to imply that one cannot perform an SA without having an explicit performative at one's disposal. It just serves to demonstrate the differences that obtain between SAVs with respect to their use and usability. One could say that the 'explicit performatives' are the most extreme cases of SAVs, in that they can perform, and necessarily perform, certain SAs for which they are designated (given that the proper conditions are met, among which are, in our case, the use of the present tense and of the first person).

But couldn't we generalize the argument, and maintain that properly speaking all verbs, inasmuch they express an 'activity' of some kind, in principle are SAVs? Such a generalization would not hold water in most cases, even with SAVs that otherwise are beyond any suspicion of non-performance. Consider the following pair of sentences:

I believe in God
I believe that the Earth is flat.

While the first utterance is an 'act of faith', typically performed by an SAV 'to believe', as in the *Credo in unum Deum* of the Nicene Creed, the second is no more than the expression of a (rather unsubstantiated) opinion or 'belief'. I might as well have said (and would maybe have been better off saying) that I suppose, or think, or conjecture that the world is flat. However, such is precisely the 'normal', everyday use of the verb 'to believe', and we should perhaps not even call it an SAV in such an everyday context.[62]

Among the more standard SAVs (i.e., the ones having, among other things, the privilege of always being quoted by the established speech act theoreticians) we find such verbs as 'to announce', 'to declare', 'to inquire' and so on.[63] But are these always 'performative', i.e., performing something? If a person says:

I hereby declare this bridge to be opened,

then (provided he or she is endowed with the proper authority) there is some kind of performance: viz., that of opening a bridge. But what if I say:

He declared himself to be innocent/that he was innocent/his innocence?

One would be hard put (especially in the context of the judiciary) to accept this utterance as containing a performative verb: any criminal could let himself or herself off the hook by this kind of verbal magic.

Many speech act theoreticians, having noticed that sentences such as the above often contain, or may contain, an adverb such as 'hereby', as in:

I hereby declare the bridge to be opened,

have used this adverb as a practical criterion for a true, 'performative' SAV. Compare also the fact that one cannot easily or felicitously utter sentences like:

I hereby love you

or:

I hereby know that the Earth is flat.[64]

However, the fact that one can legitimately say, e.g.:

I hereby declare my innocence

seems to indicate that the use of 'hereby' at best is an indicator of SAVs in general, not exclusively of performativity; and also that the two categories, SAVs and performatives, in most cases do not coincide.

Finally, there is the strange category of verbal expressions that have the property of denying what they are doing, or doing what they explicitly are denying. Consider:

I don't want to bother you, but could you please have a look at my program?

or

I'm not threatening you, but if I ever see your face again around these parts . . .

Here, the speaker explicitly 'performs' an act of not wanting to bother or threaten the addressee, while he or she in actual fact does precisely that (and probably wants to as well). Conversely, in such cases, the use of the verbs 'to bother' or 'to threaten', taken by themselves, would not have the same effect as it had above; one would hardly consider utterances such as:

I am (hereby) bothering you . . .
I (hereby) threaten you . . .

or even:

I (hereby) insult you (Thomas 1996:47)

as particularly expressive or performative of the acts of 'threatening', 'bothering', or 'insulting', and perhaps not even of anything at all.

We may conclude that performativity is a property that is not specifically bound up with SAVs; in Verschueren's (1979) words, we are dealing with a performativity 'continuum', spanning all the way from 'institutionalized' SAVs such as 'to baptize', to everyday verbs that occasionally can take on a performative character, such as the ones cited in the last two examples above.

5.3.3   Speech acts without SAVs

What was said in the last paragraphs of the preceding section could lead, rather naturally, to the assumption that we may not even need SAV as a special category of verbs. Indeed, since performativity is all over the verbal spectrum (albeit primarily residing in a small set of institutionalized verbs), we clearly do not need a (particular) SAV (or even an SA at all, as we'll see in chapter 8) to perform a (speech) act, and in many cases, we cannot even properly perform the very speech act that is 'officially' expressed by the verb, by making explicit mention of the appropriate verb. Two cases may serve to illustrate the point.

The first is that of the so-called 'Speech Act Formulae' (SAF; Verschueren 1979). These are verbal expressions that in all respects behave like SAV, except that they are not 'regular' verbs, but rather, stylistic or other variations on a common semantic theme. For instance, I can say:

I want to express my gratitude for your valuable assistance

or, with the same effect (in a more relaxed mode):

I want to thank you for your help.

Similarly, one has locutions such as 'to express one's intention', 'to utter a warning', 'to make up one's mind' and so on, where a simple verb could render the same service of 'notifying', 'warning', 'deciding' etc.

Often, too, individual languages handle the 'same' semantic units in entirely different ways when it comes to expressing them verbally. Examples include 'to study' (cf. Danish *at studere*) vs. French *faire ses études* (literally: 'to do one's studies', the same as *étudier*), Japanese *benkyoo shimasu* (literally: 'to do study'); expressions for 'please': French *s'il vous plaît* (literally: 'if you please'), Danish *vær så venlig* ('be so kind'), Portuguese *faz favor* ('do [me] the favor'), Japanese *o-negai-shimasu* ('grant the honorable request'), and so on. Even though closely related expressions may be found from one language to other, related ones, the languages in question do not always avail themselves of such options; the verb 'to realize' exists in a French form as *réaliser*; however, to express the verb's meaning 'to become aware of', French uses *se rendre compte* (literally: 'to provide oneself with an account').

The second case is somehow related to the first; it has to do with 'verbless expressions' of the kind 'Thanks'. One can doubt whether we always are dealing with a verb here, let alone an SAV; witness also the fact that in many other languages, the speech act of 'thanking' has a substantive (singular or plural) as its regular expression As examples, cf. Danish *tak* (a singular/plural, cf. *en stor tak* ('a big thanks'), *mange tak* ('many thanks'), *tusind tak* ('a thousand thanks'); Finnish *kiitos/kiitoksia* (singular/plural 'thanks'); Czech *díky* ('thanks', a plural), and so on. Other languages alternate with, or even prefer, a form of the verb 'to thank': Dutch *bedankt* ('[you are] thanked'); Swedish *tackar* '[I] thank you' (along with *tack*, of the same use and meaning as Danish *tak*); Czech (along with *díky*) *děkuji* ('I thank'); or even English *thank you* (perhaps for 'I thank you', the 'full' speech act, which under normal circumstances would seem to be over-doing it slightly). Compare also the neutral French expression (almost totally deverbalized) (*Je vous souhaite un*) *bonjour* with its literal Hungarian equivalent *Jó napot kivánok* ('[A] good day wish I').

It seems clear, from what I have said so far, that speech acts, as well as speech act verbs, only make sense when used in their proper contexts. As isolated lexical items, or members of a set, they have very little to tell us. This, of course, is nothing new; as early as 1943, the celebrated Danish linguist Louis Hjelmslev wrote as follows:

The so-called lexical meanings in certain signs are nothing but artificially isolated contextual meanings, or artificial paraphrases of such meanings. In absolute isolation, no sign has any meaning; all sign meaning originates in a context, by which we either understand a situational context or an explicit context; the distinction is, however, without meaning, since we in an unbounded or productive text (a living language) always can transform a situation context into an explicit one. (1943:41; my translation)

That is to say: even if one observes an SAV in some linguistic connection, one should not believe a speech act to be taking place, before one has considered, or possibly created, the appropriate context. That context, however, is not a sterile hull containing a dried-out seed: we may make the speech acts come alive, like the dry bones contemplated by the prophet in the field of Megiddo (Ezekiel 37:7–8), with or without the help of SAVs, by continually varying the context and expanding it to suit our communicative purposes.

The 'surface' form of a particular linguistic expression (such as an SAV or SAF) does not always and necessarily tell the truth about what it is doing. Often, when trying to determine what kind of speech act we are confronted with, we may have to disregard that form, and instead look for a 'deeper' or 'implied' meaning. On some occasions, speech act locutions (SAVs or SAFs) may substitute for one another, as in the examples given above. But in addition, speech acts may be used in ways that have nothing, or not much, to do with what they 'really' stand for. These so-called 'indirect' speech acts are the topic of the next section.

5.4   Indirect speech acts

5.4.1   Recognizing indirect speech acts

If I say to somebody:

Could you move over a bit?

I do not expect that person to 'answer my question' with:

Yes

or:

Yes, perhaps I could

and not budge an inch. On the contrary, I would consider such an 'answer' highly inappropriate, even though I did indeed utter a question (formally characterized as such by word order, intonation etc.) of the 'Yes/No' type. By contrast, if the person did move, but never 'answered' my question (as might be the case if the scene happened to be a cinema or concert hall), I would be perfectly happy with his or her reaction (or 'answer').

The reason for this apparent incongruity is found in the character of my 'question'. It was never intended as an inquiry into the physical or moral degrees of freedom of my interlocutor; what I told him or her was simply to move over, but I did so indirectly: hence we call it an *indirect speech act*. But how do we recognize such indirect expressions?

Here is an example originally due to Searle (1975:61). Suppose somebody says to a friend:

Let's go to the movies tonight

and the friend answers:

I have to study for an exam.

What is this person trying to tell his or her interlocutor? And how do we know? Searle himself suggests a comparison:

The problem seems to me somewhat like those problems in the epistemological analysis of perception in which one seeks to explain how a perceiver recognizes an object on the basis of imperfect sensory input. The question, How do I know that he has made a request when he only asked me a question about my abilities? may be like the question, How do I know it was a car when all I perceived was a flash going past me on the highway? (1975:82)

Still, this does not really solve our problem: how can we know, in the example above, that the second utterance in fact is a rejection of the proposal contained in the first, while seeming to be completely unrelated to it and not containing any overt or hidden expression of negation, denial or rejection, or even a mention of the rejected offer?

There are basically two ways of approaching this problem. The first one is the philosophical-semantic one; it is based on strict reasoning and certain basic principles of logic, such as we have become acquainted with in chapter 2.3. This is the approach followed by Searle and a number of other semanticists and philosophers of language; below, section 5.4.2, I will give an example of Searle's reasoning.

The other, pragmatic way of looking at the problem takes its point of departure in what people actually say, and 'do with their words'. It assumes, and with a certain right, that it cannot be just by accident that in our daily use of language, indirect speech acts abound, and in many cases (as we have seen in section 5.2.1 in the case of the 'promise') are far more numerous than direct ones. Moreover, as we will see below (chapter 8), the whole enterprise of assigning speech acts to particular, mostly hypothetical or imagined situations is in jeopardy, once we start thinking of those acts as performed in their proper contextual affordances, as *pragmatic acts.*

Thus, the occurrence of the imperative in orders or requests is dispreferred in many languages, including English, despite its status as the 'genuine' expression of the speech act 'order' or 'request'. Levinson remarks that "*most* usages [of requests] are indirect" (1983:264), whereas "imperatives are rarely used to command or request" (p. 275); in the same vein, Thomas observes that "in English, it is not usual to use the words *I invite you* to perform the act of inviting" (1996:47). In general, the way we recognize indirect speech acts, and process them properly, has to do with the way we are 'set up' for recognition and action by the context; this is also the deeper explanation of Searle's observation. (On 'setting up' in connection with pragmatic acts, see further section 8.3.2.)

I will deal with both approaches in the following two sections.

5.4.2   The ten steps of Searle

Searle views indirect speech acting as a combination of two acts, a primary illocutionary act (in the example above, rejecting a proposal), and a secondary one (in this case, making a statement), where the primary act operates through, and in force of, the secondary one:

> [The utterer] performs the secondary illocutionary act by way of uttering a sentence the LITERAL meaning of which is such that its literal utterance constitutes a performance of that illocutionary act. We may, therefore, . . . say that the secondary illocutionary act is literal; the primary illocutionary act is not literal . . . The question is, How does [the listener] understand the nonliteral primary illocutionary act from understanding the literal secondary illocutionary act? (1975:62)

In order to answer this question, Searle builds a ten-step pyramid of reasoning at whose summit he places his conclusion as a logically necessary keystone. The steps go as follows (A will denote the proposer, B the rejecter; both are assumed to be male):

Step 1   A has uttered a suggestion (to go to the movies); B has uttered a statement (about studying for an exam). These are the bare facts of the case.

Step 2   A assumes B to be cooperative in the conversation situation, that is, his answer is taken to be relevant, in accordance with the maxim of relevance under the Cooperative Principle.

Step 3   Relevant answers in the situation at hand (where a suggestion/request is being made) are found among the following: acceptance, rejection, countersuggestion ("Why don't we make it tomorrow?"), suggestion for further discussion ("That entirely depends on what's on") – and perhaps a few more, depending on the circumstances.

Step 4   None of the relevant answers in step 3 matches the actual answer given, so that the latter, taken at face value, must be said not to be one of these. (This follows from steps 1 and 3.)

Step 5   We must, therefore, assume that B means more (or something entirely different) by uttering his statement than what it says at face value. That is to say, his primary intention (see above) is different from his secondary one. This follows from steps 2 and 4; it is the 'crucial link' in the argumentative chain: unless we can distinguish the primary from the literal, there is no way of making sense of indirect speech acts, says Searle (1975:63).

Step 6   Everybody knows that one needs time to study for an exam, and that going to the movies may result in precious study time being lost – something many students cannot afford, especially in a pre-exam situation. This is factual, shared information about the world, carrying the same weight as the facts mentioned above, under step 1.

Step 7   Hence, it is likely that B cannot (or doesn't want to) combine the two things: go to the cinema and study; this is an immediate consequence of the preceding step.

Step 8   Speech act theory has taught us that among the preparatory conditions for any speech act having to do with proposals are the ability, and willingness, to carry out such a proposed act.

Step 9   From this, I can infer that B's utterance in all likelihood is meant to tell me that he cannot accept my proposal (this follows from steps 1, 7 and 8).

Step 10   We must conclude that B's primary intention in mentioning his exam preparation has been to reject A's proposal (from steps 5 and 9).[65]

5.4.3   The pragmatic view

Starting out from the observation that indirect speech acts (despite their name) in many cases are the most common, 'direct' realizations of what we have come to know as 'illocutionary force', one could ask whether it would not be wiser to concentrate on the pragmatic aspects of that force, rather than try and establish watertight semantic and syntactic criteria for individual speech acts and speech act verbs. Such an approach would have the advantage of being closer to what people actually do with their words; the drawback would be that in such an approach, the original insights about speech acts (such as Austin's, discussed earlier in this chapter) could be lost.

However, on closer looks, such a drawback is not real. A truly pragmatic approach would, in any case, concentrate on what users do; but it would not stop there. Users are part of a world of usage: they are never alone in their use of language, but use their language as members of a speech community that reflects the conditions of the community at large.

Among those conditions are the institutions that society, that is, the social humans, have created for themselves: the legislative, the executive, the judiciary, and other organs of the state; the various religious bodies such as faiths and churches; human social institutions such as marriage, the family, the market and so on. In all such institutions and bodies, certain human agreements and customs have become legalized, and this legalization has found its symbolic representation in language.

In this manner, language transcends the historical boundaries of the 'here and now', as well as the subjective limitations of the individual's knowledge and experience. Language, in symbolizing human life, standardizes and codifies it. Thus, we are able to speak of language as defining, indeed 'constructing', social institutions (while we, on the other hand, maintain that the social reality, in a deeper sense, is the basis of the phenomenon of language; see further chapter 11). Thus, we can (with Berger and Luckmann 1966) speak not only of the 'social construction of reality' but of the 'linguistic construction of social facts':

> [l]anguage . . . constructs immense edifices of symbolic representations that appear to tower over the reality of everyday life like gigantic presences from another world. Religion, philosophy, art, and science are the historically most important symbol systems of this kind. To name these is already to say that, despite the maximal detachment from everyday experience that the construction of these systems requires, they can be of very great importance indeed for the reality of everyday life. Language is capable not only of constructing symbols that are highly abstracted from everyday experience, but also of 'bringing back' these symbols and appresenting them [presumably: 'abstractly presenting them to us'] as objectively real elements in everyday life. (1966:40)

As examples, we may think of the language of the law, or legal language; the language of the church, or religious language; the language of institutionalized aggression, or military language; and so on. In these languages, people have seen fit to standardize certain linguistic symbolizations in order to perform certain, appropriate functions that are pertinent to the existence and survival of the institutions and their members. Thus, we find language defining the institution of marriage, prescribing the correct ways of entering a binding matrimonial contract; there is language establishing the correct exercise of the judiciary power as it is embodied in the shape of judges, juries and courts of justices, by allowing only certain, well-defined expressions to be used and 'sentences' (in the double meaning of the word) to be pronounced; and so on.

In this connection, it is important to note that the real performative value of a particular 'constructed symbol', a linguistic 'prime' such as the speech act verb 'to baptize', is actually pretty restricted. The performance of the act of baptizing is closely bound up with the utterance of precisely the words "I baptize thee" (cf. section 5.1.3). This particular language both guarantees, and vouchsafes, the exercise of a highly specific speech act; however, it can only achieve this performance as the legalized embodiment of a highly institutionalized, and institutionally empowered, social function. But also in less fossilized, more normal situations, we find language use that relies heavily on interaction in order to be effective: institutional surroundings such as the court, the classroom, the hospital, the physician's office etc. provide ample evidence.

The case of doctor–patient 'conversation' comes to mind as a particularly good and well-studied example. A number of authors, such as Lacoste (1981), Treichler et al. Beckmann (1984) and Nijhof (1998), have shown that the power of language in a situation such as the medical interview depends on two factors: one, the power that one 'brings with one', in virtue of one's status, e.g., as a physician or a patient; two, successful negotiation in the course of the interview. This latter relation, while still asymmetrical, is nevertheless also mutual: the doctor has to rely on the patient for obtaining crucial information, just as much as the patient depends on the doctor for obtaining the remedy he or she seeks for his or her ailments.

An interesting circumstance, already mentioned in the research by Treichler et al. (1984), but brought out more clearly in recent work by Davidson (1998) on the interpretation of medical discourse, is that the exchange of information becomes more effective in an environment of *reduced* unilateral power; thus, a medical student who 'converses' with the patient ("out of curiosity", as he says) after the 'real' interview by the physician, is able to elicit vital information that would have helped the doctor immensely in her diagnosis, had she had access to it. Clearly, this shows that when all is said and done, the power you bring with you may be a major factor in determining your position as a negotiator; but your success in the negotiation process depends just as much on how you handle that power (or the lack of it).[66]

In a way, traditional speech act theory has put the cart before the horse. The case of the performatives, paraded for inspection on every occasion, is a very special one indeed, and one that is rather far removed from normal use of language. In real-world interaction, successful performance is not exclusively due to the power inherent either in the user or in his or her words or speech acts; ultimately, this power resides in the society, but is mediated and negotiated, through the use of 'pragmatic acts', in the institutional setting of a particular societal context. (See further chapter 8.)

Also when it comes to more mundane problems (such as: how to characterize a question? or: what is the proper answer to a question?), the criterion of strict 'performativity' is ruefully inadequate. In accordance with everyday language use, the only decent characterization of a 'good' answer to a question is: 'one which all the participants in a particular context of question-asking and -answering find acceptable'.[67]

But does that imply that we do *not* 'perform' things with words? By no means. However, we may perform in many ways, and the 'performative verbs' are not even a major tool in this respect, as we have seen; neither are speech acts as such, as we will see. With regard to the indirect speech acts, which were the original topic of this section, we conclude that they are not 'abnormal' cases (neither in theory nor in practice); rather, the problem cases are those that earlier were thought of as 'normal', because they seemed to conform to the standards set for speaking with the proper illocutionary force. As the case of the indirect speech acts has shown, the 'normalcy' of speech acting does not strictly depend on a particular verbalization; in fact, indirect speech can be a much more effective way of 'getting one's act together' than using a regular SA (as Thomas has shown persuasively and in great detail; 1996:142–6).

As pragmaticists, we must ask, first of all, when exercising our power of speech, what *effects* our speech acting has, or can have, when performed in the actual social (institutional and other) surroundings. This, again, will force us to revise whatever classifications we have adopted of speech acts and of their ways of being expressed, by placing greater emphasis on the ways the context creates the 'affordances' (see section 8.4.2) for our societal and linguistic conduct; in short: for our acting pragmatically. The classification of speech acts offered in the next section should be read in the light of these comments.

5.5   Classifying speech acts

5.5.1   The illocutionary verb fallacy

In his 1977 article 'A classification of illocutionary acts', Searle states the following: "The primary purpose of this paper is to develop a reasoned classification of illocutionary acts into certain basic categories or types" (p. 27). In saying this, Searle takes exception to Austin's original classification (into 'verdictive', 'expositive', 'exercitive', 'behabitive' and 'commissive' acts; 1962:109f). Among other things, Searle criticizes Austin for operating with overlapping criteria, for having incompatible elements within his categories, for including elements in his categories that do not satisfy the definition of the category, and so on. But mainly, Searle is unhappy about the fact that Austin apparently does not pay attention to the difference between speech acts and speech act verbs; the existence or non-existence of the latter cannot (and should not) be a criterion for the existence or non-existence of a particular speech act.

In the same vein, Leech criticizes Austin for committing the grave error of supposing that "verbs in the English language correspond one-to-one with categories of speech act": again, a confusion of speech acts and speech act verbs. In Leech's words, "[Austin's] classification (into 'Verdictives'[,] 'Exercitives', 'Commissives', 'Behabitives', and 'Expositives') is a prime example of what I have . . . called the 'Illocutionary-Verb Fallacy' " (1983:176), a fallacy that is closely connected to the problems I have discussed earlier in this chapter under the heading of 'performativity' and its pitfalls. As Thomas aptly puts it, "Austin had (at least tacitly) equated 'doing things with words' with the existence of a corresponding performative verb" (1996:46); the fact is that we can do many things with words without ever having to resort to a specific verb or verb phrase.

When trying to establish the differences between the different speech acts (as, e.g., in the categorization proposed by Austin), one soon discovers that there are many levels at which speech acts can differ. Searle puts it as follows: "there are several quite different principles of distinction: that is, there are different kinds of difference that enable us to say that the force of this utterance is different from the force of that utterance" (1977:27).

This being conscious of the 'differences that make a difference' (Bateson) should keep us from identifying speech act verbs with speech act types; however, in reality we hurry to conclusions of precisely this kind, as soon as we observe two non-synonymous speech act verbs seemingly performing different speech acts (e.g., 'to order' and 'to command'). Especially when doing cross-language comparisons, we tend to see differences in speech acting precisely because the other language's speech act verbing is different from what we are accustomed to 'back home'. To take a very simple example from two well-known, closely related European languages, German and English: whereas German has two verbs describing the action of 'asking' (*bitten*, when you ask for a favor; *fragen*, when you're asking for information), English has only one: 'to ask'. When evaluating such cases, we have to ask ourselves how much of the difference is due to variations in forcefulness, politeness, directness of expression etc. in speech acting, and how much to authentic differences with regard to illocutionary point.

Compare also the naïve enthusiasm that many first-time second-language (L_2) learners display for the 'richness' of the (however partially acquired) new language acquaintance, as compared to L_1, the 'poor relative' in the old country. One frequently hears such learners, after they have become relatively competent in the foreign idiom, say something like; 'Now that I've learned this second language, I just can't say anything in my own language any more without feeling totally inept.'

The psychological explanation of this phenomenon is that, as you expand your horizon, taking in the different dimensions of another culture, you acquire a language to deal with those differences. It is not always easy, or even practically feasible, to 'feed back' those new experiences into the old language. A new wording process, geared to the new realities, is taking place in the L_2 learner; the old (L_1) wording will be experienced, and quite rightly so, as inadequate for those new processes. The result is similar to the 'moving trains' effect, by which we perceive ourselves as moving, whereas it in reality is the other train pulling out of the station. In the same way, we experience the new language as 'better', only because it is differently (and, of course, better) oriented toward our current, different state of mind-in-the-world. (See further chapter 10.)

With respect to the problems having to do with the different kinds of speech acting and their relationships to illocutionary verbs, Searle issues a general warning: "Differences in illocutionary verbs are a good guide, but by no means a sure guide to differences in illocutionary acts" (1977:28). Searle goes on to enumerate twelve dimensions along which speech acts can be different, such as illocutionary point, fit of speech to world and vice versa, the psychological state of the speaker, the force of the act, and so on. Among these twelve, he then selects a few to guide him toward a definitive typology of speech acts; this typology will be the subject of the next section.

5.5.2 Searle's classification of speech acts

As we saw in the preceding section, Searle (1977) finds fault with Austin's taxonomy of speech acts for various reasons (inconsistency, incompleteness and so on). His twelve criteria (mentioned there) are supposed to lay the foundations for a better classificatory procedure. Yet, out of his twelve criteria, Searle only uses four:

- illocutionary point (the 'force' of the speech act in Austin's terminology; see section 5.1.3)
- direction of fit (the way the speech act fits the world, and/or the world the speech act)
- expressed psychological state (of the speaker: a 'belief' may be expressed as a statement, an assertion, a remark etc.)
- content (what the speech act is 'about'; e.g., a 'promise' to attend the party has the same content as a 'refusal', and so on).

As a fifth criterion (not included in Searle's dozen), one could appropriately mention:

- reference (to both speaker and hearer(s)),

since speakers and hearers are the principal actors on the speech acting scene. Curiously, while speakers are implicitly present in most discussions, hearers are never explicitly dealt with, even though they do occur in Searle's early descriptions of the individual speech acts.

A further, sixth criterion, though mentioned under the heading of 'social institutions', is never put to work in Searle's descriptive typology, even though it, too, is essential for a pragmatic understanding of speech acting. Below, in chapter 11, I will deal more closely with what I call the:

- contextual conditions of speech acting, that is, the societal framework in which a speech act has to be performed in order to be valid.

The five speech act categories that Searle ends up establishing are:

- representatives (or assertives)
- directives
- commissives
- expressives
- declarations. (1977:34)

I will discuss the categories in this order. Subsequently, I will consider the resulting taxonomy, and then compare it to the one suggested by Austin.

5.5.2.1   Representatives

These speech acts are assertions about a state of affairs in the world (hence they are also called 'assertives'; Leech 1983:128), and thus carry the values 'true' or 'false'. This is their 'point'; as to 'fit', they should, of course, match the world in order to be true.

Assertions often, maybe even always, represent a subjective state of mind: the speaker who asserts a proposition as true does so in force of his or her belief. The belief may have different degrees of 'force': it makes a difference whether I postulate something or merely hypothesize; however, the point of the speech act remains the same.

Thus, there seem to be many 'asserting' statements for which the 'true/false' criterion does not hold. Is a complaint true or false? We say that a complaint is justified if and only if the content of the complaint is truthful, i.e., represents the world in a true manner; but that is not the same as saying that the complaint is *true*.

5.5.2.2   Directives

As the name says, these speech acts embody an effort on the part of the speaker to get the hearer to do something, to 'direct' him or her towards some goal (of the speaker's, mostly). This is their illocutionary point; at the extreme end of this category, we have the classical imperatives.

As to the 'fit' that these speech acts represent, there is also a clear 'direction' in the technical sense of this term, viz., from world to words: the world is adapted to the uttered words. Thus, imperatives (at least in intention) change the world in that they (hopefully) make things happen in accordance with my wishes.

Directives differ in force: from pious wish to peremptory, harsh order. Austin places them under either 'exercitives' or 'behabitives'.

5.5.2.3   Commissives

This class turns out to be more or less identical with Austin's of the same name; Searle calls it 'unexceptionable' (1977:35). Like directives, commissives operate a change in the world by means of creating an obligation; however, this obligation is created in the speaker, not in the hearer, as in the case of the directives. As an instance, compare the difference between a request and a promise: the first is a directive, the second a commissive. As to their 'direction of fit', they are identical (world adapted to words). However, the 'locus' of the obligation created is different: whereas the promise creates an obligation in the promiser, the request does so in the 'requiree'.

It has been suggested to lump these two speech acts, requests and promises, together in one category of 'obligatives'. For Searle, the problem with this suggestion is in the nature of the obligation: requesting somebody to do something does not create the kind of obligation that a promise does.

However, one could perhaps consider the act of promising to be a particular kind of request, specifically directed towards the speaker: thus, the difference between directives and commissives would be one of *direction*; in addition, such a request would have a special, binding 'promissory force'. Such a hypothesis would square well with the varying degrees of force that one has to assign to promises anyhow: as we have seen above, there are great differences in the ways people use promises from culture to culture, something which has been the cause of much misunderstanding and has given rise to a number of cross-cultural prejudices (on promises, see my earlier remarks at the end of section 5.1.2; see further chapter 10).

5.5.2.4 Expressives

This speech act, as the word says, expresses an inner state of the speaker; the expression is essentially subjective and tells us nothing about the world. Saying 'Excuse me' when stepping on a person's toe (to use Searle's example) has nothing to do, causally or in terms of consequence, with the act of stepping as such: the words 'Excuse me' do not change anything here, done is done, and both stepper and 'steppee' will have to live with the change in world conditions that a stepped-on toe represents. In this sense, the criterion of 'fit' cannot be said to operate. (However, as we will see below, there is another sense in which we can speak of 'fit', and here world conditions do play a role.)

One might ask why on earth people would bother to utter apologetic expressions when committing social and other gaffes, when the evil is done anyway and cannot be reversed – especially in cases where an evil intention seems to be foreclosed. People do not normally step on other people's toes for fun, or with premeditation; and if they indeed should so do, they certainly will not apologize (except perhaps for fun, or in hypocrisy).

This is certainly a point to take into consideration when discussing the speech act of 'expressives': because of its subjective character, this speech act is also subject to limitations and changes according to different conceptualizations of social guilt behavior. In Japan, e.g., it is not customary to say *Sumimasen* ('Excuse me') when stepping on people's toes in the subway; on the contrary, apologizing for such a (mostly unavoidable) social blunder would make people suppose that one indeed had had evil intentions. In the same vein, only the good Lord can, strictly speaking, apologize for bad weather; common humans can only be bothered or irritated by it.

Another matter is the *truth* of the expressive speech act – or rather, the truth of the 'embedded proposition', called (somewhat misleadingly) a 'property' of the speech act by Searle. If I congratulate somebody on an exam, the presupposition is that there indeed has been an exam, and that the person has passed (unless I'm being ironical, or even sarcastic). The offering of condolences in the case of a bereavement is an expression of sorrow, supposed to be present in the speaker and to be in sympathy with the state of sorrow in the hearer; this naturally presupposes that the hearer indeed has suffered the loss I offer my condolences for (again, barring hypocrisy and the like).[68]

5.5.2.5   Declarations

This is Austin's 'original' category; the 'declarative' speech act in:

I declare this bridge to be opened

changes the state of affairs in the world with respect to the bridge. What earlier was a 'not-yet-opened' bridge now becomes an opened bridge. Similarly in the case of:

I declare you to be husband and wife,

the marriage candidates cease to be just an ordinary (albeit loving) pair of people, and become a married couple. In Searle's words: "Declarations bring about some alternation in the status or condition of the referred to object or objects solely by virtue of the fact that the declaration has been successfully performed" (1977:37).

Austin used this distinction to establish what he saw as the main divider in speech act theory: the difference between 'locutionary' and 'illocutionary' acts (which was introduced earlier, section 5.1.3). On the face of it, an utterance such as:

I just resigned

is as much a declarative statement as:

You're (hereby) fired;

however, the big difference is that while the former utterance is a purely descriptive statement (which does not change my universe of employment, only reports on such a change), the latter is the fatal utterance terminating my relationship with the firm I may have been working for most of my life; in the first case, I choose my words such that they fit the world, whereas in the second, the speaker fits the world to his or her words.

This was also how Austin arrived at the first, main distinction between purely 'constative' and 'performative' verbs (see section 5.3.2), a distinction that, despite its original popularity, subsequently came under much attack; actually, Austin himself had already abandoned the distinction in the last chapter of his *How To Do Things With Words* (1962:ch. 11; see Thomas 1996:49). The reason was that even the simplest, most neutral statement still has some effect on the world in which it is enunciated; this effect is obtained by some sort of illocutionary, 'enunciative' act. The difference between such enunciative acts and the original performative ones would then be either in the change they operate on the world, or in their respective forces (as in the case of the directives discussed above), or both, but *not* in the performative quality of one of the members of the distinction. And this is precisely the insight Searle maintains Austin arrived at:

> The main theme of Austin's mature work, *How To Do Things With Words*, is that this distinction [between locutionary and illocutionary acts] collapses. Just as saying certain things constitute [*sic*] getting married (a 'performative'), and saying certain things constitute [*sic*] making a promise (another 'performative'), so saying certain things constitute [*sic*] making a statement (supposedly a 'constative'). As Austin saw, but as many philosophers still fail to see, the parallel is exact. Making a statement is as much performing an illocutionary act as making a promise, a bet, a warning, or what have you. Any utterance will consist in performing one or more illocutionary acts. (1977:37)

When we focus on the 'fit' between world and words, however, the declaratives seem to occupy a privileged place. Even though 'declaring' that you've been fired may be a perfectly all right illocutionary act, it still isn't the declarative, in and by itself, that changed your employment situation. That declaration has to obey other conditions, such as being uttered by a person in power (recall the case of the emergency ward physician, discussed in section 5.1.3).

Interestingly, in cases where changes of the latter type are really important in the context of society, the two speech act types are assigned to (theoretically at least) independent societal institutions. This is the philosophy underlying the separation of powers in modern, secular society, or (as in the judiciary) the separation of the power of 'declaring' in the first sense (as performed by the jury in rendering a verdict: 'Guilty/Not guilty'), and that of 'declaring' in the second sense (as performed by the judge in sentencing: 'To be hanged by the neck until dead').

Notice especially that the judge's declaration (in the first sense) does change the world for the accused, and that the sentence, once executed, cannot be undone. Still, the judge has not 'declared' (in the first sense) the person to have

committed the crime of which he or she stands accused; that speech act, being
separated from the execution of the sentence, can at any time be undone. This
is the ultimate sense of rehabilitating the victims of 'persecutive speech acting' in
the world of politics: the truth cannot and should not be allowed to die, even if
people can.

5.5.3   Austin and Searle

Various criticisms have been offered of Austin's original theory of speech acts,
and in particular of his classificatory categories. The classification discussed in
the preceding sections was developed by Searle in order to overcome some of the
weaknesses inherent in Austin's system. The question is now: has Searle's proposal been successful, and if not, what is the reason?

Searle is undoubtedly right in criticizing Austin (as many others have done;
see, e.g., Thomas 1996:28–33) for the deficiencies in his classificatory schema.
For instance, the categories that Austin establishes are not mutually exclusive,
as their criteria often overlap (e.g., the speech act of 'describing' belongs at the
same time in the category of 'verdictives' and in that of 'expositives'; cf. also the
problems with 'declaring' that we discussed above, section 5.5.2.5). Further, as
we have seen, there is, in Austin's work, a rather general confusion between the
notion of 'speech act' and that of 'speech act verb'; the definitions of speech acts
that Austin provides are too wide; and so on.

Still, in order to do due justice to all parties, one should not forget that Austin
himself was not always happy with the classes of speech acts he proposed: among
others, his 'behabitives' (or 'exercitives'; Searle's 'directives') caused him a lot of
trouble. But even though Austin, in his description of individual speech acts, often
ended up describing particular speech act verbs in English, the importance of his
discovery, viz., that language is an instrument of action, not just of speaking, has
not diminished over time.

When it comes to evaluating Searle's classification, the first thing one notes is
that it in many respects resembles Austin's. Searle, like Austin, distinguishes five
classes of speech acts; and one of Searle's classes, the so-called 'commissives', is
more or less the same as the class defined by Austin under that name. In Searle's
exposition, much is made of all the different criteria that one could employ in
order to establish a coherent and consistent taxonomy; but when it comes to
applying the criteria, only a few of them are used, and not even these are applied
all the time, by Searle's own admission (cf. the case of 'complaining', discussed
in section 5.5.2.1). Also, the criterion of 'truthfulness' has a rather uncertain
status: Searle (1977:35) admits that it strictly speaking is neither necessary nor
sufficient to establish the category of 'assertives' (incidentally, the same criticism
that he had earlier directed at some of Austin's classifying characteristics).

However, in one respect Searle's taxonomy is superior to Austin's: it is more
oriented toward the real world, inasmuch as it takes its point of departure in

what actually is the case, namely that people perform a speech act whenever they use language, irrespective of the 'performative' criterion. Since all acts of speaking perform something in the world, they have an illocutionary character; therefore, the interest of linguists and philosophers should center on those illocutionary aspects of language use, rather than on the somewhat dubious distinction between locutionary and illocutionary acts (which Searle, by the way, never has accepted; cf. 1969:23).

If one wants to criticize Searle and his categorization, one cannot overlook the fact that both he and Austin, as philosophers, had certain objectives in describing language which, for linguistic purposes, did not always seem that relevant. Both Austin and Searle operate on the 'one sentence, one case principle'; that is to say, in order to illustrate their theory, they use sentences that are characteristic of the 'case' under discussion, e.g., a particular speech act. Over the years, with the development of pragmatic linguistics, the shortcomings of the 'case approach' have become more and more prominent; as an instance, consider again the speech act of promising.

Austin, in discussing promises, limits himself to one single instance, one isolated utterance of promising; Searle does the same. However, if we look at promises from a slightly wider perspective, we notice that the context in which a promise is made is of the utmost importance for its status as a promise and for its binding effects. Take the case of a young person promising his or her parents not to smoke before the age of eighteen. In this case, the social conditions surrounding the execution of such a promise can be exceedingly difficult (peer group pressure, work conditions etc.). In such a context, a 'pared-down' promise would make more sense: rather than simply saying 'I won't smoke until I'm eighteen', the young person could successfully promise not to smoke inside the house, or outside his or her own room, and so on.

Similarly, in the case of the 'vow' vs. the 'promise', it is the societal context that makes us distinguish between the two. The vow is a solemn public promise with great illocutionary force, and should only be used in contexts where society imposes a need of such a unique promising, invoking sanctions of all kinds and promising select, often recognizable, social status to the promisers (as in the case of monks and nuns, or of the Vestal Virgins of ancient Rome).

The societal context is a kind of 'preparatory condition' on vows and, in general, any kind of promise – a contextual condition that obliges both promiser and promisee to look for affordances and constraints that would create or abrogate certain rights and obligations, either to accept the promise or to reject it, to contract the obligation contained in the promise or to forego it. Why is a promise made to a person about to die considered more binding than a regular promise? Can I accept a promise from a person who evidently is not able to realize what the promise is all about? (As a child, I used to tell my mother I would never leave her; luckily, she didn't hold me to my promise.) Indeed, for promises as for other speech acts, with regard to their preparatory, essential and other felicity conditions, the condition over all conditions is the *human* condition: 'Felicity's condition', to quote Goffman (1983:53).

All this may seem fairly obvious. But how then to explain that we are only able or willing to admit the importance of such factors at times when we are motivated by other considerations, such as the need to be 'pedagogical' with regard to one's children, not wanting to bind them to promises they evidently cannot ever keep? Clearly, the problem is not one of being 'nice' or 'adult' about one's promises: it touches the very core of the speech act and the contextual (social and institutional) conditions for its valid and legal use.

Questions such as these are never brought to the fore in Austin's or Searle's discussions. Even though Searle mentions the institutional character of speech acting, he does not include this contextual factor among his criteria for classifying speech acts.

As pragmaticists, we should pay serious attention to contextual conditions when describing speech acts and, in general, people's use of language. If the contextual conditions for a particular speech act's being realized are not met, then there simply is no speech act, no matter what is said or written. In the legal tradition, this insight has furnished us with the category of 'promises under duress', which aren't promises at all; similarly, court sentences and other legal documents are invalid unless pronounced and promulgated by duly appointed magistrates using the official channels. Other speech act categories show similar examples, as does speech acting in other cultures (see further chapter 10). A general, wider framework for the success or failure of speech acts will be set out in chapter 8, where I discuss the concept of 'pragmatic act'.

Review and discussion

1. Consider the following utterances:

(a)

Do you know what time it is?

(b)

Do you have the correct time?

(c)

Can you tell me how to get to the men's (ladies') room?

(d)

Do you see the salt anywhere?

(e)

It's cold in here.

(f)

Isn't this soup rather bland?

Questions:
What kinds of speech act are we dealing with here? Name the individual utterances as being either direct or indirect, and specify their illocutionary point.

In particular, how is (a) different from (b)?

What is the difference between a question like (b) or (c) and a question like (f)?

Where does question (d) belong? How is this similar to statement (e)? (Hint: refer to section 3.2.)

2. *Of presidents and promises*
    On January 14, 1993, then President-Elect Bill Clinton spoke to journalists on account of rumors that he might go back on some of his promises made during the electoral campaign. This issue came up with particular force after a number of Haitian 'boat people' had been stopped and turned back from the coasts of Florida, and Clinton had reversed his earlier stand, made during the campaign, according to which he wouldn't turn away any Haitian refugees. When cornered by some rather insistent journalists, Clinton came up with the following statement:

> I think it would be foolish for the president of the United States, for any president of the United States, not to respond to changing circumstances. Every president of the United States, as far as I know, and particularly those who have done a good job, have known how to respond to changing circumstances. It would clearly be foolish for a president of the United States to do otherwise. (National Public Radio broadcast, 8:00 a.m., January 15, 1993)

Two days later, on Sunday January 17, National Public Radio news analyst Daniel Schorr read a mock 'pre-inaugural statement' ascribed to Bill Clinton, in which he made the president-elect take back all his promises before the inauguration "so he wouldn't have to break them afterwards". Schorr/Clinton concluded his 'address' with the words: "Campaigning is not the same as governing."

Questions:
What can one say about promises made during an electoral campaign, if you look at them from a Searlian point of view? (Think especially of the sincerity condition.)

Then consider the felicity conditions of presidential promising during a campaign (conditions that would hold for anybody who is running for office and makes speeches in connection with that). Here, an important point would be to weigh the possibility for the promiser to carry out the promise and, in general, the value of an electoral promise, as compared to a 'regular' promise between people. Can you give any explanation for the difference, if there is any?

In light of your considerations, how would you evaluate the sentence: "Campaigning is not the same as governing"? Do you agree? Why (not)?

If you were to assign Clinton's words an illocutionary label, what kind of speech act would they represent? And what would their 'force' be? ('Force' here is not to be taken as synonymous with 'point'; cf. n. 53.)

Is the 'force' of the president's words a significant factor here, pragmatically speaking? How does such a 'pragmatic' force relate to the perlocutionary effects of Clinton's utterances?

Now, going back to Clinton answering the journalists, can you point to anything in his choice of words and way of speaking that could be called unusual? (Keep in mind that the extract represents a press conference transcript; the reply was not prepared beforehand.) How would you go about explaining this phenomenon? (See also the next exercise.)

3. Consider the following text (from a bankruptcy court order, Northern District of Illinois, Eastern Division, by Judge Jack B. Schmaetterer, *in re* the petition for relief by the well-known bankrupted bicycle manufacturing company Schwinn, December 28, 1992):

> Enclosed is a form of a Proof of Claim. Each Proof of Claim must be filed . . . on or before 4:30 p.m. Chicago, Illinois time, on January 6, 1993 . . .
>
> PLEASE TAKE FURTHER NOTICE THAT . . . ANY HOLDER OF A CLAIM WHO FAILS TO FILE A PROOF OF CLAIM ON OR BEFORE 4:30 P.M. CHICAGO TIME, ON JANUARY 6, 1993, . . . SHALL BE FOREVER BARRED, ESTOPPED, AND ENJOINED FROM ASSERTING SUCH CLAIM (OR FILING A PROOF OF CLAIM WITH RESPECT THERETO).

The text above represents the kind of prose that we often refer to as 'legalese', a sort of juridical mumbo-jumbo that is as loved by the lawyers as it is detested by the general public. The latter are usually unable to understand its finesses, which is why (with an apt terminology) we speak of the 'fine print' of a contract: hard to read and hard to understand, especially insofar as it restricts your rights, and in general makes living with the contract more difficult (and of course more expensive) than you'd ever expected. Legalese excels at producing unusual speech act verbs; terms such as 'estopped' or 'enjoined' are hard to imagine being used in everyday conversation or normal literary prose.

Questions:
How many speech acts can you identify in the above text, and how are they expressed?

Looking at the speech act verbs representing those speech acts, what do you notice? (Hint: consult section 5.1.3 on illocutionary point and force.)

Why do you think the judiciary uses this kind of language? (Hint: think of the 'felicity conditions' for such speech acts as 'baptizing'.)

What does this text make clear about the difference between SAs and SAVs?

4. Consider the following speech acts:

(a)

   I promise not to keep this promise

(b)

   Do not read this sign

(c)

   Whoever reads this is crazy (*Wie dit leest is gek* – popular Dutch fence graffito from the thirties).

All the above speech acts are somehow deviant, but not in exactly the same way. For instance, in (a) a condition is violated (which?), whereas (b) is self-contradictory (but still a speech act?). In (c), we have a similar problem: some conditions are not properly met. (Hint: think of Napoleon crowning himself as emperor in the Paris Cathedral of Notre Dame in 1806.)

Question:
How do you explain these anomalies in (more or less) Searlian terms?

5. Consider the following utterances:

(a)

   Sit down

(b)

   Please sit down

(c)

Please have a drink

(d)

Please have a nice vacation

(e)

Please be good to me

(conventional literal translation of the Japanese expression of greeting *doozo yoroshiku*, more or less corresponding to 'How do you do', and given in return to *Hajimemashite*, literally: 'We have begun', the opening phrase between two people meeting for the first time, hence also translatable in English as 'How do you do')

Questions:
Notice that all five utterances contain an imperative. Would you say that means they have to be classified as speech acts of ordering? Why (not)? (Cf. section 5.3.2.)

Suppose some of the above speech acts are indeed to be considered orders, how would you rank their illocutionary force?

Why is it that we experience (d) and maybe also to some extent (c), as slightly odd? (Hint: these expressions are favorite among the Japanese; refer to the model set by (e).)

Along the same lines, consider the different wording you choose when giving a friend a book she or he has asked to borrow ('Here you are'), and the one chosen by the mayor of a beleaguered city handing over the keys to the commander-in-chief of the enemy troops ('I beg your excellency to please accept these keys as a token of our humble submission to the illustrious government your excellency represents'). Are we dealing with the same speech act? Wherein is the difference?

Against this background, can you also explain why foreigners often feel they must add a 'Please' to the handing over of banal objects such as books, pens, drinks, cups of tea or coffee, movie tickets, telephone handsets and so on?

6. What is wrong with the following speech acts?

(a)

I promise (hereby) to set fire to your house

(b)

I hereby warn you that you will be awarded the Nobel prize in literature

(c)

WARNING: Your lawn will turn brown in November

(Hint: refer to the rules enumerated by Searle for performing a successful speech acts in section 5.2.1.2.)

(d)
The following notice poses a different problem:

UNDER PENALTY OF LAW: DO NOT REMOVE THIS TAG
(text on tags attached to all bedding material purchased in the US prior to 1981)

Compare the current wording:

UNDER PENALTY OF LAW THIS TAG NOT TO BE REMOVED EXCEPT BY THE CONSUMER

Questions:

Why do you think the new formulation was chosen?

Does it contain the same speech act as the old one?

Do you think the addition was necessary? Why (not)

7. I once heard a story about some priests who had to screen a movie for their parish audience in order to see whether it contained any prurient material. When they had seen the movie six times, one of the priests said that he still needed confirmation on a couple of points, so they all went back and saw the film in question another couple of times. (I don't recall what verdict they in the end came up with: probably 'XXX'!)
    With this (possibly apocryphal) story in mind, read the following recipe, found on a package of American brewers' yeast in the 1920s:

Do not mix the contents of this package with 2 qts of lukewarm water.
Do not add 1 lb of sprouted barley.
Do not put in a warm spot (74 degrees) for 7–10 days.
Do not skim.
Do not put mixture in copper pot and heat.

Do not condense vapors.
Do not consume end product.
Do not get caught.

Questions:
The above text contains some speech acts of a particular character: on the surface,
they are injunctions, or negative orders, but in reality they seem to represent
something very different. Try and name these acts (not omitting the very last
one!). Can you say anything about the (intended) perlocutionary effect of such
negative acts?

Can you give other examples from your own experience? (Hint: What constitutes
the supreme gripe?)

How would Grice deal with a text like this?

8. *A pragmatic puzzle*
   Between the Waverley and Haymarket rail stations in central Edinburgh, Scot-
land, the train (traveling in the direction of Haymarket) enters a tunnel. Just
before entering the tunnel, the astonished traveler notices a big red billboard,
about 4′ by 6′, with large white lettering saying:

> DO NOT ENTER
> UNLESS
> IN FULL POSSESSION

Having wondered for the longest time what the train company was trying to tell
me by this extraordinary injunction, and being unable to figure out a solution, I
asked a friend, a native Scotsman from Glasgow, who often travels the distance,
if he had any suggestions. He said that he had wondered about this billboard
himself, and had asked around at stations and the like, but nobody had been able
to tell him exactly what it meant. So there really is no proper answer to the following questions, but it is worth trying to answer them anyway.

Questions:
What kind of speech act does this sentence express?

What sort of context could you figure in which this sign would make sense?
(Hint: think of a possible addressee, and his or her possible properties, such as
being in possession of X, where X could be a number of things . . .) One clue is
hidden in the very size of the billboard and its lettering; another in its striking
color scheme, which is quite unlike that of your run-of-the-mill, drab rail signs.

9. Consider the following text, being a notice from the US Department of Agriculture that greets you upon going through customs at O'Hare International
Airport's International Arrival Hall in Chicago:

AGRICULTURE'S BEAGLE PATROL
Our dogs don't bite!
They sniff out illegal food or meat in passenger baggage, in order to protect
US agriculture and livestock. Please collaborate! Report all plant, food, and
animal products to the Department of Agriculture inspectors. You will be pros-
ecuted for attempted smuggling.

US Department of Agriculture

From actual experience (Houston Intercontinental Airport, September 22, 1998),
I am able to confirm that these 'agricultural' beagles indeed don't bite; on the
contrary, they go about their business very gently (but effectively).

There is a problem with the above text, though, if you consider it from the
point of view of speech act theory.

Questions:
What speech acts are involved in this notice? (Hint: just listing them suffices; you
don't have to discuss them at this time.)

How are these speech acts linguistically characterized? (Hint: 'Report' in sentence
#3 is an imperative; and so on.)

Can you say anything about the level of politeness of the individual speech acts?
(Hint: cf. the discussion in section 4.2.3.)

In particular, if you compare the second sentence with the very last one, do you
notice anything strange?

Will people 'cooperate' upon reading this text? What do you think makes them
do so? (Hint: refer to section 4.2.2.2.)

Which parts of the text do you expect to have the correct perlocutionary effect?

Can you point to any other effects (perhaps undesired or not calculated, but still
foreseeable)?

Taking off from the discussion of 'promises' in section 5.2.1.2, try and define
some of the conditions (preparatory, sincerity, essential etc.) that determine the
(non-)felicity of (some of) these speech acts.

CHAPTER SIX
Conversation Analysis

6.1 Conversation and context

In the preceding chapter, I talked about speech acts and about the ways they are used to express our aims and intentions: what we 'do with our words', as Austin put it. In the present chapter, I want to situate those speech acts in the environment in which most of them normally and naturally occur, namely in conversation, that is, in linguistic interchanges between two or more partners, the 'conversationalists'.

Such an environment should not be restricted to the immediate context or, as it is often called, the *co-text*. It will not only have to go beyond the individual speech act and its expression, but even beyond what many linguists, including speech act theorists, have traditionally assumed to be the ideal (and correct) frame for their theory: the two-person, two-utterance interchange (A says something to which B replies). In the framework of 'conversation analysis' (CA), the various mechanisms determining people's use of language in an extended, open conversational setting are explored: who holds the right to speak (often called the 'floor', because that's where one traditionally stands when speaking in an assembly such as the House of Commons); what kind of rules are there for taking, yielding or holding the 'floor'; what makes a particular point in the conversation particularly appropriate for a 'turn' (one speaker relinquishing the floor, another taking it); and so on.

Conversation analysts have deployed a wealth of insights into these matters and have elaborated an impressive arsenal of techniques for the description and explanation of the mechanisms of conversation, as we will see in the following. However, with all due respect for their findings and results, the framework in which they operate is strictly that of a co-text, in the sense defined above; or, put in another way, CA is a minimalist approach, which allows only so much hypothesizing as is strictly required to explain the phenomena at hand.

While such a parsimonious attitude to theory building undoubtedly has its merits, it also causes certain deficiencies. The restricted co-text of utterance is insufficient for our understanding of the words that are spoken, unless it includes an understanding of the actions that take place as part of, and as a result of, those words. In order to understand people's linguistic behavior, we need to know what their language use is about; that is, we must look further than the co-text of utterance and take the whole of the language scene into our view. This means that we must extend our vision from the linguistic or conversational co-text to the *context*, understood as: the entirety of societally relevant circumstances that surround the production of language.[69] One of the weaknesses of a strictly CA-oriented approach is that those societal aspects of conversation have no place to go in a framework that primarily studies co-text, and which allows for the context to appear only as a function of the conversational interaction; chapter 11 will offer a specific treatment of these aspects.

6.2 From speech acts to conversation

What can we use the theory of speech acts for, when it comes to conversation?

Historically, speech act theory has been useful as an 'eye-opener', making us see that language is not just a bunch of sentences, and that linguistics is about other matters than merely giving a formal description of the 'sound–meaning' correspondence. Speech acts are ways of doing things with our words – our words work for us in speech acts. But how these words work, and how or where these speech acts are used (such as in conversation), is not immediately evident, and cannot at any rate be derived from a formal framework, in the way that all and only the correct sentences are supposed to be 'derived' by a grammar.

The main reason for this lack is that there, strictly speaking, is no such thing as a 'correct' conversation, in the same sense as the grammarians define a 'correct' sentence. Conversation is what happens among people; when we use language together (as in 'con-versation'), our speech acting only makes sense in our common context. The most important thing about speech acts is their function in speech; it is not crucial what the speech acts represent 'officially': what counts is how the conversationalists use them (cf. the 'indirect speech acts' that we talked about in section 5.4). An example will illustrate this. Imagine that the following remark is made by one conversational partner to another:

Why can't you shut up?

On the face of it, we could assume that this was a question. And it could be (perhaps);[70] but in any normal context of conversation we would consider this a (rather unpleasant kind of) order.

Now, let's ask ourselves if the above is the only, or only 'correct', way of ordering the other person to hold his or her tongue. Clearly, such a question makes no sense: there are simply dozens of ways of putting such an order into words. Moreover, if we look a bit more closely at what's happening, we see that the majority of those commands are not formulated as commands at all, but as remarks, statements, doubts, hints, questions etc.; and that, moreover, nearly all of them avoid using the word 'order'. Here are a few of the innumerable variants on the above theme:

> I strongly suggest you shut your mouth
> Sometimes it's a good idea to shut up
> I wonder if you really should do all that talking
> I wouldn't say more, if I were you
> Remember that proverb, 'Speech is silver, . . .'?
> How about if you just shut up[71]

and so on and so forth.

All such utterances boil down to one big order: to close one's mouth, say nothing more, keep silent, or what have you – yet, there is among them not one 'true' speech act of ordering (in the sense of 'SAV-expressed'; see section 5.3.2).

We can deal with this 'disorder' because we know how to evaluate things in context: as born and (mostly) bred conversationalists, we understand the words that others speak, the way they are intended to be understood (with certain limitations, about which later). Furthermore, we are not only *able* to do this; as conversationalists, we are placed under the *obligation* to operate contextually, that is, to recognize conversational content and intention almost in spite of their eternally varying surface shapes. Conversation is not only a human right; it is a human duty (Ruiz Mayo 1990). And Levinson even goes as far as to state that "conversation is the *prototypical* kind of language use" (1983:284; my emphasis). What is important in conversation is not a purported or (self-)imposed ideal of 'correctness', but such qualities as being entertaining, humorous, knowledgeable, witty, conspicuous (Nerlich and Clarke 2000 in press). Conversations may even (though this may strike some as strange) have a well-defined aim; viz., that of self-presentation: consider, for instance, the all-important role of conversation in Jane Austen's novels, where potential suitors may be given the boot even before they can get a foot in the door, because the heroine finds their conversation 'dull'.

6.3   What happens in conversation?

As we saw in the preceding, conversation is a way of using language socially, of 'doing things with words' together with other persons.

We can look at this use of language from two points of view. The first is that of *content* : then our attention will focus on what the conversation is about, on the topics discussed, and how they are brought into the conversation; whether or not these topics are overtly announced or maybe presupposed, or hidden in other ways; what kinds of topic lead to other topics and why; and so on. Here, we also focus on the topical organization of conversation and how the topics are managed, either by overt steering ("So, what's all this talk really about?", said, e.g., at a meeting), or by covert manipulation, often in the form of indirect speech acting, such as when Governor Felix told St Paul: "Go thy way for this time; when I have a convenient season, I will call for thee" (Acts 24:25; meaning: 'I don't want to have to listen to this talk' [about 'righteousness, temperance, and judgement to come']). A further point to be considered is the function of conversation in creating an 'ambience', a context in which the conversationalists are able to pursue their (overt or hidden) goals; this is often the function of the kind of conversation called 'small talk' or 'chit-chat'.

Alternatively, one can focus on the *formal* aspects of conversation: how conversation works, what rules are observed, how 'sequencing' is achieved (gaining and giving up the 'floor', 'turn-taking', pausing, interrupting, and so on; these terms will be explained below). These aspects are often structured in a speech act-theoretical framework: pairs such as greetings and return greetings, questions and answers, summonses and compliances, advice-givings and thanks and so on are seen as conversationally coherent on account of their underlying speech acts.

The following sections will discuss some of these formal aspects; conversational content will be taken up later in the chapter (section 6.3.3).

6.3.1   How is conversation organized?

6.3.1.1   *The beginnings of CA*

In the midst of the theoretical turmoil that followed in the wake of Chomsky's linguistic revolution in the late fifties and early sixties, a group of non-professional language workers were looking at what people did with their words, when they were not busy producing sample sentences for curious linguists. These 'non-linguists' of various observances felt that the professional linguists' custom-made examples were unnatural, since these 'utterances' were not embedded in actually occurring talk; actual talk, by contrast, was typically found in everyday *conversation*.

Moreover, it was discovered that, contrary to the received bias of official linguistics, conversational talk was not in the least incoherent or irregular; the absence of a formal set of rules for generating the set of 'all and only correct' conversational utterances was not tantamount to conversation being un-ruled, or even unruly. The rules that conversation was found to obey, however, turned out to be more like the rules that people had devised for other social activities: they were the practitioners', the local people's rules, and they resembled the rules that had been discovered by researchers in sociology and anthropology for all sorts of social interaction, much more than they resembled linguistic rules. Since the emphasis was on the methods that the members of the speech community themselves had devised for dealing with the organization of talk, the label 'ethnomethodology' was attached to these studies.

As Bilmes puts it, "[a]lthough rules are 'real', even for the ethnomethodologist, there is a sense in which they are a *resource for the member* but not for the ethnomethodologist" (1986:5; my emphasis). In other words, such rules are 'people' rules', rather than linguists': they belong to the members of a society, rather than to the practitioners of a science.

Not surprisingly, the main focus of attention for the conversation analysts became, from the very beginning, the organization and structuring of conversation, and not so much its 'correctness' (form- or content-wise). To capture the (mostly unconscious) structuring that people practice when carrying on a conversation, it was necessary to develop a technique that was in many respects rather different from the classical transcription techniques of linguistics.

To name but one example: laughter is usually not considered a linguistic phenomenon; however, in conversation, laughter often plays an extremely important role, either as a means of marking off a sequence (telling one's conversational partner that one has 'got the point' of a joke), or as a signal of embarrassment ('I don't really want to pursue this point any further'), or as a weak kind of apology, or as whatever else fits the context of a particular conversation. Since in linguistics, there were no accepted ways of transcribing laughter, the ethnomethodologists naturally had to create their own transcription systems and devices. For them, transcribing conversation was not a matter of rendering all phonetic nuances in the most faithful way, in order to describe and classify the phonemes of a language and their variants, but rather, a technique that should be able to help us identify the ways in which people establish the 'traffic rules' of talk, using linguistic (as well as other, e.g., gestural) means.

The metaphor of 'traffic rules' is a highly appropriate one in this connection, since the main point of conversational structure is to keep the flow of conversation going, to avoid conversational 'accidents' ('clashes') and conversational 'traffic jams', in which the participants feel themselves gridlocked in sterile verbal exercise. Also, the techniques of good conversation management include some form of 'road assistance', by which a conversation that has halted, or has trouble maintaining the proper speed, can be helped along.

All such traffic rules and repair mechanisms find their embodiment in what Sacks and his followers have called the 'management of the conversational turn' (see, e.g., Sacks et al. 1974). The next section will discuss this concept in more detail.

6.3.1.2 Turns and turn-taking

According to Harvey Sacks, the founder of the conversation analytic method, the basic unit of the conversation is the 'turn', that is, a shift in the direction of the speaking 'flow' which is characteristic of normal conversation (in opposition to, e.g., the conversational monologue, that well-known party horror). Furthermore, in normal, civilized, Western-type conversation, conversationalists do not speak all at the same time: they wait for their 'turn', also in this sense of the word. As Sacks puts it, "A central . . . feature [of conversation] is that exactly one person – at least one and no more than one – talks at a time" (1995:II, 223).

Yielding the right to speak, or the 'floor', as it is also called, to the next speaker constitutes a turn. But how do people go about allocating turns to each other or themselves? This is where the so-called 'turn-taking mechanisms' come into the picture.

Turns occur normally at certain well-defined junctures in conversation; such points are called 'transition relevant places' (TRPs). A TRP can be exploited by the speaker holding the floor. This may be done directly, for the purpose of allotting the right to speak to another conversationalist of his or her choice ("Now, we'd like to hear Jim's view on this"). This is what Sacks called the first general rule of next-speaker selection: "current speaker selects next speaker" (1995:II, 223). Alternatively, the current speaker may proceed more indirectly, by throwing the floor wide open to whoever feels like getting into the fray ("Any other opinions or further comments on this matter?").

The second general rule of next-speaker selection is when "a next speaker selects himself" (Sacks 1995:II, 224). Obviously, in this case one may want to obviate the possibility that a speaker just goes on self-selecting; the question is then "when somebody else can decide that they're going to start talking". This is where the concept of 'transition relevant places' becomes important.

As to TRPs, we have on the one hand, the natural breaks occurring in every conversation: a speaker has to pause for breath, or runs out of things to say, or simply declares his or her contribution to be finished: all those points in the conversation are places where a natural 'transition', a relay of the right to speak to the next speaker, may occur. On the other hand, there are the formal rules of next-speaker selection that regulate the turn-taking, as we have seen.

Obviously, a speaker may just ignore an upcoming TRP and hurry past it. Many old-time conversational practitioners (such as politicians) have the habit of ignoring a natural break that would have occurred at the end of, say, a sentence (with the corresponding intonational pattern before a full stop); instead, they create an 'unnatural break' (e.g., in the form of a mid-sentence pause). Such a break is not recognized as a TRP by the other participants, and thus allows the speaker to continue full speed across the next upcoming, real TRP. Others employ the technique of 'masking' a TRP by emitting 'turn-threatening' noises (such as 'Aaahhm') at potential transition points, thus warning other speakers of their intention to continue past the TRP as soon as they have regained their breath.

Another mechanism regulating the completion of a speaker's turn is in force during, e.g., story-telling: the current speaker announces that he or she has a story to tell, and that the other speakers are expected to wait until the current speaker has completed his or her entire complex turn (or 'turn completion unit'; see Lerner and Takagi 1999; Kjærbeck 1998). Possible occurring TRPs are also ignored here, but this time by understood common agreement: 'Let the guy/lady have his/her say.'

All such mechanisms of 'selection' (self- or other) are among the most important moving parts of the 'turn-management system', the conversational machinery owned and operated by the actual and potential floor-holders and -getters.

On the other hand, the non-floor-holders in a conversational situation are not mere silent bystanders. First of all, their contribution to the conversation is an important element of the 'traffic management' that I talked about. Depending on differences of culture and language practices, the phenomena that are often gathered by the common denominator of 'back-channeling' may vary in shape and frequency, but they are always of great importance for the flow of conversation. The 'back-channeler' provides support for the speaker in the form of short utterances ("I see", "Right", and so on), or of various, more or less articulate noises (regular phonetic ones as well as others). Certain languages have specialized in back-channeling of the latter kind; thus, Japanese reportedly has some 150 different back-channel devices (called *aizuchi*), varying from regular utterances such as *hai* or *ee* ('yes') and *soo* ('I see') to vocalic and consonantal sounds of great variety, including grunts and (oral or nasal) sucked-in breaths.[72]

Bystanders can also intervene in the conversation directly, for example by taking the floor (preferably at a TRP, so as not to be accused of interrupting the speaker). This kind of turn-taking is probably the most familiar among speakers of any language, as there are strong cultural taboos in many communities against usurping the right to speak, not only in a formal, official or religious context, but also in everyday conversational practice. 'Wait for your turn' is advice that is instilled as a maxim in children from a very young age in American society; nevertheless, the rule may not be entirely universal. In other cultures, the anathema of interrupting is not felt so strongly, and consequently not inculcated so forcefully.[73]

6.3.1.3   Previewing TRPs

Managing the conversation has a lot to do with one's ability to foresee what's going to happen around the next bend in the conversational path, the next 'turn'. The content-related aspects of this management will be dealt with later; here, I will point to some of the formal aspects of what sometimes has been called 'predictability'.

Predictability has a lot to do with what Sacks has called the "adjacency relationship" (1995:II, 43), which is a bit like the cement holding chunks of conversation together, despite their being spread out over time (and occasionally, space). Here's an ethnic joke demonstrating adjacency under rather adverse conditions:

Two silent Finns go on a hunting trip. Early in the morning, one of them says: 'Nice day today' – to which the other doesn't reply. After a couple of hours, they go separate ways. Towards evening, when the two friends meet with other hunters in the sauna at the lodge, the 'addressee' is heard to mutter: 'People talk way too much around here.'

In this 'exchange', the normal routine would be to have the second conversational partner reply something like 'Yes', or 'Right' or 'A bit chilly', or whatever else is expected in such a situation. Regular adjacency would imply for the second part of a pair not to be separated from the first by half a day's silence (as reportedly is not unusual among Finns: Sajavaara and Lehtonen 1996); certainly it would not normally allow a second pair to be entirely absent (even among Finns, as in the above joke). Normal adjacency (as in the classical case of the 'greeting') would require a more or less instantaneous response; a 'minimal pair' would be 'Hi', 'Hi', which, despite its brevity, is some kind of conversation, as Sacks remarks (1990:II, 34–6). Other typical so-called 'adjacency pairs' are question/answer, request/offer (or request/denial), order/compliance and so on: given one part of the pair, the other is normally predictable. (On the content component of such adjacency pairs, see section 6.3.2.2.)

The expectancy included in the adjacency relationship operates also in other environments. Here, we can meet more or less clearly predictable 'turn signals' in the form of changes in the speed of delivery (this is why we often are able to predict the end of somebody's speech at a public occasion), or of intonation and word-choice patterns, as in certain stylized types of conversation and other discourse. Conversational 'closers' (e.g., on the telephone: 'OK?', 'OK') serve as what has been referred to (after the article of that name by Schegloff and Sacks 1973) as 'opening up closings'; conversational starters ('Excuse me', 'Yes?') exhibit similar predictable patterns.

In telephone talk in particular (but also elsewhere), signals such as 'OK', 'well' or other 'summarizing devices' often announce an upcoming closure of the conversation. Such 'pre-closings' (or, in general, 'pre-sequences') will be dealt with in the next section; usually, such signals are accompanied by changes in intonation and/or speed that are as difficult to describe exactly as they are easy to detect.

Such 'final', or intended-to-be-final, markers can be used as manipulative devices, not only preventing others from joining the conversation, but signaling that what should have been one's next TRP should be considered the end-point of the interchange, rather than an opening up of the floor for a new speaker. If I say something like:

To sum this all up, let me add a last comment . . .

or:

Concluding our discussion, we should not omit . . . ,

I am basically telling the other speakers that enough has been said on the matter, and that no further speakers are welcomed on the floor. Such ritualized pre-closing signals are available for people leading meetings in conventional, standardized environments, where they can routinely pronounce phrases such as:

Let us all pray (*towards the end of an invocation*)

or:

None higher? First, . . . Second, . . . Third (*at auctions*)

or:

Are you ready for the question? (*Roberts' Rules of Order*'s formula for closing the discussion at a meeting)
and so on.

But also in everyday conversations, many such sequences have a ritualized character that wholly or partially excludes a 'normal' reaction. For example, greetings of the type:

How are you?

are routinely followed by the predictable:

Fine, and you?

Such utterances have lost their original content of 'inquiring about somebody's health', and have become purely formal devices for starting a conversation. Still, these formal pre-sequences can be 'revived' at will by inept conversationalists, who ignore their 'pre-character' and will answer a 'first pair part' of greetings like the one above by a lengthy and detailed account of their bodily and mental state of health.

Often, such misunderstandings are caused by intercultural differences (see section 10.2.1) in the nature of the greetings: a more elaborated inquiry into the health of the greeted person, such as:

How are you feelin' this morning, ma'am

tends to elicit an elaborate response more easily than, e.g., one of the above-cited forms. An amusing instance of such a cultural misunderstanding is found in the following extract from David Lodge's novel *Paradise News*:

> The waitress, whose name, Darlette, was displayed on a badge pinned to the front of her apron, put a jug of iced water on the table and said brightly, 'How are you this evening, sir?'
> 'Oh, bearing up', said Bernard, wondering if the stress of the day's events had marked him so obviously that even total strangers were concerned for his well-being. But he inferred from Darlettte's puzzled expression that her enquiry had been entirely phatic.
> 'Fine, thank you', he said, and her countenance cleared. (1992:129)

Here, the problem lies in the nature of the greeting, 'How are you this evening, sir?'. For Bernard, a British tourist in Hawaii, this is a question about his well-being, to be answered in some sort of (admittedly perfunctory) manner. For Darlette, his answer is baffling. Her question had not been a real question, but an instance of 'phatic communication', in Roman Jakobson's terms (1960).[74]

Similarly, if somebody asks us if we are doing anything tonight, we expect the other person to come up with suggestions as to what we possibly could do together. Innumerable jokes are built around failed expectancies of this kind (possible answers other than 'What have you got in mind?' or 'Let's get together' could include, e.g., 'Bruce's coming around', 'Mind your own business', or even a flat 'Of course, I'm always doing something'). The fact that in certain cultures, the mere expression of admiration of another person's property may construed as an invitation to an (obligatory) offering of that property as a gift, followed by an equally obligatory acceptance, points to the strength of such conventional predictability, also as regards the more content-oriented turn-allocating mechanisms that will be discussed in the following sections.[75]

6.3.2   How does conversation mean?

The next few sections will focus on questions having to do with the way conversational techniques are used to convey meaning. True conversation, of course, never is the mere exchange of formalities (even though certain conversational activities, such as greetings, come pretty close in many societies). What we want to know is how the way one talks with people functions in human communication, both through the medium of the simple formalisms that we have looked at earlier (such as turn-taking), and by including other, more elaborate techniques. The latter can only with difficulty be explained on formal terms alone; which is why it is necessary to include also the content. I do not believe (contrary to many conversation analysts, such as Lerner and Takagi 1999) that such matters should be left alone until the end of our analysis; as I will show below, content is an integrating part of our analysis of conversation, as it is of all human language activity.

6.3.2.1 Pre-sequences

As already indicated above, certain utterances are usually (in some instances, even always) felt to be 'precursors' to something else (another utterance, or perhaps a sequence of utterances). The classical examples are the so-called 'attention getters', such as:

Hey

You know something?

Excuse me

and so on, to which the usual answer would be:

Yes

What?

or something in the same vein.

After this initial exchange has been concluded, the real business can be dealt with. Utterances which serve as 'precursors' to others are often called *pre-sequences*. They can be considered as purely formal tools of conversation management, but usually, they are more than that, and occupy a position which is midway between the formal and the content aspect of conversation. Pre-sequences may include pre-announcements (such as 'Whaddya know', 'Guess what'), pre-invitations (e.g., 'Are you doing anything to-night?'), pre-threats ('Watch it') and numerous others (cf. Levinson 1983:346ff).

Some of the most frequent pre-sequences are of the type sometimes called 'inquirers'. These usually precede a request of some kind; their function is to make sure that the request about to be made is indeed, from the point of the requestee, within the limits of the possible. For example, before purchasing an item in the shop or requesting information about something, help with a task, or any favor at all, we inquire about the available possibilities of obtaining that item, information, help or favor.

For instance, a well-known pre-sequence in shopping would be:

I wonder if you have X?
Do you by any chance have X?
Does your shop carry X?

(where X is some item that I might want to purchase).

When the shop clerk answers in the negative, the sequence usually comes to an end then and there (unless some information is requested or offered as to where else to buy the desired item). However, if the answer is affirmative, the 'pre-sequence' usually (though not necessarily) changes its 'activity type' (Levinson 1979) from being a pre-sequence of an informatory kind to being a prelude to an act of buying. This act can, under the circumstances, be almost unavoidable, depending on the item (and, of course, the social conditions of the purchase). Thus, it may be all right for an American restaurant guest to inquire:

Waiter, do you have any oysters on the half shell tonight?

and subsequently, after the waiter has checked and come back with an affirmative response, decide not to have oysters after all, but lobster. In France, however, a request such as:

Are there any Coquilles St. Jacques?

normally binds the guest to consume a portion if the waiter is able to confirm that there are indeed scallops on the menu.[76]

Since pre-sequences in a way have a life of their own, they are not always counted as sequences on a par with any following, independent sequences to which they play an ancillary role; instead, they may appear to be half-submerged, somewhat 'under the surface' of the conversation, so to speak. The following exchange is an example:

Are you doing anything tonight?
Why are you asking?
I thought we might maybe catch a movie.
Well, no, nothing in particular. What do you want to see?

After the initial pre-sequence ('Are you doing anything tonight?'), the sequence is interrupted by the question 'Why are you asking?', which is answered first, before the answer to the pre-sequence question is made available. Whereas such overlapping is rather normal in the case of pre-sequences, it is by no means limited to that case. The phenomenon in question is usually captured under the label of 'insertion sequences' (Sacks 1995:II, 528), about which more in the following section.

6.3.2.2 Insertion sequences, 'smileys' and repairs

Even though the 'adjacency', or immediate neighboring relationship, typically holds for two utterances belonging to the same exchange, there are cases where such immediacy is not maintained; the resulting 'gap', however, does not damage conversational coherence, and Sacks's well-known rule 'no gap, no overlap' (1995:II, 527) remains in force. How is this possible?

Typically, what we are dealing with here is called *insertion*; often, insertion is used to effect what Erving Goffman (1967) has called a 'remedial exchange', such as a *repair* (Sacks 1995:II, 525). In an insertion sequence, the normal flow of conversation is not stopped; conversationalists behave as if they were aware that the 'turns' in their talk are operating at different levels, and thus the main stream of conversation may continue its course, even though part of it is shunted off in order to let the conversationalists attend to actual or potential, upcoming difficulties. After the obstacles have been removed, conversation continues as before; the original turn-taking counters either have not been affected by the insertion sequence or are reset following it. Thus, in the middle of a conversational exchange, one may be presented with a greeting, or a request for information, or an order, none of these having anything to do with the flow of the exchange.

In the following exchange (from Halliday 1978), different conversational goals are being pursued by different activity types: greeting, buying/selling, exchange of information about the weather (maybe just a case of 'passing the time of day') and leave-takings. All these activities are intertwined, rather than following each other strictly in sequence: e.g., in the buying sequence below, the conversationalists insert a 'weather information exchange'. Notice in particular the pre-sequence that 'pre-empts' (see section 6.3.2.3) the actual (speech) act of 'buying/selling', replacing it by an indirect speech act of 'inquiring about the availability of the item to be purchased':

> Morning Tom!
> Good morning, sir!
> Have you got a *Guardian* left this morning?
> You're lucky; it's the last one. Bit brighter today, by the looks of it.
> Yes, we could do with a bit of a dry spell. You got change for a pound?
> Yes, plenty of change; here you are. Anything else today?
> No, that's all just now, Tom. Be seeing you.
> Mind how you go. (Halliday 1978:219)

Normally, one does not perceive attending to such 'other business' (greetings, requests, orders etc.) as interfering with the business at hand; it is similar to telling your party on the other phone line that you're busy, or to uttering the standardized phrase (valid in all sorts of situations): 'Just a moment, please.'

Consider the following sequence (situation reconstructed from memory: me, the father, being home alone with a sick kid):

> I (*on the phone to departmental secretary at university*): So I think I'll be in tomorrow, when Jacob's a little better. And if you could maybe ask Bob King to take my phonetics class . . . [*in a loud voice*] HEY STOP THAT RIGHT AWAY

SECRETARY: You want me to stop WHAT?

I: Sorry, I was talking to the cat – Hold on . . .

SECRETARY: ???

I: The damn cat was fixin' to sit on the baby's face . . . As I was saying, Bob promised to take my phonetics class today if necessary . . .

While there is no proper 'sequencing' of replies in this conversation, yet, if we know the situation, its content and coherence are obvious, despite the interruption caused by the insertion sequence.

In cases where such sequences deal with non-life-threatening matters, though, we may observe other reaction patterns, with potential loss of coherence and even content. The classic case is the scenario where the shopkeeper or clerk picks up the phone and starts talking to a customer on an incoming line right in the middle of your interchange, and most of the time without so much as asking you for permission or offering an apology. While this is usually perceived as non-cooperative behavior, interestingly (maybe in part due to the relative newness and relatively recent common availability of the telephone service), there seems to be as yet no generally accepted way of conversationally dealing with such situations, even in cases where the inserted conversation (often about obviously private, non-business-related matters) tends to go on and on.

In general, telephone conversations are still largely an unexplored field, despite the pioneering work of Schegloff and Sacks in the early seventies (Schegloff 1972; Schegloff and Sacks 1973). Even though the initial interest in conversational exchanges originated in Sacks's work with telephone calls to the Los Angeles Suicide Prevention Center (see Sacks 1995:I, xlviii), one has to remind oneself that there is a crucial difference between face-to-face and telephone conversations. The former utilize a great number of non-verbal communicative methods for regulating the interchange: think of the role that eye contact plays in establishing or changing turns, or of the importance of body postures in figuring out what (or if) the other person is going to say (something); for instance, getting up from one's chair is an accepted body-language pre-sequence to saying goodbye. In contrast, there is no established way of communicating such signals by telephone. (On body moves, see further section 8.4.3.)

The same holds, *mutatis mutandis*, for another new medium of communication: the electronic message service, better known as 'email'. In this medium, only the writing component can be used to represent language, as no sounds or visual cues are available; yet, by the speed and immediacy of the electronic medium, the illusion of a fast-paced, 'real' conversation is created, which, despite its written character, is very different from the customary slowness and distance in other forms of written communication, such as letters. Even so, the intimacy it creates is in many ways deficient and illusory, especially when it comes to expressing one's emotions (cf. the 'failing middle register' that Janney mentions: on the email, one can only talk (in small letters) or SHOUT (in capitals); 1996:204).

The way people have been trying to deal with this problem indirectly illustrates the importance of body language as an accompanying and modifying feature in all conversation. Especially in the fast-developing types of electronic communication known as the 'multi-user domain' (MUD) or 'chat room', the need for a 'wired' substitute for such language has made computer buffs invent the 'smileys', viz., combinations of regular ASCII symbols and alphanumerical characters, standardized to express a certain feeling or attitude towards what is being written. In some cases, this attitude is equivalent to a smile; hence we have the name 'smiley' for this 'code', originally formed as a vertical implementation of the ubiquitous smiling figure of the seventies: :-). Putting a 'smiley' (a.k.a. an 'emoticon', with an interesting neologism for this communicational category) next to what you're writing means something like: 'Don't take this too seriously'; in other words, a 'smiley' is a visual mitigating device. (There are reportedly close to 150 such codes around among computer users, and a whole new subculture of 'emoticons' is developing.)

As we see from the examples given, sequencing may be interrupted, or even stopped altogether, whenever other business needs to be attended to (which may or may not be related to the conversation at hand). Evidently, natural disasters, or even minor mishaps (like in the cat example above), need immediate attention and require that the conversationalists adjust their interchange to the emergent situation in the outside world. In general, although interruptions and insertions may happen at all times during all kinds of conversations, many of the actual phenomena are related to a particular culture (for instance, the above-described 'telephone intrusions' are much more familiar in the US than in Europe), and cannot be properly understood without some insight into the particular pragmatic presuppositions that are at work.

In many cases, an insertion is motivated by a need to repair a 'damaged' conversation. Damages can be of various kinds: misunderstandings (including 'material' failure to understand what is being said due to noise etc.), failure to observe normal sequencing (as in the case of non-adjacency, or of speaking out of turn, or whenever the conversation is hampered by 'non-sequiturs' of a more pragmatic kind (as when I ask a friend whose husband has recently passed away, 'And how's John?'); in all such cases, a repair sequence may be initiated.

One distinguishes between self-initiated repairs (where the speaker momentarily relinquishes the current floor, and erects a temporary structure where repair operations can be performed), and other-initiated repairs, the latter mostly consisting in corrections offered to the speaker, e.g., 'You mean of course . . .', inserted directly into the speaker's discourse, correcting his or her vocabulary or pronunciation, questioning the utterance's presuppositions and/or setting them right, and so on. In general, self-initiated repairs are 'preferred' to other-initiated ones (Schegloff et al. 1977; see further the next section).

Repairs are also used as strategic devices: correcting oneself, in particular, can be a way of gaining time for thinking, or a means to prevent somebody else from jumping into the conversation at an upcoming TRP. At other times, what seems to initiate a repair sequence by force of a request for information, an apology etc. contains in reality a speech act of a totally different kind.

As an example, consider the other-initiated repair in the following (constructed) conversation between a Macho Male (MM) and a Feminist Female (FF):

MM: So I was trying to pick up this chick when . . .
FF: Excuse ME, did I hear that right?
MM: Awfully sorry, I mean, *woman* . . .
FF: PICK UP?
MM: Awfully sorry, I mean, *meet* . . .
FF: So you're trying to imply that there actually are women around who would go out with a MALE CHAUVINIST PIG LIKE YOU?

In this case, both repairs are other-initiated, and the speech acts of 'asking for confirmation' or 'excusing' are in reality threats, acknowledged as such by the speaker in his apology-cum-repair. The dialogue ends with a rather heavy-handed 'presupposition correction'.[77]

6.3.2.3   *Preference*

Imagine you're in a foreign country, where you speak and understand some of the language, without being fluent. You're staying in a friend's house and the phone rings. What do you do?

My guess is that you'll leave it alone. Not only are there the difficulties in speaking a foreign language on the phone (always more complicated than in face-to-face interaction), but what are you expected to say? And even if you know how to deliver the first line of a telephone interchange (the 'first pair part' of an adjacency pair; see below), what does the other person say in return? And what comes next?

A typical telephone exchange in English could go like this:

C[ALLER]: [Phone rings]
R[ESPONDENT]: Hello
C: May I speak to Alexander Kirkwood, please
R: Just a moment, please

There are, of course, numerous variations on this scheme – but as a general rule, there is minimally a two-part interchange before the caller can proceed on business. Let's consider some of the possible variations of the first pair part: R may start with a self-identification (either by name or by phone number), in addition to the 'Hello'; the initial formula itself may be more or less explicit, in accordance with local and familial custom. Thus, in Italian, one says *Pronto* 'Ready [to take your call]', in Czech, the opening gambit is *Prosím* 'I beg [the favor of your call]', in Spanish, one says simply *Diga* 'Say [your message]' or the more old-fashioned *Mande* 'Command [me to answer you]', and so on. Some of my older Norwegian acquaintances used to answer the phone by naming themselves by their family name, followed by the expression *Værsågod*, literally 'Please (or: Feel free to) [say something]'.

The follow-ups (or 'second pair parts') of such opening sequences are more controversial. For instance, does the caller have to offer proof of identity beyond a (perhaps recognizable) voice? How does it feel for the respondent to have to deal with an unidentified caller? Many respondents prefer to know who their caller is before they go any further into the conversation; on the other hand, many callers prefer to remain anonymous as long as they don't know who is at the other end of the line: "Do I have the party with who I am speaking?" (as Lily Tomlin, in the *persona* of Ernestine, used to say in her famous telephone opening in the long-defunct American, show *Laugh-in*).

In general, what we notice is that there are relatively uncomplicated cases, where the second part of an opening is expected in the context and goes straight through, whereas other sequences trigger a need for checking, backtracking, 'mental searches' ('I know this woman/man, but where did I meet her/him and what the hell is her/his name?'), and so on.

This observation does not hold for telephone interchanges only, but for all conversational interaction. Take a first-part greeting such as 'How are you?' Here, a second part in the form of a simple return greeting (e.g., 'Fine – and you?') is expected, whereas a lengthy account of sleepless nights or boring highway travel on the way to work is clearly to be avoided.

The next question is whether we can say anything about the form that such interchanges preferably take.

Consider the following two conversations:

(*In the liquor store*)
(a)
SALES CLERK: You're over 21, aren't you?
CUSTOMER: Sure.
SALES CLERK: OK, here's your beer.

(b)
SALES CLERK: You're over 21, aren't you?
CUSTOMER: Well, er, yes, my birthday was actually yesterday, and
               we're having a party tonight . . .
SALES CLERK: All right, may I see your ID?

The customer's return in (b) is clearly problematic, given the circumstances (the case may serve as an illustration of what happens to those who break the First Rule Of Dealing With Authorities: 'Never volunteer information' – actually an instantiation of Grice's maxim of quantity; see above, section 4.2.2). The fact that superfluous information is offered in the second part of the turn makes this type of answer inappropriate, as well as ineffective. As a result, the salesperson gets suspicious and wants to see an ID.

But the story doesn't end here. If we look more closely at the customer's utterance in (b), we notice a couple of other things. The elaborate response in case (b) is in stark contrast to the simple 'Sure' in (a). In (b), there is hesitation in the customer's reply, and he starts his sentence over again (a 'false start': 'er'); there is an expletive ('yes'), there is a so-called 'hedge' (showing a certain insecurity: 'Well'), there is a lot of irrelevant information (what does the sales clerk have to do with the customer's birthday and his party) – all this is against the norm and beside the point, and serves as an indicator of something being 'glossed over', conjured away by talk.

Generalizing from these examples, we get the following picture: in conversational interchanges, not all second parts in an adjacency relationship are of equal structural complexity. Some are extremely simple, such as acknowledgments or confirmations ('Yes', 'OK'), others show various degrees of structural build-up (like elaborate excuses, long explanations etc.).

Here are some further contrasting instances; this time the interchange has the form of a request and an (indirect) denial:

[Simple-structured second part]
A: Could you help me lift this box, please?
B: OK [*goes over and helps A lift box*]

[Complex-structured second part]
A: Could you help me move tomorrow morning?
B: Well, er, let me see, I have to take Cindy to nursery school and take my mother-in-law who just has broken her arm to the doctor and Fred my handyman is coming over to fix the attic window, so . . . couldn't we make it some other day, perhaps, or does it have to be tomorrow?

Such complex, negative responses to requests are different from positive ones in a number of respects: structure, word count, 'hedges' and hesitations (like 'er'), and probably with regard to some other features as well, such as articulation, speed of delivery, pitch and so on. The ranking 'acceptance–rejection' from structurally simpler to structurally more complex implies that one has to work harder, use more linguistic resources to say 'No' to a request than to say 'Yes'. A 'No' (as in the example above) may have to be shored up with lots of background material, in order to convey the impression that one does not just decline to perform the requested action, but that the 'No' is due exclusively to circumstances beyond one's control, which then have to be specified. This specification takes time and requires a greater effort – something which may surface as hesitation, pauses, false starts, repairs and so on.

The term used for this ranking is *preference*; another, perhaps more suitable term would be 'markedness'. A 'marked' sequence is structurally richer and more complex than an 'unmarked' one (often termed the 'default'): it's what we do when nothing else is specified, like driving along at 55 m.p.h. when there are no stop signs around, children to watch, speed signs to observe, and all the traffic lights are green. Marked behaviors (like making a turn, going at excessively slow speeds, stopping in the middle of the highway, not driving on when the light turns green and so on) have to be announced, preferably before they happen (e.g., by turning on one's signals). Marked behaviors are, furthermore, *dispreferred* because they require more effort on the part of the users, which usually results in a noticeable deviance from what is expected or accepted. For the same reason, finally, dispreferred behaviors are often lacking in effectiveness.

Some of the features mentioned above appear also in other contexts where dispreferred responses turn up. Most conspicuous are pauses (self-interruptions, possibly followed by self-repairs with or without explanation, e.g., 'what I really want to say is, er, yes . . .'), the already-named 'false starts', repetitions, wordiness, as well as features of a 'prosodic' kind: speed of delivery, stress, intonation, irregular breathing (both in and out); maybe even such extralinguistic features as flushing, trembling and the like.

All such phenomena could lead one to believe that the whole matter of preference had its original seat in the physio-psychology of the individual language user. However, as Levinson remarks, this is not so: preference is a *format* of utterances, not a psychological state of the uttering individual. And he defends himself against accusations of circularity by pointing to a well-established correlation between the external phenomena I just mentioned, and the facts of '(dis)preferredness': we find 'recurrent and reliable patterns' of correlation between the two domains, that of 'preference' and that of the 'kind of action' performed. Thus, e.g., in the case of offers or invitations, an acceptance is in preferred format, whereas refusals normally are in dispreferred format. Here is an illustration of the correlation that Levinson has in mind (1983:336):

FIRST PARTS

	request	offer/ invitation	assessment	question	blame

SECOND PARTS

	request	offer/ invitation	assessment	question	blame
Preferred:	acceptance	acceptance	agreement	expected answer	denial
Dispreferred:	refusal	refusal	disagreement	unexpected answer	admission (or non-)

On the whole, one can say that certain kinds of openings and responses are always and definitely preferred, while others are usually and more or less definitely dispreferred. On the telephone, a complex opening such as 'Who is the party I'm speaking to there?' is dispreferred (compared to a simple 'Hello'); similarly, a complex and self-contradictory answer such as 'There is not a soul here right now' is normally dispreferred, and only acceptable either as a joke, or in a particular context such as the answering machine (especially if followed by instructions like: 'Please identify yourself, stating name, business, time of day and telephone number'). The same goes for complex responses and responses that carry too much information (like in the request denial quoted above), or suggest dubious or undesired intentions by prolonged silence or significant heavy breathing, and thus do not allow the gradual building up of a conversation. Here's an example of such an (unsuccessful) informational overload on the second part of a telephone greeting:

> [*Phone rings*]
> BRUCE: Hello
> CALLER: Hello, I'm Julie from the *Patriot Ledger*. How are you today?
> BRUCE: I'm fine, thanks, but I already take two newspapers and I think a third would be superfluous.[78]

Here, the caller, by providing full self-identification and affiliation information, precludes further business; if she hadn't mentioned the name of the newspaper, she probably would have been able to continue the conversation and perhaps persuade Bruce to subscribe.

6.3.3   From form to content

The previous sections concentrated on the formal means conversationalists have at their disposal for structuring their talk, measuring their interventions and controlling the 'floor'. As became apparent already there, these formal devices (in particular those having to do with what is called 'sequencing'; see below) often are inseparable from what the forms in question express. A request is followed by a compliance or a rejection, not only on the formal level: there is a reason for pairs occurring together, to wit, the fact that both members of the pair deal with the same content.

In the following, I will examine some of the content-oriented mechanisms of conversation. Doing this will also provide some insight into the pragmatics involved; a fuller discussion will be reserved for later.

6.3.3.1   *Cohesion and coherence*

Intuitively, we are able to distinguish coherent talk from incoherent babbling. Linguists distinguish between 'cohesion', which is the way words formally hang together in sentences and the like, and 'coherence', which captures the content-based connections between the words that make them produce sense. Stubbs expresses this distinction as follows: "Cohesion has to do with relations between surface linguistic forms . . . whereas coherence refers to relations between communicative acts" (1983:126–7).

In other words, cohesion establishes *local* relations between syntactic items (reference, concord and the like), whereas coherence has to do with the *global* meaning involved in what we want to express through our speech activity.[79] As to conversation, while the local sequence of turns creates a certain amount of cohesion, it is by no means sufficient to guarantee coherence. To be coherent, a text must obey the *Coherence Rule*, as defined by Tsui: "in order for an utterance to form a coherent sequence with the preceding utterance, it must either fulfil the illocutionary intention of the latter, or address its pragmatic presuppositions" (1991:111; cf. 123).

While local cohesion certainly is a valuable help in detecting and managing textual coherence, it is by no means a guarantee. Below, I provide a piece of text that shows no coherence at all, although it is locally pretty well organized as a sequence of 'turns'. (I will address illocutionary intentions below; pragmatic presuppositions and other pragmatic aspects of coherence will be discussed in section 7.2.3.2.)

The following interchange (between a psychiatrist and his patient, an 80-year-old, educated, middle-class woman) is taken from Rosenbaum and Sonne (1986); it is a typical instance of schizophrenic discourse (or maybe even several discourses):

I[nterviewer]: Is it something you have experienced?
P[atient]: No, yes, it's been said to us.
I: Aha.
P: Yes, it's been said.
I: Who said it to you?
P: Well, I can hardly remember who. There are many young gentlemen here, many young people who have been separated, and they have said it – they have told something about it. Yes.
I: Where are these young people?
P: Well, they are three hundred things after all, so we are, we had people all over space, yes. There were . . . the whole of space was filled with people and then they were put into three skins at our place.
I: Three skins?
P: Yes, they were put into the body, but I think that two of the skins are ready, they should be ready, they should be separated. And there were three hundred thousand who had no reason, or soul, or reason. But now they are so . . . , now it seems that there are some who have neither soul nor reason and they had to be helped, and people have to be helped, I can't do it here in this where we are, we have to be in . . . if I am to take care of these things. These . . . that's what the ladies say, they are aware . . .
. . .

P: I've helped them in Øster Søgade [a major thoroughfare in central Copenhagen], we helped them in that way.
I: In Øster Søgade?

P: Yes, we helped them in that way there and there were many who slid away and many who were helped. Yes.

I: There were many who slid away and many who were helped?

P: Yes, I don't know how many, I don't know. But there are many trisks and svilts, I think there are most trisks and svilts [meaningless English words calqued on equally meaningless Danish ones; cf. 'trilms', below]. That is those who are made out of svilt clay.

I: Out of svilt clay?

P: Yes, it is out on space. They make them in trilms.

I: Trilms?

P: By trilms. And then they go through three levels. Some only go through two. Some go through three. Yes. When they make them. (1986:9ff)

The coherence in this piece of conversation is strictly 'local': it turns around the limited formal organization of the talk by referring to items that have been mentioned in the immediately preceding context. Thus, while there is a certain amount of text cohesion, the patient-interlocutor has to rely heavily on the interviewer's 'prompting' role to be able to proceed in a minimally ordered fashion. Thus, whenever the interviewee halts, the interviewer can only get her started again by repeating some of her last words.

Although it is, of course, strictly true that one never completely knows what the other party is going to say in an interchange, the above 'conversation' is more incoherent and less predictable than most. What are, e.g., 'trisks' and 'svilts' and 'trilms'? Or what about 'sliding' – into what? (Later on, it turns out that the people slide into 'sugar-pools'.) What is this piece of conversation really 'about'? And even as cohesion goes, the only way to make it continue is for the interviewer to repeat some of the words that have just been uttered by the patient, more or less like a Rogerian therapist, or his or her computer equivalent, ELIZA, would do. The interviewer just keeps the speech flow going, without having an inkling of *where* it's going.[80] As the interviewee herself remarks at a later point in the conversation, it is as if there were a sound tape playing in her head:

P: . . . we have a tape that speaks. It's a tape speaking now . . . It's an old tape speaking.

I: It's an old tape speaking?

P: It's an old tape speaking when . . .

I: When you are speaking now?

P: Yes, that's a tape too. (Rosenbaum and Sonne 1986:12)

The 'tape metaphor' nicely symbolizes the 'text cohesion' that after all is present in this piece; however, there seems to be not much of a coherence in the sense defined by Tsui.

Contrast now the following interchanges, all of which, at first blush, seem to lack 'text cohesion'; yet in a bigger framework, they end up making sense.

A: What's the time?
B: (a) Twelve noon.
    (b) Time for coffee.
    (c) I haven't got a watch, sorry.
    (d) How should I know.
    (e) Ask Jack.
    (f) You know bloody well what time it is.
    (g) Why do you ask?
    (h) What did you say?
    (i) What do you mean? (Tsui 1991:115)

Of all these answers, only (a) strictly qualifies for the coherence criterion named above (a common illocutionary intent is observed in the adjacent pair 'request for information [about physical time]–compliance by giving the requested information'). However, this does not make the rest of the answers irrelevant, inasmuch as they all make sense in *some* current context (that is, they address some common presuppositions in the pragmatic background of the speaker and hearer). For example, take the 'coffee' reply, (b): people usually have coffee at the same time every day; hence 'time for coffee' equals some, more or less precise, indication of real clock time. Similarly, if one happened to live in the East Prussian city of Königsberg towards the end of the eighteenth century, a way of telling the time 'Twelve noon' would be to reply: 'Professor Kant just walked by'; Kant's daily noontime constitutionals on the city walls were so punctual that people could use them to set their watches by.

In normal conversation, even unexpected answers come as no surprise, once we're able to place them in their proper sequence, either in physical reality or in the context of the discourse. If we're unable to do either, we may ask ourselves if the person we're talking to perhaps suffers from some psychic disorder, alternatively whether he or she intends to convey a totally different content than what we seem to perceive (e.g., 'I don't want to talk to you', 'Get lost', or some other such message).

In the case of the schizophrenic discourse quoted above, some of the sequencing rules have been violated; this is something we notice while unsuccessfully trying to understand that conversation. As Tsui remarks, "the violation of the rules [governing coherent sequences] results in incoherent discourse which is *noticed* and attended to by interlocutors, and . . . the violation of these rules can usually be accounted for" (1991:111; my emphasis).

While sequencing plays an important role in the structuring of our conversations (not only on the level of formal signals, but also on the level of what the utterances mean, and of how they function), the mere fact that utterances follow utterances with a certain amount of regularity and cohesion is in itself no guarantee of coherence, as the above examples also have shown. Sequencing clearly cannot just be a matter of constructing utterances according to some abstract rules of 'conversational syntax'; the rules are at best reconstructions of what actually happens in an environment of users building up the conversation. Hence, even though "conversations are (in part) composed of units that have some direct correspondence to sentences" (Levinson 1983:294), the analytical methods of sentence grammars have only limited validity in the domain of conversation. By contrast, sequencing (in particular as manifested in Levinson's 'paired utterances'; 1983:293) is at the basis of the already-mentioned 'adjacency pairs', about which I will have to say more in the next section.

6.3.3.2 Adjacency pairs and content

As we have seen, characteristic of conversation is its adjacency in pair-wise structures. The word 'conversation' itself evokes the ritually performed and metrically codified verbal exchanges that we are familiar with from the chorus of classical Greek drama or from monastic antiphonal psalmody and hymn-singing. Here, the parties alternate in responding, the alternating, adjacent pairs being marked in the text by the symbols '℣' and '℟', for *versus* and *responsum*, respectively. The term *versus* is from the Latin verb *vertere*, 'to turn' (cf. how we refer to the front and back ('turned') side of a page: *recto*, respectively *verso*) and recalls the turning and returning of the lead in chanting that is so characteristic of choral psalmody (just as turning the pages is characteristic of reading). In the same vein, 'con-versation' consists in people's paired (turn-wise) 'col-laboration', including the repetitions and extensions that these turns naturally lead to.

This collaboration (as Harvey Sacks was the first to show us) doesn't just proceed at random, but obeys certain rules, governing not only what follows what, who can speak when, and so on, but also what a conversation is about. Thus, adjacency pairs, defined earlier as two subsequent utterances constituting a conversational exchange, or 'turn', are characterized as to function and content by their *type*. The type of a pair is given by a common illocutionary intention (or 'force', as Austin called it); pairs can thus be, e.g., 'greeting–greeting', 'order–(verbal) compliance', 'request'–'providing the requested item (e.g., information, permission etc.)' and so on.

Conversation analysts such as Sacks et al. (1974) distinguish between the 'first pair part' and the 'second pair part' of any adjacency pair. For instance, the first pair part may be a summons; then what constitutes the second pair part has to be an utterance which deals with compliance (either positive or negative), as in the following exchanges:

Could you please close that window?
Sure.

and:

Could you please close that window?
No way.

The second pair part may contain more information (e.g., 'In a minute', or 'No, I'd rather have it open'); but that wouldn't affect the exchange and thus the type of the adjacency pair.

In general, the notion of 'type' is useful when it comes to predicting what the answer could be, and how it is managed: in a way, it defines the 'base line' for the second pair parts that are possible. But it does more.

Following the theory of adjacency pairs, given a first part of a pair, a second part is immediately relevant and expectable. Furthermore, according to Schegloff (1972), if a second pair part is not found in the context of the conversation, then the first pair part is judged officially not to exist, and the first speaker may repeat the first part (e.g., by iterating the summons, maybe with some emphasis: 'I asked you to close the window', 'Would you PLEASE close that window' and so on). Such repeated first parts do not normally occur in conversation (e.g., one doesn't repeat a greeting, unless one wants to make a point: 'I have not been greeted').

The absence of a second pair part is noticeable, and has certain conversational effects, as in the case of 'pretending it didn't happen'. Suppose somebody makes a socially impossible request, such as asking the boss's wife for a date at the company outing. The painful silence which ensues makes the unfortunate requester feel embarrassed; yet it is also a means of telling him (by not giving any indication that anybody has heard what he said): 'Listen, you did something unfortunate, but we're prepared to pretend it didn't happen.'

Formally, one can express the same 'denied reality' using an explicit (and strictly speaking, self-contradictory) second pair part such as 'We didn't hear that, did we?' And an even stronger second part would contain an indirect speech act of reprimanding: 'I don't believe what I'm hearing', meaning: 'I heard you, but I can't believe my ears, since I definitely think you shouldn't have said what you did.' In such cases, as noted earlier, the most effective way of stating what is really being expressed, viz., that the speaker is a socially incompetent oaf, is *not* stating it (explicitly).

The difference between the strict notion of 'type' (based on the shared illocutionary intent of the interchange) and a more relaxed view (based on the pragmatic properties of the reply, viewed as an understanding of the effects of the interchange) may remind us of our earlier distinction between direct and indirect speech acts. While traditional speech act theory (as outlined by Austin) put great emphasis on the actual verbs expressing speech acts (SAVs), later developments allowed for speech acts to be realized in all sorts of indirect ways and still produce the same effects (cf. the classic example: 'It's cold in here', pragmatically understood as an effective request to close the door or a window).

In such a pragmatic view, neither the adjacency pair itself nor the illocution-ary intent act making up its 'type' is focused upon; rather, it is the entire (lin-guistic as well as social) user behavior that is invoked to provide an explanation. The following section will elaborate on this (see further chapter 11).

6.3.3.3 Types and coherence

A typical adjacency pair is a question, together with its answer – but what is its 'type'? To solve that problem, one has to know what constitutes a legitimate answer to a question, given its particular illocutionary intent.

Consider the following interchange:

Q. Is Lennart there?
A. You can reach him at extension 88236.

Strictly speaking, this pair does not constitute a regular 'question–answer' type: the information requested by the speaker (whether or not Lennart is 'there', i.e., at the listener's location) is not given, except indirectly. By contrast, a 'regular' answer, such as 'No, he isn't', or 'I'm sorry, he isn't', or simply 'No', while staying strictly within the bounds of adjacency pair typology ('second pair part provides the information requested in first pair part') would be very uninformative.

The easiest way out of this dilemma is to assume that whatever follows a question simply *is* the answer. Under this assumption, there strictly is no speech act of answering, no 'answerhood' (except as a notion that is so vague and all-encompassing that it is useless for describing what actually occurs as answers to questions). As Levinson aptly remarks, "there is no proposed illocutionary force of answering" (1983:293). In other words, 'answering' is not a speech act;[81] it can only be properly defined on the basis of, among other things, the preceding question.

Another way of viewing the 'answerhood' of the above reply would be to say that the question in reality was not about whether or not Lennart was at the given location, but just represented an indirect way of asking: 'Do you know where Lennart is right now?', or simply: 'Where is Lennart?' In that case, we could still maintain that the type of the pair was safeguarded and that therefore, the question–answer pair was coherent, also with regard to its illocutionary intent: 'requesting information'.

In a strict adjacency pair typology, such an interpretation of the speech acting involved here is not recognized as legal. If one takes the point of the original question to be the extraction of information about Lennart's presence in a particular location ('there'), then the 'bald on-record' answer 'No (, he isn't)' is correct, but not too helpful. By contrast, an answer that specifies *where* I can reach Lennart ('extension 88236') provides me with the information I need; whether or not Lennart is at the original, presumed location has now become irrelevant.

Conversation analysts have tried to solve the problem of 'unexpected second pair parts' by invoking the distinction between sequences and pre-sequences, introduced above. Thus, in the case of the question:

Is Lennart there?

we are dealing not with a request for information, but rather with a pre-request for something else (the permission to speak with Lennart, an effort to be put in touch with Lennart, and so on). This *pragmatic coherence*, as it is sometimes called, cannot be explained in a strictly sequential framework (Jacobs and Jackson 1983a:65). One could perhaps say that the question whether Lennart is there inquires about a 'felicity condition' for the real request: clearly, if Lennart isn't there, then it makes no sense to try and talk to him 'there'. The clever interlocutor perceives this, and infers that the real reason for inquiring about Lennart's location is the speaker's desire to see him, or talk to him on the phone; therefore, he neglects ('pre-empts') that original question and answers what he thinks is the 'real' request by indicating where Lennart may be reached:

You can reach him at extension 88236.

Conversely, there are cases where a pre-request mistakenly is interpreted as 'the real thing'. A good example of this is the following, due to Jacobs and Jackson (1983b:302):

(A customer walks up to a check-cashing counter)
CUSTOMER: Can I cash a check?
ATTENDANT: I'll be right there.
CUSTOMER: That's okay. I was just wondering whether it was too late or not.

Here, the first utterance is interpreted as a pre-sequence to a check-cashing encounter, where it in reality was just a request for information. The uptake has been too quick: cooperation took the form of second-guessing. Sometimes this results in unexpected reactions, as in the delightful example also provided by Jacobs and Jackson (1983b:301–2):

(*The scene is Sally and Scott's home in Champaign, Illinois, where Sally and Scott both teach at the university. Sally is trying to get a plane out of Champaign, and has just finished talking to her travel agent on the phone. She sits down in the living room, wearing a coat to leave for the university. Scott is in the next room, preparing for his class; he has heard some of the conversation, looks up from his books and asks:*)
SCOTT: Could you get out of here?
SALLY [INDIGNANT]: What do you *mean*, could I *get outta here*?!?
SCOTT [LAUGHING]: No, uh, heh-heh-hehhhh, could you get outta Champaign, er . . .

The above is an example of 'paranoid uptake': again, the second pair part is OK in the actual pair sequence (when Scott's utterance is interpreted as an indirect speech act of 'asking someone to leave'), but makes no sense as a sequel to a sincere request for information (which in fact it was; witness Scott's laughing reply).

To come back to the problem: given a question, what can the answer be, we note that a strictly sequential adjacency concept, based on a narrow speech act typology of 'questioning', does not provide a useful solution. Any question can have numerous 'answers', all of them relevant to the (possibly hidden) point of the question. Here is a further illustrative example:

Q. What does Joe do for a living?
A. (i) The same as always
    (ii) Oh this and that
    (iii) I've no idea
    (iv) What's that got to do with it?
    (v) He doesn't. (Levinson 1983:293)

Here, all five answers are 'to the point', meaning that they make sense as answers (depending on the context, naturally), even though they do not provide any 'real' answer to the question, except in some vague, evasive way.

But notice that while only answer (i) strictly qualifies as a typologically acceptable reply, it contains no information whatsoever about Joe's business (except in the case of a questioner who is more or less familiar with Joe and what he usually does for a living). As to the other answers, they state (appropriately, with respect to the question) that Joe doesn't do anything in particular for a living (ii); that the addressee doesn't know the answer (iii); that the question is rejected by the addressee as improper or irrelevant (iv); and that Joe is a lazy bum (v). All these answers are (again dependent on the context) perfectly acceptable, yet they are not all (especially (iv) or (v)) in strict accordance with the principle of pair adjacency.

The reason that we don't get our notion of conversational coherence upset by answers like the ones quoted above, and that such replies are considered perfectly good answers,[82] is that they somehow deal with the *content* of the question: they do not just address its illocutionary force, but also its pragmatic presuppositions (see section 7.2.3.2).

For a discourse to be coherent, it is not enough, or even necessary, that an utterance and its predecessor or successor, combined into an adjacency 'pair', abide by the strict rules formulated by the conversation analysts and based on an orthodox speech act interpretation of the utterances in question. Pairs are important because they 'steer us' toward a good understanding: "given an answer, the question is relevant" (Levinson 1983:293). But also, conversation is much more than just combining pairs in sequences (not to mention the fact that those pairs can easily expand into 'threes', 'fours' and so on, and that 'sequence' in this sense does not have to entail 'immediately following or preceding'). Tsui's 'Coherence Principle' (quoted in section 6.3.3.1), with its double emphasis on both illocutionary force and pragmatic presuppositions, is stronger than, and hierarchically superior to, the notion of paired adjacency. Adjacency is a case of coherent sequencing, but not all sequencing needs to be defined strictly in terms of adjacency.

Of the two components that make up the coherence principle, pragmatic presuppositions will be discussed in a broader, pragmatic context in chapters 7 and 10. As to the other component, illocutionary intention, this will be examined more closely in the next section.

6.3.3.4 Conversation and speech acts

The regular, 'paired' structure of conversation has a parallel to the regularity with which certain speech acts manifest themselves as institutionalized acts (cf. Austin's original discovery of speech acts of the type 'I baptize thee'), and to the "obvious regularities" that operate in speech act behavior: "answers follow questions, greetings follow greetings, etc." (Levinson 1983:289).

Consider now the following conversational exchange, in which John says to Mildred (at a party they're both attending; example modified from Levinson 1983):

It's getting late, Mildred.

Among Mildred's possible answers, we could imagine at least the following three:

Are you really that bored?
Do you want to go home?
So?

Now, if we want to determine the 'type' of this exchange pair, we have to find out what John's utterance really stands for: is it a statement about the time of day (of course relative to the usual coordinates: 'late' is not an absolute indication of time, such as, e.g., '00:15 GMT'); an expression of boredom ('Let me tell you frankly that I'm bored out of my mind'); an act of vengeance or punishment (Mildred may have been flirting with John's neighbor); a secret code for: 'Remember to take your pill'; or something entirely different?

In other words, we must try to establish the 'illocutionary intention' (or 'point') of John's remark. What kind of speech act does it represent? A statement, admonition, request, threat, confession? – it all depends on such things as: how well Mildred knows John (whether they are married, or just dating); what sort of party it is (a formal dinner, or a drop-in or gate-crashing affair); and so on. To borrow a terminology originally developed in another context: one must know the *script* for this particular interaction in order to assess the contextual value of this particular utterance.[83] A 'party script' would include information about people's conversational behavior at parties: they may joke, fight, argue, flirt, discuss linguistics, eat potato chips, get drunk, and so on; alternatively, they may even enjoy themselves.

The funny thing about Mildred's possible answers in the above conversation is that they all, in a way, are OK; that is: in the context, they make sense.[84] Especially if we look at their possible outcomes, they must certainly be valid, *effective* answers: John may get upset, and just walk off, or he may hand Mildred the car keys, or they may continue the conversation (which in all likelihood then is going to turn into an argument, with its appropriate, but equally unpredictable speech acting and its inappropriate, but equally predictable ending).

The above shows, first of all, that speech acts are not particularly good tools to work with when it comes to understanding an utterance in context: which speech act one actually is looking at depends very much, if not exclusively, on that particular context.

Second, classifying conversational adjacency pairs in terms of 'illocutionary intention' is a problem in itself (see above); however, it certainly is not going to be less thorny if we limit ourselves to situating those pairs in their immediate appropriate co(n)texts, without taking their perlocutionary effects into account.

What counts is how a speech act *functions*. If John's remark to Mildred functions as a statement, then it *is* that speech act (or some variant of it, such as a reminder); if it functions as an expression of boredom, then it *is* that expression, and so on. What we're really looking at here is a *pragmatic act* (see further chapter 8); as Levinson says, "the units in question seem to be functionally defined by the *actions* they can be seen to perform in context" (1983:291; my emphasis).

In light of the above, the discussions about the type of conversational interaction are in reality a bit beside the point. What is important is not what a speaker decides to question, order, request etc., but the effects these speech acts have on the conversational interaction.

Austin was already aware of this when he talked about the 'uptake' as a necessary condition on the 'happiness' (or felicity) of speech acts (1962:10). If we extend Austin's condition to include not only the other qualifying conditions of a speech act, but also its effective results *in context*, the problem boils down to: 'What does an individual utterance end up meaning, when considered in its total context?' For example, is a particular request (e.g., 'asking for a match') really a speech act of 'asking', or maybe a come-on remark, a plea for human understanding and sympathy or a prelude to armed robbery? Such a total context goes necessarily far beyond adjacency organization and speech act typology; for further discussion, see chapter 8.

Review and discussion

1. The following conversation transcription is due to Jan-Ola Östman (who gave it as part of an exam in the winter 1990 linguistics course at Helsinki Univer-

sity; the questions below are my own). This transcript looks very much the way you will find conversations transcribed in works and articles on conversational analysis (CA). Among the conventions used in CA, the following occur in the extract (for a full account of CA transcription conventions, see Levinson 1983:369–70, appendix to ch. 6):

!, exclamation mark: exclamatory intonation
?, interrogation mark: rising intonation
=, equal sign: latches utterances without gaps
–, dashes: pause
:(:), colon(s) (after vowel): (degrees of) lengthening
underlining as in <u>syllable</u>: stressed syllable or word
//, double slash: point of overlap (corresponding to point where next turn begins
[, left square bracket, vertically across two or more lines: alternative way of marking overlap

In this piece of conversation, four people, called here A, B, C and D, are having an after-dinner conversation in the host's living room. Two of the people have been shopping at the new mall; the two others did not come along. They exchange experiences and comments, and contribute 'small talk'.

The lines below are numbered for easy reference; they do not necessarily represent conversational 'turns'.

1. A. There was an as<u>ton</u>ishing traffic in Walnut Creek // today
2. C. Oh, <u>Bob</u>by! // Did you like the you know – <u>Bi</u>shop's <u>Bloom</u>ing <u>Mar</u>ket=
3. A. Huh?
4. A. [Well?
5. B. =<u>I</u>   [went with her?
6. C. To<u>day</u>?=
7. B. =Yeah?
8. D. Oh ex<u>cuse</u> me? – is that the <u>new</u> one=
9. C. Yeah [the one on <u>North</u> Street
10. D. [=that they were gonna open last=
11. A. =<u>That</u>'s the one –
12. A. Anyway? – They had a <u>hu::ge</u> no a <u>ma:r</u>velous parking // lot there=
13. B. For three hundred [cars
14. A.   [=with space for <u>three</u> hundred // cars
15. C. So, did you <u>find</u> yourself a typewrit // er?
16. B. A <u>tape</u>-recorder [dear!
17. C.   [A <u>tape</u>-recorder?
18. A.   [Oh <u>no</u>? They were <u>fa:r</u> too expensive // for me=
19. C. Oh yeah?
20. A. =<u>Well</u>? – These days <u>every</u>one's affected by the <u>oil</u> crisis, <u>aren</u>'t they?

Questions:

(A) Organization of the conversation:

Try to identify the various turn-taking mechanisms as defined by Sacks and his followers. In particular, pay attention to his rule that maximally one speaker speaks at the same time (see section 6.3.1.2).

How many turns are there in this excerpt? Are there cases of overlapping talk? Should the rule of 'no gap, no overlap' perhaps be slightly modified? How would you characterize the transition in lines 1–2?

Sacks talks about TRPs, 'transition relevant points', or: points where a turn shift can be expected or is possible (sections 6.3.1.2 and 6.3.1.3). Study the case of C in line 15, who 'butts in' with 'So, . . .'. How is this made possible and acceptable for the other participants? Is there any way to 'preview' this TRP? (Hint: look at who have been holding the floor for the past four lines.)

How would you characterize A's turn in 11? Isn't it strange that A 'self-selects' in line 12, and just continues with his 'Anyway, . . .'? What does line 11 do, in CA terms? (Hint: consult section 6.3.2.2 on 'insertion sequences'.)

Can you identify any clear cases of corresponding first and second pair parts? (Cf. section 6.3.1.3.)

Did you find any 'repair sequences' (section 6.3.2.2)?

(B) Content of the conversation:

Is this conversation coherent? In what way? (See section 6.3.3.1.)

In terms of turns, who are the leading conversationalists, and who are the lesser contributors? Who are the ones that interrupt most often?

In terms of speech acts, can you point to any adjacency pairs in this conversation, such as greetings, question–answers, requests for information–information provided, apologies–acceptances and so on? (Cf. section 6.3.3.2.)

Did you notice any 'back-channeling'? (Cf. section 6.3.1.2.)
    (As for 'preference' phenomena, this extract is not too clear. Refer to the next exercise.)

(C) Context:

(a) *About the conversation:*

In what way can we say that this conversation is typical of a particular kind of people?

How would you characterize the conversation in terms of 'lively', 'dull', 'interesting', 'not interesting', 'engaged', 'uninterested'? How about the conversationalists?

What is the topic of this conversation?

What are the intentions of the conversationalists?

(b) *About the people:*

Who of the four know each other, and how well? Are any of them strangers to each other? Are any of the four married (to any of the others)?

Who is the host, and who is 'Bobby'?

Does any of the four have a social position that is markedly different (higher, lower) from any of the others?

Can you figure out who are the shoppers, and who did not go? Who went out to buy ('find') what? Did this person find and buy what he or she was looking for?

Can you guess the respective ages (within ten or fifteen years) of the conversationalists?

Who are presumably male, who presumably female among the conversationalists? (Hint: consider who is most impressed by the new shopping mall vs. who is wowed by the number of cars that fit in the 'marvelous' parking lot.)

2. *Preferred vs. dispreferred responses*

While the phenomenon of '(dis)preferred' response sequences is probably universal, the way (dis)preference is realized is not. In his treatment of 'preference organization', Levinson (1983) concentrates on morphological and syntactic features; prosodic properties (with the exception of pause) are not treated specifically, even though some (such as 'in-breath') are mentioned in passing (p. 337).

Some languages have extensive prosodic means of signaling preference; breath mechanisms especially are often employed in this connection. Scandinavians manifest assent or *'aizuchi'* (see section 6.3.1.2) by producing an in-breathed *ja* ('yes'); the Japanese show the difficulties involved in what they are talking about by sucking in their breath sharply, either though the mouth (producing a hissing sound) or through the nose (producing what sounds more like an inverted snort; the behavior seems to be restricted to males). For good reasons, the utterance itself is not breathed in Japanese (like the implosive Scandinavian *ja*), as this might result in a shortage of breath and hamper normal conversation.

Below, the Japanese 'hiss' is reproduced as a number of <<<<s (the number indicating length), typically (but not necessarily) followed by an utterance such as *taihen desu*, 'it's hard, terrible, etc.' In conversation, this dispreferredness marker often assumes the shape of a short, nasal breath intake of different strength, often almost inaudible, and usually accompanied by a slowing down of the tempo and a lowering of the voice pitch. The following conversation provides several examples:

(*A and B are colleagues at work. A wants to pass on some concert tickets to B, because he can't go himself*)

A: ... *konban ongaku-wa kippu-ga arun-desu-ga, doo-desu-ka*

(I got tickets for tonight's concert, would you be interested?)

B: *Soo desu-neee* << ... [*slow delivery, pitch descending, then a short moderate nasal in-breath, followed by a pause*]

(Well, I don't know ...)

koo-yuu ongaku-wa doo<u>mo</u>-neee <<<< ... [*slow delivery, pitch and intensity decreasing, last syllable of* doo<u>mo</u> *inaudible, sharp nasal in-breath, followed by a pause*]

(That kind of music, you know ...)

Katoo-san-ni agetara doo-desu-ka. Kurashikku-ga suki-da-soo-da-kara ... [*lively speed, high pitch, engaged intonation*]

(How about Miss Kato – wouldn't it be a good idea to offer her the tickets? She is probably more interested in classical music). (Mizutani and Mizutani 1986:237; my transcription and translation)

While preference as a phenomenon of conversational organization probably is universal, its individual manifestations in different languages may display a great deal of variation. The audible markings of 'dispreferredness' in Japanese are of a very different kind than we are used to in English – yet, they are extremely effective in structuring one's conversational preferences. Small wonder, then, that many Japanese carry this marking device over into other languages, where the effect may a very different one. (See further chapter 10 for intercultural pragmatic differences of this sort.)

Questions:
Which of the following would you associate with a sharp breath intake through the mouth, when occurring in a conversation in your own language: extreme emotional upset, approaching physical danger, physical pain, other?

Do the conversationalists in the above transcript use other markers to signify pre-ferredness or dispreferredness? Which markers do they employ and where do these occur in the text? (See section 6.3.2.3 for hints.)

3. The following dialogue occurred at the US Immigration Service checkpoint in Lester B. Pearson International Airport, Toronto, Canada, on January 10, 1993:

> IMMIGRATION OFFICER: Where do you live?
> PASSENGER: Evanston, Illinois.
> OFFICER: Are you an American citizen?
> PASSENGER: No, I'm a resident.
> OFFICER: May I see your Green Card?
> PASSENGER: [hands over card]
> OFFICER: [examines card, punches something into his computer, hands back card] Do you have a driver's license?
> PASSENGER: Yes.
> OFFICER: OK, pass on.
> PASSENGER [astonished]: But don't you want to see it?
> OFFICER: No, just pass on.

Questions:
On the basis of what you have read about 'preferred second pair parts' in sections 6.3.1.3 and 6.3.3.2, how would you evaluate the passenger's question? Why was the passenger astonished?

In terms of pre-sequences (section 6.3.2.1), what kind of follow-up would one expect when one is asked a question such as 'Do you have a driver's license?', uttered by a policeman or a customs officer? (Cf. the classic example 'Do you have the time?')

Why does the 'pre-empting' of the regular second pair part (which normally happens in cases like these) not operate in the dialogue above? (Hint: ask your-self what kind of information it was that the customs officer really was eliciting, and how this relates to the actual question asked.)

4. There is a Japanese city by the name of Nikko, situated about fifty miles north of Tokyo, where one finds a great number of famous and beautiful shrines and temples, all gathered in a big complex in the foothills of impressive, cedar-clad mountains. Walking through this immense compound, a tourist sooner or later may have to respond to nature's call. Looking around for any familiar words or symbols (pictographic, architectural or otherwise), and not finding any, the tourist then addresses himself to a young, kimono-clad temple attendant, who seems to be in charge of visitor information. The following dialogue ensues:

> TOURIST: Is there a toilet around here?
> ATTENDANT: You want to use?

TOURIST (*somewhat astonished*): Sure I do.
ATTENDANT: Go down the steps.

Somewhat puzzled, the tourist then discovers the stairs, and lo and behold, there is the men's room. Now what can we learn from this little story?

Questions:
How would you categorize the speech acts being used here?

In terms of adjacency, what type(s) of pairs are involved? (Cf. section 6.3.3.3.)

Where does the misunderstanding arise?
What framework would you invoke to characterize such a misunderstanding? Could we appeal to CA for a sufficient explanation? Or should we not even try?
And if CA can't help, what would we have to invoke instead in order to obtain a 'normal' understanding of the tourist's request ? (Hint: consider the presuppositions that may be involved.)

(Note: There are additional factors involved in this intercultural scenario; for further details, please refer to chapter 10.2.)

5. Consider the following text:

The telephone rang.
'Is that Dr Bailey?'
'Yes.'
'Is Roland Michell there?'
'It's for you.'
'Who?'
'Young, male and well-bred. Who is that, please?'
'You won't know me. My name is Euan MacIntyre.' (A. S. Byatt, *Possession: A Romance*, London: Vintage, 1990:432)

Questions:
What do you think of this conversation? Is it coherent? In what sense? Does it show cohesion? (Cf. section 6.3.3.1.)

As to turn-taking, how are the different turns marked? In particular, how are the different conversationalists, referred to by the various 'whos' and 'yous', identified? (Hint: for each utterance, consider who is the addressee, in addition to who is the addresser.)

Is there anything unusual in this turn-taking, compared to regular conversation? (Hint: think of who has the floor, and how the floor rights are yielded across the wires.)

In particular, can you think of other telephone openings, not just in British but also other cultures, including possibly your own?

What do you make of the utterance 'You won't know me'? Does it represent a turn? Or otherwise, what is its status?

6. Here's an old joke:

> (*Two psychiatrists, Drs Sapirstein and Barnstone, pass each other in the hallway of the clinic. The following dialogue is reported to have occurred:*)

> DR SAPIRSTEIN: You are fine, how am I?
> DR BARNSTONE: Thanks, you're OK too.

Questions:
Considering this as a case of conversational expectancy (as in 'turn-taking'), what is normal, what is odd about this interchange? (Hint: separate out the 'formal' and the 'content' aspects; cf. sections 6.3.1.2 and 6.3.2.3.)

What kind of 'paired sequences' do we have at work here? Is the expectancy of the 'first pair part' met by the 'second pair part'?

What is presupposed for our proper understanding of this interchange as a joke? (Hint: try to describe, with the joke as your point of departure, the psychiatric profession, and what psychiatrists do for a living, to somebody from another culture.)

(Optional): What is implied in the doctors' names?

PART III
Macropragmatics

CHAPTER SEVEN

Metapragmatics

7.1 Object language and metalanguage

The prefix *meta-*, in accordance with the etymology of the Greek word, indicates a change or shift (as in *meta-morphosis*, literally 'trans-formation'). In particular, as applied to the use of language in philosophy and in the sciences, the prefix indicates a shift of 'level' in the language we are using or the activities we engage in. For instance, when I am just playing tennis, I am at the level of play; but if I start discussing with the referee whether or not the ball I missed was inside the white line, or even start berating him for his faulty judgment (as we all have seen a player like John McEnroe do), I shift, 'move up', to the 'meta'-level of tennis; what I am talking about here is the legitimacy of a particular activity on the 'object' level.

In the same way, a 'metalanguage' indicates a language that is about language, one level 'up' from the language itself, the 'object language' (the terms were originally invented by the Polish logician Alfred Tarski in the thirties). A metalanguage indicates, comments on, examines, criticizes etc. what happens on the level of the object language.

In everyday life and language use, when we put things in (verbal or literal) parentheses or in quotes, we use metalanguage. E.g., I can utter:

. . . as I was saying, it should be next week. (Wardhaugh 1998:299)

Here, we have a 'verbal parenthesis' ("as I was saying") announcing, in metalanguage, that what follows is a repeat sequence or a concluding statement; the scope of the metalanguage (even if not formally indicated) being usually understood as bounded by the internal cohesion or the content of what is said or repeated in the 'object language'.

The following literal citation is clearly marked off; the inverted commas function as metalanguage statements saying, 'This is a quotation':

> (*Annie has been seeing her shrink, who suggests she come five times a week*)
> ANNIE: I don't think I mind analysis at all. The only question is: Will it change my wife?
> ALVY: Will it change your wife?
> ANNIE: Will it change my life?
> ALVY: Yeah, but you said "Will it change my wife?"!
> ANNIE: No I didn't. I said "Will it change my life?", Alvy.
> ALVY: You said: "Will it change my WIFE. Will it change my . . ."
> ANNIE: Life. I said "Life". (from the Woody Allen movie *Annie Hall*; Yamaguchi 1997)

In the excerpt above, the actors 'state', using the metalanguage of quotes, what they consider as being the other person's exact words. They quote for the sake of argument: in order to argue properly, you have to document your adversary's words *verbatim*, just as in the medieval Scholastic disputes, where it was mandatory to repeat the exact ('object') wording of your opponent, and only then add your own ('meta-') comment or rebuttal to it, strictly *in forma*, as it was called (i.e., formally worded as a syllogism).

A metalanguage of this kind is often called 'reflexive', since it reflects on what is being, or has been said; in particular, self-reflexive comments such as 'Oops', 'you know', 'if you see what I mean', 'how shall I express myself', 'frankly speaking', and so on have lately attracted much attention; see the recent literature on 'discourse markers' and related phenomena (e.g., Schiffrin 1988).

Applying this 'meta'-thinking to the professional study of language, we may say that whenever we busy ourselves theoretically with language, in particular whenever we try to describe a language by writing up grammatical and other rules, we create a metalanguage, usually called *linguistics*. Linguistics is a metalanguage inasmuch as it is about (an object) language.

But we can move a step up. We can start discussing the linguistic rules and descriptions themselves, for instance with the aim of discovering which are the best ones for a particular language. If I say to a fellow linguist: 'My grammar is better than yours', or 'Your rules don't work', then I am talking one level up from where those rules and descriptions are located. Since the latter belong to linguistics, the characterization I give of another person's linguistic endeavors belongs to a higher level, properly called 'metalinguistic' in the sense of: 'that which deals with linguistics as its object'. (Another frequently encountered term is 'metatheoretical', implying a discussion of motivations for preferring one (linguistic) theory to some other.)

At this point, it is not trivial to ask why it is necessary to engage in this kind of metatheoretical activity. In particular, when it comes to pragmatics, what meta-level(s) are we talking about? In other words, where does 'metapragmatics' come into the picture, and what can we use it for?

The next section will provide some answers to these questions.

7.2 Pragmatics and metapragmatics

As we have seen in chapter 1, pragmatics is the study of humans communicatively using language in the context of society. Consequently, 'metapragmatics' must be, in accordance with what was said in the previous section, a discussion of 'object pragmatics' on the next higher level. This level is where we discuss the way we define and do pragmatics, and where we debate issues such as why one definition of pragmatics is better than another, what kind of relationship pragmatics has to semantics, how many principles we want to work with in pragmatics, whether or not we should include an activity such as conversational analysis in our pragmatic studies, and so on. On this level, furthermore, we can choose to focus on definitional questions (as we did in chapter 1); alternatively, we can concentrate on the conditions that govern the communicative use of language in society (and indirectly, our ways of doing pragmatics).

A simple example may clarify what I have in mind here. In chapter 5, we discussed the various speech acts that humans use in communication. Describing this human activity, we are engaging in *pragmatics*. However, if we ask ourselves what principles govern the use of speech acts, and how they relate to other human communicative activities, we are touching upon metapragmatic questions. The same is the case when we ask for an explanation why, for instance, the speech act of promising among the Ilongots or the people of Pohnpei seems to have a very different pragmatic value than it has in Western societies (as we saw in section 5.1.2).

We should be careful not to assume that a description (however painstaking) of linguistic activities automatically will lead us to a pragmatic view of those activities. To take the case of speech acts, there is no direct path from the linguistic shape of a particular act to its pragmatic value. An act of promising using the 'canonical' verb *to promise* may be pragmatically less effective than a similar act performed indirectly, perhaps not even using actual 'speech', but some standardized, pre-established convention: raising a finger or an eyebrow at a fish auction to signal an act of bidding, or even moving the entire body, as in the case of the Roman senators, who voted by marching to the right or to the left of the senate archway (*pedibus eundo in sententiam*, literally: 'letting one's feet do the voting'). As we will see in section 8.4.2, the pragmatic act of promising depends for its success not just on the 'correctness' of the corresponding speech act; a pragmatic act (specifically, a *pragmeme*) can be described as a matrix of features, among which the act's linguistic realization is an important but by no means unique element.

In other words, we cannot talk about pragmatics as if it were some simple kind of 'natural metalanguage' for linguistics. The reason is that pragmatics takes the totality of communication into account, whereas linguistics only focuses on the narrow language aspect. However, merely extending the scope of linguistics will never make it pragmatic, let alone metapragmatic; for that, we need the societal perspective, letting our gaze sweep 'top-down', so to speak, rather than 'bottom-up'.

The following sections will deal with the various ways in which the term 'metapragmatics' itself has been used.

7.2.1   Three views of metapragmatics

According to Caffi (1994a:2461), there are three ways of dealing with metapragmatics: one, as a theoretical discussion on what pragmatics is, and what it should comprise; two, as a discussion of the conditions and possibilities that enable people to act by using words, to 'do' pragmatics by *acting* pragmatically; and finally, three, as the pragmatic pendant to the metalinguistic level referred to in section 7.1, which is often captured under the label of 'reflexive language' (Lucy 1993).

Caffi's tripartite distinction is based on the following considerations. First off, pragmatics has often been likened to a 'waste-basket' in which linguists and philosophers have deposited the unusable and unclassifiable (but not discardable) items from their respective inventories (as we saw in chapter 1). As Caffi says, "pragmatics is tolerant" (1994a:2462): it does not exclude, on principle, any reasonable activity that human language users engage in (cf. Haberland and Mey 1977). But this tolerance may also result in a lack of identity: how is pragmatics different from other disciplines that deal with human language behavior, such as conversation analysis? Tolerance (even when practiced in the name of charity) may cover a multitude of sins, as another authority (St Paul) warns us. Metapragmatics needs to address this question, which comprises more than just the definitional matters discussed in chapter 1; in particular, we need to show how the methodological and conceptual apparatus of pragmatics differs from that of linguistics and (linguistic) semantics. (See further the next section.)

Second, we are faced with the fact that pragmatics, by itself, cannot explain or motivate its principles and maxims. The reason that pragmaticists operate with, e.g., a Communicative Principle, or a Cooperative Principle (with its attending four maxims) or a Coherence Rule (Tsui 1991), cannot be found inside of pragmatics; neither can such principles be straightforwardly deduced from the observation of pragmatic regularities.

Metapragmatics in this sense deals with the conditions that determine the 'sayability' of statements, promises, requests etc.; such conditions cannot be restricted to a single, local context of use, as the conversation analysts want us to believe; even less can we rely on a strictly linguistic co-text. The world in which people live is a coherent one, in which everything hangs together: none of its phenomena can be explained in isolation. For instance, in establishing and explaining coherence in utterances, pragmatic presuppositions are important factors (as we saw in section 6.3.3.3), and they need to be discussed by comparing them to simple logical or linguistic presuppositions.

In general, metapragmatics, taken in this sense, should worry about the circumstances and conditions that allow us to use our language or prevent us from using it (or from using it adequately, as the case may be). An investigation into these conditions is necessary and timely, and involves a consideration of societal import, yet it cannot be dealt with on the level of the observed phenomena alone; which is why we must refer to metapragmatics for a discussion of such problems (see further section 7.2.3; cf. also chapter 11).

A third consideration has to do with the way language is able to reflect on itself, make statements about itself, question itself, improve itself, quote itself and so on. Such reflexive, metalinguistic uses of language were what first attracted the attention of the philosophers, as we saw above; but they are also a suitable vantage point from which to consider metapragmatic language uses.

To take a simple example: we do not only specify pragmatic principles (cf. chapter 4), but we also comment on those principles from a metapragmatic point of view (in Caffi's first sense; typical question: why do we need a Politeness Principle?). Moreover, we want to interpret and apply the principles in actual use, which includes a metapragmatic discussion (in Caffi's second sense) of their validity in particular cases (typical question: under what conditions is it OK to disregard the Politeness Principle?). As users, we can, within limits, make and break the rules of language: for instance, we can choose not to be polite, and 'flout' the Politeness Principle, if our circumstances are such that we think our aims and goals are better realized by not being polite. And finally, we may even publicly announce our flouting by saying, e.g.:

You did a great job, and I'm not being polite,

making the latter half of the utterance into a typical self-reflexive, metapragmatic statement (in Caffi's third sense; typical question: what did you mean by saying that?).

The three aspects of metapragmatics highlighted here will guide us through the remainder of this chapter. In particular, I will come back to the question of reflexivity in section 7.2.4.1.

7.2.2 | Metatheory

Above, I quoted Caffi as saying that pragmatics is 'tolerant': it does not exclude any activity that has to do with the users of human language, considered as users.

But this tolerance should not be misinterpreted or abused: pragmatics should not engage in methodological looseness, in the sense of 'anything goes'. Only a serious metapragmatic reflection on itself, its aims and methods, can prevent pragmatics from becoming the infamous 'waste-basket' – conceptually akin to Alan Perlis's famous characterization of the 'universal tar pit' of computation: the Turing machine as a model of the human mind, in which everything is possible, but nothing interesting ever happens.[85]

The metatheoretical concerns of pragmatics have manifested themselves in the attention that has been paid, from the very beginning, to questions of *rules* and *principles*. Earlier (in chapter 4) I discussed these from a more practical point of view; here, let me add some thoughts on their metapragmatic function and character.

7.2.2.1   Rules

Interestingly, the term 'metapragmatics' does not occur in several of the major reference texts on pragmatics which have appeared during the past twenty-thirty years, such as Gerald Gazdar's *Pragmatics* (1979), Stephen C. Levinson's *Pragmatics*, Geoffrey N. Leech's *Principles of Pragmatics* (both the latter from 1983) or Jenny Thomas's *Meaning in Interaction: An Introduction to Pragmatics* (1996). In his recent addition to the pragmatics textbook literature, *Understanding Pragmatics* (1999), Jef Verschueren devotes an entire section to what he calls 'metapragmatic awareness'; however, his treatment covers mainly the problem of "making linguistic choices", as well as our awareness of those choices and our ability of reflecting on them (1999:187); in other words, we are facing the third possible interpretation of the term in Caffi's schema.

Outside of linguistics proper, the notion of a 'metapragmatic stance' in matters of language use emerged early, and attracted the attention of a number of anthropologists and anthropological linguists such as Michael Silverstein (in publications from 1976 onwards; see especially 1992, 1993) and Alessandro Duranti (1996). Often, these authors tie the metapragmatic issue in with 'indexicality', in a further development of what Charles S. Peirce had called the 'indexical meaning of signs' (Duranti 1996:37ff; Silverstein 1993; see further section 7.2.4.2).

As an exception to the lack of involvement in metapragmatics on the part of most of the pragmatic linguists mentioned above, one of them, Leech, offers an interesting metatheoretical discussion on the concept of rules in grammar and their motivation; in this connection, he also mentions the term 'metagrammar'. While maintaining the arbitrariness of language (in accordance with Saussure's theory of the linguistic sign), Leech points out that the assumption of arbitrariness *in* the grammar does not necessarily entail the absence of a non-conventional motivation *of* the grammar: the rules are conventional (or arbitrary), but the reason *why* we have those rules involves what Leech calls "extralinguistic considerations"; and he continues: "The rules of a grammar (that is, of the grammar of a particular language) are arbitrary [read: conventional]; but there is also a 'metagrammar': an explanation of the typological or universal characteristics of grammars in general" (1983:25). As an example, Leech quotes the imperative in English: since the 'subject' of an imperative is always understood as 'you', there is no harm in not expressing this subject, since "nothing [is] to be lost by its omission" (p. 25).[86]

While the argument in itself does not carry too much weight, either from a grammatical or from a typological point of view, the case aptly illustrates a typical 'metapragmatic' kind of reasoning about grammar, in particular about grammatical rules. What Leech calls 'metagrammar' is in fact a reasoning about rules, an effort to 'rule' certain rules in order (that is to say: being in accordance with the conventions of grammar), even though they may seem motivated nonconventionally.

There are, says Leech, two ways of talking about such cases: "the first states the rule as a matter of convention, and the second states that given that this rule exists, it is a reasonable [assumption?], on *extralinguistic grounds*, that it does so" (1983:26; my addition and emphasis). Even though he does not use the term, Leech's 'metagrammar' thus becomes a *metapragmatics* in Caffi's first sense, as defined above. The grammatical rules themselves are conventionally placed inside the grammar; but if we want to discuss whether or not such a convention is 'reasonable', we have to move up to the metalevel. In addition, the moment he starts discussing grammatical rules in relation to their users, Leech must have recourse to the 'extralinguistic considerations' that he 'reasonably' (and perhaps a trifle apologetically) appeals to; such metapragmatic considerations are properly subsumed under Caffi's second sense (see further section 7.2.3). Finally, there is the question of the users' reflexive awareness of such considerations, in particular to what extent "*language users know more or less what they are doing when using language*" (Verschueren 1999:187; original italics); this is a metapragmatic question in Caffi's third sense.

As we see, Leech's metagrammar, being part of metapragmatics, fundamentally involves *metapragmatic* reasoning and reasonability (metatheoretical, extralinguistic and reflexive, respectively). The reasonability of the metagrammar is, furthermore, a *user* reasonability: it is the users that deem the rules reasonable. This is established by the simple fact that no rule can be used without a user; for a pragmaticist, the use of the rules of grammar is by definition subject to a general metarule incorporating the users and their (linguistic and extralinguistic) context.

7.2.2.2 Principles and maxims: the case for 'economy'

What holds for grammatical rules is *a fortiori* true of the pragmatic principles and maxims that were mentioned in chapter 4: their rationale cannot be discussed within pragmatics (and is, on the whole, seldom discussed). In particular, the principles according to which people cooperate in their use of language, are polite to each other, or make economic use of scarce linguistic means – Grice's Cooperative Principle, the Politeness Principle, as propounded mainly by Leech, or the Economy Principle, as well as a number of others – are invoked by many authors, but their motivation or explanatory force are almost never questioned; the same holds for the maxims subsumed under these principles. (An exception is found in Sperber and Wilson's 1986 work, which explicitly criticizes the Gricean Cooperative Principle; cf. above, section 4.3.2.)

Leech is among the few who roundly take the metapragmatic aspects of the principles and maxims into account. According to him, "[p]art of the essence of Grice's CP [Cooperative Principle] is its extralinguistic motivation in terms of social goals" (1983:27). If the essence of a pragmatic principle such as that of cooperation is in its 'extralinguistic motivation' and its 'social goals', then that principle belongs on the metapragmatic level, as we have seen in the previous section; chapter 11 will go into more detail as regards the social character of these goals, and how they function as extralinguistic motivation of the various principles. For now, I will leave the Cooperative Principle aside, as it has been discussed and criticized extensively elsewhere in the literature (cf. Mey 1987b), and rather focus on the seemingly less controversial, since less often disputed, principle, that of 'economy' in language use.

Often, a 'Principle of Economy' is formulated (e.g., by Sperber and Wilson 1986) as the human propensity toward achieving maximum effect with least possible effort. If we want to apply such a principle (whose validity is said to be general, and whose rationale is strictly outside pragmatics) to the area of pragmatics – that is, if we want to maintain that a principle of economy is at work in people's use of language –, then we have to ask ourselves under what conditions and in which contexts of language use the positing and application of such a principle would be acceptable, or even plausible. In other words, we will have to invoke metapragmatics.

As a behavioral norm, a principle is something by which we abide no matter what: a 'person of principles' is not easily swayed; a 'principled account' is one which holds up in the face of even serious objections and so on. Consequently, we should expect 'economical use of language' to be the norm, not the exception, in language use. In actual language use, however, such is not the case, and naturally enough: language economy is practiced only where it is economically necessary or desirable. Thus, in the old days, when we used the services of companies such as Western Union in the US or KDD in Japan to send a telegram, where every word cost money, a 'Principle of Economy' imposed the well-known 'telegraphic style' on our communication, and for a reason: our economy.

But how about everyday use of language? When we see competent language users in action, it makes little sense to talk about 'economy'. Good speakers or able stylists take pride in expressing themselves in well-wrought, ably crafted poetry or prose; their clever use of insightful similes and judiciously applied tropes, of ornate embellishments and effective repetitions, is a far cry indeed from all sorts of economy, principled or not.

Contrariwise, the person expressing himself or herself 'economically', that is, in as few words as possible, may be obeying certain self-imposed or externally motivated restrictions, but is certainly not going to be complimented for saving on words. The noble savage speaking in monosyllables or uttering a final 'Howgh' is by no means a role model for the modern, civilized language user, whose corresponding 'penurious' speech acts of solemnly confirming what has been said (using expressions such as 'Amen', 'So help me God' etc.) are severely restricted as to their allowed usage, both contextually and content-wise. Which leads me to believe that the whole idea of an 'Economy Principle' is based on the same kind of misunderstanding that elevates simple language and restrained behavior to the level of virtues, in force of some ill-understood notion of a frugal life-style as the ideal of good housekeeping, linguistic or otherwise.

In spite of its conceptual poverty, the Economy Principle carries an amazing prestige. It is often used as a kind of final, incontestable argument – whatever it appears under the guise of the 'Law of Least Effort', the 'Efficiency Principle' or a general 'Principle of Economy'. Here is Searle, discussing one of the prepara-tory conditions for the speech act of promising: "I think there is operating in our language, as in most forms of human behavior, a principle of least effort, in this case, a principle of maximum illocutionary ends with minimum phonetic effort" (1969:60). And to quote an older source, this is what a celebrated French linguist, the late André Martinet, had to say on the subject: "the linguist must keep in mind . . . the principle of least effort, which makes him restrict his output of energy, both mental and physical, to the minimum compatible with achieving his ends" (1962:139).[87]

Compare also the following: "PRINCIPLE OF EFFICIENCY: Given nothing to suggest the contrary, whenever a further utterance would be redundant one can infer that the speaker need not make the utterance but that he will operate as if he had made it and will expect the hearer to operate similarly" (Fraser 1975:195). Here, the crucial question has to do with the word 'need': what kind of 'need' are we talking about here, and where does it come from? A need for 'economy', efficiency, or other kinds of verbal parsimony does not exist unless it is imposed by outer circumstances that are not only 'extralinguistic', but outside of the normal conditions of operating linguistically.

For instance, a need for 'economy' in language use typically arises whenever the difference between life and death is a matter of seconds. Speed and efficiency in communicating are crucial in such a setting: one calls out "Fire!", and not "I hereby announce to you that a great fire has broken out in the dining-room." Similarly, where other restrictive conditions, such as the state of one's postal expense account or one's balance in the bank, impose an 'economical handling of scarce resources', a 'Principle of Economy' in one's use of language may make sense; in all other cases, it doesn't. (For a more detailed critique of the 'Principle of Economy', see Mey and Talbot 1989.)

7.2.3   II Constraining conditions

Metapragmatics (in the second sense defined above) specifically studies the conditions under which pragmatic (i.e., users') rules are supposed to hold. That is to say, metapragmatics worries about the conditions that allow us to use our language or prevent us from using it, or from using it adequately. It comes as no surprise that such conditions may vary greatly from times to times and from places to places, and that there cannot be any truly 'universal principles', in the sense of principles that are valid for any linguistic practice anywhere at any given time. At most, we can say that there are, in any given culture or group of language users, certain principles that the members of the culture, the users of the language, agree on as working guidelines in their language practice.

Saying this does not make a metapragmatic discussion of principles uninteresting for the study of language use; however, it puts such studies in their proper perspective. That is to say, it provides a healthy antidote against all forms of ethnocentrism that so easily creep up on the linguist or pragmatician who is looking for correspondences across languages, and (almost unavoidably) tends to establish such correspondences using terms deeply anchored in his or her own culture or language.

The much-quoted and widely accepted Cooperative Principle is a good example of this tendency. In particular, some of its maxims, such as that of 'quantity', can be questioned for their ethnocentric bias towards what sometimes is called 'Standard Average (Western) European/North American'. In many other cultures, the virtues of linguistic parsimony are not extolled to the same degree as is allegedly the case in our society. As examples, compare the research (referred to in section 4.2.2.3) that has been carried out on Malagasy language and culture regarding the alleged universality of conversational implicature (Elinor Ochs Keenan 1976), or the studies done on many of the peoples of the Caribbean and the Pacific, who respect and value verbal proficiency more than efficiency (see, among others, Allwood 1976; Reisman 1989; Keating 1998; Sidnell 2000 in press; on the intercultural aspects of pragmatics, see further chapter 10).

The following sections will deal with metapragmatic conditions as *constraints* embedded in the circumstances of our linguistic practice.

7.2.3.1   *General constraints*

The world of pragmatics is not predictable in the same way as morphological or syntactic worlds are. That is to say: no strict rules and conditions can be set up for a pragmatic universe, neither can any stringent hypotheses be formulated and tested that would create the illusion of a well-formed world, as it is done in a rule-based grammar ('regular', in the original sense of the word).

A pragmatic approach to language cannot be captured by the exact methods of mathematics or physics. As Nunberg has observed in a thoughtful (but unfortunately little-quoted) article, the criticism that pragmatic explanations on the whole lack the rigor of explanations in syntax and phonology is "inappropriate, as it arises out of a native [naïve?] conception of what a pragmatic explanation should look like, based on the assumption that semantics and syntax ought to have the same methodology" (1981:199).

As the main reason for this misdirected critique, Nunberg mentions the impossibility of using the scientific testing procedures of linguistics on phenomena such as conversational implicature: the allegation that we are dealing with a pragmatic phenomenon, rather than with a 'genuinely' linguistic one "is not subject to empirical confirmation in the sense of the natural sciences" (p. 220). The ultimate reason that we need an 'understanding' (*Verstehen*, in the sense defined by Max Weber 1978), rather than a scientific explanation in the traditional sense, is that the pragmaticist "has to be able to put at least part of his foot into his subject's shoes" (p. 220). Or, to quote Caffi's elegant aphorism, "The program of metapragmatics (its manifesto) might be the sentence that Socrates would have added to his motto 'I know [that] I don't know', had he not been forced by the tyrants to drink the hemlock: 'I don't know enough that I do know'" (1994a:2465).

Pragmatics views the world as a world of language users (Nunberg's 'subjects'); metapragmatics tries to capture the general conditions under which these users work. Rather than speculating on what the user possibly could (want to) say, it investigates what the user actually can and normally will (be expected to) say. Instead of imagining the 'possible worlds' of abstract semantics, we focus our attention on the feasible world of down-to-earth pragmatics. In other words, we constrain the world of use in accordance with our (explicit or implicit) knowledge of the users and with the expectations that follow from that knowledge.

Efforts at computer modeling of human language behavior have made us aware of the importance of user goals, as embodied in devices such as *scripts* (cf. Schank and Abelson 1977). Scripts have very little to do with rules in the traditional sense; rather, they are realizations of certain general constraints which guide us as we strive to realize our goals under normal conditions. The goals and expectations that are incorporated in such constraints are essential to a pragmatic understanding of human activity, much more so than are correctness of sentence construction and observance of the rules of grammar (cf. Mey 1991b). Of course, we may choose to deviate from the normal case, while staying within the general set of expectations, but then we have to qualify the constraining conditions. Alternatively, we may want to create a new set of constraints, another script.

Carberry, who works with computer modeling of human search strategies in information retrieval, observes that such strategies:

utilize *pragmatic* knowledge, such as a model of the information-seeker's inferred task-related plan and expected *discourse goals*. The power of this

approach is its reliance on knowledge gleaned from the dialog, including discourse content and conversational goals, rather than on precise representations of the preceding utterances alone. (1989:76; my italics)

Linguistic actors rely on what is implicit in the scenario (the 'script'), as well
as on what is explicitly stated (in the dialogue). However, their activities do not
necessarily obey the rules for using certain distinguished, 'canonical speech acts'–
on the contrary: in order to 'state' something, I usually avoid using the speech
act verb to state, as Caffi perceptively remarks (1984a:456). Thus, what we are
looking for in metapragmatics is, in Caffi's words, those "units of action which
are constitutive of a given interaction" (p. 464). That is, the whole framework
of discourse is invoked, both on the general level of a story, an argument, a report
etc. and on the individual level of this particular story, argument, report etc., all
within the limitations of the interactants and the conventions agreed on between
them (see also Caffi 1984a).

The problem with the available models (both computational and other) is that
they tend to be "deterministic and idealistic" (Borutti 1984:445), and that they
are valid only for the general cases. In pragmatics, however, we are not always
and only interested in people following the normal route; an elegant error can
be much more interesting than a plain truth, as Nietzsche said. What route we
choose depends not only on what goals we pursue, but also on what we want to
do along the way. As Borutti reminds us:

> in order to understand discourse, the procedures of making meaning normal
> and constant are very important . . . To obtain a correct representation of the
> subject's discourse, we must consider the linguistic strategies of the speaker,
> the effects he or she is planning, the anticipation of the hearer'[s] mental reac-
> tions, his or her pre-existing context of speaking, etc. (1984:445)

7.2.3.2 Presuppositions

The notion of presupposition was originally developed in a semantic environment; as such, it does not hold up to our pragmatic expectations. For one thing,
semantic presuppositions deal with truth or falsity: they are defined as 'holding'
(that is, being true), even if the sentence containing the presupposition is false (as
we have seen in section 2.5).

Such a strictly truth-conditional definition of presupposition fails on several
counts: first, there is more to sentences than the abstract truth value they carry,
when viewed as logical propositions. Second, sentences, when spoken, cannot be
considered in isolation from the speaker and the listener(s), who are relevant
factors in any situation of language use. Third, we do not live our lives, or speak,
by truth conditions alone: 'truth' is at best one among many other concerns
that people have. Pertinent questions such as 'What good does it do?' or 'What
is it to me?' cannot be answered in a purely semantic theory of presuppositions.

Characteristically, one of the first to discover this pragmatic fact was not a linguist, but a philosopher, Robert Stalnaker, who introduced the term 'pragmatic presupposition' in an influential early article (1977 [1974]). Stalnaker established the fact that an utterance needs a context in order to be correctly interpreted, also with respect to its truth or falsity (which was what Stalnaker, being a philosopher, was mainly interested in). Take every philosopher's favorite example:

The cat is on the mat.

This sentence, regardless of whether it is true or false (that is, whether or not there is a certain cat on a certain mat), presupposes that there is some cat, and some mat: namely, the cat and the mat that the sentence refers to. But the sentence doesn't tell us a thing about what this particular cat represents in a particular connection (such as what this cat means to its owner), or about the context in which somebody (e.g., the owner) could have uttered the sentence in question. The owner may have cried out in despair: 'The cat is on the mat!', thereby conveying a message to the person in the household who was closest to cat and mat; the message may have been the equivalent of 'Quick! Joey is doing it again – get him off Aunt Euphemia's mat!' (said about a particular cat who, under certain conditions, such as being in an agitated state of mind, sees fit to spray on a particular mat, a precious heirloom from a much-cherished, long-deceased great-grandaunt). This utterance is quite different from the 'same' sentence pronounced by the philosopher who uses it as an example, when musing about the nature of presupposition.

Speaking of cats, the following notice could be found on a lamp-post in Evanston, Ill., one day in late August of 1992:

FOUND: GRAY CAT
LOST SINCE JULY
PHONE: 491-7040

What do we make of this? Suppose the usual, semantic presuppositions hold: we know that there is a cat, and that the cat is gray. We know furthermore that people when they say things like 'Gray cat found' usually speak the truth; when they put up a sign like the one above, they normally do not play tricks. This we can conclude by way of conversational implicature (see section 3.2.3). Similarly, by a conventional implicature (see section 3.2.4), we can safely assume that the author of the message is the same person as he or she who actually found the cat (the utterance 'found' conventionally implies 'found by someone' – usually the utterer).

In the terminology of speech acts, the message counts as an act of informing the community about the fact that a cat has been found; and it also counts as a speech act of offering, namely, to give the cat back to its owners (that's why there is a phone number included in the message). But we still have a long way to go before we can understand the real 'meaning' of this rather strange message.

We need, first of all, to explain the situation itself: what do people do when they find a cat? Or maybe even more fundamentally: what do cats do when they start touring the neighborhood, and find themselves new homes? (I'm not asking *why* they do it; that is beyond our pragmatic universe.) In our society, there are a number of unwritten conventions that deal with 'pet behavior', understood as both the behavior of the pets themselves, and that of the humans dealing with them. As to the latter, it is tacitly assumed that on finding a stray cat on the streets, or on discovering that you have acquired a new house guest who turns up every morning and asks for milk and loving care, you do something about it: you ask around who might have lost a cat, you maybe insert an ad in the local free paper and you put up notices around your house.

These are all pragmatic presuppositions: they have to do with, or 'index' (see below, section 7.2.4), the metapragmatic conditions in which the language users and their cats live and exercise their linguistic and human, respectively feline rights; such conditions are often gathered to the common denominator of so-called 'shared' (or 'common') knowledge.

However, this tells us only part of what's happening in his situation: the denominator in question is strictly a mis-nomer. The knowledge we are speaking about has not just to do with knowing things, but should rather be understood in the broader sense in which the Bible talks about 'knowing' (as in 'carnal knowledge'). In Caffi's words, "[p]ragmatic presuppositions not only concern knowledge, whether true or false: they concern expectations, desires, interests, claims, attitudes towards the world, fears etc." (1994b:3324).

Furthermore, the word 'shared' in the expression 'shared knowledge' contains a possible misunderstanding as well. Take the case of our 'gray cat'. When I first read the message, the last sentence had me truly puzzled: 'Lost since July'. What is that supposed to mean? How could the person who wrote the notice at the end of August have known that the cat had been lost for at least one month? Did the cat speak to him or her in human words, like cats do in fairy tales? Or did the person possess preternatural insights, or have a revelation, or did he or she conclude from the state of emaciation the poor animal was in that it had been on the road since July? 'Lost since July' conventionally implicates that there was a time before which the cat was not lost; but how can one determine that point of time with sufficient confidence to go officially on record, on a lamp-post on a public street, as maintaining this to be 'true'?

Clearly, if we choose to limit ourselves to this much of available information, we must give up. The shared knowledge that we possess does not allow us to deal with all the implications and presuppositions of the sentence, either in a truth-functional or in a pragmatic (let alone a metapragmatic) sense.

A semantic notion of presupposition (which includes, despite their name, some of Stalnaker's original 'pragmatic presuppositions') merely links sentences together on the basis of what is true or false. A serious theory of pragmatic presuppositions goes beyond this, and inquires *metapragmatically* into the ways an utterance is understood in the context of the language users' 'common ground'.

Here, it is important not only to record *what* people say, but to figure out *why* they say things, and why they say them the way they do. In the 'cat' example, our metapragmatic inquiry rests on the pragmatic presupposition that pet lovers will do anything to save a cat from a fate worse than death, namely: living in the animal shelter on borrowed time. But consider now the following example, an advertisement in the 'For Sale' section of the Chicago weekly *Reader* (August 29, 1992):

MOVING OUT OF country. Everything must go. Husband, dog, microwave, tv, vcr, personal word processor, appliances. Great deals. Call Ori, 312-404-2391.

For brevity's sake, let's disregard the obvious presuppositions here (such as: there are certain items that are put up for sale; 'moving out of country' means: 'leaving the US'; and so on), along with the usual conversational implicatures (the author of the ad intends to sell certain items: 'must go' means in this context: 'I want to sell'; something which also can be independently inferred from the fact that the ad appears in the 'For Sale' section of the paper). Even so, there are still a number of pragmatic presuppositions that have to be sorted out.

One of the latter could be clarified by referring to the institution of the 'Sayonara-sale', best known from Japanese contexts, where servicemen and others going back to the US (or whatever their home country happens to be) will sell absolutely everything they have. The Japanese expression *sayoonara* means 'goodbye'; and indeed, the advertisement in question seems to represent a farewell: to a previous life, to the current place of abode, to a lot of valuable possessions – which is precisely the difference between this type of sale and, say, a regular garage or yard sale, where one usually only sells things one doesn't need any more, or at least can do without.

In the case of this particular 'Sayonara-sale', however, another, higher (or metalevel) consideration enters the picture. What we register is a conflict of pre-suppositions: under normal assumptions about buying, selling and advertising in our society, one does not usually buy, sell or advertise husbands (and dogs only under restricted conditions). So, how to understand this 'sale' of a husband? Is the ad a polite invitation – to whoever happens to be first in line or on the phone – 'to take this husband of mine off my hands'?

In fact, none of our 'shared' (or 'common') knowledge assumptions and cor-responding presuppositions seems to be able to explain the story behind this par-ticular ad. Apparently, some conversational maxim has been broken; and, as in the case of conversational implicature, our task is to figure out which maxim has been infringed upon (most likely that of relation), and what inference we are sup-posed to deduce from this breach. In the case at hand, the infraction turns out to be governed by a *metapragmatic* constraint on the conditions for speaking (or, as in our case, the writing of an ad or notice). In the case at hand, these conditions are in the last analysis subject to an extralinguistic influence, namely the personal circumstances and motives of the person inserting the ad.

One suitably constrained context in which this prospective 'sale scenario' could be realized is the *joke*: the whole thing could be a spoof, with nothing to it, and the ad writer no more than a prankster(-ess). However, we run up against yet another metapragmatic constraint here: in US society, there are certain things you don't joke about, at least not in public; among them are marriage, death, defecation, sex, religion and money.

But now what if the ad were *meant* to announce an upcoming divorce? In this case, we would be able to assign the proper speech act ('announcing for sale') to the ad; still, indirectly, it would seem to convey a strange message. Metapragmatically speaking, the reason is that an advertisement such as this one contradicts what Caffi calls the "shared metapragmatic knowledge . . . of culture-bound and group-bound action frames" (1994a:2463). An advertisement such as this is not the usual 'action frame' for telling your friends that you're splitting up. Even so, depending on the circumstances, this could indeed be a very nasty way of saying that your marriage was on the rocks (especially if hubby didn't know he was up for sale).

To conclude this section, a word about how presuppositions and implicatures are different, from a metapragmatic point of view. Analyzing the seemingly innocent texts above has shown us three things: one, pragmatic presuppositions are necessary in order to understand what people are doing with their language; two, in order to reach that understanding, we need to use our skills both of conversationally implying and of pragmatically presupposing; and three, even with the best of wills and the cleverest techniques, it sometimes is impossible to ferret out all the pragmatic presuppositions and construct all the necessary implicatures in order to make sense of what is being said or written. What we need to invoke here is a metapragmatic rationality of the kind defined by Caffi as "a reflection on the possibility conditions of action and interaction" (1994a:2462).

The metapragmatic moral to be gathered from the above is that the 'shared' or 'mutual knowledge' that conversation presupposes is not always given; indeed, only through conversation are we able to build up this knowledge, to supplement it and to refine it. In this way, the hidden pragmatic presuppositions may be brought out into the open, if necessary. But notice that there is an important metapragmatic difference in this respect between such presuppositions and conversational implicatures: valid presuppositions tend to remain mostly implicit, while valid implicatures rise to the surface and become visible in the course of conversation.

In daily life, we never think much about what is presupposed; we don't have to go 'presupposition-hunting' in order to understand an utterance. This happens only when we get stuck and perhaps (triggered by some conversational implicature) have to invoke a metapragmatic constraint; however, metapragmatically questioning an interlocutor's presuppositions is a dangerous sport, inasmuch it may threaten the 'face' of my conversational partner.

Contrariwise, in the case of conversational implicatures, we are able to understand the utterance only if we make the proper inferences, based on our conversational activity. Also, while we are obliged to act on those inferences, the nature of this action, precisely because its necessity is manifest, is subject to discussion. What is conversationally expected or requested may be refused or denied without conversational penalty; our action can be a negative one, and the conversational implicature rejected without prejudice to either myself or my partner(s).

Whereas pragmatic presuppositions (as all presuppositions) are here to stay once they are accepted (and not explicitly cancelled), conversational implicatures share the shifting framework of conversational interaction. We may put presuppositions to work to create an implicature; but we cannot use an implicature to create a presupposition (unless the implicature is ratified by all parties and becomes a new presupposition in its own right). Implicatures are mainly the individual's own business; presuppositions require a collective, sometimes even metapragmatic justification. As Caffi remarks, in her lucid treatment of the subject, "presuppositions are grounded on complicity ... ; communication is somehow like sitting down at the card table: presuppositions can be a bluff" (1994b:3321, 3323).

7.2.3.3 Speech acts and discourse

The problem of language use is as old as language itself: how to connect the words of our language with the things of our world? All human language activity consists in 'doing these things with those words', that is, uniting what is said with what is done, joining speech activity with world action. But even if historically, the discovery of speech acts has been instrumental in paving the way toward a better understanding of our use of language, the actual input of speech act theory to the analysis of 'real' language use has not always been impressive. The reason for this failure lies in the purely philosophical, abstract character of the speech acts as defined and described by the original theoreticians, Austin and Searle. In metapragmatic terms, the never-asked, yet crucial question can be formulated as: what are the societal (and other 'extralinguistic') conditions that determine whether or not a particular speech act succeeds, is 'felicitous' or 'happy'?

A recurrent problem with speech acts has been how to isolate and identify them in relation to the actual utterances. As we have seen in section 5.3, there certainly is nothing like a simple, one-to-one correspondence between the words uttered and the speech acts performed (let alone the latter's perlocutionary effects). Speech acts function always in dialogue: requests are granted or refused, promises are accepted or rejected, threats are acknowledged or ignored, questions are (normally) answered and greetings returned; and so on. The appropriate speech acts enter the language scene, play their roles, and exit again, in a kind of mini-scenario for what is happening in language interaction in general. In this way, speech acts assist us in making sense of the more-or-less predictable sequences that we all know from normal conversation. Rarely, if ever, is a greeting not returned (except by oversight); a congratulation is normally not rejected; and so on. Thus, speech acts play a structuring role in the baffling diversity of human talk.

According to the canonical theory, as set forth in chapter 5, certain theoretical conditions have to be fulfilled in order that speech acts can play this role; however, most of these conditions are not met in normal contexts of language use. The situation reminds one of what Jan-Ola Östman once remarked about the Cooperative Principle: no ordinary conversation would ever be cooperative if the speakers strictly followed the CP (1981:37). To take just one example: in the case of a bet, we can list a number of expressions that count as correct verbal 'uptake', but there are at least as many unpredictable, maybe never-heard-before (sometimes not even verbally expressed) ways of acknowledging a bet that still would count as correct uptakes. It is the result that matters: once an utterance is properly placed in its linguistic co-text as well as in its entire world context and its effects have become visible, the speech activity in question is established and recognized as a situated, *pragmatic* act.

Thus, there is more between speech acting and the user's world than what is contained in speech act philosophy; the reason is that all human language activity ultimately underlies the laws of the greater universe of *discourse*, understood as the entire context of human language-in-use. Metapragmatics thus goes beyond the philosophy of speech acts: it reflects on the discursive context of the users and examines how it is active in the production of human language acts; it regards the latter as conditioned by this context, inasmuch as they are, in essence, *pragmatic acts*. (See further chapter 8.)

Such an 'active' production naturally presupposes the existence of a particular society, with its implicit and explicit values, norms, rules and laws, and with all its particular conditions of life: economic, social, political and cultural. These conditions are often referred to collectively by a metaphorical expression: the 'fabric of society', understood as the supporting element for all societal structures and the necessary context for all human activity. Inasmuch as this fabric operates and becomes visible (mostly through language, but also in other human activities), it is captured by the term 'discourse'.

Discourse is here taken as a *metapragmatic* condition which not only refers to the immediately perceived context of, e.g., a conversation, a job interview, a medical consultation, a police interrogation and so on; it also comprises the hidden conditions that govern such situations of language use. It raises questions such as: how do people use their language in their respective social contexts? What kind of freedom do they enjoy in their use of language, and how is that use constrained?

Discourse is different from *text* in that it embodies more than just a collection of sentences; discourse is what makes the text, and what makes it context-bound.

But discourse is also different from *conversation*. Conversation is what most people do naturally, do socially and, so to speak, do all the time; it is the most wide-spread form of language use and, in a sense, the embedding of all our linguistic activities, both in our personal history and upbringing and in our daily lives. All the same, even if conversation is among the most important functions of human language, it still is but one particular type of text, governed by special rules of social use.

Thus, while it seems natural to use the term 'discourse' specifically in connection with conversation, 'discourse analysis' and 'conversation analysis' are not the same. The former includes the latter (cf. Stubbs 1983); hence, discourse analysis should not (as is sometimes done) be understood as being a particular, grammar-oriented kind of conversational analysis.[88]

In order to understand this better, let's consider how discourse is treated by the French philosopher Michel Foucault (whose ideas are at the origin of much of contemporary thinking on discourse). Foucault has characterized discourse as the practice of making sense of signs. This practice goes beyond the mere interpretive activity of understanding utterances: 'making sense' should be understood here as an *active* creation of meaning, as "practices that systematically form the objects of which they speak" (1972:44). The discursive space is a fertile chaos, a *tohuwabohu*, ready to accept the impact of language, of the Word (cf. Genesis 1:2; John 1:14). Conversely, the discursive space furnishes the metapragmatic wherewithal for the production of meaning. Outside of this space, the medium in which Foucault's 'objects' are created, nothing happens: no human practice is possible, since, literally, nothing makes sense.

The metapragmatic conditions that Foucault places on the human practice of meaning production make discourse different from a simple collection of (isolated or co-textualized, 'live' or transcribed) sentences or utterances. Since these conditions are embodied in the language users, they cannot simply be identified with the restrictions imposed by grammar, by content (e.g., in the shape of truth conditions) or even by the rules of conversational practice; transcending all these, they represent the whole of human sociality. The practice of discourse is the practice of society: the creative space in which Foucault's 'objects' emerge, are constituted and transformed *is* society (1972:32). Among the 'objects' produced by society in its discursive practice, human social relations are paramount; discourse is thus simply "the ensemble of phenomena in and through which social production of meaning takes place, an ensemble which constitutes *society as such*" (Mumby and Stohl 1991:315; my emphasis).

Discourse creates and re-creates society's bonds; it transcends the individual user and enables the single individual to exist and coexist with other individuals. Objects can be arranged in *systems* according to their distinctive features (as, e.g., phonemes in phonology), or according to their distributional properties (as morphemes in morphology and syntax); these same objects can then form *structures*, in which the classified items change their status and character by the fact of being structured into, conditioned by, a totality. Thus, a word is more than a sequence of phonemes; a sentence more than a number of morphemes and words strung together; a text more than a concatenation of sentences. As represented in all of these, discourse transcends both the systems it emanates from and the societal structures it creates (Foucault's 'objects'), allowing them "to emerge and [be] continuously transformed" (1972:32), in everlasting creation and re-creation. Discourse cannot be considered in isolation from the systems and structures that support it and whose fulfillment it constitutes.

On the other hand, and in a very real sense, discourse has to do with 'speaking'. In particular, discourse is a speaking *about*, specifically understood as speech-mediated *acting*. In Foucault's own language, French, *discours* is often used in the sense of 'official address, speech' (as for instance in *les discours chez Thucydide*, 'the speeches in Thucydides'). In this interpretation, speaking is a *societal* speech act, a pragmatic act of entering an official scene and delivering an official message, like the one Pericles transmitted to the Athenians in his famous discourse on the occasion of the first funeral ceremony for the war heroes of the Peloponnesian conflict in 431 BC (Thucydides, *Hist.* II:35–46), and in which he dealt with what he saw as the unique political and cultural mission of the Athenian commonwealth.

But also more generally, speaking is more than an idle pastime, a way of getting to know your neighbors or of 'passing the time of day', as the somewhat old-fashioned expression has it. All speaking connotes, and derives from, the power that Foucault talks about. Metapragmatically, all speaking reflects, and is dependent on, the structures of society, whose discourse is characterized by the existing relations of power.

The following may serve as an illustration of how societal power structures discourse, and conversely, how discourse supports the power conditions it creates and re-creates. Current social discourse in the US is blind to the issue of class, and concentrates instead on such variables as race, gender, income, education (and lately also fitness). The tenet of the 'classless society' pervades all our speaking about issues of social equality, discrimination, minority rights and so on. "Class is for European democracies or something else – it isn't for the United States of America. We are not going to be divided by class" (from a speech by former US President George Bush; quoted Navarro 1991:1).

When we focus on some particular aspect of US society, however, as for instance the relationship between mortality rates and class, it becomes clear that class issues indeed are important. According to Vicente Navarro himself, who works in the area of medical sociology, heart diseases with mortal outcomes strike about two and a half times more frequently among workers in the steel industry than among corporate lawyers (1991:4; the figures are 86 vs. 37 per 10,000, according to the 1986 US census).

These figures do not take into account that the steel industry is predominantly Black, while corporate lawyers are usually white. A race-based discourse interprets the higher mortality among steel workers as related to their being (mostly)

Black, whereas the lawyers' low mortality is taken as having to do with their being white. However, the class realities of society paint another picture: the white steel worker's chances of longevity are closer to his Black colleagues' in the industry than to what his race-mates in the upper echelons of society can look forward to.

In health matters, race is not the main issue; class is. A racial misreading of the above figures may be (and often has been) exploited by the corporate-political structure – the big companies, organized medicine (as represented by the ultra-conservative American Medical Association, AMA), a Republican-dominated Congress and so on – to block the establishment of a universal health care. If one succeeds in creating the illusion that white workers' health prospects are better than the Black population's, a major incentive for reform is neutral-ized in the awareness of a large segment of the class which needs it most: the American workers.

Considered from a metapragmatic viewpoint, all discourse happens on the premises and conditions laid down by the powerful; consequently, the powerless can only change those conditions (including their own) with great difficulty, as long as their only way of speaking and acting is by submitting to the discourse of the powerful. The facts and observations offered above bring out the metapragmatic conditioning of discourse in a twofold fashion: by either not speaking at all about social issues, or by addressing them in a certain way, our discourse creates categories and attitudes that are conducive to keeping those in power who created the current discursive space in the first place. (See further section 11.1.4; Mey 1985.)

7.2.3.4 Worlds and words

The notion of 'constraint', introduced above, at the same time embodies the metapragmatic conditions that naturally and necessarily surround the human potential of language use, and the ideals of constancy and consistency that guar-antee a consistent and well-functioning mechanism of discourse.

As an example, consider the world of art, in particular that of the literary work. The essence of participating in a literary universe is, for both 'consumers' and 'pro-ducers', for readers as well as for writers, the acceptance of a set of constraints, in particular such as relate the literary universe to language, and vice versa.

The metapragmatic problem of 'making up' a literary world – that is, of estab-lishing the proper 'script' for one's characters – is closely related to that of setting up conditions for the way we use language in conversation. In both cases, the constraints have to respect the individual actors' idiosyncrasies; moreover, as authors or conversationalists, we have to keep those constraints constant as well as consistent throughout the entire (literary or conversational) enterprise, on the penalty of becoming unintelligible or misunderstood, and possibly losing our audience (our readers or interlocutors). Literary constraints function as necessary and sufficient conditions on writing and reading; they are, in fact, *metapragmatic* constraints on our use of language.;

On opening a book, readers deliver themselves wholesale into the hands of the author (Mey 1994d). Entering the author's world, they voluntarily accept the constraints that are imposed by the text: "reading is born as a cooperative agreement between the reader and the text" (Eco, as quoted in Lilli 1990). Such constraints need not be explicitly stated in order to be effective: they are inferred from what we notice about the characters by comparing their behavior, as described, with our own familiar ways of being, and by applying the inference schemas that we use in our own daily lives.

In a literary environment, the usefulness of constraints as metapragmatic explanatory devices (by comparison to rules or even principles; cf. section 7.2.3.1) is borne out by the ease with which readers manipulate such constraints (and in turn, are manipulated by them), in contrast to the cumbersome application of syntactic and other co-textual rules (cf. Halliday and Hasan's rule for finding the nearest acceptable referent of a deictic expression, mentioned earlier; 1976). As to principles, with the exception of the Cooperative Principle (to be discussed in section 9.4 under the heading of 'contextual cooperation'), most principles (such as that of politeness or tact) have but a dubious validity for author and readership. By contrast, the constraints present in a literary production allow us, as readers, to balance on a tightrope connecting two domains: the world as we know it (where everything is the same, as a rule), and the literary universe (where nothing is the same, on principle): *Ceteris paribus, nullis paribus.*

Pragmatics being the science of the unsaid, however, what *is* the same, and what different, is never explicitly stated; nor is one told how to handle these samenesses and differences, that is, how to interpret a particular constraint. Literary universes are introduced and established in vastly different ways, using means that are widely divergent from period to period, from culture to culture. For instance, compare the detailed descriptions of time, space, actors, geography, characters, physiognomy, apparel etc. that were customary in the Romantic period with the extremely frugal and indirect lighting of the literary scene by modern novelists such as Alain Robbe-Grillet or Jorge Luis Borges. Reading a novel by Sir Walter Scott in 2000 is quite a different cup of tea than reading the same book over 150 years ago, when his work first saw the light of day. Even in today's literature, no amount of elegant and skilful pastiching (as an example, take John Fowles's *A Maggot*) can obscure the fact that authors and readers must work with their texts. Manipulating textual and dialogical constraints is dependent on the contemporary conditions under which these constraints are defined and understood by authors and readers: constraints that will have to be redefined by each new generation. (A fuller treatment of these problems will be provided in chapter 9.)

This point of view has consequences for our metapragmatic dealings in our everyday lives and usual surroundings. The way we accept or reject the constraints in a literary work, and make decisions on our own goals and expectations in reading by incorporating those constraints in a script – possibly having first unearthed them from the dark chambers of our subconscious – reflects on our dealings with language on a day-to-day basis. The playwright 'sets the stage', in the literal sense of the word, that is, words the plot on stage by manipulating the constraints of dialogue and stage directions; likewise, we model and change the world of our lives, using the words that are at our disposal to 'word the world', as I have called it (Mey 1985:179ff).

This 'wording' poses a double metapragmatic problem: that of matching and that of changing. As to the first, the matching problem comes up, for instance, when we start to realize that our use of language reflects the real-world situation rather poorly. This can be either because the words belong to another, earlier period (this, we normally can live with: nobody thinks of 'sailing' as an unorthodox activity, even when mentioned in connection with such definitely 'sail-less' contraptions as atomic submarines), or because the words do not match our altered consciousness of the world. If we feel constrained by such a state of affairs, it usually means that either we or the constraints aren't right. There just is no way we can 'sail to Byzantium' in an atomic submarine. And this leads us directly to the other problem, that of changing, as the following example will show.

One of the constraints of contemporary English concerns the so-called 'generic' use of the personal pronoun third person masculine: *he*. The metapragmatic (mis-)'match' here is that half the world's population is female; so how can we refer to them by the masculine?, people say. A solution ('change') is to introduce the hybrid form *s/he*; alternatively, one could declare the feminine to be the proper generic form and uniquely use *she*, also when males are around.

In this case, the change concerns not the real state of the world (which remains more or less the same all the time), but the constraints we place on our use of language in describing that state – clearly a metapragmatic affair. What we do is to change the discourse about the world, in a limited scenario, more or less as we are wont to do in the case of the literary universe. We don't change the world (at least not directly) by using the generic *she*; at best, we may change (or 'raise', as it used to be called) our consciousness about the problem. And of course there is nothing wrong with that, as I have argued elsewhere (e.g., Mey 1985:365–8).

However, a naïve belief in the 'magic' of the metalevel in pragmatics could lead to such absurdities as the proposed use of the 'generic' feminine in universes where the majority or even 100 percent of the population are masculine (e.g., the military or the Catholic priesthood). The existing world is one in which more or less half of the inhabitants are female, half are male; and the function of a feminine form, under the constraints that operate in that world, is first of all to denote a female being. However, our world is also a world in which the societal power is distributed neither fairly nor in accordance with a more or less equitable sharing among the sexes. To change that, we will have to employ other means

than (however meaningful) pragmatic insights and (however artful) metapragmatic constraints. (See further section 11.3.3.)

When discussing the metapragmatic conditions of language use, we should
remind ourselves that they reflect not simply the world as it is, biologically or
ontologically, but rather the world as we have made it and have learned to see
it. However, in discussing our societal state of mind, our human meanings as
expressed in language, we cannot avoid reflecting also on the words embodying
those meanings. Talking about the metapragmatic constraints that tell us how to
use, and how not to use, the words that go with our world and minds naturally
leads us to a reflection on the words themselves and on the ways we use them.
The following sections will examine these metapragmatic constraints of the third
kind (following Caffi's tripartition), paying special attention to the phenomena
of indexing and 'indexicality'.

7.2.4   III Indexing

7.2.4.1   Reflexivity and simple indexing

What is usually called 'reflexivity' in linguistics has to do with a particular kind
of linguistic construction: the case of 'reflexive reference', as evidenced in the
reflexive pronouns of many languages. If I say: 'Real men shave themselves', I
am using a reflexive form (the pronoun 'themselves' refers to the subject of the
sentence, the noun phrase 'real men'). But we can 'index' reflexivity also in other
ways, even without an explicit reflexive form, as when St Paul admonishes the
married couples in his congregation: "Wives, submit yourselves unto your own
husbands, . . . Husbands, love your wives" (Col. 3:18–19). Here, the reflexive
pronoun 'yourselves' refers to the vocative expression 'Wives!', the 'subject' (as
it is sometimes called) of the imperative 'submit'. In contrast, 'your own', without
being technically 'reflexive', refers to the same subject: 'wives'. Similarly, 'your'
in the next sentence refers to the subject of the admonition 'love your wives',
viz., 'Husbands'. We see that these latter forms fill the same function as does the
reflexive in the first sentence: they are functionally equivalent (in this case, have
the same kind of referentiality). Other languages have similar, sometimes very
elaborate ways of denoting reflexivity, using pronouns, particles, verb forms and
other linguistic devices such as stress and intonation.

In cases like these, a particular form of the language carries with it a kind of
'index' telling us where to look for the appropriate reference. However, such
'indexicals' can do only part of the job. Without an appropriate context of users,
even the most sophisticated deictic systems break down. As an instance, take the
case of conversation.

From a metapragmatic point of view, the presence of actual or potential
conversational partners is a necessary condition on any use of language in
conversation. On the intuitive level, this is borne out by the fact that people
actually smile and gesture while speaking on the phone: they need to make the

presence of their conversational partner explicit to themselves, even though their partner cannot see them, and they cannot see their partner. The smiles and the gestures continue to exercise their functions of maintaining and supporting the user context, whether or not there are any conversational partners physically present.

A classic instance of this 'invisible partnership' is found in a famous example, originally due to Fillmore (1981:151). A person speaking on the phone is giving instructions to his conversational partner; in the course of the conversation, mention is made of a certain box, the size of which the conversationalist indicates by using the American English word *yea*, accompanied by a gesture indicating (more or less exactly) size or height. Now, an expression like *yea* belongs to a group of words that make no sense without such a corresponding gesture. While normally people use their hands to suggest the measure that the *yea* stands for, in the case of a telephone conversation, one's interlocutor cannot see this gesture. Hence the utterance:

I need a box *yea* big,

when spoken on the phone, is meaningless under a strictly linguistic interpretation (since it reflects no visible or retrievable referent). Metapragmatically, however, by reflecting on itself, *yea*, especially in tandem with the corresponding gesture, serves to remind us that in conversation, things make sense only when the presence of a (visible or imagined) conversational partner is taken into account.

The earlier-mentioned case of the 'shifters' (pronouns and adverbs that change their reference in relation to the speaker's center of orientation; see section 3.3.1) further illustrates the importance of partner presence in any normal conversation. To use an example provided by Levinson (1983:55), it is useless to say to one's interlocutor:

Meet me here a week from now with a stick about this big

without some contextual 'anchoring' of the pronouns and adverbs (*here, now, this*) in question. Deictic pronouns such as *this, that* presuppose a center of orientation; if nothing is said, we assume that the center is in the neighborhood of the speaker, or has somehow something to do with the speaker (*this* is close to the speaker, *that* is further away); analogously for adverbs of time and space, including elements such as *yea*.

The conversational participants and their shared 'coordinates' are an integrated and necessary part of the language act; hence the obligatory assumption of the always already "co-present conversational participants" that Levinson (1983:284) singles out as essential to the pragmatic organization of texts. This general organization may be further highlighted by the use of so-called 'discourse markers' (also named 'pragmatic markers', 'pragmatic particles', 'discourse particles' and so on; Verschueren 1999:189). Their use is defined as facilitating the production and reception of discourse by assigning its individual parts their relevance and weight in the context; for instance, if I preface my utterance with 'Honestly', my interlocutor knows not only that I will speak my mind, but also that the following utterance may be of a controversial or unpleasant nature. Prefixing 'However' to a sentence signifies that its content is in a certain opposition to what preceded; and so on.

Discourse markers, along with other direct indexes of discourse, belong to the explicit level (Caffi's third) of metapragmatic awareness. This is in contrast to the cases where indexing, especially deixis, being implicit, is not contingent upon direct interaction between co-present partners: the agents may be invisible, distant in time or space (as in the above example of *yea*, or even (as when we are reading, or enter an Internet chat room), 'virtual'. Rather than launching into a full-size description of discourse markers (the literature has been growing steadily for the past fifteen years or so; see Schiffrin 1988), I will concentrate in the next section on some aspects of this implicit metapragmatic awareness, as seen in indirect or 'invisible' indexing.

7.2.4.2   Invisible indexing and indexicality

One could call the deictic pronouns (see section 3.3.2) instruments of 'direct deixis': they indicate reference straightforwardly, and do this in force of their linguistic properties as indexing elements. If I know what the English word *this* means in relation to *that*, I will not look the wrong way when given directions. The same goes for *here* and *there* and similar terms indicating place and time. Again, other languages may exhibit more complicated systems than does English; for instance, Finnish distinguishes between a 'where' that merely specifies the 'whereabouts' and a 'where' that is exactly 'to the point'. Thus, when picking blueberries in the woods, a mother may call out to her kids 'Where(abouts) are you?' (because she doesn't know the exact location), whereas the children would reply, not *Täällä* ('hereabouts') but *Tässä* ('exactly here' – since that's what mothers want to know when they ask a question like the one above; Östman 1995a).

Such formal complications do not compromise the general, denotational value of the deictic elements involved. However, there is more to indexing than being "denotationally explicit", to borrow Silverstein's term (1993:45ff): there are always other, implicit factors that need to be recognized. To use an analogy: the speech act of 'promising' presupposes implicitly the existence of a promisee: a promise is always a promise to someone. In a sense, there are no promises as such; a promise is always *some* promise, a promise uttered by somebody in a particular context to somebody else. All this is implicitly contained in the *pragmatic act* of promising, as opposed to the 'naked' speech act and its corresponding verb (see further section 8.3.3). Similarly, an indexical expression implicitly refers to a lot more than just the element indicated by the pointing finger or its linguistic equivalent. To see this, consider the following.

It is always (and trivially) true that *I say this*, if taken as a logical proposition: 'What I say, I do say' (paraphrasing Pilate's famous utterance; John 19:22). In the context, however, such an utterance always conveys something more and different, something which, moreover, usually is not altogether trivial. Just as *Dixi* (said at the end of a speech) means 'I have finished', rather than 'I have spoken' (which is always true, not only at the end of a speech), Pilate's *Quod scripsi scripsi* ('What I have written I have written') is by no means merely tautological, but indexes the procurator's official unwillingness to change his written text (from: 'The King of the Jews' to the formulation demanded by the high priest: 'He said: "I am the King of the Jews"').

Here's another example, taken from work by Mikhail Bakhtin. While it is trivially true that *sentences* are repeatable ("Sentences are repeatable. Sentences are repeatable"; Bakhtin 1994:108; cf. Morson and Emerson 1990:126), it is not the case that I can utter a sentence twice in the same way: *utterances* are not repeatable, but are always different depending on who says them and under what conditions. By the very fact of being uttered, the utterance indexes a person who utters; this indexicality is, however, *implicit*, and has to be brought out by an analysis of the discourse in which the utterance takes place (see Hanks 1992). These implicit properties of the utterance reflect on the utterance itself, by indexing its *user* relation: that is to say, they tell us something about how the utterance is produced, respectively received. In other words, the utterance's implicit indexicality is *metapragmatic* in nature.

For our understanding of the ways speech acts (and more generally, pragmatic acts) build up the discourse, this metapragmatic indexicality is of the highest importance (see further section 8.4.2). A particular instance is the case of *reading*. When we are confronted with a written text, the universe of discourse is given by that text and its metapragmatic 'contextualization cues'.[89] The way we identify a particular character and his or her contribution to the dialogue is by way of such cues; in particular, the concept of *voice*, understood as the placing of the character and his or her utterances within the narrative, is of prime importance here. 'Voice', in this sense, is a *metapragmatic indexical*; it will be discussed extensively in section 9.4.

Review and discussion

1. Consider the following quotation from Levinson (1983:103–4):

the reason for linguistic interest in the maxims is that they generate inferences beyond the semantic content of the sentences uttered. Such inferences are, by definition, conversational implicatures, where the term *implicature* is intended to contrast with terms like *logical implication, entailment,* and *logical conse-quence* which are generally used to refer to inferences that are derived solely from logical or semantic content. [footnote omitted] For implicatures are not semantic inferences, but rather inferences based on both the content of what has been said and some specific assumptions about the *co-operative nature of ordinary verbal interaction.* (last emphasis mine)

What Levinson is telling us here is that our utterances (with their concomitant implicatures and presuppositions) are not simply objects in the physical world, nor do they belong exclusively to the domain of logic and philosophy (like the 'judgments' of the School and the 'propositions' of mathematical logicians and formal semanticists). The Gricean maxims deal with *utterances,* that is, *linguis-tic* objects which imply, first of all, other linguistic objects, other utterances. As a result, utterances cannot simply be subsumed under the laws of physics or logic, or allocated a place in the semantic universe by means of a simple indexing ('ostensive' or referential) function. The implications of utterances, considered as linguistic objects (including their relationships to, and effects on, the world), are much more intricate than perceived by most philosophers of language and logi-cians, and even by many linguists. In particular, they have to do with the coop-erative nature of our everyday use of language.

On the background of this quotation and its explication, try and answer the following.

Questions:
If metalanguage, in general, is defined as opposed to 'object language' (cf. section 7.1), then how can we say that utterances are 'linguistic objects', and what does this mean?

In what sense is an assumption about the 'cooperative nature' of language part of our linguistic metalanguage? (Hint: ask yourself how Grice reasons about establishing his 'Cooperative Principle', and cf. the Levinson quotation in section 4.2.2.2.)

And in what sense can the CP be said to 'transcend' that linguistic metalanguage? (Hint: ask yourself if there would have been a Cooperative Principle if Grice hadn't 'invented' it.)

2. Metapragmatics deals with pragmatics on the metalevel. That is to say, we speak about pragmatics and decide, among other things, what its relationship is to other parts of linguistics.

Various models for this relationship have been proposed. In section 1.3.1, we discussed the difference between a 'component' and a 'perspective' approach. The US linguist Georgia Green uses a metaphor from the domain of marital relations, when she talks about 'the uneasy courtship between semantics and syntax' (1986:6); her metaphor could be extended, in an admittedly Pollyannaish way, to comprise also pragmatics and the other linguistic disciplines. In this rosy view, they all would make up one merry household, with all the members of the linguistic family living happily together ever after.

Contrast this now with British linguist Ruth Kempson admitting that "pragmatics has been the Cinderella" of her *Semantic Theory* (1977), and ask yourself the following.

Question:
On the basis of Caffi's remark that "pragmatics is tolerant", quoted in section 7.2.1, how could you define a minimal condition for a happy 'cohabitation' between pragmatics and the rest of linguistics to take place? (Hint: refer to section 7.2, end, and the beginning of section 7.2.1.)

3. In the Roman senate, it was customary to have voting performed not by individual voice count or a roll-call type of vote, but by having the senators (the *patres conscripti*) 'vote with their feet', by going to the one or the other side of the hall in order to indicate their preferences. In recent times, I have seen this kind of voting (in Latin called *pedibus ire in sententiam*, literally 'use your feet to indicate the direction of your opinion') practiced in a televised high school popular song contest on a beach near Kyoto, Japan.

Question:
Which of the conditions defined for 'classic' speech acting could be made to hold for this kind of 'pedestrian speech act'?

4. In the spirit of the preceding exercise, consider how, in our age of shopping by Internet, it becomes more and more common for people to have access to copyrighted merchandise by mail and electronically. The legal problems involved have spawned a whole new breed of 'Internet lawyers', whose main function it is to watch over copyrights that are potentially violated by Internet and other users (as an example, take the 'sampling' of copyrighted music that goes on widely among people crafting home pages or creating new works of art from electronic bits and pieces salvaged on the net; cf. I. Mey 1996). Conversely, manufacturers and copyright owners do their best to protect their products and themselves, in the process creating a new species of 'speech act', as evidenced by the following examples:

(*Found on a package of Microsoft software for the Macintosh, purchased in January, 1998*)

NOTICE:
Please read the enclosed license before using the software. By using the software, you are agreeing to be bound by the terms of this license.

(*The Danish version of this 'speech act' is even more explicit, see below; my translation*)

IMPORTANT
Read the license agreements in the accompanying booklet before breaking the
seal and starting to use the software. By breaking the seal you oblige yourself
to respect these license agreements.

While the intent of these messages is clear ('Don't use the software except under
the conditions we have set'), the way these orders are communicated is something new. You are invited to reflect on the metapragmatic character of the messages above, and to answer the following.

Questions:
What kind of speech act are we dealing with here?

How is this speech act formulated? What are its conditions for 'felicitous' performance, as compared with the conditions stated in section 5.2.2?

From a metapragmatic point of view, how can we argue that the particular conditions for this license agreement to be put in place are in accordance with a
pragmatic view of speech acts? (Feel free to say that they are not; but provide
some form of argument.)

In particular, try to imagine how one could go about otherwise enforcing a
condition that is unilaterally imposed as a particular interpretation of an
act which is not in itself a speech act. (See also chapter 8, on 'pragmatic
acts'.)

5. In her 1992 article 'Indirectness: A gender study of flouting Grice's maxims',
Suellen Rundquist brings statistical evidence for the fact that men, much more
than women, tend to 'flout' the maxims laid down by Grice for conversation.
(Refer to section 4.2.2.3 for the notion of 'flouting'.) The following is one of the
situations that Rundquist invokes to justify her claim.
   During a mealtime conversation, family members talk about field hockey, and
how 'Mum' has allegedly been active in this sport for a very long time. 'Dad'
sees fit to offer some ironic comments on Mum's sporting achievements, and he
does this by flouting a particular maxim, that of quality: in other words, he exag-
gerates to the point of ridiculing the whole business. Here is the relevant excerpt:

[Mum:] I used to spend a lot of time playing field hockey, good sport.
[Dad:] Yeah, Mummy was probably playing field hockey when Herbert
Hoover took office.
[Mum:] Yeah
[Dad:] Woodrow Wilson and Teddy Roosevelt.
[Mum:] Mhm
[Dad:] George Washington
[Child:] Abraham Lincoln
[Dad:] Aristotle and . . .

[Child:] Thomas Jefferson
[Mum:] Yeah, . . . even when they bombed Pearl Harbor I was. (Rundquist 1993:437)

As Rundquist remarks, Dad not only instigates the flouting, but manages to engage everybody, including a child participant and finally 'Mum' herself, in this bout of 'Mummy-bashing'. Thus, Rundquist's hypothesis is corroborated that in general, "men initiate flouting of maxims much more than women do" (p. 445). This implies, according to Rundquist, that the classic theory of speech acts (as shaped by Grice and Searle) fails to recognize one of its own preconditions, namely the limited access to social power for women, as compared to men. In particular, as in this case, a principle or maxim can be disregarded, or 'flouted' in different ways and under different conditions, depending on whether the speaker is male or female. The males, being socially more powerful, are able to define the conditions that prevail in a given social situation, including the right to 'flout' a maxim: to be polite or not, to be relevant or not etc. Such a breaking of maxims says less about cognitive content or conversational importance than about who is in control of the situation. Rundquist's conclusion is that principles such as Politeness, Relevance etc. cannot be discussed in terms of cognition only, and that therefore, conversational inference cannot "be based entirely on a cognitive foundation" (ibid.).

Questions:
In what respect is Rundquist's last remark a metapragmatic one?

In what sense can her whole piece to be said to constitute a metapragmatic statement? (Hint: consider Rundquist's stance on the 'preconditions' of speech act theory, as quoted above.)

What is the impact of Rundquist's findings on a pragmatic theory of cognition, viewed in relation to societal parameters? (Hint: refer back to Rosaldo's and others' critique of the notion of the speech act of 'promising', as mentioned at the end of section 5.1.2.)

What particular societal factors do you think have come into play in this particular context of a family conversation? (Hint: consider the 'historical pattern' dictated by the male initiator, and what it takes to follow that lead.)

(Optional, cf. chapter 4): Discuss Rundquist's findings in terms of (a) the Politeness Principle, and (b) the Principle of Relevance.

6. On presuppositions and shared knowledge
In the following episode from *Peanuts* by Charles Schultz (*Austin American Statesman*, September 6, 1990), Linus is trying to borrow a sheet of paper from his nerdic classmate Marcie. Marcie turns down his request. The following dialogue is found in the three frames of the cartoon in question:

LINUS: Quick, Marcie, I need to borrow another sheet of paper ...

MARCIE: Polonius said, "Neither a borrower, nor a lender be."

LINUS: Point that kid out to me and I'll teach him to mind his own business!

Questions:
Try to identify the presuppositions and (lack of) shared knowledge that this cartoon builds on. (See section 7.2.2.2.)

How much of this can be said to be 'universal', and thereby account for these cartoons' extreme popularity, not only in their homeland, the US?

7. Indexicals

In section 7.2.3, I talked about the metapragmatics of indexing, and referred to indexical elements as being dependent for their proper understanding on the presence of contextual factors. The following is the text part of a cartoon in the well-known *Blondie* comic series by Young and Drake (*Austin American Statesman*, September 6, 1990). The dialogue is between Dagwood and his perpetually irascible boss:

BOSS: Dagwood, what *is* this?

DAGWOOD: *What* this?

BOSS: *This* this!

DAGWOOD: Oh, *that* this

BOSS: You keep *that* out of this!

DAGWOOD: But that's the this that this *is*

BOSS: (aside) I came *this* close to giving him one of *these*

Questions:
Try to determine the reference of the indexicals in the above dialogue. You may want to do this by visualizing a situation in which the original dialogue could have happened. The actual cartoon has four frames; try to picture them for yourself, allocating each interchange to one frame, and describe the chosen frames briefly.

What does this dialogue tell you about 'invisible indexing'? (Cf. section 7.2.3.2.)

8. Motivating the 1989 Panama campaign, President George Bush, in a TV newsreel interview, said the following:

When American servicemen's wives are being sexually molested, this President isn't going to sit with his hands in his lap. (*The Panama Deception* (1992), a documentary directed by Barbara Trent, written and edited by David Kasper)

Questions:
How to account for the deictic 'this' in 'this President'?

Contrast this use with that of 'reminder deixis', discussed in section 3.3.3.

What does such a form for 'self-deixis' usually connote? (Hint: try to find more examples, of the type: 'this administration'.)

8. Consider the following advertisement for a book:

Blue Cross
What Went Wrong?

Prepared by the Health & Law Project
University of Pennsylvania

Sylvia Law, Principal author

Here is must reading for legislators and anyone with the slightest interest in health and hospital insurance. Professor Law's important study of the Blue Cross presents some shocking facts and figures . . . she examines the development of Blue Cross into a web of local hospital insurance agencies . . . [and] arrives at the conclusion that the Blue Cross is not serving the public well. (*New Republic*, June 29, 1974)

Questions:
If somebody asks: 'What went wrong?' what is the immediate presupposition, and how is it confirmed in the text? (Hint: what does this study 'present'?)

How does the ad build its appeal on this presupposition? (Hint: ask yourself how it argues for this book being 'must reading'.)

What presuppositions are contained in the words 'the slightest interest'? (Hint: refer to section 7.2.2.2; what do we know about people who 'have an interest' in something?)

Why does the ad say 'the slightest interest'? Can you detect an implicature here? (Hint: do I, as a reader, have to buy into this sales pitch? What is the ad trying to tell me?)

What does this superlative add to the presupposition, and how does it strengthen the implicature?

To understand this ad, do we rely mostly on its semantic or on its pragmatic presuppositions?

Which of the presuppositions you have discovered are semantic, which are pragmatic?

CHAPTER EIGHT
Pragmatic Acts

8.1 What are pragmatic acts all about?

If you want to know what a particular human activity is all about, you may start out asking questions like: 'What are the rules of baseball?' or 'What is cricket like?' But pretty soon you'll get to the point where you want to figure out what these sports enthusiasts actually are doing out there in the field. And, while it may be hard enough to explain a sport such as baseball or cricket to someone who doesn't know the first things about ball games, certainly it will be impossible to explain, or understand, anything interesting about baseball or cricket without having access to watching people play.

Similarly, if you want to know what a particular religion is all about, you are of course entitled to ask what its beliefs are; but you will be more interested in, and enlightened by, the practices that are characteristic of such a religion. The same goes for politics and politicians. 'Read my lips' may be a useful election slogan for somebody who promises lower taxes; but 'check my acts' provides a better indicator of what that politician really stands for.

We could apply this line of thought to the fast-developing field of pragmatics. Ask any pragmatician at a cocktail party what pragmatics is all about, and he or she will tell you that it is a science that has to do with language and its users, or some such thing. But if you want to know what pragmatics really stands for, you must try and find out how the game is played, what pragmaticians do for a living, and how they are different from the people active in other, more or less related branches of language studies. So, the question is: what would be a typical pragmatic look at people using language? and the answer is: look at them as performing *pragmatic acts*.

Consider the following example. The Chicago alternative cultural weekly *Reader* had an advertisement in its August 21, 1992, issue for a downtown cocktail lounge called Sweet Alice. The ad carried the text

'I brought some sushi home and cooked it; it wasn't bad.'

Now what are we going to make of this?

Of course, this sentence is a joke: everybody knows that sushi is eaten raw, and that you're not supposed to cook it. Cooking sushi may strike one as funny, or stupid, or outrageous, depending on one's point of view. In an informal way, we could say that the above utterance makes no sense. And a linguist might want to add that, since everybody knows that sushi is defined as being eaten raw, a sentence such as the above is wrong, in the same way as are sentences such as the earlier mentioned 'Colorless green ideas sleep furiously', which made a certain American linguist famous in the sixties (cf. section 2.1; the example is from Chomsky 1957, and is by now one of the classics of the linguistic repertoire).

When asked about the odd wording in the advertisement quoted above, the linguist might go on to say that the sentence above contains a semantic clash, and that's why it doesn't make sense: the semantics of one of its parts (the sushi) contradicts the semantics of another part (the cooking). So far, so good. Still, one could ask, why use such a silly sentence in an advertisement for a cocktail bar?

This is where pragmatic acts come into the picture. Pragmatics tells us it's all right to use language in various unconventional ways, as long as we know, as language users, what we're doing. That implies letting ourselves be 'semantically shocked', if there is a reason for it, or if it is done for a purpose. But what could that reason or purpose be?

In this particular case, the joke has a euphoric effect, similar to that of a disarming smile; it invokes the silly state of mind that becomes our privilege after the first couple of drinks. Which is precisely why this ad is effective as an invitation to join the crowd at Sweet Alice's: the invitation is in fact a *pragmatic act* of inviting.

Such a pragmatic explanation of a linguistic fact will by some (mainly linguists) be ascribed to an inability to explain linguistic matters in normal ways, making use of the standard methods of semantics or syntax; this kind of attitude has led to the well-known characterization of pragmatics as the 'waste-basket of linguistics' (as I have mentioned *inter alia* in section 2.1). Other, more sophisticated approaches consider pragmatics to be the study of language in relation to its users, as compared to the science of language in its own right: grammar as studied by the linguists, or marketed as a corrective device, bringing out the hidden schoolmarm in all of us. By contrast, pragmatics studies language as it is used by people, for their own purposes and within their own respective limitations and affordances.

8.2 Some cases

Pragmatics starts out from a conception of language as being *actively* used. One could say that pragmatics is where the action is; but what is the action? Clearly, the ad in the preceding section is an attempt to sell us something: a cocktail bar, a particular ambience, a particular clientele, a promise of good times, and so on. It does this by inviting us in, so to speak. But it doesn't do that by saying: 'Come into my parlor, my cocktail bar' – such an invitation would be too blatant to be effective – nor does it invite us in by appealing to our baser instincts of greed, sex, violence, getting plastered, or what have you. (Never mind that certain estab-lishments do just that: they and their customers get what they are in the business for; so it can certainly be done.) No, Sweet Alice uses a more roundabout technique.

The ad talks to us in a voice that appeals to us as individual language users with a particular history, a living context. As such, we have been exposed to certain kinds of language that we feel comfortable with, e.g., the footloose language that people like Goldie Hawn or Lily Tomlin ("Gracious Good Afternoon") taught us to appreciate. It is precisely this kind of talk which Sweet Alice invites us to enjoy, in the kind of company that we associate with such language. The cocktail bar is sketched as a desirable place, but the invitation is by innuendo only: a *pragmatic act* of inviting, rather than a specific, codified language formula of the speech act type that we discussed in section 5.3.

Another example in the same category concerns an advertisement for the cig-arette brand of Winston (*Austin Chronicle*, August 20, 1999:72–3). Even though the word 'cigarette' only occurs in the obligatory warning text ("The Surgeon General has determined . . ."), and in the 'tar blurb' ("14 mg per cigarette"), and even though the visual presence of the displayed cigarette pack is almost diminu-tive, being reduced to an 'icon' on the right side of the two-page center spread, there is no doubt as to what the message is: 'Buy Winston!'

To understand the workings of this act of advertising, let's have a look at the pictorial representation that the ad displays. The scene is a birthday celebration. One notices an enormous, three-tiered cake on the center table, to the right of which two persons are standing: an elderly gentleman, dressed in formal attire, red carnation in lapel buttonhole, and next to him an attractive young woman, wiping off the remains of what apparently was a piece of cake from the gentle-man's mouth. While doing this, she approaches him very closely, mouth wide open (as is the gentleman's – waiting to be wiped off, and maybe kissed?), in the most ingratiating and seductive of manners, showing quite a bit of cleavage in the process. Briefly, the woman looks and acts as if wiping old men's cake-lined mouths is the kind of activity she enjoys most of all in life.

Now the caption. It says simply this (in large black letters, on the right-hand page of the colorful spread):

"She's after my money.
Like I care."

What are we going to make of this? The clue is in the two words adjoining
the small 'icon' that I mentioned above: "Straight up." The old gentleman manifests his sophisticated understanding of the situation (the gold-digger doing 'it'
for the money, whatever 'it' takes), at the same time as he tells us that he really
doesn't care, as long as he gets her to do 'it' (most likely, too, the only possible
way to get her to, given his age and general condition). This, then, is read together
with the neutral 'frame' that appears on the same page (next to the Surgeon
General's warning, and in exactly the same black-and-white layout and format):
"No additives in our tobacco does NOT mean a safer cigarette." The idea is that
Winston doesn't make bones about cigarettes being dangerous, and that Winston
is not going to tell you anything else: "Straight up." The pragmatic act of advertising materializes as an appeal to the male in us, who likes to be 'straight up' in
matters such as women, cigarettes and other dangerous things. The appeal is
never made explicit: it does its job by the (preferably male) viewer's implicit inclusion in, and identification with, the situation of the message and its wording, just
like it happened in the case of Sweet Alice.

Among the most common pragmatic acts are those of 'implicit denial'. Here's an
example from the 1992 Republican National Convention, where a backer of
George Bush's gave a speech praising the president's concern for people with
AIDS. The speaker's credentials were above any doubt: not only was she a
staunch Republican, a friend of Vice-President Quayle's, but she also was HIV-
infected herself: she was introduced as "having contracted the infection from her
former husband". The speech emphasized, among other things, the necessity of
not being judgmental in matters of AIDS, in particular of not falling into the
well-known moralistic (clap-)trap of regarding the disease as a punishment for
people's sins; when a person has cancer, so the speaker said, we don't ask him
or her how many packs of cigarettes he or she has smoked a day. In other words,
we should treat the disease, not condemn the patient.

    However, in her speech, the woman denied implicitly what she had just explic-
itly stated: that one should not worry too much about how one had contracted
the infection. This could be seen from the fact that she had herself introduced as
having contracted AIDS in a 'legal' way: she had been married, her husband had
given her the disease, so she was not to blame. In addition, since she was now
divorced, any links to immorality were further weakened, while the former
husband and his way of life were being implicitly characterized as doubly bad,
both for himself and for the virtuous, innocent victim.

    All of these implicit assertions and judgments contradict the explicit message:
'Don't worry about where your AIDS came from: there is no reason to
be ashamed.' As it turns out, the speaker herself was pretty much concerned
about the origin of her disease, by wanting to establish clearly that she had con-

tracted it practicing a legal form of intercourse, viz., involving permitted, non-adulterous, 'normal' sexual activity.

The pragmatic act involved here is one of denying. But notice, first, that no explicit denial takes place, that is to say, no actual speech acts of denying are encountered; and second, that as far as the speaker's use of language goes, solely her background (as a card-carrying Republican with AIDS) can explain her concerns having to do with the origin of her disease, as these were expressed in the press releases. In this connection, it is worth noticing that the reporters consistently used the unconditional affirmative: "Mrs X had contracted the disease from her former husband", not: "Mrs X, who allegedly had contracted the disease ..." or: "Mrs X, who said/stated/maintained ... that she had contracted the disease from her former husband."

8.3   Defining a pragmatic act

8.3.1   Co-opting, denying and the CIA

As we have seen in sections 8.1 and 8.2, a frequent pragmatic act is that of implied identification with the reader or viewer, 'co-opting', as it were, the target of the advertising act. This act – which cannot be reduced to, or pinpointed as, any (number of) specific speech act(s) – is a frequently used (not to say overused) element of advertising techniques which basically try to seduce the viewer or reader through a promised identification with some prestigious environment or a set of 'right people': young, smart and rich. Like the 'implicit denial' discussed in the previous section, this technique of persuading relies primarily not on what is said, but on the 'unsaid', as the anthropologist Stephen Tyler called it over thirty years ago (1967). In both cases, a common denominator can be identified: namely, a situational 'setting up' in which the context of the acting carries more weight than the spoken act itself.

In order to see the importance of this 'setting up' as an integrated, constitutive element of the pragmatic act, consider the following case, as told by Jacobs and Jackson (1983b:285). In their famous analysis of the so-called 'Watergate' affair (the scandal which eventually led to the demise of US President Nixon in 1974), authors Carl Bernstein and Bob Woodward refer to a situation in which one of them (Woodward) was exposed to what Jacobs and Jackson call a 'conversational influence attempt' – for short (surprise, surprise) a 'CIA'. Woodward perceived this particular CIA as an effort on the part of the Nixon lawyers to 'strike a deal': they seemed to offer him some information that he could use in his reporting, in exchange for his keeping out of some particularly sensitive areas (Bernstein and Woodward 1974:328–9).

The point of the story is that at no time is such an offer explicitly made; in particular, no speech acts of 'offering' or the like can be detected in the lawyers' discourse, as narrated by Bernstein and Woodward. Thus, when Woodward voices his impression of being 'conversationally influenced' toward making a deal, the three lawyers are able to protest their innocence in unison: nothing was farther from their minds, such a course of action would be totally reprehensible and immoral and so on. Whereupon Woodward muses that the only way he could have perceived the offer was because he had been listening for it; in other words, he was 'set up' by the conversational context for hearing an offer being made. In the terminology of speech acts: in such-and-such a context, when such-and-such is said, the wording may *count as* an attempt to bribe, and is understood as such.

The case is analogous to the trick that you were taught on going into Mexico in the old days: when the *Federales* pulled you over, you had to be sure that there was a $20 bill tacked to the back of your driver's license. Whether or not this 'counted as' a bribe depended entirely on whether the policeman in question was 'set up' to expect a bribe (and was willing to accept it: the 'uptake' is essential). Technically speaking, no bribe was offered, except in retrospect: if the policeman did take the money, then there had been an effort on my part at retroactively bribing him. However, if the policeman then proceeded to arrest me for allegedly attempting to bribe an official in function, I could have proclaimed that I never had had the slightest intention of offering a bribe, but that the bill somehow had got stuck to my license in the Mexican sun.

The next section will go into more detail as to the mechanics of 'setting up'.

8.3.2 'Setting up'

The cases cited above illustrate three things:

1 For sequences like the ones described to 'count as' a particular pragmatic act, the circumstances (the 'setting up') must be right.
2 There need not be any speech act involved (of either bribing, making a request, or whatever else); it is the context that determines the nature of the pragmatic act.
3 Without 'uptake', there cannot be a pragmatic act; however, the uptake can be canceled by another, subsequent act. For instance, the policeman could try to stuff the money back into the driver's pocket if he had a suspicion that this might be a 'sting' operation; this pragmatic act might be combined with certain speech acts, e.g., of protest or of explicit denial.

An amusing instance of how to exploit such a 'setting up' is found in the well-known comedy by the Norwegian-Danish playwright Ludvig Holberg, *Erasmus Montanus*. Erasmus, a village lad with philosophical aspirations, newly created *Baccalaureus Philosophiae* at Copenhagen University, irritates everybody in his village by trying to involve them in the absurdest of philosophical 'disputations'.

His favorite approach is to 'demonstrate' that people are not people, but stones, bulls, roosters etc. In between, he preaches that the world is round, not flat (as everybody in the village believes), even giving up his sweetheart for Dame Philosophy in the deal.

Having alienated the poor girl, and having made his mother cry because he has 'proven' that she in reality is a stone, he eventually gets entangled in a discussion with an army recruiter passing through the village. (Unbeknownst to him, some of the villagers have conspired with this lieutenant to try and rid themselves of Erasmus by having him inducted into the army.) During the conversation, the recruiter successfully involves Montanus in a proposition according to which children should beat their parents. He feigns disbelief in Montanus's disputational qualities, and wagers a ducat on his not being able to prove such a ridiculous proposition. The other rises to the bait, and produces an elegant syllogism proving his point: "What one has received he ought, according to his ability, to return. In my youth I received blows from my parents. *Ergo* I ought to give them blows in return" (Holberg 1914:172; Act V, Scene 2).

Upon which the lieutenant proffers the agreed-on ducat, which Erasmus, being an honest person, refuses to take – it had only been a joke, he says. The lieutenant insists – his honor is at stake, and as an officer and a gentleman, he must pay his debts. Erasmus finally agrees to take the money, and in the same instant, the recruiter clamps the manacles on him and declares him to be properly inducted into the Royal Army. No matter how Montanus tries to argue that he did not take the ducat as press-money (*distinguendum est inter nummos*, i.e., 'one has to distinguish between money and money'), and that hence his 'uptake' did not count, the officer has the last word, and 'proves' that Erasmus Montanus now is a true soldier ("Whoever has taken press-money is an enlisted soldier. You have done so, *ergo* –") and, aided by his corporal, drags him forcefully away, to the amused discomfort of poor Erasmus's fellow villagers.

Clearly, the effects of the 'setting up', that is, of the contextual conditions in this case, are such that there is only one possible outcome of the situation. Normally, this uptake cannot be rescinded, except (as in the case at hand) by an extra-contextual agency, a *deus ex machina*. And so, at the end of the play, the poor lad is liberated from military service, having recanted and promised "never to bother any one with disputations any more" (p. 176).

8.3.3 Pragmatic acts and speech acts

Pragmatic acts do not necessarily include specific acts of speech. In the cases above, there were no uses of language that could 'count as' any particular illocutionary act such as 'co-opting', 'denying', 'bribing' or 'enlisting'. This is not to say that language could not have been, or never is, involved in such cases; only that there are no *specific* speech acts that can be held accountable for the action.

'Fishing for compliments', for example, or 'soliciting invitations' can perfectly well be performed verbally without ever saying anything that could be identified as 'a speech act' of soliciting a compliment or an invitation. Jacobs and Jackson (1983b:303) give the following example of such an interchange ('soliciting an invitation'):

(*Fran, one of Sally's friends, has called Scott, Sally's husband, on the phone after Sally (who just had a baby) had returned from her vacation. The baby is two-and-a-half months old.*
Below, // indicates overlapping speech)
FRAN: How's the *baby*?
SCOTT: Oh, he's fine. He's starting to crawl now.
F: Oh *really*?
S: Well, not really *crawling*. He just sorta inches along.
F: Wow! I haven't even seen him yet.
S: Yeah, he's down in Granite City right n//ow.
F: Oh, with //Sally's folks.
S: With the grandparents.
(*3 second pause*)
S: Jus' a second Fran, I've gotta get my hot dogs off the stove.
F: Okay.

In this case, nothing is said at any time about 'coming over'; neither is the word 'invitation' ever mentioned. Even so, the tenor of the conversation is clear: Fran tries to secure an invitation from Scott to come and see the baby; Scott doesn't want to commit himself (or maybe Sally) to what he sees as a somewhat importunate intrusion into their private sphere.

Levinson (1983:279) has the following example of 'fishing for compliments':

(*Interviewer to candidate for job*):
Would you like to tell us, Mr Khan, why you've applied to Middleton College in particular?

Here, the interviewer's intention is clear: he wants to give the applicant an opportunity to say something nice about Middleton College. Mr Khan cannot very well say that it was the only place he thought he had a chance, or that it was the only job offering in the *Higher*; he knows damn well he is expected to say something positive about the institution he is applying to: it's all part of the game.

To explain what's going on here, Levinson (1983:264) suggests that we might add an 'indirect force' to the literal force of utterances, so as to account for their 'indirect effects'. However, such an explanation won't do. First of all (as we have seen in section 5.4.3), most usages of speech acts happen to be indirect, so this additional feature will not be sufficient to separate out the true pragmatic acts. Second, such an addition seems totally *ad hoc*, as there is no motivation for adding a particular 'force' beyond what we can read off from the indirect, pragmatic aspects of such situations.

What I propose, instead, is to consider these cases in the light of a *theory of action* that specifies, for any given situation, the limitations and possibilities the situation is subject to or opens up, as the case may be. What is wrong with speech act theory, in general, as has often been remarked, is that it lacks a theory of action; and even if it does have such a theory, the action in question "is thought of atomistically, as wholly emanating from the individual" – to quote an author (Fairclough 1989:9) who, among others, has singled out precisely this lack as one of the main weaknesses of early pragmatic thinking.

In general, human activity is not the prerogative of the individual, setting 'goals' and devising 'strategies', or charting out courses of action like a captain on his ship, a Platonic rider on her or his beast of burden. Rather, the individual is situated in a social context, which means that she or he is empowered, as well as limited, by the conditions of her or his life. The idea of the person as a 'free' agent, engaging in all sorts of 'free' enterprise and deciding 'freely' on means and ends – that idea was never anything but fiction, even in the days of Enlightenment and pristine undiluted capitalism, when 'Live Free Or Die' seemed to represent a serious alternative.

The next section will discuss pragmatic acts from the point of view of a theory of action.

8.3.4   Pragmatic acts and action theory

We can look at pragmatic acts from two points of view: that of the agent, and that of the act. As far as the individual *agent* is concerned, there are his or her class, gender, age, education, previous life history and so on. These are the factors identified by the ethnomethodologists under the caption of 'MR' ('member resources'), namely, the resources that people dispose of as members of the community; with regard to communication, these resources are "often referred to as background knowledge" (Fairclough 1989:141). Another way of characterizing such resources is as constraints and affordances, imposed on the individual in the form of necessary limitations on the degrees of freedom that he or she is allowed in society.

The other point of view is that of the *act*; here, we are particularly interested in the language that is used in performing a pragmatic act. The question has two aspects: from the individual's perspective, I can ask what language I can use to perform a specific act; from the perspective of the context, the question is what language can be used to create the conditions for me to perform a pragmatic act.

As to the former perspective, following Verschueren (1987, 1999), we may invoke the *adaptability* of language, by which the individual members of society rely on language as their principal tool to adapt to the ever-changing conditions surrounding them and, in doing so, "generate meaning", as Verschueren calls it (1999:147). As to the latter perspective, the traditional speech acts are among the tools that we have at our disposal to control our environment, respectively adapt to it in various ways. As Levinson aptly remarks, the function of a promise as a speech act is to put one context to work to change another: speech acts are functions from context to context (1983:276).

More specifically, Verschueren (1999:149), in dealing with adaptability and linguistic choices, distinguishes among three ways of choosing the appropriate ('well-adapted') linguistic means: one is to appeal to the actual circumstances legitimating a particular choice, as they appear in the presuppositions that I am able to recognize (e.g., uttering 'I'm sorry to hear about your dog' presupposes that something bad has happened to the other's dog); another is to create, or invent, the circumstances that make a particular choice appropriate, as it happens in the case of conversational implicatures (e.g., asking at a newsstand 'Do you have the *Herald Tribune?*' implies that I want to buy the newspaper); and finally, an utterance may be well adapted only to certain circumstances that have to be actualized before the act becomes possible, suitable, legally binding or otherwise effective. For a typical case, consider the administering of the sacraments in the church, where the speech act 'I baptize thee' becomes effective *ex opere operato,* that is, contingent upon the pragmatic 'act having been performed': the baptismal formula depends, for its effect, on the actual flowing of the water on the body of the person to be baptized.

In all these cases, the pragmatic acting can be considered as *adapting* oneself, linguistically and otherwise, to one's world. And rightly so: in the final analysis, all our acting is done in that world, and within the *affordances* it puts at our disposal. (See further sections 8.4.1 and 8.4.2.)

A pragmatic view of speech acting serves to replace, or at least readjust, the earlier focus on the individual speech acts as our unique (or at least, chief) means of verbal control of, and adaptation to, the environment. As the examples given above have shown, in pragmatic acting it is impossible to pinpoint a particular, predetermined use of any canonical speech act. Thus, when people practice 'indirect denial' or 'co-opting', the speech acts used are not commensurate with the pragmatic acts performed (just like when I invite people into a community of consumers by asking an innocent question such as 'What kind of man reads *Playboy?*').

For the same reason, pragmatic acts cannot be simply considered to be some particular subtype of the indirect speech acts discussed in section 5.4. For example, in a dinner-table situation, there is a difference between an indirect request such as:

Can you pass me the salt?
(compare the direct request 'Pass the salt')

and 'hints' or 'prompts' such as:

I'd like some salt

or:

Isn't this soup rather bland?

Both the latter utterances can be seen as efforts to have somebody pass the salt, yet neither of them 'counts as' a request; rather, they are pre-sequences to requests ('pre-requests', to be exact; see section 6.3.2.1), that somehow obtain the desired result most of the time, even without having to be developed into full-blown requests: the salt is passed on.

While speech acts, when uttered in contexts, are pragmatic acts, pragmatic acts need not be speech acts (not even indirect ones). A theory of action explains this by appealing to the "underlying goal orientation" among the participants in the discourse (Jacobs and Jackson 1983b:291), and which manifests itself in their interactional goals. The interpretation of a particular utterance relies on these interactional goals, a less interesting subset of which are the purely communicational ones. Thus, the hinting and prompting utterances in the example above are interesting not as informative statements (A: 'I'd like some salt'; B: 'Thank you for sharing this with me'), but as pre-requests to a request which is usually not formulated, and maybe not even needed for the interaction to be successful.

The developmental aspects of language use seem to bear this out as well. Children learn to deal with pragmatic acts long before they discover the existence of 'real' speech acts. The proper framing of a pragmatic sequence is often sufficient to obtain the right result, as every educator knows. In this context, even 'doing nothing' can figure as a recognized (pragmatic) act; compare the familiar story of Joshua and his mom:

> MOTHER (*calling out the window to child in yard*): Joshua, what are you doing?
> JOSHUA: Nothing . . .
> MOTHER: Will you stop it immediately!

Joshua's pragmatic act in this interchange could be described as trying to get out ('opt out') of a conversational minefield. And since there is no speech act (let alone a speech act verb) 'to nothing' (even though the philosopher Martin Heidegger did invent a word for it: "*Das Nichts nichtet*", literally: 'The nothing nots'; which can happen only in German), the next best thing is to use words that say as little as possible, in fact 'nothing'. One is reminded of Christopher Robin going off 'to do nothing':

> What I like best is doing nothing . . . It's when people call out at you just as you're going off to do it, 'What are you going to do, Christopher Robin?' and you say, 'Oh, nothing", and then you go and do it. (A. A. Milne, *The House at Pooh Corner*, ch. 10)

Learning how to manage speech acts, including their 'correct' verbal uptake, occurs later in the child's life than learning to respond to them in the form of an appropriate action. The individual speech acts, such as literal responses to requests, are acquired later than are appropriate reactions to pragmatic acts. As Jacobs and Jackson conclude, "children have to learn that a literal response is possible" (1983b:295).

8.4 Pragmatic acts in context

8.4.1 The common scene

In the preceding chapter (7.2.3.3), I talked about the necessity of situating our speech acts in context, especially when analyzing people's conversation. No conversational contribution at all can be understood properly unless it is situated within the environment in which it was meant to be understood. 'Quoting out of context' is a well-known means of manipulating a conversational partner, and the proper use of conversational techniques pre-empts such manipulation precisely in the name of good conversational behavior.

In the present section, I want to explore the background of the social behavior that conversation, seen as pragmatic interacting, represents. The actors in this conversational play fulfill their roles on a common 'social scene', as it is often metaphorically expressed; let's for a moment look more closely into this metaphor and its implications for pragmatic acting.

The French sociologist Jacques Rancière (1995), starting out from the notion of 'common scene' in the political domain, has defined politics as the "battle for the common scene of understanding". The common scene is not simply a matter of agreeing on a common ground, or establishing some common definitions or some common conceptual framework. Rather, we are dealing with a contest here, a *battle*: while trying to establish their common ground, people incessantly engage in fights about issues thought to be 'common', but in reality originating in various kinds of misunderstanding.

One has to distinguish, says Rancière, between a simple misunderstanding (French: *malentendu*, or *méconnaissance*, i.e., a wrong understanding, or even a lack of understanding) and a misunderstanding on a deeper level (French: *mésentente*), where understanding is not only difficult, but even impossible, because there is not, and cannot be, any common platform where all the involved parties can meet; which, according to Rancière, is the usual, unfortunate situation in politics (1995:12–13).

In politics as in daily life, it frequently happens that one person does not understand what the other is saying, not because the words are not clear or the phrasing ambiguous, but simply because the one interlocutor doesn't *see* what the other is talking about, or because she or he interprets that which the other is talking about as something entirely different. In Rancière's words:

The cases of misunderstanding are those in which the dispute on 'what speaking means'[90] constitutes the very rationality of the speech situation. In that situation, the interlocutors both do and do not mean the same thing by the same words. There are all sorts of reasons why a certain person X understands, and yet does not understand, another person Y: because, while he perceives clearly what the other tells him, he also doesn't *see* the object of which the other speaks to him; or even, because he understands, and must understand, sees and wants to make seen, another object represented by the same words, another reasoning contained in the same argument. (1995:13; my translation and emphasis)

Rancière's 'scene' is more than just a context, understood as a common background, or platform, of conversation. Rather, the question is about the underlying presuppositions making this very context possible. This context of common possibilities is a 'scene', on which the actors can perform within the limits of their roles and the action of the play. Their entire rationality in acting rests on the *affordable* ('what can I do, given the context?') rather than exclusively on the *thinkable* and *cognizable* ('what can I say and understand, given this context?'). The 'common scene' is thus 'transcendental' in a deeper sense than Kant's: not only the possibility of thinking and cognizing is questioned, but the very possibility of *acting* on the cognitive scene. And this is why Rancière's notion of 'common scene' is so important when it comes to understanding pragmatic acts.

On a scene, one's understanding depends entirely on the actions performed. To understand 'actively' means: to have an idea of what to do, how to act, not just of what to say or think (these latter, while important, still are subordinated to the acting). The understanding one has of others, too, depends on their acting and on the role they assume on the scene. What may appear as crazy behavior outside of the theater (cf. expressions such as: a 'theatrical laugh', to 'assume a tragic posture', to 'indulge in histrionics' or even to 'put on an act') is perfectly understandable and rational when viewed on the scene. Here, role and rationality merge: acting outside one's role is not only irrational, but strictly speaking impossible for actors who want to keep their places, to stay active, both on the scene as actors and in real life on the payroll of the theatrical company.

Pragmatics establishes the common scene squarely within the societal context, by making it clear that not only in politics, but also on the social scene at large, a 'battle' for domination is going on, and that without an understanding of the domineering forces of society, our understanding of the common scene will always be limited. To use a term originally coined in psychology (Gibson 1979; see further the next section), the scene's 'affordances' are also the affordances of our actions. Our acting is determined by what the scene can afford, and by what we can afford on the scene. Common affordances create a common platform for action; a lack of common affordances eliminates the possibility of acting socially, be it in speech or otherwise. Our acting on the scene, inasmuch as it depends on that understanding, only makes sense, and is possible, if the scene has been established as *common*, that is, 'affordable' for us and by us.

But not only does the scene determine our acting; conversely, our actions determine and reaffirm the existing scene. We profess adherence to our common platform by acting within its confines, by obeying its limitations, by realizing our possibilities on the scene. Our acting (and this includes the speaking of our roles, our 'speech acting') is always a *situated action*, that is, an action made possible and afforded by and in a particular situation, on a particular scene. The next section will explore in more detail what this has to say for the question of pragmatic acts.

8.4.2 Situated speech acts

Earlier (section 5.4.1), I have drawn attention to the so-called 'indirect speech act problem': how can it be that our speech acts more often than not are executed by verbal expressions having very little to do with the literal interpretation of those expressions, but rather much with their conventional interpretation (either as idioms, or by using certain rules of inference; Levinson 1983:268–72)? What I would like to suggest in the line of an answer is, in accordance with what has been said in the previous sections, that those so-called 'indirect' speech acts derive their force not just from their lexico-semantic build-up, but from the *situation* in which they are appropriately uttered. And I want to generalize this solution to comprise not only indirect speech acts, but speech acting in general, that is, any way of using words in order to do things.

Speech acts, in order to be effective, have to be *situated*. That is to say, they both rely on, and actively create, the situation in which they are realized. Thus, a situated speech act comes close to what has been called a *speech event* in ethnographic and anthropological studies (Bauman and Sherzer 1974): speech as centered on an institutionalized social activity of a certain kind, such as teaching, visiting a doctor's office, participating in a tea-ceremony, and so on. In all such activities, speech is, in a way, prescribed: only certain utterances can be expected and will thus be acceptable; conversely, the participants in the situation, by their very acceptance of their own and others' utterances, establish and reaffirm the social situation in which the utterances are uttered and in which they find themselves as utterers.

The emphasis is thus no longer on describing individual speech acts (as it was for Searle and his followers). What the speech event does is understandable only in terms of the language used; conversely, the individual speech acts make sense only in the event. More recently, this view has gained further support among anthropologists and linguists; thus, Hanks states that "meaning arises out of the interaction between language and circumstances, rather than being encapsulated in the language itself" (1996:266), that is to say, encoded in semantic units and administered by way of syntactic rules.[91]

In such a "radically pragmatic view" (Levinson 1995), the indirect speech act dilemma is resolved by moving the focus of attention from the words being said to the things being done. In the sense that 'indirectness' is a straight derivative *from* the situation, and inasmuch as all speech acting depends *on* the situation (with its dialectic coupling and 'back-propagation', as we have seen in the previous section), one may say that in a situational sense, there are only indirect speech acts; alternatively, that no speech act, in and by itself, makes any sense. *A fortiori*, there are, strictly speaking, no such 'things' as speech acts. What is left, then, are what I will call *instantiated pragmatic acts* (for short: 'ipras' or 'practs'); I will have more to say on these below.

If there are no speech acts as such, but only situated speech acts, or 'ipras', it follows that it is a mistake to believe (as most philosophers and linguists do) that one can isolate, and explain, our use of words by referring to individual speech acts having well-defined properties (such as illocutionary force), to be assigned strictly in accordance with philosophical and linguistic criteria (semantic, syntactic, perhaps even phonological). It further implies that all efforts expended in trying to break out of this linguistic and philosophical straitjacket, such as the ingenious theorizing surrounding Horn's two principles, or Sperber and Wilson's much-admired theory of relevance (both discussed in section 4.3.2), in the end must be frustrated, since no single theory of language or of the mind will ever be able to explain the activities of the human language user *in a concrete situation*. Such a situation depends neither on the mind nor on language exclusively, and cannot be expressed in terms intended to specifically operate within, and describe, the mental or linguistic.

By contrast, a pragmatic approach to speech acting will always, as its first and most important business, raise the question of the *user's possibilities* in a given situation. According to the psychologist James J. Gibson, the exercise of the human faculty of perception, such as that of vision, is not just a simple matter of an object reflecting itself in the mind and processed by some specific psychological mechanisms. Such a basically Cartesian view of the mind and its operations is at a loss to explain what happens in actual human perception and thinking.

Varying Kant's famous dictum about the blindness of the mental categories, we can say not only that the eye is blind as long as it is not governed by visual categorizing, but also that the visual categories themselves (shape, color etc.) aren't just workings of the mind, but are prefigured in the objects the eye sees, or expects to see, in a given situation. On entering a room, for instance, I will automatically 'see' what looks like a window as a window, because the situation 'ROOM' is one in which there are normally found objects called 'WINDOWS'. It is the situation that (along with the active perceptive categories) creates the objects of perception, in accordance with the possibilities afforded by the situation (which is why Gibson called them 'affordances'; 1979).

Applying this to the case at hand, situated speech acting, we conclude that in using language for communication, what we can (and actually do) understand is what we can afford to hear. 'Jumping to conclusions', 'inductive thinking', the *demi-mot* that the good listener, according to the French proverb, is satisfied with, verbal allusion, indirect speech acting, are all instances of such 'situational affordability'.

The theory of pragmatic acts does not try to explain language use from the inside out, that is, from words having their origin in a sovereign speaker and going out to an equally sovereign hearer (who then may become another sovereign speaker, and so on and so forth). Rather, its explanatory movement is from the outside in: the focus is on the environment in which both speaker and hearer find their affordances, such that the entire situation is brought to bear on what can be said in the situation, as well as on what is actually being said.

In this line of thought, the emphasis is not on conditions and rules for an individual (or an individual's) speech act, but on characterizing a general situational prototype, capable of being executed in the situation; such a generalized pragmatic act I will call a *pragmeme*. The instantiated, individual pragmatic acts, the 'ipras' or *practs*, refer to a particular pragmeme as its realizations. Since no two practs ever will be identical (being realized in an actual situation, and every situation being different from every other), every pract is at the same time an *allopract*, that is to say a concrete and different realization of a particular instantiation of a particular pragmeme. Most importantly, there is no way of determining *a priori* what an allopract should look like (and, *a fortiori*, what it cannot look like); which explains why indirect speech acts, one of the most important classes of allopracts, are, within limits, pretty unpredictable.[92]

Thus, the Israeli linguist Dennis Kurzon, who has worked specifically on the pragmeme of 'incitement', is able to conclude his deliberations by stating that "any utterance may constitute an act of incitement if the circumstances are appropriate to allow for such an interpretation" (1998:28). Similar considerations hold for the cases that we have looked at earlier, where we had to do with pragmemes of inviting, co-opting, denying, bribing and so on.

In studying practs, we are not concerned with matters of grammatical correctness or the strict observance of rules. What 'counts as' a *pract* (that is, what can be subsumed under a pragmeme as an allopract of a particular pract) is determined exclusively by the understanding that the individual participants have of the situation, and by the effects that the practs have, or may have, in a given context. Schematically, this can be represented as follows:

PRAGMEME

ACTIVITY PART   TEXTUAL PART

(INTERACTANTS)   (CO(N)TEXT)

SPEECH ACTS   INF REF REL VCE SSK MPH 'M'...

INDIRECT SPEECH ACTS

CONVERSATIONAL ('DIALOGUE') ACTS

PSYCHOLOGICAL ACTS (EMOTIONS)

PROSODY (INTONATION, STRESS, . . .)

PHYSICAL ACTS:

  BODY MOVES (INCL. GESTURES)

  PHYSIOGNOMY (FACIAL EXPRESSIONS)

  (BODILY EXPRESSIONS OF) EMOTIONS

  . . .

Ø (NULL)

PRACT

ALLOPRACT

PRAGMEME, PRACT, ALLOPRACT

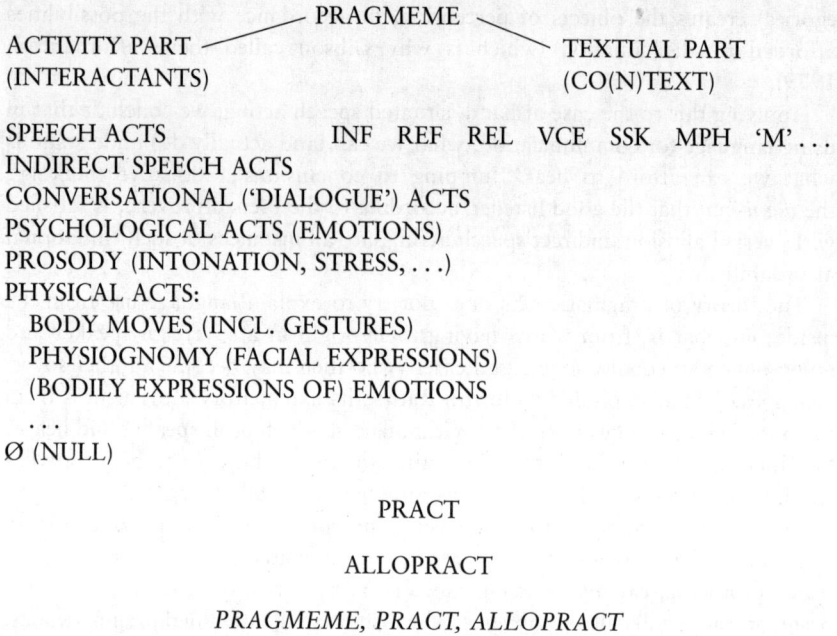

In the above scheme, the column to the left lists the various choices that the language user has at his or her disposal in communicating; it should be considered a feature *matrix*, whose cells can be either filled or empty. The language user may choose one or several of the available options; if all the cells are empty, the matrix goes to zero ('Ø'), representing the borderline case of 'silence' (which is not the same as 'zero communication'; see Jaworski 1997; Kurzon 1997. On 'dialogue acts', see section 8.4.3). The right-hand side of the schema symbolizes the elements that are present in the textual chain; the listing is not complete, but in any ordinary length of text most of the elements will be found concurrently existing.

In the row to the right, 'INF' stands for 'inferencing', 'REF' for '(establishing) reference', 'REL' for 'relevance', 'VCE' for 'voice', 'SSK' for 'shared situation (or dialogue) knowledge', 'MPH' for 'metaphor', while 'M' denotes a 'metapragmatic joker', an element that directs our attention to something happening on the metapragmatic plane. Here, the notion of 'indexicality' that we discussed in section 7.2.4.2 plays a major role. For instance, a German subjunctive has the potential of indicating that the text is attributed to another source; a particular use of tense in English may indicate that the speaker is embarking upon what is called 'free indirect discourse' (see further section 9.3; more on this in Mey 1999:ch 5.4); in many languages, a different word order may tell us that the center of attention has shifted to the transposed element; and so on. Since it is not possible to catch all of the manifestations of the 'joker' in one formula, I refer to this element by the innocent abbreviation 'M' (for 'metapragmatic').

A welcome corollary of looking at speech acting as 'practing' is that the venerable and vexing dilemma of 'illocutionary' vs. 'perlocutionary' force vanishes entirely. As Yueguo Gu has remarked, "perlocution is not a single act performed by S[peaker]. Nor is its effect being caused by an utterance. It involves a [rhetorical] *transaction*" (1993:428; my italics), involving minimally both a speaker and a hearer, as well as a number of other agents or factors. Another contemporary pragmatician, Kurzon, confirms that perlocutionary acts "are not a separate issue in speech act theory" (1998:41). But even if perlocutionary acts should not belong in speech act theory, they are still part of pragmatics; also for this reason, it would be better just to call them what they really are, namely *pragmatic acts*. There is only one force in any act of uttering, whether illocutionary or perlocutionary, and it is pragmatic: the force of the *pragmeme*.

8.4.3 Pragmatic acts and body moves

Pragmatic acts engage the whole individual in communication, not just the speech portion of his or her contribution. Moreover, in the metapragmatic dimension, pragmatic acts are essential in establishing and maintaining the metacommunicative framework for communication.

What is lacking in most accounts of speech act production and reception is the aspect of interactive feedback, that is, the way we communicate about the act being performed: whether or not it is received properly, whether or not we are in agreement, whether or not we are going to perform in accordance with the act and so on. This feedback can be linguistic (Allwood et al. 1991), or be given by a movement of the body (in the widest sense of the term, incorporating gestures but not limited to them).

The term 'body language' is often used to denote this aspect of interaction. It is usually thought of as an accompaniment to the more important verbal signal. Recently, however, researchers have come to realize (cf. Good 1996) that body language is a powerful tool in communication, because it may restrict (constrain) the delivery of the speech signal and facilitate the choice between the different interpretations that are open to the listener.

We should distinguish here between body language serving only to *illustrate* what is said (such as shaking a fist in accompaniment to a verbal threat) and a body movement that is *taking part* in the dialogue (as in the 'I Want You' poster, Uncle Sam wagging his index finger at 'you'). While both are legitimate parts of the pragmeme, only the latter enters into the dialogue as a potentially independent unit, a *body move* (BM). This is why some researchers have chosen the name of *Dialogue Act*, or *Composite Dialogue Act* (Gill et al. 1999) for situations where, to vary Donne's immortal words, 'one could almost say, the body speaks' (1615). And when the body speaks in this fashion, its movements, the body moves, form an integral part of the interaction (e.g., in a conversation); as such, they represent, or are part of, a *pragmatic act*.

Clearly, the idea of non-verbal communication being a simple supplement or aid to verbal exchange is too narrow. Rather, one must admit that bodily communication (and this includes, e.g., such poorly researched factors as emotions) is able to 'set the scene' for total communication. In other words, if your body does not follow you, your listener will not either. Non-verbal communication, in its broadest sense, will not just be one of the 'messier aspects of interaction which result from the co-presence of speaker and addressee' (Good 1996:310), but enables the interactants to 'constrain the set of possible computations which [they] might undertake' (ibid.: 312).

When it comes to assigning the non-verbal language a role of its own, some have taken their cues from the techniques and insights of conversation analysis (CA). Body moves are seen not as just movements of the body, but rather as 'moves' in a well-scripted play (typically a verbal interaction), just as conversational moves (such as turn-taking) are part of the overall structure of a conversation. And just as the moves of a conversation are enacted pragmatically on the 'common scene' shared by the conversationalists (see section 8.4.1), BM are executed in what has been called an 'engagement space' or a *field of engagement*: "The body field of engagement is set as the communication opens and the bodies indicate and signal a willingness to co-operate" (Gill et al. 2000:97). This field of engagement is a "variable field and changes when participants are comfortable or uncomfortable with each other". For instance, "[d]isagreement or discrepancy can necessitate a *reconfiguration* of the body field of engagement" (ibid.). (Something similar occurs when people who do not even intend to explicitly communicate experience an intrusion into their potential fields of engagement, as, e.g., in an elevator, when people automatically move away from anyone getting too close.)

Gill et al. distinguish several kinds of body moves that can play a role in the pragmatic interaction. I will limit myself here to discussing two of them: the BM *take-turn*, which operates in the same fashion as CA turn-taking, and occurs mainly as interactants enter or leave the common engagement space; and the *focusing* BM, involving a movement of the speaker's body into the common space, accompanied or followed by a corresponding movement of the interlocutor. Below, I will consider some examples of these moves. The sketched frames are based on videotaped recordings of an actual interaction sequence (Gill et al. 1999).

First, an example of a body move of *turn-taking* (Gill et al. 2000:106; see figure 1).

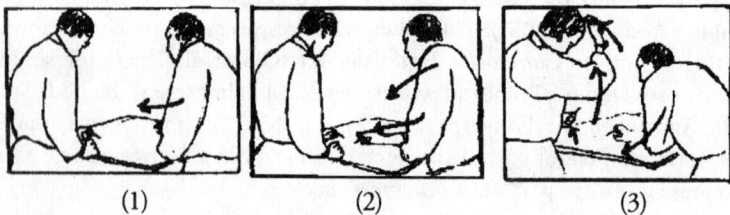

(1)   (2)   (3)

Figure 1

B You could start the trim from the
corner couldn't you. If you had trees or
something in your paving something
in the paving that cuts

A *[A moves his hand in]*　　　　　　　　*A: BM Take-turn*
But looking at it from a very
practical point
*[A's elbows go down on the
table, B moves back]*
of view if people getting if you get
out of the car here how do you get
to the office, . . .

The two interactants are members of an architect firm: A (senior, to the right in the picture) and B (junior, to the left). They discuss the outlay of a parking lot to be constructed for a client. There has been a suggestion on B's part to plant a line of trees across the lot to create a pathway to the offices ("If you had trees or something . . ."). At this point, A cuts in, 'self-selects' the next turn (probably because he thinks B's suggestion is not addressing the matter properly), and starts to talk about how people actually will get from their cars to the offices ("from a very practical point of view . . . how do you get to the office").

Looking at figure 1, we see how in frame (1), B is bringing in his proposal, assuming a neutral body stance: body relaxed, hands down. This stance is proper to the pragmatic act of 'plain assertion' or 'suggesting'. When A wants to interrupt, he prefaces his turn-taking by moving his hand into the engagement space in frame (2), at the same time bringing his body closer to B's, and in the end plunking his elbows down on the central part of the common work space, the table. These three body moves together produce a very forceful result: B almost retires from the scene, lifts his hand and pencil (frame 3) and moves his body away, and his arms up. Thus, the turn-taking is not only prefaced by, but also accompanied, and in fact realized, by, the bodily movements of the interlocutors.

Notice that in CA terms, the point at which A interrupts has not the slightest affinity with or similarity to a transition relevant place (TRP; see section 6.3.1). The interruption cuts straight across B's line of talk; B isn't even allowed to finish his sentence (recall that A is the senior partner in the firm where B is employed). To execute such an irregular, non-TRP turn shift, more is needed than just an announce or a verbal interruption: the body move not only supports but in fact *realizes* an otherwise difficult, perhaps impossible change of turn.

In the next example (figure 2, which follows on in the video sequence from the previous one), we see how the pragmatic act of *focusing* the interaction is realized with the help of body moves. In a focus move, the interactants agree on a point to be discussed. Focus may involve a reconfiguration of the engagement space, for instance when one of the participants has attempted to withdraw, or

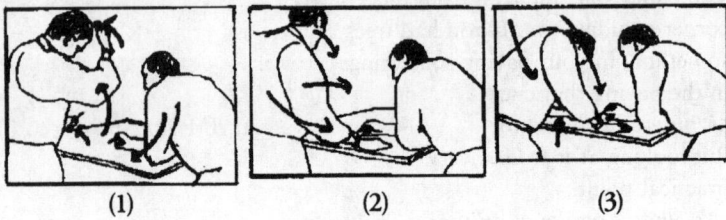

(1)   (2)   (3)

Figure 2

actually has withdrawn, at least temporarily, from the interaction (as in the previous example, where B moved out, following A's forced turn shift and 'invasion'
of the common space). What A does in the present sequence is (with the help of
a focusing body move) to bring B back into the active engagement space. In frame
(1) of figure 2 (which is the same as the third frame of the previous sequence),
B has moved out bodily from the field of engagement; A stays where he is (keeps
his elbows on the table, leaves his hand in the forward position, but does not
move it further toward B; Gill et al. 2000:110).

A if people getting if you get
    out of the car here how do you get
    [A keeps elbows on the table]   A: BM Focus
    to the office,
                [B bends down]   B: BM Focus

A signals that he is there, ready to discuss factual matters, and that he does
not intend to threaten B or further interrupt him. The turn shift being successfully completed, things have reverted to normal, as far as A is concerned,
and B is welcomed back into the common space by A's neutral stance and his
pragmatic act of 'focusing' (the chief ingredient of which is to maintain the same
position); this is then reciprocated by B (who bends down to meet and accept A's
overture).

In terms of pragmatic acts, A creates a 'focus of attention' by staying in his
previous position, implicitly inviting B to join him by asking him a question:
"how do you get to the office". In this way, A's pract of 'inviting in' overrides
and neutralizes the previous one ('get out of my way'); one could also say that
by focusing on the matter at hand (i.e., the way people are getting to the offices
from their cars), A shifts from the object level to the metalevel, where the basic
action can be described in pragmemic terms as '(re-)establishing the level of talk'
(possible associated speech acts are 'excusing' and 'minimizing negative effects':
"I don't want to interrupt . . .", "Please ignore my interruption . . .", "Let's talk
business . . ." and so on). Subsequently, B follows this lead and moves back into
the engagement space, first with his hands and arms, along with a slight incli-

nation of the head, in frame (2), then with his full body in a 45-degree inclination, with one elbow down on the table, hands very close to A's in frame (3). In this way, A's and B's body moves have successfully achieved the pragmeme of '(re)focusing the ongoing interaction'.

It is important to note that the BM described above are not just illustrative movements of the body, serving to underline a particular act: they are an integral part of the action. In this connection, one should recall that BM, unlike speech acts, have no intrinsic 'content'; they can, but need not, be associated with a particular verbal act. But even in case they do, they still make sense only in the total context of the pragmatic act, of which the verbal act also is a part.

As integral portions of pragmemes, body moves are naturally part of, and may naturally represent, the whole pragmatic act which realizes a particular pragmeme. (Compare what happens in the case of (direct or indirect) speech acts in the classical theory, whenever the context, or 'interactive space', is constrained enough to permit the making of inferences about what is meant by the act). In pragmatic acting, strict 'linguistic feedback' (in Allwood et al.'s sense; 1991) is not the main, let alone the only thing; it is the overall contextual affordances of the pragmeme that pave the way for a correct interpretation of the body move (as also shown in related work on interactive moves in constructive dialogue situations: Goodwin 2000; Hindmarsh and Heath 2000; Roth 2000; Streeck and Kallmeyer 2000 in press).

8.4.4 Pragmatic acts as social empowerment

If pragmatics is about human adaptability (as we have seen in section 8.3.4), pragmatic acting can be defined as *contextualized adaptive behavior*. In this view, a pragmatic act is an instance of adapting oneself to a context, as well as (on the basis of past situations and looking ahead to future situations) adapting the context to oneself. In all this, language helps us identify and execute, in any given context, the appropriate situated acts. In this sense, language is the 'generalized script' (see section 6.3.3.4) for all human action, since it functions both as a repository of earlier experience and as a tool-box for future changes.[93]

In section 8.3.1, we saw how Jacobs and Jackson (1983b) interpreted this adaptive behavior as 'conversational influencing', meaning: the ways in which speakers try to influence each other through the use of language in order to realize their goals. What these authors correctly emphasize is the importance of situational information in establishing the expectations that will allow the various influencing patterns to yield the desired result. What they do not underscore sufficiently, though, is the extent to which the situational context already is pre-cast, so to speak, in the mold of society. It is society itself that speaks through the interactants when they try to influence each other: this 'speaking' may take the shape of felicity conditions, conventions, culture, social structure, or what have you. Any approach which bases itself exclusively or predominantly upon rational actions performed by single individuals must fail, inasmuch as it does not take into account the degree to which this rationality itself is supra-individual, 'pre-set' by society.

As to the rules and principles that were discussed in section 4.1, neither of these notions does justice to the concept of pragmatic acting. A rule specifying the conditions for a particular speech act (requesting, promising etc.) cannot collect all the forms of speaking we encounter when people actually perform requests, promises etc. Similarly, a principle defining cooperation cannot explain why an act that 'flouts' a maxim under that very principle may be a highly successful cooperative move, as in the case where I choose not to comply strictly with a certain request (e.g., for information), if I perceive that complying with the request is not relevant to the real intention of the requester (cf. the example in section 6.3.3.3: 'Is Lennart there?'; 'You can reach him at extension 88236').

In section 7.2.2, I proposed to replace the notions of principle and rule with that of 'constraint'. Rather than letting a principle tell us how to cooperate in executing a speech act, or having a rule define what counts as a particular speech act, we pick a *constraint* which, given the actual speech situation, will identify the possible ways of obtaining our interactional goals.

A metapragmatic constraint is not imposed by conversational structure or conversational context. True, we have rules that prescribe the correct sequence in conversation (such as the so-called 'adjacency rules'); while such rules are able to tell us what can happen in conversation, they tell us nothing about the outcome of a conversation, its success or failure. By contrast, a constraint that represents the wider structure of society is based upon, and reaffirms, the relationships of dependency and hegemony that exist in any actual speech situation, and thus guarantees the outcome of my pragmatic acting.

Applying this to our discussion, pragmatic acts are pragmatic because they base themselves on language as constrained by the situation, not as defined by syntactic rules or by semantic selections and conceptual restrictions. Pragmatic acts are situation-derived and situation-constrained; in the final analysis, they are determined by the broader social context in which they happen, and they realize their goals in the conditions placed upon human action by that context. As such, they correspond pretty closely to what Levinson, in an early article, has called 'activity types' (or, with a less felicitous term, 'social episodes'): "they [the 'prag-memes'] constrain what will count as an allowable contribution to each activity [or 'pract'], and on the other hand, they help to determine ['set up'] how what one says [one's 'speech acts'], will be 'taken'" (Levinson 1979:393; my additions). In other words, the 'setting up', as I call it, both creates the affordances for the pragmatic act and tells us what kind of pract we're dealing with.

As examples, consider the pragmatic act of 'co-opting', as realized in the ad text 'What kind of man reads *Playboy*?' This pract is only effective in a situational context setting up prototypical, prospective male *Playboy* readers. Hence, the visual display exhibited along with the ad reinforces this prototypical 'setting':

racing cars, expensive clothes, good-looking women and so on. Only in that context, and given those conditions, does the pract effectively address a particular audience as consumers of particular products.

Or take the case of somebody saying: 'Real programmers do it on the console.' Here, a situational context is evoked in which a self-styled 'real programmer' spurns the use of computer language to facilitate contact with the machine, and goes the rugged way of talking to the computer in (what at least comes close to) machine language.[94] By this evocation, I invite in, and 'co-opt', all those who are supposed to feel the way I do: I establish a 'little circle of friends', one of the most powerful ways of discriminating socially against outsiders. Again, no speech acts (direct or indirect) are being used that could be made responsible for exactly this discriminating effect.

I conclude that pragmatic acting is exploiting one's societal empowerment, rather than exercising 'power' in the usual sense. 'To empower' means: investing somebody with power, to put a person into a power position. Since my position derives from society, society's empowerment limits my acting potential at the same time as it enables me to act as a free agent, operating within the constraints that society has imposed. The pragmatic act is the 'social default' in a given situation.

This paradox of 'institutionalized freedom' reminds us of the way in which Herbert Simon (one of the founding fathers of Artificial Intelligence; 1969) used to describe his famous ant. The ant is said to display intelligent behavior when he goes about finding his way back to the ant-hill; yet, since the ant has nowhere else to go, his intelligence is merely an instance of social and pragmatic 'ant default'. The ant acts *socially* by obeying the laws of the hill; and he acts *pragmatically* by staying within the ant colony's empowering limits, by which the complexity of his task is simply allocated to the environment (cf. the related notion developed by Gibson under the name of 'affordance'; see section 8.4.2, above).

Using Bolinger's colorful image (1980), if our pragmatic use of language can be likened to the firing of a 'loaded weapon', then we should take care to remind ourselves where, and by whom, and for what purpose those pragmatic cannon balls were cast. In other words, the question is: 'Whose language are we using?' (Mey 1985).

The next chapter will examine one particular instance of pragmatic acting, namely, as it is realized in the world of writing and studied in literary pragmatics.

Review and discussion

1. You are in Pisa, Italy, and want to have a meal in one of the local restaurants, La Stanzina, which has been recommended to you by some of your friends.

Unfortunately, neither the owner of the restaurant, Roberto, nor his genial and voluminous wife, Simonetta, speak a word of English. Also, the menu is in Italian only, and you understand very little of its culinary terminology. When you sit down to order your meal, you will nevertheless have certain expectations as to what is going to happen (based on your previous expectations from eating out), such as that there will be a waiter, he or she will give you a menu, you will make a choice, you will be served, you will eat your meal, you will pay and leave. All this is contained in what is often called the 'restaurant script' (a notion originally due to Marvin Minsky and further developed by people like Schank and Abelson in their efforts to build computer models of human activity; 1977). The script serves as a blueprint of the situation, and enables you to navigate through it, even if some details may change or are unknown, as in the present case. Hence, the general context of the restaurant will enable you to interpret and perform certain pragmatic acts taking place in the restaurant, even if you may be at a loss as to how to interpret the actual Italian words (or 'speech acts') used. Thus, e.g., when Roberto comes to your table, all smiles, and welcomes you in Italian, you need not understand the exact wording of his greeting. And when he hands you the menu, you will understand this as a pragmatic 'pre-sequence' (cf. section 6.3.2.1) to 'taking your order'.

On the basis of all this background information, now consider the following.

Questions:
What further pragmatic pre-sequences and acts are likely to take place in this context of La Stanzina, as part of the restaurant script?

What particular pragmatic act is the menu a part of? What is the pragmatic value of the spatial arrangement of the menu?

Let's say you are familiar with the term *pasta*. You also remember having eaten something with seafood in it, going by the name of *marinara*. How can you figure out an entry like *penne alle vongole*, supposing it is placed under the heading *Paste*, and before the item *linguine marinara*?

Explain how the notion of 'script' (mentioned above, and discussed in section 6.3.3.4) would be useful in dealing with this situation, in particular by pointing out which pragmatic acts are involved in this script.

You could, of course, avoid all the above problems and whip around the corner to Borgo Stretto or Piazza Cavour, and get your every wish fulfilled at one of the American fast-food places. What (apart from the lousy food) would mainly make this situation different in terms of pragmatic acting?

2. The famous sage-cum-buffoon Nasreddin Hoca, a figure familiar in popular culture from Serbia throughout the Middle East, reportedly once had a visit from an importunate neighbor, who wanted to borrow a length of rope. This is how

the Hoca managed to get out of the bind without offending his neighbor too much:

NEIGHBOR: *Efendim*, could I borrow your rope?
HOCA: Sorry, my friend, the rope is in use.
NEIGHBOR: But I cannot see anybody using it.
HOCA: Of course not, my *harem* is using it.
NEIGHBOR: *Hocam*, what could your *harem* possibly be doing with a length of rope?
HOCA: They're putting flour on it.
NEIGHBOR: *Allah Allah*! How could anybody be putting flour on a rope?
HOCA: Clearly, that's what one does when one doesn't want to let one's neighbor have it. (Anonymous, *Nasrettin Hoca'nın letaifi*. Istanbul 1956)

One could discuss this episode from a variety of viewpoints. One would be to itemize the speech acts that are being used. Another could be to look into the cooperation that is going on here and how the Cooperative Principle is being put to work (if at all). Finally, if the focus is on pragmatic acting, we could ask ourselves what is going on in this situation *pragmatically*; and from that perspective, try and answer the following.

Questions:
What purpose do the speech acts being used here serve?

In particular, what is the metapragmatic value of the Hoca explaining what he is doing with his rope?

What pragmeme is involved? Can you locate the different parts of the schema shown in section 8.4.2 in the individual parts of the dialogue?

Given the situation, could the Hoca have acted differently? If yes, how? Would he still be operating within the same pragmeme?

(Optional): Discuss the Principle of Cooperation on the basis of this case.

Notes:
Hoca is originally the same word as the Arabic *hadji*, 'pilgrim who has visited Mecca'; in Turkish, it is used as synonymous with 'sage, teacher'.
Hocam, Efendim: the suffix *-m* denotes the first person singular possessive: 'my'. (Cf. in French: '*mon général*' as form of address to a four-star officer.)
Harem means both the actual collection of wives that are allowed a man under Koranic law and the location where these wives are found (the usual interpretation in Western texts).
Allah Allah: exclamation of astonishment etc.: 'for God's sake'.

3. In January, 1998, the following two-page spread could be admired in the *Swissair Gazette*: an aproned, mini-skirted waitress in a semi-fast-food restaurant is depicted, tray in hand, looking straight at you with a quizzical, sexy half-smile, like you just had said something to her which wasn't quite in the line of duty or obligation. The caption reads:

I'M A DAMNED GOOD WAITRESS.
IF YOU WANT TO SEE AN ACTRESS, GO WATCH A MOVIE.

In the extreme bottom right-hand corner of the right-hand page, a barely visible vignette reads:

Winston. Reliable

This text is formed as a circle, in the manner of an official imprint (e.g., a customs or post office stamp), suggesting an impression of 'reliability' (or 'warranty').

The advertisement's only mention of the word 'cigarette' or 'tobacco' is in the customary 'Surgeon General's Warning', appearing in a white box in the top left-hand corner of the left page, stating that "cigarette smoking is detrimental to your health" etc.

Questions:
How do we know that this picture in fact is an advertisement?

How do we know that the ad is for a tobacco product (cigarettes), even though no cigarettes or cigarette-smoking people are shown, and not even the words 'tobacco' or 'cigarette' are mentioned (except in an official, non-sponsored, 'negative' way)?

On the basis of what has been said in section 8.4.2, establish the character of this text as a pragmatic act. What kind of situated acting are we looking at? How do we know this? In other words, how do we know that this act is an instantiation of a particular pragmeme, and which?

As far as speech acting goes, are any speech acts being used here? What kind?

How do they relate to the situation's pragmeme? Are they part of the pragmeme's instantiation? (Refer to the schema in section 8.4.2.)

How does the reader establish the link between the visible image and the 'invisible' content of the message? What specific role does the waitress play in this linking? What does her utterance contribute to the pract in question?

4. *Of bulls and briefs*

In the late eighteenth century, after much pressure from a number of European (in particular, the Portuguese and French) governments, the Holy See decided to dissolve the Order of Jesuits (the *Compañía de Jesús* or Society of Jesus, founded by Iñigo (St Ignatius) de Loyola in 1536) world-wide. Without going into the particulars of this unique event in the history of the church and in the practice of canon law (other 'suppressions' of religious orders had been mostly local, such as that of the Carthusians by Emperor Joseph II of Austria-Hungary in 1782), one can safely say that the disbanding of the Jesuits was a political, rather than a disciplinary act of strictly religious character.

The instrument chosen to effect this suppression was a so-called 'papal brief'. For a papal brief (or bull) to be valid as a legal instrument (e.g., of proclaiming an interdict,[95] of condemning a heresy and so on), it has to be read publicly in the presence of those whom it concerns. Without such a reading (called a 'promulgation'), the document is null and void, as far as its legal effects are concerned.

The interesting point about this particular legal instrument, the papal brief *Dominus ac Redemptor*, issued by Pope Clement XIV in 1774, was that it could not be promulgated world-wide, as intended by the pope. In Russia, the strong-willed and hard-headed Empress Catherine the Great was not going to allow the intrusion of any papal nonsense onto her territory – which, at the time, after Poland's third partition, contained most of 'Polonia Minor and Mazovia', corresponding to those parts of present-day Poland that are closest to Russia. In those newly acquired parts of the Czarist empire, being predominantly Roman Catholic, there were several Jesuit residences; and these continued to function without special interference from the Orthodox Church or the Russian authorities. Thus, Poland's partition, a disaster to the nation, became a blessing for the Jesuits: since the brief never was promulgated in any of the Polish Jesuit 'houses', these residences could not formally be dissolved, and continued in effect to exist until the Order's glorious restoration by means of Pius VII's papal bull *Sollicitudo omnium Ecclesiarum* in 1814.

The point that this story is meant to emphasize is that no speech act by itself can be of any effect if the circumstances are not right. The act of suppressing the Jesuits could not be effected by the papal words alone; the words had to be spoken as part of a *pragmatic act* of suppressing, incorporating the various conditions that hold for such legal documents to become effective (such as their public promulgation, or their being published in an official source such as the British *Hansard*).

Questions:
The first question then is: how do the various elements present in the schema in section 8.4.2 figure in the pragmeme of 'suppressing'? Before you start answering this question, a few further comments are in order. First, as to the pragmatic acts performed by the popes under various nomenclatures, one might ask why a 'brief' was used for the Jesuit Order's suppression, as against a 'bull' for its

restoration. The question is of interest both legally and practically. To take the latter first: as the name indicates, in the hierarchy of documents, a brief ranks lower than a bull; in speech act terminology, a different *force* is at play in the two cases. So perhaps Pope Clement wanted to speak and 'walk softly' because, after all, he was 'carrying a big stick'? This may well be part of the explanation since, given the controversial nature of the papal measure, it seemed important not to make too much noise while executing it, or to attract too much attention. In connection with this, consider also the other important, legal, difference between the two papal kinds of order: whereas a brief requires only two signatories to be valid, a bull needs twenty. Hence it seems likely that His Holiness Pignatelli preferred not to have to shop around for too many signatures, and therefore stayed with a brief, rather than do it the bullish way. This latter difference has directly to do with the *pragmatic* character of the papal act. In speech act terms, we are looking at the 'felicity conditions' that govern the issuing by a pope of a particular legal instrument.

Hence the second question: how would you fit in the elements that derive from classic speech act theory with the theory of pragmatic acts as explained in this chapter? (Refer again to the schema in section 8.4.2.)

As a final characteristic of papal pragmemes, one could mention their need to bring the order of speech acting into correspondence with that of pragmatic acting. Whereas within executive documents such as bulls and briefs, the various speech act verbs are used in more or less normal fashion, a remarkable thing happens toward the end of the document. There, all the SAVs that have been used throughout the bull are repeated in their nominalized forms. For instance, if the bull has 'commanded' somebody to do something, then at the end you will encounter the phrase: 'Let nobody dare to go against this command'; if there has been a speech act of 'revoking', then the corresponding verbal noun ('revocation') is mentioned in the bull's final clauses; the verb 'abrogate' is matched by the noun 'abrogation'; and so on and so forth. The 'legalistic speech acting' which is characteristic for briefs or bulls is apparently felt to be insufficient (as it in fact is) without a formal appeal to the grand context in which these acts are executed. For this reason, the final clauses of any papal bull are of the following, standardized form:

> If anybody should be so bold as to go against these letters of command, admonition, abrogation, revocation, . . . , let him know that he will incur the wrath of Almighty God and of His Holy Apostles St Peter and St Paul. Given in Rome, at the Holy Apostles Peter and Paul's, in the Year of Our Lord . . . , in the . . . th year of Our Pontificate.

This solemn coda places the addresser and the addressee in a larger, worldly as well as celestial, legally binding context, by which the pragmatic act receives its situated seal in terms of place and time, invoking the power relations that constitute its affordances.

The last question is, then, whether you can use what has been said above to have the pragmatic act subsume, but not abolish, the speech act. Just as the papal word is powerful, but has to be heard to be effective, a pragmatic act has to be executed using the means of language and other communicative devices that we have at our disposal. Explain how this is done.

5. An ad for Miller Lite Beer runs as follows:

MILLER LITE
IT'S IT AND THAT'S THAT

(*Reader*, Chicago, August 28, 1992)

Question:
What do 'it' and 'that' refer to here? How come we have no problem identifying their referents (see section 3.3.2) even though no in-text clues are provided? (Hint: the sentence is for all practical purposes tautological, i.e., contains no information whatsoever and is always necessarily true.)

6. On the shuttle bus that carries you to and from the city parking lot at George Bush Intercontinental Airport in Houston, Texas, you will notice a sign saying:

No *tipping, please*

Underneath this sign, to the right side of the driver's seat, there is a small plate, half filled with coins and one-dollar bills. You, as a pragmatic linguist, will immediately notice the discrepancy between what the sign says and what in fact happens. Hence the following.

Questions:
How would you characterize this situation in terms of 'pragmatic acts'? (Hint: focus especially on the 'setting up' effect, discussed in section 8.3.2.)

Which of the two 'notices' do you think has the stronger effect? (Hint: if you are unable to decide, consider the next question first.)

Does the 'set-up' offer you a real choice?

CHAPTER NINE
Literary Pragmatics

9.1 Introduction: author and reader

In chapter 6, I raised the question of how useful pragmatics (in particular, speech act theory) is in explaining the human activity commonly known as 'conversation'. Whereas conversation can be regarded as one of the principal ways in which humans produce *oral*, spoken texts, in addition to this 'oracy' (as it is often called), we have the phenomenon of 'literacy', interpreted either as the ability to read and write, or as the actual production and consumption of written texts. And while in the preceding chapters, our emphasis was on language as it is spoken (especially in conversation), the question now up for discussion is whether the pragmatic mechanisms that we uncovered have any validity, or explanatory significance, for literary texts.

The question: what is the significance of pragmatics for the study of written text?, or more broadly: how does literature relate to pragmatics? has to be seen from the angle of the *user*, in keeping with the general notions about pragmatics that I introduced in chapter 1. But who is this user, when it comes to literature?

At first glance, we seem to recognize the reader as the user *par excellence*: it is he or she who acquires the products of someone else's literary activity, and by consuming ('reading') them, satisfies a personal need, and indirectly, provides the author, the producer of the text, with a living. As I have argued elsewhere (Mey 1994d, 1995), this relationship is not just one of buying and selling a regular commodity; authors and readers, while being distinguished by their different positions on the supply side, respectively the demand side, of the literary market, have more in common than your regular sellers and buyers. It is the degree and kind of *collaboration* which is displayed in the literary 'market' that makes it different from a pure exchange of commodities.

Buying goods in the marketplace puts me under no special, direct obligation to the producer. Of course, for my own benefit, I must respect the intentions of the producer, often expressed in 'Directions for Use', 'Consumer Manuals' or similar pieces of documentation. As to my further relationship to the producer, there is the warranty, a document that (provided I follow all the rules and regulations) guarantees my product against production faults and producer negligence. Apart from that, no real cooperation is either necessary or desirable: producer and consumer part ways, and probably never will meet again, unless something untoward happens. The ideal sales situation is that in which post-sale contacts are reduced to a minimum.

In the literary world of producing and consuming, the situation is very different. You don't just buy a book: you buy an author to take home with you. The work that the author has done in producing the text has to be supplemented and completed by you, the reader. Reading is a collaborative activity, taking place between author and reader: reading is an innovative process of *active re-creation*, not just the passive, pre-set and pre-determined use of some 'recreational facility'.

As a contemporary novelist has expressed it cogently and succinctly: "[A novel] is made in the head, and has to be remade in the head by whoever reads it, who will always remake it differently" (Byatt 1996:214). Similarly, Morson and Emerson, writing in the Bakhtinian tradition, state that: "the potential of great works is realized by an act of creative understanding from an alien perspective reflecting experiences the author never knew, and so Shakespeare grows in meaning by virtue of what his works contain but could only be realized by active understanding from a new perspective" (1990:310).

It follows that the reader, as an active collaborator, is a major player in the literary game. His or her influence extends beyond the acquisition of a text and its subsequent assimilation through the visual and psychological processes that we usually associate with reading. The reader's contribution consists in entering the universe that the author has created, and by doing so, becoming an actor, rather than a mere spectator. By acting, however, the reader changes the play: what the reader reads is, in the final analysis, his or her own co-production along with the author. I have called this interaction a *dialectic* process (see Mey 1994d, 1999), inasmuch as the author depends on the reader as a presupposition for his or her activity, and the reader is dependent on the author for guidance in the world of fiction, for the 'script' that he or she has to internalize in order to successfully take part in the play.

The pragmatic study of literary activity focuses on the features that characterize this dialectic aspect of literary production: the text as an author-originated and -guided, but at the same time reader-oriented and -activated process of wording. The reader is constrained by the limitations of the text; but also, the text provides the necessary degrees of freedom in which the reader can collaborate with the author to construct the proper textual universe, one that is consonant with the broader contextual conditions that mark the world and times in which the reader lives.

In the following, we will look more closely at the mechanisms that language makes available to realize this joint textual production. The first question to consider is that of the literary product as the telling of a story, a *narrative*.[96]

9.2 Author and narrator

In her novel *A república dos sonhos* ('The Republic of Dreams'; 1989, originally 1984), the contemporary Brazilian author Nélida Piñon tells the story of an old woman, Eulália's, last days. Telling this story implies giving an account of Eulália's long life, an account which is provided through 'flashbacks' and retrospective narrative, attributed, among others, to a young woman, Eulália's granddaughter Breta. In telling her story, Breta assumes a double narrative perspective: for one, she lets the life-story unfold through the voice of her grandmother (as 'heard' by Breta herself); in addition, Breta tells us how she experienced her grandmother's final hours. One can easily determine these two levels of narration as representing a story within the story, the classical device favored especially by the Romantic writers of the nineteenth century (Mikhail Ju. Lermontov's *A Hero of Our Times* is a prime example).

Neither of these narrative levels is directly linked to the *author* of the book: Piñon speaks, as it were, through the voice of her characters, among which Breta is the central figure. Breta is given a crucial part in the telling of the story, the process of narrating; Breta is a major narrative 'voice', distinct from the author's own. But there is more.

Toward the end of the book, Breta remarks to herself that she, when all the funeral fuss is over, will sit down, and tell the story of what happened in grandma's bedroom – that is, the story she just has been telling us! Breta the narrator suddenly becomes another person: Breta the author. This new 'author' has, so to speak, caught us unawares in a flying start, organized by the real author, Nélida Piñon. Before we have had time to realize it, we have already met the author Breta, who enters the fictional world of *The Republic of Dreams* to become the new, 'prospective' narrator (or should I say: narratrix?) in the literary universe created by author Piñon. Thus, Breta is at the same time an author *and* a narrator; however, she can only be this by the grace of the real author and, as we will see, by the reader's active acceptance of this division of roles. (I will have more to say on this below, in sections 9.3.3 and 9.5.)

What this example illustrates is the important difference that exists in a literary production between author and narrator. Strictly speaking, the author creates the narrator, either explicitly or implicitly; an egregious example of the former is the stories that are called 'homodiegetic', that is: told in the first person (as opposed to 'heterodiegetic' stories, that are told in the third, or more rarely, in the second person; see Mey 1999:ch 6.2.3). Other examples are found in the Romantic 'stories within stories' that I referred to above (as an instance, consider the 'junior captain' Maxim Maximych in Lermontov's *A Hero of Our Times*, whom the homodiegetic narrator meets in the first chapter, but who then takes over to tell his own story).[97]

In a sense, the narrator always *is* a 'character' in the story, whether or not he (or she?) explicitly manifests himself or herself on the scene; which is why many literary critics prefer to talk of a 'narrative instance', to be referred to not by 'he' or 'she', but by the impersonal pronoun 'it'. Whether we choose the one or the other terminology, the narrator (or narrative instance) cannot be held responsible for the actions and opinions of the other characters (including a homodiegetic 'I'); neither (and *a fortiori*) can the author be identified with the actions and opinions of the characters (including, again, a homodiegetic 'I').

The pragmatic relevance of our distinction is in the different uses that author and reader make of it in producing, respectively consuming, a piece of text. It is important that the reader be made to understand that the narrator's *persona* is not identical with that of the author or any other character; which explains the occurrence of the familiar disclaimers found on the inside of the front cover of novels, to the effect that 'all the characters occurring in this book are fictitious, and any resemblance to any living persons is purely coincidental'. Such a statement need not be 'true', in the sense that the author may indeed have drawn on actually existing persons, sometimes even letting this fact be known, by subtle or not-so-subtle hints, as in the *roman à clef*. While a writer, as a narrator, may be permitted to actually portray her or his persons as real characters, as an author (crudely defined as the person who gets the royalties), she or he is not allowed to draw on actual experiences to depict living persons unfavorably; doing so would inevitably earn him a lawsuit for libel.[98] With a variation on D.H. Lawrence's famous *bon mot* (quoted by Toolan 1994:88): "Never trust the teller, trust the tale", we could say: 'Never trust the narrator (or author), trust the text, and your own ability as a reader to make sense of it.'

As we see, the pragmatics of authorship vs. 'narratorship' are of the utmost importance for the successful cooperation between the users involved in the production and consumption of the literary work. Narrativity, however defined, is always a pragmatic quality of *texts*. The next sections will go into some detail as to the underlying mechanics of these pragmatic presuppositions (as defined in section 7.2.3.2).

9.3 Textual mechanisms

The following sections will deal with some of the pragmatic mechanisms that were discussed in chapters 3 and 7, and relate them to the question raised in the previous section: how does the consumer of a text go about understanding the narrative, as it has been situated in place, time and discourse by the text producer?

I will start out with the phenomenon of reference (including deixis); following that, I will discuss the role of tense; and I will conclude by saying something about discourse. (For more detail, the reader is referred to chapter 3 of Mey 1999.)

9.3.1 Reference

Consider the following extract:

> [H]e returned home only to find her the wife of his hated cousin and mother of many little ones with his features but not his. (Byatt 1992:176)

The above assertion is made about a sailor, who has been at sea for many years, and whose return was not expected – least of all by his wife, who had remarried a cousin of her husband's (referred to as "hated" in the extract). The marriage had been successful, one could say, at least in the way of fertility (hence "the many little ones"); but to the original husband, the sight of all these children bearing the features of the despised cousin rather than his own must have been pretty appalling, and have made his homecoming a sad one.

All this information we glean without special difficulty just by quickly perusing the above text. Yet, the phrase "the many little ones with his features but not his", taken by itself, sounds a little odd, not to say contradictory, and is not easy to understand, taken out of its context. The question is now: what precisely is this context, and how do we go about interpreting it? In particular, who are the various occurrences of 'his' referring to?

In spite of the efforts of many linguists and text theoreticians, no sure-fire ways of resolving reference have as yet been found (cf. section 3.3.3). In the anaphora at hand, we are guided not by some mechanical rule of thumb, such as Halliday and Hasan's (1976) 'last occurring suitable antecedent', or by some technique of 'stepping back through the text until we find a suitable candidate', but by our understanding of the whole world in which things like the events described in the passage can take place. By entering the world of the text, by becoming participants in the drama enacted in the narrative, we become at the same time understanders of the ways in which the *personae* interact, and how they are textually referred to. In this particular case, many of us have read about, and have maybe even known, people who were thought to have perished and still came back 'from the dead', as the expression goes; post-Holocaust Europe was full of happenings like these.

Here, it is important to see how our understanding of the fictional world is contingent upon our acceptance of the author as an 'authority', as an *auctor* in the classical sense: a creator who speaks the word by which the creatures become alive; or at least one who, having been "present at the Creation" (Proverbs 8:22–31), is allowed to share this experience and wisdom by acting as a mouthpiece for the creative force. Such an understanding is prior to, and a precondition for, any further or deeper understanding of the text; the establishment of the correct references (such as the several occurrences of "his" in the above passage from Byatt) is a consequence of this understanding, not its effective cause.

The above is not to say that we can disregard the linguistic evidence or somehow bypass it. The way we have learnt to use reference in our language is an indispensable help in our understanding of texts; however, it is never an absolute guarantee of a particular understanding. As Michel Riffaterre has expressed it with admirable stringency, "a given linguistic characteristic . . . can be employed for a variety of presumed purposes, as well as for none at all" (1960, 1961; as quoted in Fludernik 1993:349). Riffaterre's observation goes under the name of the 'principle of polyvalence', and it "needs to be insisted on most emphatically", as Fludernik rightfully observes (p. 349).

Having seen how the textual world is both pragmatically dependent upon, and preconditional to, the establishment of linguistic reference, let's spend a few moments considering the problem of *tense* in a literary text.

9.3.2 Tense

In section 3.3, I talked briefly about the indexical functions of tense, considered as a means of situating an utterance in time relative to a user. The relationships between tense as a linguistic category and time as a physical reality are extremely complicated, and have been the subject of many philosophers' and linguists' often fruitless speculations. With regard to tense in literary works, the situation is no different: briefly, the question is how to determine, using the resources that the language puts at our disposal, who is saying what at which point of time in the narrative.

A simple schema is that proposed by Ehrlich (1990), following a well-known distinction introduced by the logician Hans Reichenbach (1947). Ehrlich establishes the following distinctions: first, we have the time at which the utterance is spoken: this is 'speech time' (ST). Then, there is the time at which the event that is spoken about took place: this is called 'event time' (ET). And finally, we have the time that is indicated by the temporal indicators of the utterance (that is to say, both verbal tense morphemes and adverbs of time). This temporal perspective is called 'reference time' (RT). To show the contrast between the different 'times', Ehrlich provides the following example:

John had already completed his paper last week.

Here, "the RT is last week, the ET is an unspecified time prior to last week, and the ST occurs after both RT and ET" (Ehrlich 1990:61).

What this example does *not* show is the influence that a possible context may have on the use of tense. Or more precisely, it does not tell us anything about how to understand a particular tense in a particular context of use, i.e., in a *pragmatic* environment. Here, the relations between RT, ST and ET may not follow the standard pattern, or even be entirely disrupted, so that we can only understand what's going on by appealing to our understanding of the pragmatic world in which the interplay between the tenses is taking place.

The problem reminds us a bit of what we're confronted with in so-called 'flashbacks' in literature or on the screen. A story unfolds in time, but suddenly the time perspective is broken, and events anterior to those related are 'intercalated', inserted into the stream of events. In the early days of the movies (Sergey M. Eisenstein's *Potemkin* is a classic example), these shifts were overtly indicated by the appearance of a frame bearing the date and place, such as 'Odessa 1905', 'May 5', 'Below Deck', 'In The Sailors' Mess', 'There Are Maggots In The Meat' and so on. Later cinematographers started using various other techniques, such as letting a picture fade out, contrasting black-and-white with color sequences, or using special audio effects (a 'signature' theme, underlying music of a special character and so on). Today's movie-makers can limit themselves to an appeal to our understanding and cinematic know-how: flashbacks are almost never explicitly introduced any more, and it is left to the reader to sort out the different changes in cinematic time.

In contrast to a motion picture narrative, written text has a specific morphological device called 'tense' available to indicate the various canonical times: ET, RT and ST. In most of the languages that I am familiar with, a narrative cannot do without this linguistic category of tense, even though its use may vary enormously from language to language. One well-known instance involves the absence of the present tense of the common verb 'to be' in certain, highly frequent Russian sentential constructions. As an example, take Anna's famous contribution to the discussion on whether to marry for love or for convenience in Tolstoy's *Anna Karenina*:

Ja dumaju ... esli skol'ko golov, stol'ko umov, to i skol'ko serdec, stol'ko rodov ljubvi.

(I think ... [that] if [there are] as many minds as [there are] heads, then [there are] also as many kinds of love as [there are] hearts.) (Tolstoy 1962:155; my translation).

In translating this *bon mot*, I have been forced to introduce four occurrences of the phrase 'there are', all of which are absent (and cannot even be reproduced as such) in the Russian text.

Naturally, this can cause complications in understanding, especially in cases where translators are not aware of the intricate differences between the grammars of Russian and English. Here's an example in which the translated tense misfires:

(*In the beginning of Mikhail Bulgakov's classic satirical novel* Master i Margarita *('The Master and Margarita'), two gentlemen, Ivan and Berlioz, appear on the scene, walking and talking with each other in a Moscow park. Their discussion is interrupted by the purchase of some soft drinks at a nearby stand, and by a momentary fit of dizziness, accompanied by a hallucinatory experience, on the part of one of the conversationalists, Ivan. When things are back to normal, we are told that*):

. . . – povel reč, prervannuju pit'em abrikosovoj. Reč èta, kak vposledstvii uznali, šla ob Isuse Xriste.

(. . . – [he (i.e., Ivan)] continued the discussion interrupted by the drinking of the apricot soda. This conversation, as we learned subsequently, was about Jesus Christ.) (Bulgakov 1969:13; English trans. Mirra Ginsburg, 1967:5)

On reading this fragment in its English translation, the baffled reader asks himself or herself how to reconcile the two conflicting time indications expressed here. The time adverb *vposledstvii* 'subsequently' refers to a point of time in the future. This reference time (RT) is posterior to event time (ET), that is, it must occur some time after the events depicted in the preceding passage; more specifically, after the two interruptions in the gentlemen's conversation, caused by soda drinking and hallucinating. Finally, and uncontroversially in the case at hand, speech time (ST) and ET are simultaneous, the conversation occurring more or less at ET.

However, by any account, the RT established by 'learned' (a past tense) has to be *prior* to ET, according to the rules for the use of the past tense, both in English and in other languages (including Russian), and hence would exclude the use of an adverbial expression such as 'subsequently', denoting *posterior* time. This conundrum can only be solved by appealing to the understanding that we have of the situation: the conversation (about whose content we have not been informed so far) will, at a future point of time (RT), be disclosed as having had to do (at ET/ST) with the person of Jesus Christ. This is what our common 'readerly' sense tells us has to be the meaning of this obscure passage.

But had we not been forced to rely exclusively on a particular translation of Bulgakov's work, but instead been able to consult the Russian original, we would have found the solution to the problem right away, on condition that we recalled certain peculiarities of the Russian morphological and grammatical system. For one thing, Russian verb forms such as *uznali* exhibit what is technically called a 'perfective aspect'. Furthermore, since Russian grammar has no forms for the future tense, these perfective verb forms do duty for that which we call the 'future' in English grammar.

Much simplified, we can say that the English opposition 'present tense' vs. 'future tense' is rendered in Russian by a difference in aspect: 'imperfective' vs. 'perfective'. The following two (constructed) examples demonstrate this Russian technique:

Ty znaješ [imperfective] *kak mir postrojen*
('You know how the world [is] put together'; e.g., said by a friend to some-body who is complaining about a lost love or job),

and:

Ty uznaješ [perfective] *kak mir postrojen*
('You will know/learn how the world [is] put together'; e.g., said by a parent to a son or daughter who refuses to listen to expressions of parental wisdom).

In our case, the use of the past tense *uznali* (which is an 'impersonal' form of the third person plural, commonly used in many languages in this fashion, and to be translated as 'one', 'you', or 'we') in reality expresses a *future* point of reference: 'as we *were to learn* subsequently'.[99] In the context of the novel, this makes sense: part of Bulgakov's story is a fictionalized enactment of Christ's last day on earth, containing, among other things, a lengthy theological/philosophical debate with Pontius Pilate.

The Bulgakov example that I have analyzed here shows two things:

1 The occurrence of a linguistic anomaly (such as a verbal past tense, combined with a future time adverbial) can only be explained by reference to a larger frame of narration, in which such a combination makes sense. This is the 'readerly', pragmatic interpretation of the difficulty.
2 While the occurrence of a particular linguistic form is not sufficient, by itself, to make the correct inferences ('Riffaterre's principle'), linguistic forms are certainly a much-needed help in the analysis of a text's pragmatic content. The Russian text contains more clues in this respect than does the English translation I have quoted (the insufficiencies of which we would be tempted to attribute to a faulty understanding of the workings of the Russian verb system, if it weren't for the fact that the translator is a native-born Russian).[100]

Let us now have a look at how textual understanding works in the totality of contextual conditions that are often gathered under the general heading of 'discourse'.

9.3.3 Discourse

In section 7.2.3.3, discourse was defined as "the ensemble of phenomena in and through which social production of meaning takes place" (Mumby and Stohl

1991:315). Since a text is a typical social product, created by users in an environment of socially determined conditions, discourse looms large in all textual interpretation. The "ensemble of phenomena" referred to here is what I call the *universe of discourse*; it comprises, but not exclusively, the textual phenomena usually dealt with in logic or linguistics. It follows that linguistic and logical considerations have no claim to textual priority, and hence never will take interpretive precedence over, or go beyond, the mechanisms of discourse. The present section illustrates this aspect of text interpretation by appealing to our understanding of 'incorrect', 'illogical', 'impossible' or even 'counter-textual' phenomena occurring in a text.

Generally, on entering the world of a novel or a play, we deliver ourselves into the hands of the author, who is going to act as our cicerone through the textual maze (Mey 1994d). Reading is always a gamble: you trust the author to deliver a story that may or may not interest you; luckily, the odds are usually restricted to a couple of hours lost to an uninteresting or even boring text.

On the other hand, the discourse aspect of a text is not just a passive one, a reader being (more or less successfully) entertained by an author; on the contrary, the success of the text depends on the reader's active collaboration in creating the textual universe (Mey 1995). The reader is party to the textual discourse as much as is the author: only in the meeting of their 'heads' (using Byatt's earlier quoted expression; 1996:214) will the real story be successfully delivered and see the light of day.

How does the reader go about this process of (self-)activation? The key word here is *credibility*: the writer has to establish a universe of discourse that the reader is willing to accept on the author's 'authority'; that authority in its turn is dependent on how skillfully the author manages to arrange the events and persons she or he is depicting, and how cleverly she or he manages to assign the characters their proper 'voices' (on this, see the next section). Let me give an example.

In William Faulkner's short novel *As I Lay Dying* (1964, originally 1930), the main character is an old woman, Addie Bundren, who at the time of the novel's beginning has been dying for several days. The novel tells the story of how her relatives and neighbors comply with her last wish: to be buried at her birthplace, in the county of Jefferson, Southwestern Mississippi ("I made Anse promise to take me back to Jefferson when I died"; p. 165 in the 1964 edition). Doing this involves their undertaking a journey of around sixty miles, taking place under the most adverse conditions imaginable: swollen rivers, submerged bridges, drowned mules, an unwanted pregnancy, a broken leg, a barn set on fire, and so on – all this while maneuvering a mule-drawn cart with a coffin on top, containing Addie's slowly decaying corpse.

But the story is not only *about* Addie: she *participates* in it, both through the pull she exerts on her family, who have to brave incredible hardships and near-insurmountable obstacles in order to fulfill her exorbitant last wish, and through the physical presence of her dead body, which in a way is the chief protagonist of *As I Lay Dying*.

The unexpected course of events connected with Addie's ultimate odyssey, her 'going back to her roots', culminates in chapter 40 of the book (called 'Addie'), where the corpse suddenly is given a voice in the form of a monologue, containing a kind of confession-cum-apology. This chapter is essential for our understanding of Addie's bitter life and joyless marriage, as it leads up to her dying and being buried (or should we say: finally exorcised?) in safe territory. What's more, it is a necessary ingredient of the story as such: without it, our readerly understanding would be greatly impaired.

Faulkner's unlikely description of a person holding forth over nearly eight printed pages (pp. 161–8), five days after her death, has been remarked by many critics as lacking in 'verisimilitude' (thus Bleikasten 1973:54). However, to put it this way would run counter to the understanding that we have of Addie Bundren, as it has been built up through the successive chapters, leading us up to a point where her entrance on the scene is quite natural, in fact expected. Her "talking body" is not likely to "scandal[ize]" (Felman's expression; 1980) any of the readers, at least no more than the thoughts expressed by the deceased would have scandalized the participants in this rural drama, had they had access to them.

The universe of discourse that has been erected around Addie's corpse is symbolized by the coffin that one of her sons, Cash, is making for her while she still is alive ("hammering and sawing on that goddamn box", p. 14). This coffin, the sounds of whose manufacturing punctuate the initial chapters of the book, serves as a home-made scaffolding, a rustic throne, from which the defunct matriarch finally, after a lifetime of enforced silence, can address the readership (and implicitly, her faithful but confused relatives). Moreover, she *needs* to do this, since the story wouldn't make sense to us unless we knew what is behind her remarkable request for post-mortem relocation: Addie's alienation, her feeling of having been a stranger to her family all her life, and her wish to punish her husband Anse for being the unintelligent, devious, inflated, self-centered and loveless man ("Anse. Why Anse. Why are you Anse"; p. 165) that the development of the story shows him to be. In addition, Addie's indirect confession of her marital infidelity, a secret she takes with her into the grave, has to be interred, not in a foreign graveyard, where the 'stones might speak' (cf. Luke 19:40), but in the safe environment of her home county, where the earth is loyal to its own offspring. "And then I could get ready to die" (p. 168).

Thus, the pragmatically oriented reader is both able, and forced, to live with the lack of verisimilitude that the voicing of a dead person normally entails. It's a bit like what happens in the world of fairy tales: nobody takes offense at a talking fox, or a puss in boots. And even in the 'normal' world of telling tales, that of the time-honored novel and other 'straight' forms of literature, we do not take umbrage at the omniscience of an author – a person whom we in normal life might not trust to tell us the exact time. In the same vein, we accept the author's ability to wake up the dead, to make the past life speak. Using Donne's beautiful conceit, Addie's "eloquent blood spoke through her cheekes", and the competent reader will agree with Faulkner's illustrious predecessor "that one might almost say, her body thought" (Donne 1958:258).[101]

Our knowledge about what can happen in narrative is conditioned by our pragmatic (including cultural and social) presuppositions, as well as by the particular 'contract' that we enter into upon opening a novel. Just as the time of the narrative event need not coincide either with real time, or with time as it proceeds, in orderly fashion, through our lives, so the levels of the narration need not coincide with those of reality. The following may serve as an illustration.

Above, in section 9.2, I mentioned the case of Breta, the granddaughter of Eulália, another matriarch who, in the very first pages of Piñon's book, is depicted as approaching death. The old gentlewoman's gradual demise is protracted until the very end of the novel (1989:615); in between, we have been exposed to innumerable flashbacks, remembrances, and different 'points of view' (on which more in the next section) – indeed of changes in the narrative progression in its entirety. Nothing of this is likely to embarrass the modern reader, who has been trained to hold on to the thread of a narrative despite many hitches and near-breaks. As to the character Breta, there is a clear distinction between the things she says in her own voice, such as the novel's last sentence: "I only know that tomorrow I will start to write the story of Madruga" (p. 663), and the actions that are attributed to her in the narrator's voice, such as: "Breta grew tired. She threw off the sheet and went to the window" (p. 647), or the things that are said about her by others, such as when Eulália asks Breta's mother: "And where is Breta?"; "In school, happily. I need to be alone" (p. 653).

Confronted with passages like these, readers are guided in their interpretation by asking themselves the all-important question: 'Whose voice is it we are hearing?' The next section will deal with this question (and its possible answers) in detail.

9.4 Voice and 'point of view'

As we have seen, readerly control of the narration's vagaries is sustained though a variety of devices, some of which are linguistic, while others belong to the domain of what one could call 'reader pragmatics'. Among the latter, there is one that stands out by its importance and frequent use: the contextual phenomenon I will call *voice*. (A similar notion was recognized by the French narratologist Gérard Genette (1980) as 'focalization'; by others also called 'point of view').[102] Despite its importance for the analysis and understanding of text, 'voice' and its related contextual concepts have found no accepted place in the deliberations of those pragmatically oriented researchers who hail from various linguistic backgrounds: in most cases, their span of attention is limited by the purely grammatical, co-textual phenomena.[103]

In the traditional view of narration, authors create a text by inventing some characters, who then proceed to act out some sequences of events, called 'stories'. The characters are the author's 'creatures': we attribute the creational origin of a particular character (e.g., Huckleberry Finn) to its creator, a particular author (here: Samuel Clement, a.k.a. Mark Twain). It is essential for the author (as it is for any decent creator) that his or her creatures stay in line and do not transgress the boundaries of the story or of the parts they have been assigned in the play; in particular, the characters should preferably stick to their authorized roles.

However, characters do not always 'behave'. Authors frequently complain that their *personae* assume independent lives and voices, and that the plot starts to develop by an inner logic of its own, with the author as a bemused spectator on the sidelines, following the antics of his or her creatures and chronicling them as best he or she can. In extreme cases, the characters may confront the author with their demands and enter onto the stage by themselves, as real, live persons, as has been immortalized in the famous play by Luigi Pirandello, *Six Characters in Search of an Author* (cf. Mey 1994d).

My use of the stage image is more than a facile illustration. It serves to highlight some of the points that I have been trying to make with regard to the process of narration. A stage play basically consists of characters speaking in the *voices* that have been assigned them by the playwright. These voices are used in the context of an actual setting, that is, a context created by the physical stage, by the director's interpretation of the text, but most of all, by the wider ambience of the literary playhouse and its temporary inhabitants, the audience, the latter representing the broader context of society.[104]

The process by which (theatrical or literary) voices are created is called *voicing*. The voices appearing on the scene are embodied in the *dramatis personae*, originally 'personified' by the masks worn in the classical theatre (as the word indicates: *persona* is Latin for 'mask'). Voices are made possible within the *universe of discourse*, that is, they neither represent independently created roles, to be played at will as exponents of the actor's self-expression, nor are they strictly grammatically produced and semantically defined units, to be interpreted by linguists and text analysts according to the rules of grammar. Rather, voices have to be understood in an interactive process of ongoing collaboration between all the parties involved. It is this *contextual cooperation* that the process of 'voicing', in the final analysis, presupposes and represents.

Consider the following extract from Tolstoy's *Anna Karenina*:

(*Levin has just blurted out his proposal to marry Kitty, and feels he has been rejected by her uttering:*)

– Ètogo ne možet byt' . . . prostite menja . . .

Kak za minutu tomu nazad ona byla blizka emu, kak važna dlja ego žizni! I kak teper' ona stala čužda i daleka emu!

– Èto ne moglo byt' inače. – skazal on, ne gljadja na nee.
On poklonilsja i xotel ujti.

("This cannot be . . . Forgive me . . ." A minute earlier, how close she had been
to him, how important for his life! And now, how aloof to him and distant
she had become! "This could not have been otherwise", he said, without
looking at her. He bowed and prepared to leave.) (Tolstoy 1962:57, my
translation)

In the above extract, the reflections on the contrast between 'closeness' and 'distance' that are sandwiched in between the two pieces of dialogue (attributed to
Kitty and Levin, respectively) are not ascribed to either of the characters by any
explicit device, linguistic or otherwise. The preceding context has directed our
attention to Levin's doubts and anxieties about proposing to Kitty, and how the
outcome of the proposal would affect the rest of his life. Though by nature a
timid person, Levin has decided to wager everything, to put all his spiritual energy
into one decisive move. When things go terribly wrong, we instantly recognize
the voice of the reflecting character as Levin's. Thus, on reading the indirectly
'quoted' commentary on what has happened ("A minute earlier, how close she
had been to him, how important for his life! And now, how aloof to him and
distant she had become!"), the reader understands these reflections as being
'uttered' in Levin's voice by considering the content of what is reflected upon.
Similarly, it is Levin's inner voice that utters the words "A minute earlier . . .",
depicting, in what is usually called 'free indirect discourse', the horrible contrast
between the situation just a moment ago and the present point of time – just as
some of us remember the wistful comment on a lost love from Paul McCartney's
famous song *Yesterday*:

> Yesterday
> Love seemed such an easy game to play.

We see how successful voicing depends on the interplay of the agents in the
narrative process, narrator and 'narratee' in concert making up the successful
narration. In the following, I will illustrate the crucial role of 'voice' in a pragmatic approach to text by showing the interplay of voices, as it is acted out in
another contemporary novel.

Going back to the story of Breta, as told by Nélida Piñon in *The Republic of
Dreams*, let's try to come to grips with the rather confused and complex narrative structure that this book deploys. Whereas in the Faulkner novel, the various
voices are distinctly marked by having their names affixed to the top of the
chapter in which they appear ('Cash' heads the chapter attributed to his voice,
'Addie' the one in which she appears as the speaking 'I', and so on),[105] in Piñon's
story the readers are more or less on their own when it comes to figuring out
whose voices are being heard.

The parallelisms between the two stories are obvious, as are their differences. Not only do we again have a dying grandmother (corresponding to Addie's dead *persona* in Faulkner's story), surrounded by a whole gallery of living and dead persons, all related, or otherwise belonging, to the extended nuclear family founded by grandfather Madruga and grandmother Eulália upon arriving in Brazil from Galicia. But in contrast to Addie's, Eulália's death is not a single event: it is protracted throughout the story, featuring flashbacks to Eulália's earlier existence in various parts of her home country and in Brazil. Also, compared to Faulkner's heroine (who actually dies at the very beginning of the story), Piñon's Eulália is both alive and dying all through the book. Her actual death is mentioned in passing, a little bit off-hand, towards the end of the story ("After Eulália's death . . ."; "Grandmother left us quietly, without making a great show of it, a week later than the time she had stipulated"; p. 648); earlier, Eulália's death had only been implicitly referred to (such as on p. 619 by her being "placed inside [her] red and black casket").

In addition, we meet a host of other characters from the family album, popping in and out of the narrative, each with her or his own 'point of view' and 'voiced' contributions: Madruga, the patriarch-grandfather and husband of Eulália; the various second-generation sons and daughters; the grandchildren; friends of the house; servants; and so on. In addition, as is usual in Latin American fiction nowadays, some of these persons appear both in real life and as ghosts, in their actual lives and after their deaths; furthermore, there are important revelations contained in a half-crazed old family friend's diary and in a secret box kept by Esperança, Breta's mother. To tease out all these happenings and threads of events is no mean task; if the reader did not have a way of perceiving how the different voices interact, Piñon's labyrinthine prose would be totally impenetrable. It is here that the notion of 'voice', understood as: the verbal expression of a particular character's role, can be shown to have decisive weight.

In the following, I will sketch out in more detail how a particular character, the granddaughter Breta, is being given different 'voices'. I will use the commonly used (here slightly modified) narrative schema that has been popular among various authors following the publication in 1972 of Genette's seminal work *Narrative Discourse* (Genette 1980).

First of all, we have the *author*, Nélida Piñon, who is responsible for the literary work as such. She speaks to us indirectly, as it were, as a *narrator*, through the device of story-telling. As the 'narrative instance' in charge, she has all the attributes that we ordinarily associate with a story-teller: omnipotence, omniscience (specifically, knowledge of what goes on in the heads and 'inner sancta' of the persons described), omnipresence and so on. In this narrative, as is usual, the narrator remains *implicit* (see Mey 1999:ch. 8.4.2): we are told that "Eulália had started to die on Tuesday" (the opening sentence of the book; p. 3), but no official, *explicit* 'sender' of this message is provided. The *voice* we are hearing is the voice of the narrator, not that of the author: the latter only speaks to us through the former.

Similarly, we are introduced to Breta as Eulália's granddaughter by the same implicit narrative voice (p. 14: "Eulália watched them [the grandchildren coming into her room to say goodbye].... Eulália noted Breta's presence.... She had always handed over this granddaughter to her husband").

Later on in the book, some of the *character*s tend to become narrators in their own rights. This starts already a couple of pages down from the previous quotation, where the grandfather introduces himself as a narrator by saying: "The story of Breta, and of this family, began at my birth" (p. 16). As to Breta herself, she assumes her role as a first person narrator on p. 66, with the words: "When I was a little girl, Grandfather surprised me with presents and unexpected proposals."

These continuous shifts between 'heterodiegetic' (or third person) and 'homodiegetic' (first person) narration are characteristic of this particular novel; but in order to pin down the 'I' of a particular piece of homodiegetic narrative, we not only have to invoke the grammatical or linguistic resources at our command, but in addition, we have to enter the 'fictional world' (Mey 1994d), the world of narration, by identifying with the particular voice that is speaking. For instance, in the case of Madruga, the grandfather, introducing himself as an 'I' on p. 16, we are at first uncertain whom the narrative voice belongs to: Eulália (who also has been present throughout the preceding section) or Madruga, her husband. As we read on, it turns out that the voice is that of a boy: his passion for fishing, his burgeoning attraction to women, all bespeak the gender of the young Madruga.

When, toward the end of the book, after many allusions to her future role as a family chronicler (e.g., on p. 17, where her grandfather muses: "What if she were to be the first writer in the family?"), Breta 'comes out' as an author ("I will write the book nonetheless"; p. 662), it is the voice of Breta, as a *character turned narrator*, telling us this. And when we close the book on the last sentence ("I only know that tomorrow I will start to write the story of Madruga"; p. 663), we are in the presence of a narrative voice that tells us that what the Breta character is going to do as an *author* is to write the story, parts of which she has just told us in her own, character-turned-narrator's voice. By this narratorial trick, Breta the presumptive author hands back the narrative relay to the actual author who has created her, Nélida Piñon, thus closing the narrative score on a final, impressive flourish.

It is only through an active, collaborative effort, shared between reader and author, that this interplay of voices can be successfully created and recreated. The question naturally arises of whether it would not be reasonable to assign a 'voice' to the reader as well, and what implications this assumption would have. I will deal with this question in the next section. (For a comprehensive treatment of the problems of 'voice', see Mey 1999.)

9.5   Reading as a pragmatic act

The notion that there is power in words, and that among our words certain are more powerful than others, is not new; in fact, it is at the basis of some very old and fundamental beliefs about language being an instrument of force. The priests of Old India and Rome carefully guarded the verbal expressions of their ancient rituals, out of fear that mispronouncing them might result in nullifying their force.

Perhaps acting on a similar (mis)apprehension, modern philosophers and linguists have tried to capture the notion of 'power in words' by creating the concept of 'speech act' as representative of a particular, so-called 'illocutionary force': that is, a power thought of as residing 'in' certain well-defined words and (il)locutions. Examples are the force inherent in formulaic expressions such as "I pronounce thee man and wife", or in the formulas used by people in everyday language when making commitments, statements, promises, predictions, and so on, using the appropriate, recognized language for each particular purpose. (Details were given in section 5.1.3.)

Like all verbal expressions, what such speech acts need, in order to be valid, is a proper *context*: considered or spoken by itself, no speech act makes any sense. Conversely, we have a wide variety of linguistic expressions that, given the proper context, all may serve to express the point that the speech act utterer is trying to make. I can express a promise in dozens of different (direct or indirect) ways (cf. sections 5.2, 5.4); and even the humblest speech act in narrative, the 'parenthetical' *inquit* ('he or she said'), can be varied *ad libitum*, an art which some authors have practiced with great versatility and sometimes exaggeration.[106]

As I intimated in the previous chapter, the theory of *pragmatic acts* may take this thinking several steps further. If the context is so important for our pragmatic understanding of an utterance, as I argued in section 8.4.3, can we then not say that it not only is an important, but *the* most important, element of our dealings with language, and through language with the world? After all, our linguistic acting is part of our overall human activity; we act in concerted co-operation with other humans, in their co-presence and in the co- and con-texts of word and world. Basic to pragmatic acts (as distinguished from speech acts) is the fact that the former (as opposed to the latter) depend not so much on the actual words being used as on the circumstances that lead up to, and accompany, those words. For this reason, by embracing the notion of 'pragmatic act' one does not have to do away with speech acts; one merely emphasizes the fact that as such, i.e., out of context, speech acts are not valid instruments of action. Conversely, a particular choice of words may not even be necessary or substantial for effective action, as the examples of pragmatic acts of advertising have shown. Here are some further examples of how the contextual conditions are instrumental in helping us read a text, by allowing us to co-create a particular pragmatic act.

A recent advertisement for a Brazilian brand of milk, called 'Parmalat', shows a picture of a baby clutching a carton of Parmalat milk, while dressed up as a 'little prince' à la Saint-Exupéry, and uttering the words: 'You have never seen a king cry. But you will, if you don't stop ravishing the Amazonas.' Neither the picture nor the text has anything to do with milk as such, and not even the word *Leite* ('milk') on the carton can be made out clearly. The actual wording (if one can call it that) of the advertisement is printed so small and unobtrusively that it escapes one's attention at the first couple of readings ('Parmalat. Because we are mammals': *Veja*, Special Issue: *Amazônia, um tesouro ameaçado*, São Paulo, December 24, 1997). Similarly, a picture of a Carlsberg beer truck making its way up a road in the Grand Tetons is as much an advertisement for that brand of beer as would be an explicit invitation to take home a six-pack. Many readers will also recall the famous (some would say: infamous) 'United Colors of Benetton' advertisements of a decade ago, in which socially sensitive issues (poverty, racial segregation, undernourishment, even AIDS) were used as back-drops for the brand name.

The reason that displaying such minimally worded pictures can function as pragmatic acts of advertising is that they are 'set up' (see section 8.3.2) as ads by the environments in which they normally occur. An advertisement is what we expect to see on billboards, as displays in magazines, on posters etc. Moreover, since the names identifying the advertised products (Parmalat, Carlsberg, Benetton) are known as the names of particular brands (of milk, beer, clothing), the omission of any overt message of invitation, exhortation, instruction, admonition etc. is warranted: given the brand name, an act of advertising is expected.[107]

Generalizing from this premise, we can further say that given the correct circumstances, pragmatic acts are *pre-defined*: a pragmatic act is a kind of self-fulfilling promise, threat, excuse or what have you, the exact nature of the act depending on the circumstances, the 'setting-up', that the context does for us.

The next question is how to apply the concept of 'pragmatic act' in the context of *reading*. Here, I can only deal with this question in a general way; the specifically *textual* implications of reading, viewed as a pragmatic act, are discussed elsewhere (Mey 1999:ch. 10.4.2). If it is true that: "Upon entering the fictional space, the readers more or less resign their autonomy and follow the instructions of its creator, the author, as the textual authority is suitably designed" (Mey 1994d:154–5), it is also the case that successful reading depends on the readers' willingness to accept their share of the text work, on their ability to take their proper seats in the fictional theater, to become true *lectores in fabula* (Eco 1979). The readers' ability to do this, however, depends to a great extent on an author's ability to create this theater, to give the readers a possibility to assume their stance in the fictional space; it is in this 'setting up' of the readers that the pragmatic character of the act of reading becomes all-important.

Consider the following excerpt from Virginia Woolf's novel *Jacob's Room*:

(Jacob Flanders, his painter friend Edward ('Ted') Cruttendon and Jinny Carslake, an English girl who is living with the latter, are sitting at a table outside a little café in Versailles, having drinks.)

"But he's quite different," said Jinny, folding her hands over the top of her glass. "I don't suppose you know what Ted means when he says a thing like that," she said, looking at Jacob. "But I do. Sometimes I could kill myself. Sometimes he lies in bed all day long – just lies there . . . I don't want you right on the table"; she waved her hands. Swollen iridescent pigeons were waddling round their feet.

"Look at that woman's hat," said Cruttendon. "How do they come to think of it? . . . No, Flanders, I don't think I could live like you. When one walks down that street opposite the British Museum – what's it called – that's what I mean. It's all like that. Those fat women – and the man standing in the middle of the road as if he were going to have a fit . . ."

"Everybody feeds them," said Jinny, waving the pigeons away. "They're stupid old things."

"Well, I don't know," said Jacob, smoking his cigarette. "There's St. Paul's."

"I mean going to an office," said Cruttendon.

"Hang it all," Jacob expostulated. (Woolf 1978:129)

The linguistic competence of a reader is commonly understood as comprising the ability to assign the correct reference to textual elements such as pronouns, deictics, subjects of verbs and so on. Various rules of language usage serve as auxiliary devices in our exercise of this competence. One of these is the existence of a 'normal' word order (subjects occur before verbs in English, adjectives before nouns, and so on); another is the fact that pronouns usually occur in close proximity to their referents. Yet another technique that we rely on heavily for solving textual riddles is that of conversational implicature, as we have seen in section 3.2.3. Finally, in any normal text we may expect a certain syntactic and semantic continuity that encourages us to stick with an interpretation, once adopted (this is often referred to as the 'obstinacy principle'; Fludernik 1993:285).

In the excerpt above, grammatical and syntactic 'props' of the kind described are not of much help: they are either absent or ambiguous. For example, how do we know who Jinny is talking to when she says "I don't want you right on the table"? Clearly, it cannot be Jacob, even though he is the most suitable immediately preceding candidate, grammatically and co-textually. Similarly, the "them" in Jinny's next contribution to the conversation ("Everybody feeds them") cannot possibly be the head of the immediately preceding, grammatically and co-textually closest accessible noun phrase, "Those fat women . . .". By contrast, we are not in doubt as to the reference of "that woman", even though no particular woman has been explicitly mentioned or is present (with the exception of Jinny); or as to what Cruttendon refers to by "it", or who are meant by "they" in his remark "How do they come to think of it?" In the general context (rather than in the restricted co-text), we know what to expect and what to exclude, even without the usual support of strict pronominal reference and anaphora.

The contextual mechanisms by which such expectations and exclusions are governed constitute what I have called the 'setting-up' that is required as part of a pragmatic act. In our case, it is the entire pictured backdrop that functions as the set-up: a café in a by-street in a French provincial town, "where people sit drinking coffee, watching the soldiers, meditatively knocking ashes into trays" (p. 129). Whoever has been in a scene like this will also remember the ubiquitous pigeons "waddling round" the feet of the patrons, sometimes attempting to snatch a crumb of cake or a piece of bread from the tables; the town women parading the streets in impossible hats; and all the rest of a typical French small town, Sunday afternoon scenario.

It is on this scene that the protagonists become alive, and their speech and actions achieve meaning: the men engaged in philosophizing; the women trying to make sense of their lives and relationships by talking about them. In between these strands of dialogue, the references to the general framework, the 'backdrop', of the story serve to set up the acts of talk. The coherence of the conversation is not just a matter of thematic consistency (in fact, there is precious little of that, as in most conversations); in order to understand what is going on in the talk, we must take the whole scene into account.

Reading Woolf's dialogue is thus possible only if we read and understand the actual scene; in fact, the dialogue would not have made any sense unless we had been 'pre-set' for the various snatches of talk by entering the scene ourselves and becoming acquainted with its various inhabitants. When the referent of "you" in Jinny's remark is formally identified as a pigeon, we as readers had already set up a 'pigeon-hole' for it in our minds. When Jinny says "them", we know what she is talking about, even before she starts "waving the pigeons away". Into the slots of our scenic understanding, the instantiating elements drop like keys into well-oiled locks.

The pragmatic act of reading implies an open-ended invitation to the reader to join the author in the co-creation of the story, by filling in the holes that the text leaves open. Just as the 'said', the speaker's explicit verbal act, in many cases is dispensable, given a sufficient backdrop and the listener's pragmatic act of understanding the 'unsaid', so the reader's act of understanding is not dependent on what is found in the actual text (or co-text) in so many words, but on the total context in which those words are found – and are found to make sense, through an active, pragmatic collaboration between author and reader. It is this spontaneous, mostly unconscious 'plugging' of the textual gaps that characterizes us as competent and 'versatile' readers (see Tsur 1992: Mey 1999:ch. 9.1.2); conversely, this characteristic carries with it an obligation on the part of the author to offer us a readable, 'pluggable' text. Needless to say, 'pluggability' is always relative: modern authors like Paul Auster or Don Delillo differ quite a bit in this respect from, say, Jane Austen or William Thackeray; similarly, the 'retardation' of the narrative that characterizes Homer's epic poetry, where everything is told and no gaps are left unplugged, was already remarked on by Schiller and Goethe in their early correspondence (Auerbach 1998:19).

In reading, as in other pragmatic acting, it is the general contextual conditions and presuppositions that make any understanding (literary or otherwise) possible. Naturally, these conditions, inasmuch as they represent the constraints of society, will manifest themselves differently in different social and cultural settings. The next chapter will deal with these cross-cultural differences in some detail.

Review and discussion

1. A popular 1940s tune ran:

> Open the door, Richard,
> Open the door, Richard,
> [percussion rolls to imitate knock-knock-knocking]
> Richard, why don't you open that door?

According to English grammar rules, the pronoun *that* (as opposed to *this*) refers to something which is removed from the addresser and close to the addressee.

Questions:
Will this explanation be satisfactory when explaining the deictic element *that* in the song above?

What does *that* refer to? (Clearly a door, but what kind of)?

How does *that* exercise its deictic potential? (Hint: look for the possible context that this element can occur in.)

What if the songwriter had chosen *this*, rather than *that*? Wherein would the difference mainly lie? (Hint: does *this* have contextual functions similar to (or even the same as) *that*?)

What is this kind of deixis often called? (Refer to chapter 3.)

2. The passage below contains the opening paragraphs of Bruce Chatwin's short novel *Utz* (London: Chatto and Windus, 1988):

> An hour before dawn on March 7th, 1974, Kaspar Joachim Utz died of a second and long-expected stroke, in his apartment at No. 5, Široká Street, overlooking the Old Jewish cemetery in Prague.

Three days later, at 7.45 a.m., his friend Dr Václav Orlík was standing outside the Church of St Sigismund, awaiting the arrival of the hearse and clutching seven of the ten pink carnations he had hoped to afford at the florist's. He noted with approval the first signs of spring. In a garden across the street, jackdaws with twigs in their beaks were wheeling above the lindens, and now and then a minor avalanche would slide from the pantiled roof of a tenement.

While Orlík waited, he was approached by a man with a curtain of gray hair that fell below the collar of his raincoat.

'Do you play the organ?' the man asked in a catarrhal voice.

'I fear not,' said Orlík.

'Nor do I,' the man said, and shuffled off down a side-street.

Questions:
Since this is the beginning of a story, we expect to be immediately introduced to the main character. How is this done in the text? How are the side characters introduced? (Hint: notice especially the difference between the two introductions in the second and third paragraph. Speculate about the reason why the latter character is introduced in a more elaborate manner than the former.)

Deictic elements are found in plenty throughout the excerpt. Identify them and their functions.

What types of deictics do you find and how are they different as to function (pronouns, articles, demonstratives etc.)?

Given that this extract covers a little over one page out of a book of 154, one cannot expect to learn too much about the characters from what is actually given as the immediate co-text.

Show how our understanding ('shared knowledge') of the entire context in which this story is set contributes to our understanding. (For instance, we all know what a funeral is like, even if it happens in Prague rather than in our own hometown. From this contextual knowledge, we can make certain inferences about the occurrence of a textual item such as 'the organ' in the interchange between Dr Orlík and 'the man'.)

3. Consider the following dialogue:

A: She's the type to take control, show strength and affirmation.
B: Actually she falls apart. She fell apart when her mother died.
A: Who wouldn't?
B: She fell apart when Steffie called from camp with a broken bone in her hand . . .
A: Her daughter, far away, among strangers, in pain. Who wouldn't?
B: Not her daughter. My daughter.
A: Not *even* her daughter.
B: No.

A: Extraordinary. I have to love it. (Don Delillo, *White Noise*, New York: Viking/Penguin, 1986, pp. 19–20; my emphasis)

Since this dialogue is part of a story (in which 'A' and 'B' are some of the characters), one may surmise that the interchange is coherent, that is, makes sense in that wider context.

On the other hand, one could focus on the strict local cohesion of the dialogue and ask how it is constructed.

Questions:
Referring back to section 6.3.3.1, examine this extract for cohesion, indicating where and how the co-text creates the fabric that keeps the interchanges together.

The text should also be compared with the sample of schizophrenic discourse given in section 6.3.3.1. That text, though passing the 'cohesion test', is not coherent. How does the present text rank in relation to coherence? What is typical of the coherence in this particular dialogue? (Hint: look at A's attitude towards the character referred to as 'she', compared with B's.)

From the wider context of the novel (and implicit in the co-text as given here), it appears that B is the husband of 'she', while A is more or less secretly in love with her. Would this knowledge in any way affect your analysis of the excerpt's coherence? Whose daughter is the girl at camp? Is B really ignorant of this fact? How would you argue?

What makes for the final 'knockout' effect (clearly demonstrated in A's 'even')? Who is the winner of this dialogic game of chess?

4. *Adam in the garden*

During the election campaign of 1970, incumbent Congressman Adam Clayton Powell, Jr, of the 18th Congressional District, was giving a press conference outside his opponent's headquarters at 135th Street and 7th Avenue in Harlem, New York.

A heckler interrupted him, asking him if he was going to be present at the narcotics parade to be held the following Saturday, "like he'd promised". To which Powell replied that of course, nothing would keep him from attending.

A moment later, the heckler interrupted again, wanting to make absolutely sure that the Congressman would be present at the parade. Powell, visibly irritated, reiterated his assurance, and went on with his speech.

The heckler then intervened a third time, stating that "Well, Mr. Powell, sir, you ain't gonna be at that parade, 'cause there ain't gonna be one and we never spoke of one". (*Harper's Magazine*, April 1971)

The technique developed by the heckler in this extract is often called that of the 'garden path': leading an unsuspecting listener (or reader) into a verbal trap, which is then sprung at the crucial moment. Sometimes (as in the case above) this is done with the intention of making a fool of the listener and humiliating him or her publicly; in other cases (often in a literary context), the idea is to jolt the reader and obtain some kind of narrative 'shock effect'. (Refer to section 4.2.2.3, where I mention a classic example: Julio Cortázar's 'spider story'; see also Mey 1992b.) The reader or listener must go along the path with his or her 'seducer', the heckler or story-teller; otherwise the trap at the end of the path will remain unsprung, and no 'garden path' effect is obtained. Thus, the necessity of an active cooperation by listener and reader in the pragmatic act of understanding (in the broadest sense) becomes clear.

On the background of the above, answer the following.

Questions:
Which speech acts can you identify in this interchange? How can they be said to be subsumed under some textual 'pragmeme(s)' (and which)?

Is there a way back from a 'garden path'? Can you indicate an alternative path, an escape route or a loophole?

In the extract above, where did the Congressman go wrong?

What should he have said instead of what he actually did? Were there alternative speech acts that he could have used, while staying within the original pragmatic situation (possibly described as: 'gaining support for his candidacy')?

In all this, does the Cooperative Principle apply? How? (Refer to chapter 4.)

5. Story time and real time
In the British-Japanese author's Kazuo Ishiguro's *The Unconsoled* (1996), we meet a hotel porter by the name of Gustav, who in the course of his duties takes a late-arriving guest to his room, and in the process harangues him about the life and duties of a porter according to Gustav.

The monologue takes place while the hotel elevator moves up four floors; however, the 'transcript' of Gustav's discourse fills over three pages in the novel. At no point of time is there a mention of an elevator stop, or some other pause in the guest's trek to his room, something which could explain the strange lack of congruence between the time things take in the reality of the story (in 'story time'), and the time those same things are standardly allotted outside of the narration (in 'real time'). In other words, the question is how a person can utter the equivalent of three printed pages (something which, without interruption, would take at least ten minutes) in the amount of time needed to go from a hotel lobby to a room on the fourth floor. We are here confronted with an extreme case of the discrepancy that sometimes holds between what has been called 'speaking time' (or, from the point of the reader, 'reading time') and 'story time' (the time that things take, more or less realistically, in the narrated course of events; Toolan 1994:49f).

Questions:
Referring back to the Faulkner story excerpted in section 9.3.3, how would you judge this lack of temporal 'verisimilitude' (which of course could be complemented by a lack of similar verisimilitude on the local plan)?

Is there any objective reason for the reader to follow the events of the story in 'real time', as it were?

How would you characterize the cooperative reader in a situation where narrative time and real time don't match up (as in the Ishiguro case)?

How much leeway should a reader give an author?

Discuss this problem from your own experiences as a cooperative, yet pragmatically oriented reader. Think especially of the differences between the above kind of narrative and the classical novel, where time proceeds apace with the action (or if it doesn't, one is at least given some temporal guidance in the form of a remark such as 'It is now five years later . . .', or some other such helpful instruction, preferably at the beginning of each new chapter).

Are you familiar with any modern literary works that do not respect 'real time', in the sense discussed above, and at the most construct one or several small textual universes in which events are minimally cohesive, time-wise? (Hint: think of Proust, Joyce; see further Mey 1998.)

6. Truth and fiction and their consequences
Discussing the ways in which the press characterizes certain politicians, depending on the way their political fortunes change, Michael Toolan has remarked on the pragmatically versatile reader's need to 'control' the correspondences between story reality and the outside world. For instance, Boris Yeltsin as the mayor of Moscow used to be the press's pet version of a politico, whose frequent visits to the city's gutters were the *risée* of the educated Western world. After his stand-off against the putschists in 1993 and his subsequent (re)turn to power, he was hailed as a wise, elderly statesman of great personal courage and insight, a picture that despite his many relapses into alcoholism has not substantially changed in the eyes of the international press. Similarly, Gerry Adams used to be a senseless Irish nationalist and IRA-connected terrorist; but the moment he became a key player in the talks about ending domestic strife in Northern Ireland, he was suddenly accepted as what he probably had been all the time, in both his own and many of his fellow countrymen's eyes: a serious political worker striving to attain better conditions for his people.

Consider now the following quotation by Toolan (here slightly modified) and say whether or not you agree with his view of these differences, and why.

If [Yeltsin or Adams] were character[s] in a novel, such drastic shifts in presentation [would be regarded] as reflecting a grossly unreliable, if not incompetent narrator who doesn't seem to know his own story. But this is one major way in which press narratives differ from literary ones. Unlike a literary narrative, press narratives are never 'finished': there is always tomorrow's edition, which may have to assimilate new and awkward events, even to the extent of revising the newspaper's background construction of events. . . . Reading newspapers for the truth is in part at least a bit like religious belief – an act of faith. (Toolan 1994:237–8)

7. A voice from the grave?

André Bleikasten, in his study of William Faulkner's *As I Lay Dying* (1964, originally 1930), comments on the deceased matriarch Addie Bundren's appearing on the novelistic scene after her death as follows:

Addie's confession, crucial as it is to an understanding of the book, is quite unwarranted from the point of view of verisimilitude, since, when she starts to speak, Addie has been dead for five days. Not only has her monologue no immediate local connection with the current action but also there is no way of locating it in space and time. The voice we hear in it is timeless and bodiless, conjured up by the author's necromancy. (1973:54)

Elsewhere, Bleikasten mentions the concept 'verisimilitude' (see above, section 9.3.3), literally: 'the semblance of truth', as being in conflict with this 'personification'. (108)

Questions:
Discuss the apparent contradiction between a person's being dead and being given a 'voice' in the novel by the author.

In particular, ask yourself whether 'truth' can be enforced as strictly in a narrative context as, e.g., in a courtroom or in a scientific account. (Hint: stress the internal coherence of the narrative, and check whether this is endangered by the Faulkner technique. Refer also back to the notion of 'literary constraint', as explicated in section 7.2.2.4).

What does Bleikasten mean by 'necromancy', and how would you defend Faulkner against such charges?

CHAPTER TEN
Pragmatics Across Cultures

10.1 Introduction: what is the problem?

Suppose you are a newly appointed teacher at the University of Ibadan, Nigeria. Your salary not being that grand, and the general situation in the country being what it is, you decide to get a cheap apartment close to the university, so you can ride your bike to school. However, not being prepared for the state of the local roads, on your first trip you hit a big hole, you and your bike are toppled and your books are all over the pavement.

As you begin to reassemble yourself and your belongings, a friendly local passer-by stops up and says: 'Sorry for that, man.' Whereupon he proceeds on his way, without offering any further comments or help. You are puzzled, to say the least. Why did the guy say he was sorry, when it wasn't his fault in the first place?

Here's another situation, this time from Japan. You and your Japanese girl-friend are having a house-warming party at which you expect a lot of guests. Not to overload the dishwasher, you decide on paper cups to go with the beer and the soft drinks. Your friend and yourself go to the local beer outlet, where the following conversation is heard to occur:

(*Your friend places the order and requests home delivery*)

LIQUOR STORE CLERK: *Nan-ji made ni?* (By what time [do you want the stuff delivered]?')

   YOUR FRIEND: *Goji sanjippun goro.* ('Around 5:30 [p.m.].') *A, ato kami koppu 50-ko onegaishimasu.* ('Oh, and besides [I'd like] 50 paper cups, please.')

CLERK: *1,4800-en desu.* ('That'll be ¥14,800'). *Kami koppu wa saabisu sasete moraimasu.* ('The paper cups are on the house [lit.: are being offered as a service].')
→FRIEND: *A, sumimasen.* ('Oh, I'm sorry'). [Tends the money]
CLERK: *Arigatoo gozaimasu.* ('Thank you very much'). (Kumatoridani 1999:636; adapted)

In the above interchange, we see how the Japanese expression *sumimasen* 'I'm sorry' appears unexpectedly at a point where we in English assume an expression of gratitude to be in order, such as 'Thanks a lot.' Why is it that the Japanese seemingly have to apologize for other people's services rendered, by saying that they are 'sorry for your kindness' (Ide 1998)? It is not that *sumimasen* normally, and taken by itself, expresses thanks; it is widely used to apologize in cases where we in English, too, would use an apology: for instance, when addressing a stranger on the streets of London to ask for directions, one would normally say 'Excuse me . . .' before embarking on business proper.

Similarly, in the Nigerian example, we notice how a passer-by shows his empathy with the unfortunate bicyclist by using an expression which he knows is used in English to render a feeling of commiseration (albeit not always in exactly the same circumstances). The intercultural difference of use here is that uttering 'Sorry' in English often implies that one somehow feels guilty, while this is not necessarily the case in the Nigerian context.

What we are dealing with here is not a matter of what expressions 'mean', abstractly taken, or one of how a speech act such as 'thanking' or 'apologizing' can be defined, in accordance with the standard accounts that we looked at in chapter 5. Rather, the question is one of the *pragmatic* appropriateness of a particular expression in a particular context of use. The problem is that those contexts of use tend to be rather different from culture to culture, and consequently from language to language.

What appears as an apology in Japanese may be considered an elaborate form of thanking, if 'translated' into an English context; however, this may not be the right, or only, explanation. The Japanese may experience the rendering of a service that is not in the line of duty (such as offering paper cups as an unpaid *saabisu* ('service') to a good customer) as necessarily and principally triggering not a 'thanking', but an apology of the kind we have seen above. In fact, the apology pre-empts, or subsumes, the 'thanking', as it were. The basic character of a particular speech act, such as that of apologizing or thanking, is thus seen as culture-dependent; put otherwise, the pragmatic validity of a speech act (as of any other use of language) will vary, when considered in an intercultural perspective.

The next section will look into the pragmatic presuppositions of the problem sketched here.

10.2   Pragmatic presuppositions in culture

That cultural presuppositions can be major stumbling blocks on the road to understanding may sound like a truism; yet, it is often overlooked what these 'presuppositions', in an actual setting, have to say as preconditions to understanding. In
section 5.5.1, we saw how the discussion on the number and kind of SAV (speech
act verbs) suffered a great deal from this oversight, the particular verbs and their
plausibility of occurrence being modeled on whatever the Standard Average European (or North American) finds plausible in his or her culture. One can easily get
people to applaud the idea that probably no language in the world would contain
an SAV expressing the act of 'asking for a quarter to make a phone call to your
maternal grand-uncle' – yet, there is no principled reason why such a verb could
not be found; in any case, the borderlines are not easily drawn.[109]

To shed some light on the pragmatic presuppositions that are hidden beneath
the surface of our cultural varnish, one has to look for those places where the
varnish cracks and the underlying substance becomes visible. In section 5.5, we
encountered some examples of intercultural misunderstandings that were due
to the presence of a non-acknowledged, and hence not shared, pragmatic presupposition (cf. also section 7.2.3.2). Here, I will discuss some further cases from
this angle.

Challenging the presuppositions of an offer or a request is not easily done in
our culture (unless, of course, one wants to ascertain that the speaker is in his or
her right mind – to promise a casual acquaintance the moon or a rose garden is
usually not taken as a serious speech act). The following is a real-life example of
an intercultural misunderstanding based on such different, hence unfamiliar, pragmatic presuppositions; the example (earlier given as exercise 4 in chapter 6) shows
the need to highlight and question such presuppositions in intercultural contacts:

(*A Western tourist visiting a Japanese temple compound addresses a female
attendant*)

TOURIST: Is there a toilet around here?
ATTENDANT: You want to use?
TOURIST (*somewhat astonished*): Sure I do.
ATTENDANT: Go down the steps.

Clearly, the tourist (who happens to be the author of these lines) did not ask
his question because he was conducting a comparative study of toilets, West and
East, or some such thing. In the tourist's own culture, the 'insertion sequence'
'You want to use?' is highly unexpected, under the given circumstances, and
would probably never have occurred in this form.

However, the pragmatic presuppositions in Japanese culture are different;
which is why it made sense for the attendant to ask the question. One could

capture this 'making sense' as the need to ensure that the 'type' of the speech act involved (or, in terms of our discussion in the previous chapter, the nature of the ongoing 'pract') was correctly perceived; the attendant made sure of this by asking a question that would be able to disambiguate the tourist's question as a pre-sequence either to a question about toilets, or to a request to be directed, respectively taken, to the toilet.

Alternatively, and perhaps more plausibly, it could be the case that the attendant wanted to find out whether the tourist's question could have anything to do with the different kinds of toilets that are now available in Japan: 'Japanese' or 'Western' style. Under this assumption, if the tourist wanted to use the toilet himself, he would supposedly have to be directed to another place than if the desired information concerned, e.g., an accompanying Japanese friend. A further dimension of 'pre-sequencing' might have to do with the general distinction between male and female toilets, notoriously difficult to establish in the Japanese context for one who is not familiar with the characters denoting gender in Sino-Japanese script (*kanji*).

As to the incident in question, the attendant, having resolved her presuppositional dilemma by obtaining an appropriate answer to her inserted question: "You want to use?", then decided to direct the tourist to what she thought was the proper place for him, viz., a 'Western-style', male toilet facility.

Cases of this kind occur, of course, also among members of the same culture. The following example is due to Tsui (1991:122):

(Two secretaries meet in the hallway of their common office)

A: Would you like a piece of apple cake?
B: Have you got some?

Normally, in cultures such as ours, inquiring whether a person would like a piece of cake would be equivalent to offering him or her one. Furthermore, this indirect offer of a piece of cake would imply that one has some – otherwise, one would be playing games.[110] Likewise, in certain cultures the fact of inquiring, in a sales context, whether a particular item can be had amounts to ordering that item, as in the case of the Coquilles St Jacques, quoted earlier (section 6.3.2.1).

Tsui's explanation of the presumed oddity is quite regular, and consists simply in revealing the piece of real-world information that we need to, one, understand why the expected speech act of 'accepting' is pre-empted (see section 6.3.2.3), and two, properly deal with the corresponding pragmatic presupposition: "this presupposition was *challenged* because the conversation took place in an office corridor and [A] did not have an apple cake with her" (1991:122–3).

As we see from this example, the pragmatic presuppositions of a dialogue constitute the indispensable link between the spoken words and the world of their users that is needed to form the appropriate pragmatic act.

10.3 Ethnocentricity and its discontents

While most of us will agree that there are differences between peoples and cultures, very few of us are prepared to accept the full consequence of such a view. Often, we hear people say that 'some of my best friends are . . .' (where one may replace the dots by 'Black', 'gay', 'Mexican', 'women' and so on); nearly always, such utterances mask the fact that the speaker really doesn't like whatever the '. . .' stand for, but is duty-bound to deny that implicit dislike by an explicit assertion of the kind I mentioned when I introduced the notion of 'pragmatic act' in section 8.1. Such an approach to the problem of cultural and linguistic diversity could be called 'ethnocentric' or 'ethnopetal' (on the analogy of 'centripetal'): as native speakers of a particular language and as members of one particular culture, we instinctively assume that all other cultures are 'strange', in the particular sense that this term has acquired in addition to its original denotation of 'foreign'.

When we mock the Ancient Greeks and Romans because of their extreme 'ethnopetal' attitude toward the people surrounding them, we should keep in mind that many of the expressions we use to refer to (and ridicule) foreign languages and customs are in fact nothing but 'funny' ways of reproducing the barbarians' unfamiliar idioms. After all, we indulge in the same discrimination when we refer to ethnic minorities as 'redskins' or 'spaghettis', using a particular ethnic attribute to defame the entire group. The very terms we use to refer to other people and cultures bear this out: the Greek word *bárbaros* is the same as the Latin term for 'one who has a stammer', *balbulus* (compare the French *balbutier*, 'to stammer'); similarly, the word 'Creole', in reality a term denoting a particular stage of language development, is now also used to refer to groups of people at the same time as it is a way of characterizing those people's speech as " 'bad talk' and 'broken talk' " (Le Page and Tabouret-Keller 1986:236).[111]

At the other end of the spectrum, to this 'ethnopetal' view of other languages and cultures there corresponds what one could call an 'ethnofugal' view, that is, an attitude to other tribes and nations which in principle assumes that they are 'better' than us – closer to nature, more healthy, more original, more community-oriented, more open, more spontaneous and a lot of other good things, most of which have to do with a vaguely Romantic notion of what it is to be 'original,' 'natural' and so on.

Enter the 'noble savage' (more recently known as the 'native speaker', the one 'who is always right'; Mey 1981), the chimeric prototype of natural human ethos and language that anthropologists and linguists of the late nineteenth and early twentieth centuries went out to find in the farthest reaches of unknown continents and countries. Their attitude was a natural reaction to their colonialist predecessors' brutal disregard for primitive cultures and their carriers, as well as to earlier centuries' efforts to bring these primitive people to conformity with

Western ideals of humanity, education and not least Christianity. In our own days, such representations of 'naturalness' have experienced a revival of sorts in the 'back-to-nature' movements of various shades and colors, beginning in the sixties and continuing into our present decade.

In linguistics in particular, the notion of the 'native speaker' as the final arbiter in every debate on language and language use has always had, and still has, a strong appeal (but see Mey 1981 for a critique). More recently, the question of the so-called 'endangered languages' has occupied the minds of linguists and anthropologists. Often, such a worry is motivated not by a genuine concern for the plight of the people speaking 'exotic' languages, but rather by a desire to keep as many varieties of languages as possible alive in the name of a linguistic 'ecology', understood as the need to protect diversification in the world of speaking, as in the other parts of the human habitat. But the real appeal of such notions lies elsewhere.

Both ethnopetalists and ethnofugalists seem to derive the strength of their convictions from deeper-lying notions than just professional worries about a particular deteriorating or disappearing culture, language or dialect. What is really at stake here is the very private, ever-present anxiety that people have about their own existence. For any culture that vanishes into the depths of history, for any language that becomes weakened beyond recognition and finally dies, our own human existence is diminished. At the same time (as the success of many popular religious persuasions and political teachings has demonstrated), such an existential *Angst* may be obviated (or, minimally, palliated) by convictions about individual human immortality, or at least about the continuity and universality of life in its various forms: race, class, faith, culture, language and so on. Among these convictions, the belief in the universality of human language and speech occupies a prime position.

For the ethnopetalists, this universality is assumed to be located in the closest, most familiar idiom: the native tongue. Clearly, if what I say is right for me, why shouldn't it be right for everybody? The ethnofugalists, by contrast, try to find out what is right in matters of language by going back to language's 'roots': what is right now is only right because it still represents some of the primeval condition, the Golden Age (*aurea aetas*) of Ovid and others, with its uncontaminated, pristine speech. Thus, a typical early answer to the question of what it the most original, hence 'universal', language was, for the ethnofugalists, Hebrew (the language supposedly spoken by God to Adam and Eve in the garden, on a literal reading of the Bible), while for an Antwerp-based, ethnopetal amateur linguist of the sixteenth century like Goropius Becanus (a.k.a. van Gorp) it had to be Flemish.

In the following sections, I want to argue that there must be a middle way of looking at the problem of universality across cultures, by taking under scrutiny some of the various areas of research in which these issues have been raised and discussed. I will not consider approaches to language universals and universality that go under the names of 'formal' or 'semantic'; the first referring to what is often, rather misguidedly called 'universal grammar', in the sense of a body of identical syntactic relationships, thought to hold across languages; the second identified with the desire to establish a 'universal semantic vocabulary' independent of language and/or culture: the 'linguistic algebra' or 'calculus' that was the aim of such thinkers as Leibniz or Hjelmslev. While such approaches may be of value from a purely methodological, grammatical or philosophical point of view, they are not relevant to our question, when viewed from a pragmatic angle.

10.4   Cases in point

10.4.1   Politeness and conversation

In section 10.1 we saw how certain forms of behavior may count as polite in some cultures, but as impolite in others. The question is, then, whether there exists something called 'inherent' politeness (certain forms always being considered polite), or even 'universal' politeness (the very idea of politeness being common to all people, and realized in more or less the same way across cultures and languages).

To the first question, the answer is probably negative, as already suggested earlier (section 4.2.3): there is nothing inherently polite or impolite about an order given in the military, and the sergeant who would 'politely ask' a subordinate to fall in line would not be understood properly, let alone obeyed. As to the second notion, that of universality in politeness, many (if not most) of the discussions dealing with this topic have been cast in the framework of what Brown and Levinson (following Goffman) successfully defined as 'face' early on in the debate (1978). Extending the traditional development of the theory (as outlined in section 4.2.3), one could postulate that the 'turn-taking' mechanisms on which Conversation Analysis from its very beginning has been based (see section 6.3.1.2) represent a form of underlying politeness: I respect my conversational partner's speaking turn, just as he or she respects mine. In terms of the terminology introduced earlier, I will not threaten the other's conversational face, either negatively (by not responding to his or her face needs) or positively (by overtly threatening his or her face).

As regards the universal nature of the notion of 'face' itself, a case could be made for universality, as people all over the world seem to share a desire to be left in peace when they wish to, and to be supported when they need to. Such feelings have found their classical expressions in formulas such as the 'Golden Rule' ('As ye would that men should do to you, do ye also to them likewise'; Luke 6:31) and in official documents such as the French Revolution's *Déclaration Universelle des Droits de l'Homme*, the 'Universal Declaration of the Rights of Man [sic]', or the United Nations' Freedom Charter, specifying both freedom *from* (oppression) and freedom *to* (enjoy a decent life).

But apart from these generalities, on which everybody agrees, there are innumerable differences as to the nuances and details appropriate to the individual cultures, and consequently as to the way these universal rights are expressed in language. Consider again the case of 'face': whether we prioritize 'negative' or 'positive' facework depends more on our cultural preferences than on our linguistic abilities or competence. As Gudykunst and Ting-Toomey observe:

> While one might expect both negative facework and positive facework to be present in all cultures, the value orientations of a culture will influence cultural members' attitudes toward pursuing one set of facework more actively than another set ... Facework then is a symbolic front that members in all cultures strive to maintain and uphold, while the modes and styles of expressing and negotiating face-need would vary from one culture to the next. (1988:86)

A general problem with the notion of 'face', as it is usually defined and elaborated upon, is that it basically and rather exclusively reflects the individual position. The individual, moreover, is conceived of as a rational being whose actions are more or less predictable on the basis of a commonly accepted model. In our culture, the generally acceptable model is that of the 'perfect consumer', one who knows his or her place in the market, one who understands that nothing is free but that, in order to get something, one has to give something in return and that both the giving and the returning must proceed in an orderly, societally acceptable fashion.

This extended-politeness 'turn–return' model is not only at the basis of the notions of face and facework; it also determines the ideology of cooperation and 'turn-taking' in Conversation Analysis, as Silverstein has remarked (1996:626; see also 1992). The next section will go into more detail.

10.4.2   Cooperation and conversation

As we have seen in section 4.2.2, much of current pragmatic thinking is based on Grice's 'Cooperative Principle'. Over the years, many criticisms have been uttered of this principle, often based on the assumption that not everybody is willing, able or obliged to cooperate. In certain cases, a maxim may be violated in the name of a higher-order principle which tells us to avoid a taboo, or not to smite somebody with the language equivalent of the 'evil eye' or a 'manual curse',[112] bringing on death or misfortune by putting on the 'evil ear'.

The discussion on the so-called universality of cooperation (a better wording would be: the ways cooperation is realized in different cultures) often focuses on the phenomena of conversation (including conversational implicature; see section 3.2.3). As to the latter, it has been pointed out that withholding information (and thereby violating the maxim of quantity) may be completely in order in certain cultures and contexts, given certain conditions. For instance, not mentioning the name of a person I know does not always lead to the implicature that I do not know the person's name (the normal case); the reason may be that I do not *wish* to say the name (perhaps with the intention of misdirecting my listener, as during a police interrogation), or because I am prevented by taboo from saying the name (as in Navajo culture, where one may not mention the name of a dead person for fear of retribution from the defunct's *chindi*, or ghost; see Thomas 1996:76–7).

When it comes to actual conversation, the assumption is again that people across cultures will obey certain rules of collaboration in order to make conversation happen and have the flow of talk to progress as smoothly as possible. This is the principle behind the well-known rules for turn-taking that conversation analysts must be given due credit for having formulated in much persuasive detail. Still, a lingering doubt remains. What if people decide not to be cooperative?

Some cultures are inherently geared toward verbal confrontation (such as the Jewish East Coast Americans described in Tannen 1984); others are extremely averse to such conflicts and prefer silence to a heated, tendentially interesting (but also potentially face-damaging) conversation (here, the 'silent Finn' is an egregious example; see Sajavaara and Lehtonen 1996). In such cross-cultural contrasts, any comparison between degrees of cooperativity must fail, since major overriding factors of cultural background are at play, just as in the case of the Navajo.

Still another case is that of the 'deliberate' flouting of all cooperation, where the interlocutors want to have a fight, or at least want to bring some things out in the open, and are willing to sacrifice both politeness and cooperation to that higher objective. Haviland (1997) has proffered a wealth of evidence from various cultures to show that such is indeed sometimes (often?) the case; the acid test being that conversational turns simply are not respected, and that everybody tries to get a word in, not just 'edge-wise', as Victor Yngve called it a long time ago (1970), but preferably in a frontal attack on their interlocutors.

The amusing example that Haviland gives at the beginning of his article is so obviously non-cooperative that the naïve reader first thinks she or he is being taken for a ride. A transcript is provided of an actual 'dialogue' between ten native speakers (below called a through j) of Zinacantec, a language of Guatemala; their contributions appear in ten lines of exactly the same shape and format, as follows:

1 a: ((unintelligible))
2 b: ((unintelligible))
3 c: ((unintelligible))
4 d: ((unintelligible))
5 e: ((unintelligible))
6 f: ((unintelligible))
7 g: ((unintelligible))

8 h: ((unintelligible))
9 i: ((unintelligible))
10 j: ((unintelligible)). (Haviland 1997:548)

Although we may assume that the ten speakers knew what they were saying, and perhaps even were able to make out what the others were uttering (though I rather doubt it), it remains a fact that the transcript as such reveals a very low degree of conversational cooperation: no turns are taken or respected, and the intent of the contributions to this conversation is not an orderly exchange of ideas, but simply a way of 'shouting the others down' until the mediators of the conflict (the 'dispute settlers'; p. 555) deem the time ripe to intervene and make recommendations that will end the dispute and solve the problems.

Confronted with cases like these, it becomes pretty difficult to postulate the existence of a universally valid 'principle' that would prescribe the same kind of cooperation in language for everybody in every culture and community. As Haviland pointedly queries: "How do we know when our interlocutors are co-operating? Are there times when we are not even *supposed* to cooperate, either at taking turns or at promulgating 'rational' talk exchanges?" (1997:551; emphasis original).

The answer, evidently, is: we do not know unless, or until, we are part of the culture. As long as we look at intermezzos like the one described above with the eyes of a monocultural Western(ized) linguist or conversation analyst, we cannot detect anything but a blatant violation of all the principles and maxims in the book. But we could be wrong, as a cross-cultural look at collaboration shows. And the reason for our wrong beliefs might well be located in what Silverstein (1996:626) has called "Western ideologies of autonomous mind and agentivity essentialized as some kind of mental stuff" – exactly the stuff of which both rules and principles, taken in the abstract, are made.

The next section will consider the role of cooperation from another angle, namely that of the activity of 'addressing', which is part and parcel of any attempt at human contact, including conversation.

10.4.3 Addressivity

The term 'addressivity' was originally coined by the Russian linguist and semiologist Mikhail M. Bakhtin. In his understanding, it denotes a constant quality of speech: namely, the fact that any utterance is addressed to somebody, every utterance is 'dialogic'. Basically, addressivity is the "quality of turning to someone" (1994:99), a quality which Bakhtin then uses to develop his theory of 'speech genres'. (See further Mey 1999:chs 4.3.3 and 6.2.3.)

Here, I will concentrate on those aspects of addressivity which concern the *act* of addressing. How do people go about striking up a conversation, for example? How do you address a stranger or 'turn to' somebody that is passing by on the street? Calling out "Hey, you" (or its equivalent in other languages) is certainly one way of doing it, but hardly one that is universally accepted. In particular, the question of how to use the proper forms of verbs and the (often accompanying) proper personal pronouns has been in the focus of interest of linguists and sociologists alike. The following sections will deal with some of the problems involved in addressing, viewed from an intercultural point of view.

10.4.3.1   Forms of address

The way we address people is a matter of great importance in most cultures. In certain conservative societies, addressing may happen only indirectly, and never to the addressee's face; a remnant of this is found in countries such as Sweden, where the normal form of addressing persons of respect (like: children to older relatives, employees to their superordinates, store clerks to customers, students to professors etc.) was, prior to World War II (and in some places even today), the third person singular, together with the addressee's 'title': *Vill farbror titta på min kattunga?*, 'Will uncle come and see my kitten?'; *Vad önskar direktören?*, 'What does the Chief Executive Officer wish?' and so on.

The earlier languages of the Indo-European family did not have a distinctive possibility of showing respect through the use of lexical or morphological categories: thus Cicero expostulating with Catiline in the Roman senate, the dying Caesar speaking to his assassin Brutus, the ghost of father Anchises addressing Aeneas (Vergil, *Aen.* VI:851), Horace rejoicing in his former lover Lyce's lost looks (*Od.* IV:xiii) and 'Yeshua Ha-Notsri' (alias 'Jesus the Nazarene') confounding Pilate (in Mikhail Bulgakov's *The Master and Margarita*) all use the uniform Latin mode of addressing a singular interlocutor, viz., *tu* 'you (sg.)': *tu Catilina, tu Brute, tu Romane, tu Lyce, tu Pilate.*

As we all know, the situation in today's European languages is rather different: with the exception of English, where the *you*-form has come to dominate the entire spectrum of addressing, most languages possess a distinct 'deferential' form, used in addressing persons of higher social status or in order to mark distance. In many of the cases, this form (sometimes capitalized in writing) is identical with the second person plural: thus, French has *vous*, Czech (and certain other Slavic languages) *vy* (or its morphological equivalent), Finnish *Te*; all being used for both singular and plural addressees of respect. (In Brown and Gilman's (1961) terminology, the difference is described as 'V' vs. 'T'; more on this in the next section.)

In other languages, the forms of respectful address are based on a third person verbal form (singular or plural), with a possible subject represented either as a morphological category (a pronoun) or as a specialized lexical item. The first case is exemplified by plural forms such as German *Sie* or Danish/Norwegian *De*, both originally meaning 'they'; earlier, the third person singular was also employed in these languages in order to mark a non-respectful distancing, as in the case of an army officer addressing a private. (Until quite recently, the Copenhagen Police

Ordinance contained a paragraph making it unlawful and punishable by a fine to address a policeman on duty using the Danish pronoun *han* 'he', with the third person of the verb.)

The second case is where the third person pronoun is replaced by a 'frozen' paraphrase of an original honorific, such as the Spanish *Usted*, plural *Ustedes* (written *Vd.*, *Vds.*), which is short for *Vuestra(s) Merced(es)*, 'Your Grace(s)'; an identical term is in use in English for addressing nobility of a certain rank. Similarly in Lithuanian, where the word *Támsta* ('(respectful) you, sg.') represents an earlier *Tàvo Mýlista*, 'Your Affability'; this expression is used in the plural as well: *Támstos*, 'y'all' (but without the familiar or dialectal connotation that the English expression carries).

In all these cases, what is at stake is the marking of a reverential distance, a way of paying respect to people who socially are placed above oneself. No wonder then that one of the first things successful revolutionaries, the advocates of 'new things' (*res novae*, the Latin expression for 'revolution'), are committed to is introducing novelty also in this domain, thus extending into the use of language the proposed or impending abolition of all privileges of rank and order. Thus, the Bolsheviks introduced the familiar *ty* throughout the command lines of the Red Army upon its creation in 1917: this innovation did, however, not last long, as the disciplinary requirements of the army context made it necessary to have the leadership distinguished also linguistically.

The French Revolution instituted the term *citoyen* for all citizens, irrespective of birth or rank, and had everybody address everybody else with *tu*. Similarly, after 'Victorious February', the 1948 takeover in Czechoslovakia, the term *soudruh*, 'comrade', and its feminine counterpart *soudružka* were established as common forms of address, to be used to everybody, along with the familiar pronoun *ty* 'you' (sg.). The latter form of address, however, never caught on, and although I heard the cleaning women in my Prague university dormitory in 1961 address each other quite unostentatiously, in the course of their daily chores, with *ty* and *soudružka*, in 1965 Karel Vlk, the courteous shopkeeper at the store across the road from my building, where I used to buy my *housky* ('salted rolls'), cheese, milk and (occasionally) eggs, would address me in the third person, even when he was using the prescribed 'comrade': *A co si přeje ten soudruh?*, 'And what does the comrade wish?', he would invariably say to initiate our interchange. Also at the other end of the socialist hierarchy, in venerable Charles University, it was still *de rigueur* in 1962 to address top officials at occasions such as honorary doctoral promotions with expressions like *soudruhu rektoře*, 'Comrade Rector' (but using *vy*, not *ty*!).

10.4.3.2   *Social deixis*

If one asks what is behind the various manifestations of reverence in reference, an obvious answer would appeal to the distinction in forms of addressing proposed as early as the sixties by Brown and Gilman in a classic article (1961), to wit, that between 'familiar' ('T') and 'reverential' ('V') (the labels were inspired by the French forms *tu* and *vous*). These distinctive and discriminating forms of address evince the underlying structures of society, where power relations on the one hand are offset by their 'mitigating' counterparts of personal, non-power-determined relationships (such as in a family surrounding), but on the other hand also manifest themselves in the imposition of a 'familiar' form in cases where no true familiarity, but only subservience and obedience, are expressed and expected.

Both forms are pre-determined as to their use, both in the social context and in the users' awareness; for example, in an official surrounding such as the court-room, the accused's being addressed as 'T' merely reflects the mechanisms of power as they surface in the judicial apparatus, and overrides a person's natural desire and right to be given the 'V' addressing. As an instance, consider the following.

Duranti (1996) cites a case (following Jacquemet 1994:307), in which a Neapolitan court witness, a former member of the local mafia called *Camorra* who had decided to turn king's evidence,[113] objects to the judge's addressing him with the familiar Italian *tu*, rather than with the respectful, formal *Lei*. The question that the witness in this connection puts to the judge stresses the fact that there is no common, familiar ground between the two of them which, under normal circumstances, would allow for a familiar form of address. Hence, its use under the circumstances denotes a lower social placement of the addressed than would be normal between equally placed adults, and is consequently felt as objectionable by the addressee. Here is a snippet of the dialogue:

JUDGE: If you talk (*tu parli*; T) . . . about supporters . . .
WITNESS: Excuse me (*scusi*, V), but you (*lei*, V) – have [you] (*ha*, V) ever met me?
JUDGE: You (*te*, T)? Never.
WITNESS: But why then are [you] using (*dà*, V) 'you' ('*tu*', T)? (Duranti 1996:204; square brackets added by me, as in [you], to indicate the facultative 'dropping' of the pronominal subject, a common phenomenon in Italian)

What this Italian speaker is trying to convey to his interlocutor is that he does not accept the other's positioning of himself, the addressee, in a lower position just because he happens to be in the witness stand, or because of his previous connections with the Camorra. In other words, the question is one of respect; in particular, of the respect due to the witness's 'social standing' as a human. He is effectively saying: 'How dare he be familiar with me when he has never met me?' Or, in other words: 'Who does this judge think I am?'

Let's for a moment go back to the 'circumlocutory' forms for address in the 'V' mode, quoted earlier. Apart from the plural (which has a well-known function in imparting 'high standing'; recall the 'majestic plural' commonly used by popes, royalty and other dignitaries), there are the various forms of address that are based on abstract substantives denoting some 'outstanding' properties of the addressed persons. Along with the already-mentioned 'Your Grace' for persons of ducal origin, there are, for example, 'Your Eminence' (used for cardinals of the Roman Catholic Church), 'Your Holiness' (for the pope himself), 'Your Excellency' (for major civil officials, such as governors of states, ambassadors and so on). Lesser-known variations on this theme include the address forms used for the heads of certain more obscure religious denominations; thus, the Uniate Maronite Church of Eastern Rite ('uniate' means that the adherents of this denomination follow the Orthodox liturgy, but recognize the Roman pontiff as the supreme head of all Christendom) has a spiritual leader who goes by the name of *Votre Chasteté*, literally 'Your Chastity' (possibly referring to the fact that higher dignitaries in this as in several other branches of the Eastern Church are not supposed to marry).

What all these appellations do is to transfer, from the office to the office holder, a property (eminence, holiness, excellency, chastity and so on) that is supposedly inherent in the office of the person addressed. This transfer acquires a *metonymical* value, so that the possessed attributes ('your eminence, holiness' etc.) are made to stand for the supposed possessors of these qualities ('Your Eminence, Holiness' etc.). The result is that, in addition to indicating the person named (via the office that the person is holding), the circumlocution has the 'indexical' value of denoting respect for the supposedly eminent, excellent, holy, chaste etc. qualities of the person addressed.

Since this respect is intimately bound up with the status of the addressed person in the immediate subset of society, in his or her community, it is a *social* respect, a respect for a social quality. The address form thus indicates social standing in addition to identifying the person addressed; this is why these forms represent a form of 'social deixis', to use a term coined by Levinson (1982:109). Just as regular deixis indicates the person 'indexed' as to reference and identity, social deixis indicates, 'indexes', the position this person has in the social context of which he or she is a part (cf. section 7.2.4). In addition to what happens in regular deixis (where the indexing normally is a matter of course), the social character of the deixis makes it imperative that the recognition be not only given, but also accepted: forms of address are not just *per*ceived, but have to be *re*ceived. In addressing, as elsewhere, there is no perception without reception: as the latter is socially determined, so, too, is the former.[114]

10.4.4 Speech acts across cultures: the voice of silence

The purported universality of speech acting was already touched upon earlier. In section 5.2.1.1, I raised several questions, two of which are of interest in the present connection, viz.: 'How many speech acts are there?', and 'Are there any speech acts that are common to all languages?' In light of what has been said in the preceding, both questions seem to be basically ill-formed and hence unanswerable. As to the first, it is predicated on an abstract notion of 'speech act', as if a speech act were some physically discernible and identifiable object, such as a word or a sentence. As to the second question, it disregards the importance of the proper context by which any decent answer would have to include the point of departure of the questioner, that is, his or her social and cultural background. It is precisely this context that plays a decisive role in the assignment of any significant pragmatic value to a particular speech act; in other words, the proper context (or 'affordances') is what establishes the speech act as part of a pragmatic act, as we have seen in chapter 8. And it is in the light of the proper context that the second question achieves meaning, and can be answered, as we will see below.

Many researchers have worked on the problem of 'speech acts across cultures', asking themselves how speech acting is carried out in different cultures by people using different languages. One of the most influential approaches is that by Blum-Kulka and her collaborators (Blum-Kulka et al. 1989; Kasper and Blum-Kulka 1993). In their work, these authors concentrate on the speech acts of 'apologizing' and 'requesting'; the way they go about their investigation is to propose a particular, incomplete utterance that fits a more-or-less constructed situation in different cultures (for example, you are a student and want to borrow a pencil from a fellow student, a professor, a family member and so on, respectively in the US and in Japan). By completing the utterance in different ways, the subjects disclose their different stances toward the speech acts in question, in the process telling us how they realize them in their own languages and cultures. The following are examples of what Blum-Kulka et al. call the 'Discourse Completion Test' (DCT) (Blum-Kulka et al. 1989:273):

At The Professor's Office
The professor had promised to return the student's term paper that day.

Student: I was going to talk to you about my term paper, if it's all right.
Professor: _____
Student: Uhu. When do you think you'll have it marked then?

At The Professor's Office
The student has borrowed a book from the professor, which she promised to return today. However, she realizes that she forgot to bring it along.

Professor: Miriam, I hope you brought the book.
Miriam: _____
Professor: Okay, but please remember it next time. (Blum-Kulka et al. 1989:176)

The DCT may be practiced with advantage when the surrounding contexts are relatively similar and homogeneous; however, if fails to operate whenever the partners' presuppositions (most of them pragmatic, but also linguistic ones; see section 7.2.3.2) fail to even remotely match, as has been demonstrated to be the case for cultures as different as the American Indian and the Standard American English ones. (See Enninger 1987.)

Another problem with the DCT as practiced in this kind of research is that it only succeeds for those speech acts that possess a recognized, more-or-less stable (though not necessarily canonical) form in the language(s) involved. If we try to apply the test to, say, a speech act such as 'baptizing' (in which the canonical form of the act is pretty much fixed), the test becomes automatically vacuous. If, on the other hand, we apply it to indirect speech acts or to pragmatic acts, the field is so wide open that one cannot possibly pinpoint one language's peculiarities as compared to another's in terms of the words spoken ('discourse', in Blum-Kulka et al.'s sense); instead, we must take the entire societal context into account (that is, 'discourse' in its socioculturally and pragmatically oriented acceptance; cf. sections 7.2.3.3 and 9.3.3).

The principle behind all these studies, to wit, that there exists a certain, rule-governed linguistic behavior that allows us to deal with similar situations in similar ways across cultures (such as requesting, apologizing, thanking etc.), is certainly plausible enough. However, as soon as we get down to the individual speech act, the problems start coming. What is polite in one culture may not be polite in another. Some cultures require thanking in contexts where others don't. Apologies are in order in certain situations in culture A (as when you step on somebody's toes in England or the US; cf. section 5.5.2.4), while in culture B, where the same situation is evaluated differently (such as in Japan), silence could be required (cf. above, section 10.1). Here, I want to briefly focus on the notion of 'being silent', silence being an act that for many people barely would qualify as a 'speech act' in the technical sense (since there is no 'speech' involved).[115]

Silence, or the absence of spoken language (by some called 'non-phonation'; cf. Enninger 1987), can be used in a variety of ways, and is given varying values across cultures. If we consider the mechanism of 'turn-taking' in CA, we will see that the rules that allow a speaker to 'jump into' the ongoing conversation at a 'transition relevant point' (TRP; see section 6.3.1.2) vary from culture to culture. What's more, the very notions of what constitutes a valid TRP are rather different. Silence, or the fact that somebody stops speaking, is by many conversationalists interpreted as a sign that the speaker is relinquishing the floor, and that another conversationalist may grab a turn. The problem is that the *length* of the silent pause is crucial for determining the validity of such an interpretation, and that this length varies considerably across cultures.

An early study by Scollon and Scollon (1981) has shown that many of the misunderstandings in dialogue between speakers of American Indian languages (such as those of the Athabaskan family) and speakers of mainstream English are due to the fact that a silence of more than one and a half seconds is considered by the English speaker as a 'legal' point of entry (a 'TRP'); for the Athabaskan speaker, however, this silence has the normal duration of an 'inter-sentence', but not an 'inter-turn', pause. In other words:

> [w]hen an English speaker pauses he waits for the regular length of time, and if the Athabaskan does not say anything, the English speaker feels he is free to go on and say anything he likes. At the same time the Athabaskan has been waiting his regular length of time before coming in. He does not want to interrupt the English speaker. This length of time we think is around one and one half seconds. It is just enough that by the time the Athabaskan is ready to speak the English speaker is already speaking again. So the Athabaskan waits again for the next pause.

And so on and so forth, until in the end: "the Athabaskan feels he has been interrupted and the English speaker feels the Athabaskan never makes sense, never says a whole coherent idea" (Scollon and Scollon 1981:25).

As this study indicates, silence is not interpreted in the same way in different cultures. Rather than being exclusively a sign of the 'all clear – you can speak now', keeping silent could be an indication of disinterest, or a signal of concentration on one's own thoughts, or just a regular pause-filler. When such discrepancies are not only codified in the users' mental systems, but become incorporated into the *legal* systems of society, the effects on the individual can be disastrous. Consider the following example (due to Gumperz 1998).

In a famous early eighties' court case in Northern California, a Native American was indicted on the charge of murder, having allegedly killed a police officer during a shoot-out. Not only that, but the charges against him were compounded by an accusation of 'conspiracy to murder', on the grounds that when some other participant in the shoot-out had yelled 'Kill the cops', the accused had remained silent. When the accused was brought to trial, his silence was construed as an admission of his guilt, and the Native American was therefore found guilty of conspiracy with intent to murder, rather than of simple manslaughter.

The case was then appealed and fought in the lower courts and all the way up to the California Supreme Court, where in the end, most of the charges were thrown out. Curiously enough, the conspiracy charge (despite being the hardest to document) was the only one that was upheld throughout the fifteen years that the process dragged on; hence, when the defendant was freed on probation, parole was made subject to his refraining from 'conspiratory conduct'. Six months later, the man was arrested again, and indicted on precisely those same charges, his conspiratory offense being that of accepting a marijuana cigarette at a local party.

Significantly, the conspiration charges that it took the California courts more than fifteen years to debate and finally quash were all based on an act of being silent, of 'non-speaking', on the part of the accused. What is even more amazing is the fact that ever since the 1964 *Griffin* v. *California* case, it had not been permissible, under the California legal system, to construe an accused's silence as evidence against him or her (Kurzon 1997:52ff). In the events under discussion, the fact that the accused was a Native American undoubtedly contributed to the way the law was interpreted and applied to him.

More generally, as this example also demonstrates, the act of silence is labeled in different ways in different cultural contexts. The Native American's culture recognizes silence as a way of announcing that one is busy preparing an answer to a given question, or that one needs time to think matters through during a discussion. There is no way that the accused's silence could be construed, in his own culture and language, as an assent; however, popular wisdom in many cultures explicitly determines that 'silence is consent'. And even the penal codes in a number of countries allow for legal procedures to be initiated and carried through, building on that assumption, with grave consequences of prejudice for the accused. (See, e.g., Article 114 of the French *Criminal Procedure Code*, as quoted in Kurzon 1997:64.)

Compare also the fact that in cultures such as the Japanese, silence may count as consent under certain circumstances. Enninger cites the case of the Japanese bride-to-be who, upon being addressed by her fiancé (who is holding her hand) with the words 'Please marry me', keeps her silence, and her head down, thus signifying acceptance of the proposal (Enninger 1987:295; example originally due to Saville-Troike 1982:159).

What these examples show is that the act of keeping silent (we can hardly call it a 'speech act') is highly dependent, as to its interpretation, on the cultural context in which it is performed or 'uttered'. Just as regular speech acts need a proper context of utterance to be validly performed, the act of silence doesn't properly make sense unless it is *situated*, as to both its linguistic and its cultural context. We may go one step further, and say that it is the context of culture and language which 'sets up' the language user to deal with a particular act of speaking (or non-speaking, as the case may be): in the Japanese example of the bride remaining silent in the face of one of the most important decisions in her life, or in the 'French' interpretation of an accused's silence – potentially a matter of life and death under certain circumstances – the 'speech act' of non-speaking doesn't make sense unless it is pragmatically founded in the social set-up of the language users. In other words, silence (like the other, 'proper' speech acts) is in reality a *pragmatic act*, as I have defined it in chapter 8.

Depending on the context of a particular culture and language, and thus ultimately of society, speech acts, given this pragmatic foundation, may be societally equivalent even though their actual appearances vary quite a bit. For this reason, it is inherently impossible to define the linguistic and cultural value of a particular speech act 'across cultures': the notion contains a contradiction in itself. For a speech act to be valid, it has to be located in a particular cultural context; since that context, by definition, is different from another context belonging to a different culture, so too is the speech act.

What the pragmaticist does find, though, are contexts that are broadly equivalent as to their *societal* impact. There will always be certain acts that humans perform when they wish to enter into a stable relationship (whether we call it marriage, partnership or something entirely different); similarly, there will be certain needs that the individual perceives as relevant to himself or herself in a particular social surrounding. Here, among other things, the notion of 'face' that was discussed earlier re-enters the picture; humans will always need a certain amount and kind of 'addressivity'; conversation is a human right as well as a human duty, as we have seen; and so on and so forth. Since all these different activities, in the final analysis, are *pragmatic* in their nature and execution, whoever wants to talk about pragmatics across languages and cultures should keep in mind that, as cultures are different, so are the manifestations of the pragmatic acts that make it possible for humans to live in a particular 'lingua-cultural' habitat.

The next chapter will focus on some social features that are typical of the pragmatics of this habitat.

Review and discussion

1. *Speech acts and style*

The speech acts we use when saying certain things are often more important than the contents of what is being said. A colleague of mine, in response to a question in a seminar, once flatly told the questioner "I don't understand the status of your question." In the context, this answer 'counted as' (Searle 1969:36; cf. section 5.1.3) a put-down: what was said had this particular effect because of the *style* of what was said. Furthermore, if (as the French say) *le style, c'est l'homme*, 'the style is the (hu)man', then style will differ in accordance with the particular men (and women) engaging in speech acting.

One of the big dividers between people from different cultures is precisely style. Wars have been fought over matters of ritual and style: the Sepoy rebellion in India in the late 1850s started because the native soldiers feared they might get contaminated by biting an unclean bullet (the British were rumored to have used pork fat to grease their ordinance). A stylistically doctored telegram (the infamous *Emser Depesche*, 'sharpened' (*zugespitzt*) and altered by Bismarck himself) provoked the French into declaring war on Prussia in 1870. When it comes to language use, some cultures are more direct than others: Americans often perceive Israelis as being 'rude', while the Americans themselves are being considered ruder than others by most people (including Israelis!). In some cultures, directness is associated with male behavior; in others (like the Malagasy) it is a feature of women's talk and connotes less careful language use, not straightforwardness or other virtues.

The reply quoted above could well be an illustration of this tendency; in general, speech acts need to be put into their cultural and stylistic context in order to be evaluated properly. For instance, a simple question like:

What do you mean by that?

can be the famous piece of red cloth that sets off some people's wildest aggressions ('What do you mean, "What do you mean?"?!'), while others perceive nothing but an innocent query. If particular speech acts in certain cultures are considered to be inherently more aggressive than others, linguistic field workers must take this into account when studying languages in far-away places. In certain cultures, it can be difficult to elicit responses such as, e.g., answers to questions, because the asking of questions in those cultures is perceived as improper. It has happened that linguistic field workers came back from 'their' people with the astonishing report that 'they don't have questions in that language'. This would be just as true as a report by a Victorian lady linguist on the language of London dock-workers: 'They never use swear words' – which would be more correctly phrased as 'I haven't ever heard them swear in my presence' – probably an accurate description of the factual situation in nineteenth-century England.

Questions:
On this background, consider the matter of question-making in your own culture. Enumerate the various ways questions can be put to use, and the ways they differ. (Hint: think, e.g., of 'questioning' vs. 'interrogating'.)

Do you know of any 'illicit' uses of questions in your own language? In other languages?

What does this mean for the speech act of 'questioning' as such? (Hint: ask yourself if the 'second pair part' (cf. section 6.3.2.3) of a question is always obligatory. When is it not?)

2. Compare the following warnings, printed on the coarse brown-paper wrapping bags that the OLLB (Ontario Liquor Licensing Board) provides its customers with, so they may conceal their shameful purchases when venturing out into the street:

English: 'Don't drink and drive'

French: 'Si vous buvez, ne conduisez pas' (lit. 'if you drink, don't drive')

Another French variant on the same theme (this one from Québec) is: 'Si vous buvez, ne prenez pas le volant' (lit. 'if you drink, don't take the wheel')

Questions:
Clearly, in the context of purchasing liquor and the possibility of people mixing 'bottle' and 'wheel', the intent of these messages is clear, despite their rather different wording. Would you say they share an 'illocutionary point'? (Cf. section 5.1.3.)

In terms of speech acting, how would you characterize the difference between the two (or three) messages?

Is this difference 'intercultural' (notwithstanding the fact that they are issued by the same authority)?

What kind of an 'order' would you say the second French version represents – or does it?

How could one, acting pragmatically (cf. chapter 8), express the same message? (Hint: refer to the Carlsberg beer truck in section 9.5.)

3. *To thank or not to thank?*
In 1976, the Israeli colonel Bar-Lev, on a special mission to Uganda, placed a telephone call to the country's dictator Idi Amin in order to thank him for his cooperation during a successful operation in the airport of Entebbe (special units of the Israeli army had freed the hostages held by a Palestinian guerrilla group after a hijacking). The following is a transcript of this telephone conversation, as found in Verschueren (1980:65–6, 1999:53–4; the original source is William Stevenson, *90 Minutes at Entebbe*, New York: Bantam Books, 1976, pp. 215–16):

> BAR-LEV: Sir, I want to thank you for your cooperation and I want to thank you very much.
> IDI AMIN: You know I did not succeed.
> BAR-LEV: Thank you very much for your cooperation. What? The cooperation did not succeed? Why?
> IDI AMIN: Have I done anything at all?
> BAR-LEV: I just want to thank you, sir, for the cooperation.
> IDI AMIN: Have I done anything?
> BAR-LEV: I did exactly what you wanted.
> IDI AMIN: Wh – Wh – What happened?
> BAR-LEV: What happened?
> IDI AMIN: Yes?
> BAR-LEV: I don't know.
> IDI AMIN: Can't you tell me?
> BAR-LEV: No, I don't know. I have been requested to thank you for your cooperation.
> IDI AMIN: Can you tell me about the suggestion you mentioned?
> BAR-LEV: I have been requested by a friend with good connections in the government to thank you for your cooperation. I don't know what was meant by it, but I think you do know.
> IDI AMIN: I don't know because I've only now returned hurriedly from Mauritius.
> BAR-LEV: Ah . . .

IDI AMIN: ... in order to solve the problem before the ultimatum expires tomorrow morning.

BAR-LEV: I understand very well, sir ... Thank you for the cooperation. Perhaps I'll call you again tomorrow morning? Do you want me to call you again tomorrow morning?

IDI AMIN: Yes.

BAR-LEV: Very well, thank you sir. Good-bye.

In order to understand what is going on in the above conversation, I will first provide an annotated account of the events preceding it, then follow up with a number of questions.

As to the event, we should recall that the Israeli paratroopers actually operated inside another sovereign country, Uganda, contrary to international laws and conventions (no state of war existed between Israel and Uganda). The only way this operation could have a semblance of legality was to 'legalize' it by directly involving the head of the Ugandan state, the dictator Idi Amin. However, the clever politician had (maybe following a leak) seen fit to decamp for Mauritius, thus leaving the field wide open to the Israeli operation. On coming back from his visit, Idi Amin finds that the 'embarrassing' situation has ceased to exist: the hijackers have been liquidated, and the hostages freed. Moreover, Idi Amin has not lost 'face' (cf. section 4.2.2.2), because he obviously cannot be held responsible for what people did in his absence. But if he isn't responsible, then he cannot accept a 'Thank you' from the Israelis either.

The Israeli commander, on the other hand, is highly concerned about the international image of the state of Israel. Actions like these tend to confirm the impression, already existent in much of the Third World, of Israel as an aggressive nation, without respect for international law and order. Therefore, the best thing for Israel to do is to involve the Ugandans *post factum*, so to speak, and obtain an official 'absolution' from their head of state. If Idi Amin knew about the impending Israeli strike, and even better, if he had said he would cooperate, then Israel could not be accused of international terrorism and adventurism.

So the Israeli colonel tries to involve Idi Amin in an act of 'thanksgiving', by which the operation would be acknowledged as a cooperation, hence more or less legalized. If the Israeli soldiers went into Uganda with the full knowledge and blessing of the Ugandan government and its head, no blame would be attached to Israel's handling of the affair.

But conversely, if Israel is not to blame, then Uganda could be accused of having allowed the Israelis into Entebbe airport. For Idi Amin, this accusation must be avoided at all costs; which is what explains his 'hedges', pretended ignorance, and in general, his rather non-cooperative behavior.

As to the *form* of this conversation, it represents the symmetrical, synchronized speech acting (such as greeting, thanking and so on) which has been studied extensively in Conversation Analysis (cf. chapter 6): a second pair part is expected once a first pair part has been uttered (the pair in question might be called 'imposition and avoidance').

As to its *content*, the various 'Thank yous' represent an endeavor to impose co-responsibility, and hence blame, on the other party; conversely, the addressee's profession of ignorance can be interpreted as an effort to reject and avoid the imposition, by not allowing oneself to be thanked.

Questions:
With this in mind, try to answer the question raised by Verschueren (1980:66) in his account of the episode: "Did Bar-Lev thank Amin?"

Notice that Verschueren's question may be read in two different ways: either as a question of as to the occurrence of the proper second pair parts in the thanking sequences, or as a question of whether any real thanking occurred.

The latter question can itself be considered from either a political or a(n) (inter-)cultural angle. As to the first, you want to ask yourself whether the surface acts of 'thanking' were performed as *bona fide* speech acts or as manipulatory maneuvers of 'blaming'. Similarly, were Idi Amin's protestations of ignorance meant to counteract an 'effort to blame', originating in the addresser? (Hint: refer back to the 'failed bet', discussed in section 7.2.3.2, and ask yourself whether or not there was an 'uptake' in the present case.)

As to the second, there is the likelihood of Idi Amin and Bar-Lev talking from different cultural backgrounds, such that 'thanking' simply doesn't mean the same thing in both cultures. Such a 'contrastive' view of intercultural communication is usually difficult to prove; in the present case, are there any signs that this could have been the case? (Hint: try to find places where the interlocutors' handling of the language may lead one to believe that they didn't quite realize the particular 'force' or 'point' of their speech acting. For similar cases, cf. the next exercises.)

4. At the end of section 5.3.2, I mentioned the case of the 'speech act that isn't': i.e., a speech act that professes not to do what it in reality does. These cases are notoriously hard to handle, especially if you have not been exposed to them all your life. Many non-native speakers therefore either exaggerate the use of them (thereby over-killing their purpose), or underplay the 'force' of the speech act by placing it in an interculturally unacceptable context.

Here is first an example of the former case. An author is writing to the editor of a professional journal to inquire about the status of an article he has recently submitted for publication:

Well, this mail is just to find out whether you have any word from the reviewers of my paper [title]. Please this mail is NOT in any way meant to put pressure on you.

Questions:
How do you evaluate the message in the sentence beginning with 'Please'?

What is the effect of capitalizing 'NOT'?

What purpose does the word 'Well' at the beginning of the excerpt serve?

(Hint: when trying to answer these questions, confront the utterances in the messages with how *you* would express yourself in a similar situation.)

Next, an example of an author writing to the editor of the same journal, apparently to inquire about the whereabouts of a manuscript. But the letter does much more:

> Thank you for your letter which left me somewhat confused. I will put aside the fact that it is dated Jan. 22 while the date of the postmark is Feb. 20. Anyway, you note that my submission has been returned to me for revision. Unfortunately, I have not received anything.

In this letter, the addresser makes it known that he is 'putting aside' something which he then proceeds to account for in detail, with dates and postmarks and everything!

Questions:
Again, try to establish the 'faults' in this piece, revealing the underlying intention: where does the author go wrong, as to both the 'force' and 'point' of his speech act(s), and more generally, as to the main intention of the letter (an inquiry about a manuscript)?

Interculturally, what do you suggest as explanation for this behavior? (Hint: some cultures value personality traits which other cultures regard as offensive or 'priggish'. Even though this letter is written in English, you will agree that it definitely is not an English letter. Any suggestions as to its origin?)

5. In the same vein, one has to be careful when engaging (consciously or without being aware of it) the powerful device called 'implicature' in languages other than one's own. Here is an example of a (supposedly not intentional) humorous implicature:

> (*The text below describes possible cheap accommodations for those participants of an international congress who wouldn't mind living in student dormitories for the duration of the congress*)
>
> Both these dormitories have rooms only with *shared* toilet, and showers. There are showers and toilets on each floor. The number of showers and toilets is

admittedly very low, approximately 20 people per one showertap or toilet. One just has to hope that not everyone wants to use the facilities at the same time. There are no sinks in the rooms.

Questions:
Do you think the authors of this message realized how the last sentence would be open to an unhappy implicature? (Which?)

The feeling for this kind of subtlety is one that is not easily acquired, even by native speakers; non-natives are rarely successful at this game. Your assignment is now to try and rewrite the text in such a way that it avoids involuntary implicatures of the above kind. (Hint: many implications are heavily dependent on location and other external circumstances, as when an exceedingly fat British MP, claiming that he has nothing against immigrants, but on the contrary works to their benefit, tries to underpin his credentials by publicly stating that he "had sixteen of 'em for lunch at the House of Commons last Tuesday" (Thomas 1996:15).)

6. *Apologizing across cultures*
In section 5.5.2.4, the speech act of 'excusing oneself', as well as some of the cultural differences surrounding this act, were discussed. Searle states that excusing oneself does not change the world, since there is no real contextual effect to an apology. According to him, excusing oneself is an 'expressive' speech act, whose only valid criteria are that of sincerity (in the utterer) and that of truth as to what the apology is about (its 'propositional content', as he calls it).

Searle ignores the fact (as do most speech act theoreticians) that there are other factors involved in world changes than merely those having to do with propositional content; changes, moreover, that may well be the real purpose of the speech acting. As we have seen in section 10.1, in certain parts of the world, such as West Africa, the use of an excuse (or equivalent expression) does not necessarily or uniquely connote any guilt or direct responsibility on the part of the speaker (as it would do in our culture). Similarly, in Japan one can utter *Sumimasen* (the multi-purpose 'Excuse me') in situations where an excuse would be highly inappropriate in our culture, such as when we are offered a gift, or when we accept an invitation (Ide 1998).

What really happens in cases like these is an *adjustment* of the 'fit' that Searle talks about, namely, a realignment of the world in the wake of a temporary disturbance in which the speaker and the hearer have been somehow involved (as spectators, as givers or receivers of gifts, as some who have been exposed to an objective or subjective wrong, and so on). The speech act of 'excusing' serves to make sure that all social and psychological mechanisms are set back to 'normal', and the green light is given for further, safe interaction at the 'unmarked' level: 'Business as usual.'

Felix Ameka, commenting on the relationship of apologies to other speech acts (especially expressions of sympathy) among the Akan, a West African culture, comments on this as follows:

> This raises one fundamental question which I think the kind of cross-cultural study of apologies and requests reported on in Blum-Kulka et al. (1989) wanted to address, namely, what situations count for triggering apologies. My investigations among Akans reveal that stepping on someone's toes is not a situation that calls for apology. It calls for sympathy – it focuses on the bad thing that has happened to the person and not on the one who caused the bad thing. This is an important point for cross-cultural studies of apologies. (1998; pers. comm.)

Questions:
On the background of these remarks, return to the example given in section 10.1, and try to come up with an alternative explanation for the passer-by's behavior.

Can this behavior be generalized across cultures? In other words, do you think that all apologies necessarily contain some element of sympathy? Give examples both *pro* and *con*.

How would an English person react to the situation described in section 10.1? (Hint: you probably will want to distinguish between different kinds of speakers of English.)

7. On silence
In section 10.2.4, I discussed the role that silence plays in communication across different cultures.

Questions:
Looking into your own cultural behavior, can you list some situations that you would characterize as appropriate for 'silent communication'.
   How varied can these uses of silence be, in your view?
   Does silence have to reflect any particular (non-)use of language?

Now have a look at the cover of this book, *Pegwell Bay* by William Dyce. Would you say that any or all of the people in the picture are silent? How would you argue one way or the other? (Hint: ask yourself who, in the picture, would (not) be able to speak to whom, and for what reason.)

Looking closely at the painting, you may discover the comet at the top (called 'Donati's'), which may well have been the reason Dyce went out to paint exactly then and here, viz., at Pegwell Bay, Kent, on October 5, 1858.
   Do you think that any of the persons in the picture is commenting on this phenomenon?

In your opinion, why did Dyce call his painting a 'recollection' (*Pegwell Bay: A Recollection of October 5th, 1858*)? What do you think he wanted to remember especially?

In addition to the visual imagery, what sounds (or silences) would you assume could have been heard? (Hint: refer also to the present book's *Epilogue*.)

CHAPTER ELEVEN

Social Aspects of Pragmatics

11.1 Linguistics and society

11.1.1 Introduction

The question of a societally sensitive pragmatics is intimately connected with the relationship between linguistics as a 'pure science' and the practice of linguistics as applied to what people use their language for, to 'what they do with their words', to use a formula that may be on the verge of becoming trite. Traditionally, in linguistics this split reflects itself in the cleavage of the discipline in two major branches that do not seem to speak to each other: theoretical linguistics and applied linguistics.

Traditionally, too, the former kind of linguistics has carried all the prestige of a 'real' (some would say: 'hard') science, whereas the latter was considered the soft underbelly of linguistics, prone to all sorts of outside and irrelevant, since 'extralinguistic', impact.

It has been one of the hallmarks of pragmatics, ever since its inception as an independent field of study, to want to do away with this split. Pragmatics admonishes the linguistic scientists that they should take the users of language more seriously, as they, after all, provide the bread and butter of linguistic theorizing; it tells the practical workers in the applied fields of linguistics, such as language teaching or remedial linguistics, that they need to integrate their practical endeavors toward a better use of language with a theory of language use. However, despite much good will, many efforts and a generally propitious climate to unification, linguistics as a science is not easily integrated with its applications. Pragmatics will probably, for a long time to come, be considered in many quarters not so much a scientific endeavor in its own right as an aspect (albeit a valuable one) of, and a complement (albeit a necessary one) to, traditional linguistics.

The *user* aspect has from the very beginning been the mainstay of pragmatics. Already in the first mentions of the term by Charles Morris (1938), following earlier work from the 1860s onward by Charles S. Peirce,[116] the term
'pragmatics' was closely tied to the user of language; in this way, pragmatics was
clearly distinguished from both syntax and semantics.[117]

But the users had not only to be discovered, they had to be positioned where
they belonged, namely in the societal context that makes their language activity
possible in the first place. For instance, a question such as 'How do people acquire
their language?' is more of a social issue than a strictly developmental problem,
only to be discussed properly in a strictly psychological environment (as had been
maintained by many psychologists and educationalists). Pragmatics opened up a
societal window on language acquisition and language use, and pretty soon pragmaticists found themselves joining hands with the psychologists, sociologists and
educationalists who had been working in these areas for many years.

The question naturally arises of what distinguishes pragmatics from those
neighboring disciplines (in addition to which one could mention anthropology,
sociology and various branches of applied linguistics, such as the study of languages for special purposes (LSP) or professional languages, the study of problems of translation, language pedagogy, language politics, language planning and
maintenance and so on).

The answer to this question (as we have seen in the preceding chapters) is that
pragmatics places its focus on the language users and their conditions of language use. Moreover, the language user is not just one who possesses certain facilities, either innate or acquired (or a combination of both), to be developed mainly
in *individual* growth and evolution; in a pragmatic view, such a development
depends on specific *societal* factors (the institutions of the family, the school, the
peer group and so on), which influence the use of language, both in the primary
acquisition stage and later in life (e.g., in second language learning).

Whereas classical faculty psychology maintained that the use of speech could
develop only if the language faculty was stimulated during the so-called 'sensitive period', pragmatics underscores the social aspects of this stimulation as
opposed to its purely psychological character. The social conditions for language
use are 'built in', so to say, into the very foundations of language acquisition and
use, and therefore are difficult to detect and determine as to their exact effect:
the results of an individual's linguistic development in very early life become
evident only much later, when the young person enters the first stages of his or
her formal education by joining the school system.

It is therefore not surprising that some of the earliest pragmatic research
focused on the problems of school vs. home environment. As early as the late
fifties and early sixties, Basil Bernstein was able to establish a positive correlation between children's school performance and their social background (see
Gregersen 1979 and references quoted there). It turned out that school achievement in important respects depends on the learner's earlier development in the
home. On the whole, white, middle-class children were seen to be significantly

better school performers than their peers from the lower strata of society (that is, from non-white, non-autochthonous and in general non-mainstream environments).

Social theory, as it was practiced in those years, had no explanation to offer for its own statistical results, and the pragmatic determinants of the learning process remained hidden from observation. It was not until the covert structures of societal domination were looked into that certain pragmatic features could be identified as important for language use in education. One of the most crucial of these turned out to be the question of the 'ownership' of cultural goods, and how this ownership was administered through various patterns of 'hegemony', in cultural as in other respects.[118]

The young person's school achievement thus not only furnishes a good illustration of what pragmatics is about, it also very clearly demonstrates why the pragmatic pattern of thinking originally met with such resistance, and why many of the earliest impulses to pragmatic research had to come from the outside, from the ranks of educationalists and sociologists such as Paulo Freire and Basil Bernstein. The next sections will deal with their important and innovative work.

11.1.2   Language in education

11.1.2.1   Who's (not) afraid of the Big Bad Test?

'Morals are for the rich', Bertolt Brecht used to say, echoing an earlier saying by another German playwright, Georg Büchner (*Woyzeck*, 1838). With a slight variation on this dictum, we could say that education is for those who can afford it. Here, I am not only thinking of the prohibitively high costs of education in countries such as the US, where the best educational facilities often operate under a kind of 'free enterprise' system,[119] but also (and mainly) of the privilege of coming from the right social background. The same classes that have established the institutions of higher education have also been instrumental in structuring that education and organizing its curricula; we are faced with a co-opting, self-perpetuating system that favors those who are most similar to those already in it, *pares sibi*, as the expression used to be.

One of the requirements for those who aspire to participate in any college or university program in the US is to take the appropriate tests, such as the SAT ('Scholastic Aptitude Test') before entering college, and the GRE ('Graduate Record Examination') as a prerequisite to entering graduate school. These tests, although apparently devised as standard measures of intelligence and scholastic ability, are in reality disguised roadblocks on the way to higher education, designed to eliminate all those who (for whatever reason) have not been sufficiently exposed to American mainstream culture and thinking. Most serious educationalists agree that the tests are worthless as measures of aptitude for academic work;[120] still, the tests are maintained, because they allow undesirable elements to be weeded out, while promoting those who promise to cause least trouble for the establishment in their later professional lives.

Characteristically, the tests are geared to the values of the white, middle-class, male-dominated segments of society; minority students and foreigners taking these examinations do less well. It is not uncommon to observe an intelligent foreign student performing relatively well on the mathematical parts of the GRE, but near-failing the verbal part; this alone should induce a healthy skepticism toward the value of such testing as a whole, and draw our attention to the part that language plays in devising, administering and taking these tests.

At stake here is, among other things, what many educational researchers have dubbed the 'hidden curriculum'. Schools are not only supposed to impart professional knowledge through their teaching; equally important are the attitudes and beliefs that are fostered and reinforced through the educational institutions. If one asks what these attitudes are about, one has to go back once more to the question of societal power: the prevalent attitudes reflect the attitudes of the powerful segments of society and are geared toward perpetuating the possession of that power by the ruling classes. With respect to language, the people who are able to decide what language can be deemed acceptable in the schools, which uses of language should be furthered and encouraged in education, respectively demoted and discouraged, are the same people who, from their position of power, oppress large segments of the population, not least by controlling their language behavior.

A familiar instance of this linguistic oppression is that of 'low' vs. 'high' prestige dialects of one and the same language, or that of 'pidgin' vs. 'standard' languages, where low dialects and pidgins are considered to be mere deteriorated variants of some 'high naughtiness' called 'the standard', or simply 'the', language.[121] Gross cases of oppressive linguistic behavior control include the total or partial criminalization of local or vernacular idioms, as in the case of the 'Basque stick' (a punitive device used in the schools in the Basque region, where pupils were forced to carry a stick on their outstretched arms as punishment for having used a Basque word or expression, to be relieved only by the next trangressor in line; see Mey 1985:27).

In a more profound sense, the question of 'whose language' is the controlling norm and standard of our language use harkens back to the Brecht quotation at the beginning of this section. If standards, moral or linguistic, are supposed to be compulsory for everybody, then they should be affordable for everyone, and not only for the rich and privileged. Moral behavior, like correct language, is something you should be able to afford.

The reality of life is different, though. While appealing to some universally valid laws of justice and equity (which are valid only in a perfect, but nowhere existing society), we allow the rich to engage in corruption and embezzlement, but string up the petty thief and the poacher: 'One man can steal a horse and another cannot look over the hedge.' In a pragmatic-linguistic application of this principle, former US Foreign Secretary Henry Kissinger could get away with murder, speaking his peculiar, German-tainted brand of English, while as recently as January 1998, four Hispanic women were fired from their jobs in a Dallas, Tex., factory for speaking Spanish among themselves during the lunch-break.[122]

What we are dealing with here is no longer the blatant oppression of the 'Basque stick', described above. Rather than attack the individual wrongdoer directly, we appeal to some higher principle; for instance, in the language case, by declaring English to be the 'official language of the US', thus indirectly penalizing the use of Spanish. This subtler, but equally pernicious form of social control through language has been called linguistic *repression* (Mey 1985:26).[123] The concept of repression plays an important role in defining and describing some pragmatic paradoxes that arise in contemporary pedagogical thinking: either the student is considered to be a completely passive receptacle for the ideas and knowledge to be imparted by the teacher – 'piggy-bank teaching', as the late Paulo Freire has aptly called it (Freire 1968; Freire and Macedo 1987:xvi) – or alternatively, the students are supposed to be in the possession of exactly those qualifications, as prerequisites to learning, that the teaching is supposed to imbue them with. In either case, the underprivileged students are doomed to lose out: either they enter the 'rat race' on the ruling classes' premises (and obtain the privilege of membership in the rat club, if they're lucky), or they will never make it in the race because they got off to a stumbling start.

The next section will focus on what causes this stumbling and on how to remedy its effects.

11.1.2.2 A matter of privilege

The concept of 'underprivileged', applied to language and its use, reflects an awareness of the fact that, first of all, the use of language is a common human privilege, a human right, and second, that this privilege, just as all other human rights, is very unevenly distributed among the people living on earth. In general, those without access to the full privileges of language are also those who miss out on other opportunities, such as education, better jobs, cultural goods, decent housing, health care, retirement and old-age benefits and so on. In particular, linguistically and socially deprived children are often scholastic underachievers and potential school drop-outs, with shorter life expectancies and no social future except a life on the street corner. Understandably, then, the concerns of socially aware linguists and educators were from the very beginning especially focused on this group of involuntary underachievers.

The first efforts at establishing 'remedial programs' of language training date back to the sixties, when the so-called 'Head Start' programs endeavored to give underprivileged children from the North American urban ghettos a chance to keep up with their white, suburban peers, by teaching them the extra skills (in particular, language capabilities) that they needed in order to follow the regular curriculum. The results of these programs, if there were any, usually did not last, because the teaching concentrated on the pure transfer of skills, without any connection to the contexts in which these skills were going to be used, or to the real reasons for the lack of culture and educational privilege of the children in question: their social condition.

The social concerns of the sixties that reflected themselves in these remedial undertakings were also the prime moving force in Basil Bernstein's work. Bernstein, originally a school teacher himself, noticed that children from lower social classes did less well in school than their peers from the middle and upper classes. As to the connection between poor school achievements and social background, Bernstein hypothesized that lower-class children, by virtue of their social origin, did not have easy access to the language of instruction used in the schools. These children, being native speakers of what he called a 'restricted code', could not identify with the school's 'elaborated' code (which simply was not theirs); therefore, their scholastic performance stayed significantly below that of the middle- and upper-class children, who knew how to deal with the school language as a matter of course, having been exposed to it all their lives.

In Bernstein's early works, the 'codes' represented clearly identifiable ways of speaking. Referring to one's parents as 'he' or 'she' (rather than 'Dad' and 'Mom') is a clear instance of restricted code (and a use of language very much frowned upon in environments such as my own, upwardly mobile, middle-class family). The same goes for feedback prompters ('back channels') such as 'you know', or 'if you know what I mean'; all sorts of 'tags' such as 'isn't it', 'doesn't it' and the like; a less varied choice of verbs and adjectives; an excessive use of slang, fixed expressions and clichés; and so on. Since this code only uses a subset of the language, Bernstein called it 'restricted' (Bernstein 1971–5).

By contrast, an 'elaborated code', in Bernstein's view, expressed an independent way of looking at things, as manifested by the use of the first person singular in describing and stating; an imaginative choice of expressions; an avoidance of cliché; and in general, a higher level of abstraction in expressing oneself. These characteristics are part and parcel of the linguistic habitus of the middle and upper classes; they also happen to embody the very qualifications that the schools traditionally emphasize as being of importance in the classroom; the absence of these qualifications is defined as a lack, in need of being remedied. Thus, the lower-class students, being by definition poorly prepared for the curriculum of the educating institution, were automatically accorded the status of 'underprivileged' learners and poor performers.

As his critics were quick to point out (and Bernstein himself admitted in subsequent writings), the term 'code' was from the very beginning an infelicitous choice: there were the connotations of other uses of 'code'; there was the confusion of the 'codes' with social and regional dialects; there was the fact that restricted ways of dealing with the world are typical of a great number of social and other contexts that have nothing to do with the concept of 'underprivileged', but a lot with that of 'specialization' (take the case of professional jargon, for instance). The later development of Bernstein's theories (e.g., 1981) takes these criticisms into account by developing a more finely grained model of socially diverse language use; in this model, the notion of 'social context' is made more specific, and 'code' is not exclusively thought of as synonymous with some particular kind of language.

In still later work, Bernstein ascribes the origins of the codes no longer directly to class factors, but to what he calls 'symbolic control', as found in religious and other systems of values (1990:111). Such control systems are centered either on a system's objective values, embodied in the controller's *position* within the system, or on the more subjective realization of these values in the *person* of the controller. Thus, a preacher may either appeal to an 'Eternal Truth', of which he is a legitimate representative and an ardent advocate, often endowed with punitive powers; or he may bare his breast and beat it in front of the audience, trying to sway his listeners by appealing to their emotions.

These different forms of symbolic control, the 'positional' and the 'personal', engender different types of relationships between the controller and the controlled; as such, they represent different attitudes to social values and behaviors like: respect for authority, obeying the laws, telling the truth to one's superiors, paying one's taxes and parking tickets and so on. With regard to the ways in which these approaches are realized linguistically, we notice important differences, too; particularly in education, the positional approach reflects the 'restricted' code, the personal the 'elaborated' one – with whatever implications there are for the social distribution of educational methods and privileges, within or outside of the school environment.

Consider the following conversation overheard in August of 1996 in the Oak Street Market, a local, 'alternative' grocery shop in Evanston, Ill., chiefly frequented by a white, middle-class, mostly academic clientele. The situation is as follows: an academic-looking young woman drags a little boy around the store while she is doing her shopping. The kid is naturally bored out of his mind, because the mother, being completely absorbed in what she's doing, has no time or energy to engage her son in her activities. Frustrated, the boy begins picking off items from the shelves. He is told not to; a reason is given, and the following interaction takes place:

MOTHER: I hate to use my money for stupid things, and if you are going to throw those jars on the floor they'll break and we'll have to pay for them and that means there will be no money to buy Christmas presents.

The child does not react at all to this homily, and continues his provocative actions:

MOTHER: I told you that we don't have much money, and if you want your Christmas presents, you'd better stop it!

When this, too, remains without result, the mother starts enumerating all the things he won't have for Christmas, and how there will be no money to travel to Grandpa's and Grandma's and so on – a whole panoply of real and imaginary threats. (Remember that all of this happened in the month of August!) At this point, the boy breaks into a howl, clutches his mother's arm and begins to kick her.

Clearly, what we see in this little interchange is a case of misused and mismatching codes and positions. The mother argues with the kid in elaborated code; she talks to him out of an understanding of herself as a responsible adult, as a thinking and reasoning academic *person*, and expects her boy to be on the same level. If she had been willing to use the power that is inherent in her *position* as a mother, she probably would have used restricted code ('Stop that, d'you hear me!') – and the educational process would perhaps have been more effective and less traumatic.

With regard to the notion of 'code', the later Bernstein prefers to consider it as an 'orientation' rather than as a fixed object of description. This 'coding orientation' consolidates the personal and the positional in an acceptance of, and an attitude toward, the societal framework (religious, social, professional etc.); such attitudes are less rigid and more 'portable' than the codes emanating from a traditional class analysis. As to the codes themselves, these can be oriented toward the societal framework, and hence be positional, as in the case of the traditional social roles: parent–child, teacher–student, doctor–patient and so on; alternatively, they can be oriented to the person and his or her particular use of language. As Bernstein rightly remarks, any such orientation requires an orienting institution, guaranteeing the relevance and legitimacy of the used code; therefore, any "[c]ode presupposes a concept of *whose* relevance and *whose* legitimacy" are considered valid (1990:102; my emphasis). The code is society's regulative instance, the producer of rules for 'good behavior' in matters of language.

Bernstein's insights served as guidelines for much of (Western) European sociolinguistics and other, pragmatically inspired educational research in the sixties and seventies. In particular, his distinction between 'elaborated' and 'restricted' code dominated the discourse of emancipatory linguistics for more than a decade. Still, the Bernstein-inspired solutions to the problem of selectively deficient school instruction did not always yield the desired results. For one thing, Bernstein's exclusive focusing on the formal aspects of the codes (phonological, morphological, syntactic etc.), rather than on matters of content and how that content was transmitted, stayed with the theoretical apparatus even after its author had adjusted its focal points: as a matter of fact, most of its practitioners never took cognizance of the amendments that Bernstein offered to his theory during the seventies and eighties. Also, some of the unfortunate implications of the original code concept necessitated a thorough rethinking of the societal background of Bernstein's assumptions – a rethinking which in many cases turned into a rejection, as the world of education, along with the rest of humanity, veered to the right in the eighties and nineties.

Whereas earlier in the period, the chief motivation for doing research in an 'emancipatory' framework had been to combat social injustice on the spot (such as in the classroom), the need for a more theoretically founded view of the social relations began to make itself felt, especially in later years. The framework provided by Bernstein did not have the conceptual stringency that was needed to convince the educational theorists; conversely, wholesale appeals to social conscience and the need for an emancipatory praxis quickly became obsolete as motivational support for doing serious, theory-based research (as Bernstein of course was well aware; witness his later works).[124]

Within the limits indicated above, Bernstein's understanding of the societal context and his theory of social stratification, despite all its weaknesses, were much better founded than the theorizing practiced by the majority of his contemporary North American (and earlier European) colleagues. The latter's 'analyses' of social class had only very tenuous connections with the realities of social life, and mainly consisted in setting up levels of social stratification, depending on how much money people made, how often they went to the theater or concert hall, how many books they checked out from the local library and so on. From a sociolinguistic standpoint, Bernstein's work was significantly more relevant than that of most of his contemporaries.

The next sections will consider the problems of underprivilege in other societal sectors, such as the media and certain social institutions.

11.1.3   The language of the media

Even though the educational system perhaps is the most obvious instance of the unequal distribution of social privilege as reflected in, and perpetuated through, language, it is by no means the only one. Among the cases of linguistic repression that have attracted most attention are the language of the media and the medical interview; in both cases, we are faced with hidden presuppositions of the kind characterized above. I will first discuss the language of the media; following that, I will deal with language as it is used (and misused) in the institutionalized setting of the medical profession.

Much has been said and written about the criteria for 'good' journalism, 'objective coverage' of the news, 'fairness' and so on, mostly with regard to the daily press, but including also other informative media, such as radio and TV (especially public broadcasting and televised interviewing). There seems to be a certain consensus (as expressed also in a number of documents with legal or semi-legal status) that although the air waves in principle are free, there should be some control on what is put on those waves; in particular, one should not allow powerful interests to monopolize the media for the sake of profit (e.g., by creating chains of radio and TV stations interlocking with newspapers). In the US, these rulings are issued and monitored by the FCC (Federal Communications Commission), and they should of course not be made light of, even though in practice, overt or hidden monopolization does occur, resulting (often) in lawsuits and (sometimes) in the breaking up of such chains, or at least the denial of ulterior licenses to the media magnates.

In Europe, the situation is fundamentally different. Historically, this has a lot to do with the development of the media culture in the European twenties, where a strong social democratic movement obtained control of a large segment of the radio media. At first blush, European broadcasting policy, when compared to that in the US, seems to be a good deal more geared toward fulfilling the idealistic demands of free access to the air waves for all opinions, groups, creeds and so on, not only in practice but also in the official law-making documents.

Thus, in Denmark and (what used to be West) Germany, the criteria for inclusion in the news are, at least in theory, tested against standards of objective reporting and 'balanced coverage'. The Danish legal document covering this issue mentions explicitly the "political, religious, and other similar groups" that should be accorded fair treatment in the distribution of broadcasting time, with respect both to quantity of time (number of hours) and to where those time slots are to be placed in the daily programming (*Guidelines for News Coverage in Broadcasting*, 1976; see Mey 1985:91ff).

Also as to content, the newscasters should strive to represent all opinions in an equitable manner, and not use language that could be prejudicial against any 'group' in the above sense. The official news and other programs should maintain a neutral stance toward all the opinions found in a democratic society; the majority should not be allowed to impose its views against the minority's wishes. (The rationale of this philosophy of newscasting becomes clearer when one realizes that until 1988, the Danish media were a state monopoly, and that private broadcasting by so-called 'pirate' transmitters was not allowed.)

On paper, all this sounds fine. Yet, if one looks below the smooth, papery surface, the picture becomes somewhat less glossy. When a major labor conflict disrupted the normal course of events in Danish society for a whole week in November of 1976, the newscasting in connection with the strike events was far removed from the ideals of neutrality and from the 'objectivity' and 'balance' that were supposed to be the hallmark of the official, state-owned media.

The reasons for this imbalance were manifold: for one thing, this particular strike (which had its origin in a wage dispute between a small oil company and a local oil truck drivers' union) ended up paralyzing the whole of the Danish economy, with effects in sensitive areas such as the supply of oil products to institutions and private homes; in the end, people even feared it might jeopardize the production of such traditional Christmas staples as turkeys and poinsettias. Thus, initial public support for the workers quickly turned sour, as people realized that their own walls were on fire.

From a more principled vantage point, there is a fatal flaw in the otherwise well-intentioned formulation of the 'objectivity' criterion, inasmuch as it is based on a concept of 'neutrality' which itself cannot be said to qualify as 'neutral'. The word 'neutral', according to its etymology (Latin *ne-uter*, 'not (belonging to) either'), denotes an equal distance from two opposites. In the case of opposed political views, alternative solutions, several parties to a conflict and so on, being neutral implies not leaning to either side. A basic presupposition for neutrality is to assume the existence of a 'zero point' between the two extremes; even more importantly, we must be able to determine, and agree on, the location of such a 'zero point'. Both assumptions are clearly hypothetical; moreover, they are to a large extent circular.

In any system of coordinates, we cannot pick the origin without knowing the range of the values represented by the system; hence, we have to determine the intersecting coordinates before we are able to establish their intersection. Setting the zero point can only be done if we know the values of the extremes; however, if those opposite values are themselves determined in accordance with what whoever sets the zero point believes them to be, and not (as neutrality demands) on the basis of their equidistance from point zero, we end up in circularity.

To take an example from politics: usually we operate with 'left' and 'right', as metaphors for 'progressive' vs. 'conservative' or (as it is now frequently called, with an interesting shift in distance) 'moderate' (see also section 11.2.1). As a quick look at history shows, what used to be 'left' now counts as 'center', or even 'right': for instance, Denmark's traditional 'Left Party' (*Partiet Venstre*) was originally formed around 1880 as a counterweight to the then-reigning 'Right' or Conservative Party, with the purpose of representing the small farmers' interest against what, somewhat anachronistically, could be called the big 'agribusiness' of the period. Yet, this same party was one of the pillars of the right-wing coalition that led Denmark for more than ten years, from 1982 to 1992.[125]

With regard to the labor conflict mentioned above, since the 'neutrality' that the media were trying to establish was based on an imaginary 'zero' point, its existence was just as chimerical as the objectivity itself that such a point was supposed to guarantee. The media coverage of the strike did not offer any objective, neutral information about the conflict, although it was served up as such; rather, the media reflected the interests of that particular segment of the population which was chiefly concerned about 'business as usual', and of the people who wanted to bring the conflict to a conclusion, no matter what the costs, and no matter how the original dispute about wage inequalities that was at the root of the strike was going to be resolved.[126]

11.1.4 Medical language

The French sociolinguist Michèle Lacoste has, in a thoughtful study (Lacoste 1981), drawn attention to the fact that the doctor–patient interview, despite its obvious usefulness and even necessity, sins gravely by way of linguistic repression. What the physician allows the patient to tell is not primarily what the patient wants or is able to tell, but rather, what is *pragmatically* possible in the doctor–patient relationship, in particular within the social institution of the medical interview where the interaction between doctor and patient takes place.

In the extreme case, this form of institutionalized discourse may be reduced to filling out forms with pre-set categories of questions and answers. For the patient, this has nothing to do with expressing oneself or manifesting one's problems; it is more like submitting oneself to a 'multiple choice' type of examination. Conversely, for the doctor this situation may result in an inability to obtain all the necessary information, as we saw in the case of the failed medical interview, described by Treichler et al. (1984), which was cited in section 5.4.3. The case illustrates the 'double bind' that doctors find themselves in while dealing with patients: on the one hand, they have a job to do, which means: getting people out of the office within a reasonable, preferably short, span of time (more patients are waiting); on the other hand, the job is people, who cannot be processed like cattle moving on a conveyor belt, but have to be talked to and 'taken care' of' in order to be treated (also in other ways than the purely medical ones).

In the case referred to by Lacoste, an elderly lady is complaining to her doctor about pains in her spleen. However, the (male) doctor rejects this complaint, and instead, locates the pains in the lady's stomach. When the patient repeatedly and rather indignantly denies his suggestion on the grounds that it is her body, and that she, if anyone, must be familiar with her own pains, the doctor cuts her off abruptly by saying that she doesn't even know what a spleen is, far less where it is located in the body.

This example shows two things: for one, a mere knowledge of technical vocabulary, and even the ability to use that knowledge correctly, are worth nothing, as long as the pragmatic conditions governing the use of that knowledge are not met. In the current doctor–patient conversation, even though the old lady is able to use a common medical term ('spleen') correctly, she is not understood, and her voice not even heard, because she does not possess the necessary professional standing and societal clout. What is most important here is the *hidden* conditions determining the use of language and steering its users, not only in the present case, but also in other connections (such as the academic tests mentioned in the previous section, which gauge verbal and other abilities in situations of unequal social power; see further below, section 11.3).

The other point to be made is that linguistic repression may have unexpected, even dangerous side-effects. The powerlessness of the repressed can easily turn into self-incrimination, by which the powerless attribute their lack of societal appraisal to factors such as fate, God's will, their own lack of capability, their predestined stance in society ('knowing one's place') and so on. Or it may result in resignation – as happened in the case of the old lady, who ended up saying: "Whatever you say, doctor", thereby possibly exposing herself to the risk of a faulty diagnosis, with all its concomitant dangers both to herself (as a patient) and to the physician (as the potential target of a malpractice lawsuit). Clearly, what is needed here is techniques and strategies aimed at providing appropriate aid to the societally and linguistically oppressed: typically a case of 'emancipatory' language education and use. (See further below, section 11.3.2.)

Summing up, then, the case of the medical interview is an outstanding instance of the institutionalized discourses in which the value of the individual's linguistic expression is measured strictly by the place he or she has in the institution. Only utterances which meet the criteria of the official discourse are allowed, and indeed registered; others are either rejected, or construed as symptoms of (physical or mental) illness, lack of knowledge or even intelligence, and in general dependent or inferior status.

The 'good patient', who knows that survival is the name of the game, quickly learns how to place himself or herself in this official discourse. A 'good' patient has symptoms; does not question his or her being institutionalized; takes the medicine prescribed by the staff; follows all the rules, including the No. 1 Rule: 'Remember Thou Art Sick'; and so on. By contrast, a 'bad patient' tries everything to get out, and as a result, is beaten back into submission by the institution and its personnel. In the extreme case, 'bad' patients are physically reduced to silence and/or inaction (the straitjacket and 'the operation', a.k.a. lobotomy, come to mind).

A 'bad' patient may end up accepting the institutional discourse and become 'good', even to the point where the possibility of a release is dispreferred in the end; the patient has become one with the institution, and does not want to leave. In a touching story by Gabriel García Márquez, a woman accidentally enters a lunatic asylum 'just to make a phone call' (as the title of the story has it; Márquez 1992b). She is immediately 'recognized' as a patient and enrolled in the discipline of the institution. Her innumerable efforts to get in touch with her husband remain without result. In the end, she begins to feel herself at home in the safety and the routine of the asylum, and when the husband finally tracks her down, she doesn't want to leave.

As Goffman remarks about mental institutions and their inmates (an observation that applies to all sorts of institutional discourse): "Mental patients can find themselves in a special bind. To get out of the hospital, or to ease their life within it, they must show acceptance of the place accorded them, and the place accorded them is to support the occupational role of those who appear to force this bargain" (Goffman 1961:386).

The following sections will look into the ways language interacts with our environment, in a constant, dialogic and dialectic opposition of word and world.

11.2 Wording the world

Wording is the process through which humans become aware of their world, and realize this awareness in the form of language. However, words are not just labels we stick on things: the process of wording is based on interaction with our environment. "We bespeak the world, and it speaks back at us" (Mey 1985:166).

The world we word is, furthermore, a world of people: we can only become language users through the social use of language. Once language is created in this social environment, once the world has been worded, our wording creates a shared world-picture. Without words, the world remains a black box, an unread picture-book. Using the common wordings that are available to us, we open that book, not just to look and make sure everything's still in place, but to see ourselves as part of the worded world.

One of the most effective ways of seeing the world in this way is through the use of analogies: understanding one thing by way of another. I remember how my physics teacher in high school used to tell us that electricity is like water: you can explain how electricity flows through wires like water through pipes; how resistance increases, the narrower the pipes we force the liquid through; how its 'potential' makes it flow from high to low and so on. Water is a metaphor for electricity; seeing electricity as 'water' is a metaphorical understanding, a way of 'seeing the world' through a metaphor.[127] The next sections will explore some of the potentials and dangers of this view.

11.2.1 Metaphors and other dangerous objects

Recently, a renewed interest in metaphors has stressed their importance as instruments of cognition. Metaphors have been assigned a central role in our perceptual and cognitive processes; in fact, we live by metaphors, as the title of an influential study on the subject suggests (Lakoff and Johnson 1980).

Discussions on the aptness and necessity of metaphorical awareness usually focus on the problem of content: what does a particular metaphor express, and how? There is, however, another question that needs to be asked, namely: how felicitous is a particular metaphor in a particular context, such as solving a problem, obtaining consensus, elucidating difficult subject matter, and so on?

As repositories of our past experiences and for guidance in dealing with new ones, metaphors are necessary for our survival. But also, metaphors may make it difficult for us to understand, and be understood by, other people: either because we cannot grasp the others' use of metaphors, or because the other party is unable to follow ours. Either difficulty reflects the fact that our ways of thinking are rooted in a common social practice. Metaphors are not individual means of conceptually dealing with the world, but means that have become current within a given linguistic and cultural community. If it is true that there are metaphors we live by, then different ways of life will correspond to different metaphors; our understanding of 'life's meaning' (in whatever sense of the expression) crucially depends on our understanding of those metaphors, and on our ability to bridge those differences.

The importance of metaphors as a means of dealing with the world has been stressed recently by researchers in various fields. One of them, Anthony Judge, in a thoughtful contribution on 'incommensurable concepts' and their comprehension through metaphor, speaks of a 'metaphoric revolution', by which he means a new openness to the diversity of beliefs and belief systems prevalent among the world's peoples and communities (Judge 1988, 1991). Drawing our attention to the multifarious uses of metaphor in different cultures and to the ways in which such 'congealed forms' of thinking are relevant to, as well as supportive of, mutual understanding, Judge maintains that such an 'openness' is necessary to avoid the conceptual or linguistic 'imperialism' (Phillipson 1991) that downgrades all those who do not think and talk the same way as we do ourselves. Emphasizing our own ways of doing metaphors, we reject the ways practiced by other people as invalid. For this reason, metaphors are always charged with high pragmatic explosives; metaphors are 'loaded weapons' (Bolinger 1980) in need of being secured.

I will demonstrate the necessity of such a critical attitude by analyzing the very metaphor that Judge, in one of his articles (1988), has selected to explain the political processes that are characteristic of Western and westernized democracies. Here is Judge:

> There is a striking parallel between the rotation of crops and the succession of (governmental) policies applied in a society. The contrast is also striking because of the essentially haphazard switch between 'right' and 'left' policies. There is little explicit awareness of the need for any rotation to correct for negative consequences ('pests') encouraged by each and to replenish the resources of society ('nutrients', 'soil structure') which each policy so characteristically depletes. (1988:38)

The basic metaphor is clear: policy-making is a kind of farming; just as in real farming, so in politics, too, one has to shift between different 'crops' in order to obtain a maximum yield from the 'soil'. Such a 'crop rotation' should not be haphazard, though, but calculated in accordance with what we know about each crop's typical features and the particular 'soil structure' of each patch of 'land'. Just as monocultural exploitation (that is, cultivating the same crops over and over again) is the root of all evil in farming, so the unchecked domination of any political system should be avoided at all costs.

Such a domination, with its unilateral, 'monocultural' exploitation of the political 'subsoil', is allowed to take place when "voters are either confronted with single party systems or are frustrated by the lack of real choice between the alternatives offered" (p. 38). The conclusion is that, rather than being confused by the seemingly haphazard changes in policy-making that, even when it is at its best, come with democracy in its Western(ized) forms, we should appreciate that the very life of the body politic is dependent on a system of rotation by which left and right policies alternate, without any of them becoming domineering for too long a period at a time.

Despite Judge's plea for openness in understanding metaphors and his avowed intention to steer a fair middle course between the extremes of political commitment, he is unable to avoid the strong cultural and historical biases that are inherent in the metaphors he uses, and thus ends up falling into his own metaphorical trap. Ironically, in doing so he demonstrates not only that the situation he sets out to describe is real, but also (albeit implicitly) that his explanation is incomplete and his suggested solution insufficient. Assimilating a change in policies between left and right to an "essentially haphazard" crop rotation leaves out the question of the metaphor's *content*: what kind of crops are rotated, and how one should plan their rotation, depending on what they do to the soil. And, contrary to the implications of Judge's metaphor, politics has never been a matter of mere rotation.

First off, 'left' and 'right' policies never were simple alternatives: neither were they equidistant points on a scale, measured from some postulated zero point. In politics, 'left' stands for planning, 'right' for turning loose the forces of so-called 'free enterprise'. In a planned-type economy, the government is supposed, with a maximum of fairness, to allocate the available resources to areas where they are most needed, whilst the societal burdens are divided equally fairly among all, according to their capacities. In a liberal-type economy, the market forces are supposed to exert their beneficial influence for the common good, so that the economy, free from all outside interference and completely 'deregulated', is able to find its natural balance. On this view, what one observes in today's politics (both on the national and on the international scene) is not just an alternation between two extremes on an imaginary scale: 'left' and 'right', but rather, a battle between those who are willing to sacrifice everything for profit (euphemistically called 'growth'), and those who realize that in order to safeguard the scarce resources on our planet, we have to do some planning.

Next, this battle cannot possibly be envisaged as a simple case of 'crop rotation', one alternative replacing the other, to be replaced again by the first, and so on *ad infinitum*. The limited resources of our finite world do not allow of any 'infinity'; which is why the crop metaphor, in addition to being inaccurate on principled grounds, represents a very concrete danger. To have a crop we can rotate, we must have a planet to plant a crop on. The forces of destruction that lead us toward the annihilation of the planet, if only by the simple depletion of its natural resources, will leave nothing to rotate if allowed to proceed by their own devices; this is a further aspect that Judge's metaphor neglects.

Third (as this example illustrates), no metaphor should be considered 'right' or 'wrong' on its own premises. In particular, the use of a simplistic metaphor, such as that of crop rotation, may well obscure the more intricate realities that are at the basis of the problems which the metaphor tries to illustrate. What we have is, in Judge's own words elsewhere, a "practice . . . in defiance of Ashby's

Law of Requisite Variety, namely that, to be effective, any governing or controlling system must be at least as complex as the system it seeks to govern" (1991:7). In the case of metaphor, this means that the metaphors we choose have to be complex and multi-faceted (or even multiple); "simplifying reality to simplify the decision process is a dangerously unsustainable way forward" (ibid.).

Applying this latter, truly pragmatic view to metaphor, we see how the biggest risk of using metaphors is not that they may promote a wrong conception of important issues. Pragmatically speaking, *all* metaphors are somehow wrong, namely, as long as they are not placed within their proper situation of use, and 'rethought' continuously with regard to their applicability or non-applicability. Only the total context of the situation that we want to characterize metaphorically can determine the pragmatic usefulness of a particular metaphor. The inherent danger of metaphor is in the uncritical acceptance of a single-minded model of thinking and its continued, thoughtless recycling, leading to the adoption of one solution as the remedy to all evils, whether their origins are in agriculture, economics or governance in general. The only way to neutralize this danger is to continually go back to the metaphor's roots, and possibly broaden its base or supplement it with other suitable metaphors. Unloading the 'loaded weapon' of language by deconstructing its metaphors is thus an appropriate task of pragmatics; the next section is an effort to set out this task in more detail.

11.2.2 The pragmatics of metaphoring

The primary function of metaphoric expressions is to represent our world through seeing and wording. Wording by metaphor thus differs from the standard, referential account of representation, according to which words merely refer to, and label, objects in what is called the 'real' world. Metaphors are ways of conceptualizing and understanding one's surroundings; as such, they make up a mental model of our world. Moreover, since the metaphors of a particular language community remain more or less stable across historical stages and generational differences, they are of prime importance in securing the continuity, and continued understanding, of our language and culture.

Metaphors are essential when it comes to explaining how people, despite differences in class, culture and religion, are able to communicate across geographical distances and historical periods. For this reason, the study of metaphors provides a unique understanding of the human cognitive capability, as well as an indispensable tool for solving problems in language understanding and acquisition. Even so, metaphors are not the last word in wording; nor do they provide the ultimate solution to the problem of human cognition.

Current views on metaphor, as we saw in the preceding section, are at the same time too constrained and too constraining. They are too constrained, because they only take in those aspects of the problems that they can handle metaphorically. If, for instance, I say (borrowing Judge's example from the pre-

ceding section) that a change of government from time to time is healthy for a
nation, because that's what we do in agriculture when we rotate crops, I limit
myself to those kinds of change that fit in with this particular metaphor, viz., the
actually occurring changes in an agricultural setting. I do not ask what these
changes are, why they are necessary or what their effects are outside the 'field'
I'm working in. People clamoring for political change just because that's what
one does in farming may be in for big surprises (as, by the way, will be the farmer
who practices crop rotation without carefully planning what to plant when,
where and why, and what the effects will be on the environment, both within
and outside of his or her fields).

Such a view is not only limited; it is also extremely limiting in that it con-
strains the depth of our metaphoric understanding as a way of wording the world.
Even if metaphors can provide some of the solutions to our problems, certain
pragmatic questions will have to be asked. It is the entire context of our lives
that determines which metaphors are available and what our wordings are going
to be like; hence metaphors, in order to be pragmatically relevant, should include
and respect their own context. An uncritical, purely descriptive view of metaphor
('Facts – No questions!') may be outright dangerous from a pragmatic point of
view (see Mey 1985:223).

As an illustration, consider the following. In their 1980 book, Lakoff and
Johnson routinely assign the human female to the metaphorical 'low' position,
whereas the corresponding 'high' is taken up by the male; this happens about ten
times in the course of one and a half pages (1980:15–16). A reasonable explanation for this curious phenomenon seems to be that the authors see our society
in terms of power: men on top, women at the bottom of a metaphorical 'power
pyramid'.

However, the conceptual path from society and its power structures to language is not a direct one; we cannot go straight from one 'universe' (that of
power) to another (that of language). The way we deal with the world is dependent on the way we structure it metaphorically; conversely, the way we see the
world as a coherent, metaphorical structure helps us to deal with that world. Put
another way, metaphors are not only ways of *solving* problems: they are, in a
profound sense, ways of *setting* the problems. As Donald Schön remarks, in an
important early study: "When we examine the problem-setting stories told by the
analysts and practitioners of social policy, it becomes apparent that the framing
of problems often depends upon metaphors underlying the stories which generate problem setting and set the directions of problem solving" (1979:255).

There is, in other words, a dialectic movement from word to world and from
world to word. Logically, neither movement is prior to the other; ontologically,
both arise at the same time in the history of human development. In particular,
as regards the development of the individual, when the child acquires its language, it is exposed to 'worlding' at the same time that it begins its 'wording'.
Ontologically and epistemologically, neither the world is prior to the word, nor
the word to the world (*pace* St John).

Applied to the case of Lakoff and Johnson, this means that the structure under-lying the metaphorical 'up' vs. 'down' both is presupposed by, and sets, the mental dispositions that make us assign those metaphorical positions to people. The terms of the metaphor are not only indicative of our thinking about people; they set our minds in the direction of the metaphor: some people are up, others down. Whereupon the actual power structures of our society, with its 'ups' and 'downs', quasi-automatically glide into place, and assign the powerless (the women) to the low position, the powerful (the men) to the position up high. In one sweeping movement, the world where men are up, women down, is both set and confirmed by the metaphor, which now seems vindicated by reality, if only in a circular way.

As Treichler and Frank point out: "language constructs as well as reflects culture. Language thus no longer serves as the transparent vehicle of content or as the simple reflection of reality, but itself participates in how that content and reality are formed, apprehended, expressed, and transformed" (1989:3). In order to determine what a particular wording is worth, therefore, one has to investi-gate the conditions that determine the processes of 'forming, apprehending, expressing, and transforming' that Treichler and Frank mention. We must ask what kind of wording the metaphor represents, and how this wording affects our thinking, and determines a particular mind-set, for which it may have been devel-oped in the first place.

The consequences of this view of wording are that one cannot understand one's partners in dialogue unless one has a good grasp of their word–world rela-tionships (including, but not limited to, their making of metaphors). In order to understand another person's wording, I have to word the world with him or her, by participating in a common social context. A pragmatic view of language use (and, in general, of all social activity; cf. Schön 1979) thus demands a 'sympa-thetic' practice of co-wording, in solidarity with the context of its users.

To understand a man, the proverb says, you have to walk a mile in his shoes. To understand a person's utterance, you ideally must be able to say it yourself, in your conversational partner's own context – which, after all, is no more than can be expected of one's interlocutors in any decent conversation. Language in use (and in particular, the use of metaphor) is at the same time a necessary instru-ment of cognition and an expression of that cognition. Metaphor, as a user's use of language, is a pragmatic precondition to understanding the user's context; con-versely, that context (which, of course, includes the other language users) makes it possible for that language to be understood.[128]

In this way, a pragmatic view of metaphoring serves to point the way to a better understanding of our fellow humans. In particular, it tells us what things other groups in society, other classes, other nations, attach weight to and prior-itize in their interaction with themselves, with their environment and with the others (including us). As an example, think of the different metaphors sur-rounding the rain forest and its destruction, when seen from a Western intellec-tual's point of view, as contrasted to that of the pre-industrial *caboclos* and *garimpeiros* (subsistence farmers and gold diggers) in Amazônia, Brazil. The difference here is not primarily one of conceptual structures organizing our world, of "metaphors structuring the actions we perform" (Lakoff and Johnson 1980:3); on the contrary, it is our activity of living in the world that structures our thoughts and concepts, including the metaphors we use. The poorer-than-poor inhabitants of Amazônia, who have to fight every day to survive the adversities created by both people and nature, conceptualize the rain forest not only as a force that has to be overcome (just as was the case in our own parts of the world in earlier times), but also as their 'nest-egg', their savings (*poupança*), that will carry them through in bad times. Rather than adopting the Western metaphor, representing the riches of the rain forest as a natural resource, a 'patrimony', belonging to all of humankind, the settlers and diggers are forced by their life conditions to exploit those resources for their immediate needs and their long-term survival; it is those activities that structure their metaphoric understanding of the 'environment'. By contrast, the Western metaphorical conceptualization sees the poor settlers and miners as a unique and serious 'threat' to the environment, whilst the big companies are said to 'protect' what is left of the forest against the 'folly of deforestation', practiced by the 'landless' (*sem-terra*).[129]

In this way, pragmatics forces us to critically understand our own position in the world, to realize the immense and mostly undeserved privileges that our Western societies are endowed with. This critical view is especially needed in cases where the privileges are, so to speak, self-perpetuating and pre-empt any changes unless we seriously examine, and make an effort to dismantle, our privileged status. The following sections will consider these aspects of a societal pragmatics.

11.3 Pragmatics and the social struggle

11.3.1 Language and manipulation

The 'special bind' that I quoted Erving Goffman for at the end of section 11.1.4 is a particularly clear case of manipulation, understood as: making people behave in a certain way without their knowing why, even against their own wishes and best interests. Often, the instrument of manipulation is language; in such cases, we speak of linguistic manipulation. The latter can thus be defined as the successful hiding (also called 'veiling') of societal oppression by means of manipulatory language (Mey 1985:209ff).

A case in point is the medical interview, as we have seen above. Another, closely related case is the professional manipulation of schizophrenic patients' speech and its classification as a 'non-language', called 'schizophasia': that is, as a symptom of a mental illness rather than as a means of communication. To see this, consider the following two, analogical cases.

Suppose that a political prisoner complains to his legal counsel about his letters being opened. Such a complaint makes sense in the context; the prisoner may not be successful in stopping the guards' practice of letter-opening, but his utterance: 'They are opening my mail' is at least taken seriously.

Not so with the psychiatric patient. The same utterance, in a psychiatric institutional environment, is registered as a schizophrenic symptom, proving that the person who utters the sentence is duly and properly a resident of the mental hospital. The patient, by complaining about his or her letters being opened, has furnished conclusive proof of the fact that he or she is not normal, hence has no right to complain. So, ironically, and in accordance with Goffman's observation quoted earlier, the only correct way of complaining is not to complain; which of course is sheer madness, and proves the point of the patient's being committed.

But we don't have to visit psychiatric institutions to find examples of such linguistic manipulation. Consider the following. Suppose I'm looking for a job. I tell myself that I must make a good impression on my potential future employer; I put on my best suit and tie, and go to the interview in the hope that she or he will 'give me the job'. Now, I may not be so lucky: the employer may tell me that the job has been 'taken'; somebody else 'got it'. That means they 'have no work' for me, and so on and so forth. In the universe of employment, employers give, and employees take. Such is 'our' world, as presented to us through the veil of 'our' language.

But what happens behind this manipulatory veil? There, we have a totally different picture: it's the employer who takes the employee's labor, and converts it to her or his own profit. The employee gives his or her labor power to the employer, in exchange for a salary offered; but there is one big catch: the wages, although they are called 'fair' and are arrived at in 'free negotiation', represent a clear case of societal oppression. To see this, consider the following.

The employer knows that she or he must make the employee accept less than the value of his or her labor, or else there wouldn't be any profits. The wages are not the equivalent of a certain amount of work: rather, they represent a period of time during which the employer is entitled to press all the labor out of the employee that she or he possibly can. Wages express the price relation between labor power and whatever else is bought and sold in the marketplace; hence the wages can be called 'fair' only in the sense that they obey the market laws, not as representing equitable remuneration for a certain amount of work done.

But as if this were not enough, the words we use hide the real state of affairs. 'Our' language manipulates us into doing whatever the powerful in society tell us to do – which is what the medical or psychiatric consultation and the job interview have in common. With regard to the latter, somebody might object that the worker doesn't have to take the employment: a job applicant is a free agent, and can refuse the employer's offer; also, once employed, the employee may give notice at any time. However, on a closer look we see how the very way we formulate this reasoning is yet another instance of manipulatory language use. We perceive a linguistic relation of symmetry between the two nouns, *employer* and *employee*; this relation is expressed by the suffixes *-er* and *-ee*, denoting respectively the 'agent' and the 'patient' of the action (cf. the pair *interviewer–interviewee*). In this way, we are led to believe that the real-world relationship between the bearers of those names is equally symmetrical: the employer is at the active end, the employee at the passive end of the employment relation, only with a different orientation: the employer employs the employee, the employee is employed by the employer. Even the language seems to tell us that this is a fair, symmetrical deal!

However, what the language does *not* tell us (and this is the catch) is which of the two, employer and employee, wields the power in this relationship. It is the employer who has the sole right to employ or not to employ; conversely, the employee has no right to be employed by the employer. Which shows us where the true power in this situation lies, despite the apparent symmetry of the employment relation and its manipulatory, linguistic correlate.

The next section will look into some ways that we can use language to thwart this linguistic mis-representation of reality.

11.3.2 Emancipatory language

The growing interest in pragmatics as a user-oriented science of language naturally leads to the question: in what sense is pragmatics useful to the users? In particular, given that a sizeable portion of the users of any language are underprivileged in their relation to language, and are so because of their underprivileged position in society, a deeper insight into the causes of social underprivilege may trigger a fresh view of the role of language in social processes; conversely, a renewed consciousness of language as serving social inequality may lead us toward a liberating, or 'emancipatory', use of language.

In the wake of the European 'student movement' of the sixties, there have been many attempts at making linguistics 'socially relevant', as the slogan went. Many of these efforts have not yielded the expected benefits, such as the earlier-mentioned Bernstein-inspired reforms of the school curricula. More recent setbacks include the cuts in bilingual education programs (not only in the US, but also in many European countries such as Sweden, Germany and Denmark), and the failure to achieve a consistent and internationally accepted policy toward minorities and their linguistic rights. Two of the flagrant examples that come to mind here are, one, the total lack of respect that the Turkish government shows for the language spoken by the Kurdic minority (the government even tries to deny the language its independent status by calling it 'Mountain Turkish', an appellation that flies in the face of all factual and linguistic evidence); and two, the 'English as an official language' movement that has gained momentum in many states of the US, and which aims at more or less outlawing the use of minority languages (in this case, mostly Spanish) in official and other (public as well as private) contexts.[130]

On the other hand, some programs have had a modicum of success, at least on matters of principle: consider the various efforts at improving communication between public offices and the people. Thus, in Sweden, the government has appointed an official commission to investigate the use of 'public language', whose recommendations for rather drastic changes have then been put into effect; in the US, various measures have been adopted that aim at reducing the amount of paperwork and simplifying the language of official documents (cf. the 1980 'Paperwork Reduction Act'); and so on.

On balance, the important question is maybe not what actually has been achieved, but whether there is a movement in the right direction, a light at the end of the tunnel. Are there any hopes of practicing pragmatics in the sense of what I have called, perhaps somewhat optimistically, an 'emancipatory linguistics'?

How we deal with this question depends, of course, to a great extent on what we understand by 'emancipation'. If that concept is understood as the elimination of social injustice, as a getting rid of the 'bonds' that are inherent in the very word 'emancipation' (from the Latin word *mancipium*, 'slavery, bondage'), then language is not the only, or principal, tool to use. Whether we like it or not, the world is governed by politicians, as Chancellor Axel Oxenstierna told his king, Gustavus Adolphus of Sweden, over three and a half centuries ago. Linguists have no political clout. So what can a linguist do, given the 'bondage' that is in effect in our society, and which is instrumental in creating and maintaining its divisions: between haves and have-nots, between rich and poor, between male and female, young and old? What are the opportunities for pragmatic linguists to step into the fray and join the struggle to abolish those divisive patterns and distribute society's goods more equally?

The answer to these questions is implicitly contained in the definition of pragmatics that I offered in section 1.2.1. If "pragmatics studies the use of language in human communication as determined by the conditions of society", then the task of pragmatics in linguistics is to turn the attention of the linguists toward the greater context of society, and away from focusing exclusively on their own scientific and professional interests. Geared toward a greater social consciousness of problems in the use of language, the linguists will want to spend part of their time suggesting and devising remedial treatment of socially caused linguistic problems, as well as of linguistically preserved and perpetuated social inequality. Using Einar Haugen's metaphor, first coined in the sixties, one could speak of a new concern for our common linguistic environment in the sense of an ecology of language (Haugen 1972).

Such a pragmatic reorientation of linguistics implies a conscious focusing on the users of language. Moreover, this consciousness on the part of the linguists contributes toward making the language users more conscious of their language as well. In particular, it can help underprivileged users transcend the boundaries of their underprivileged, restricted language use, without having them buy into the elaborated myths and fantasies of the privileged classes. Conversely, the privileged users' consciousness should be raised, too, so they no longer consider the privileges of their societal position as natural and non-controversial. (On 'naturalness', see further section 11.3.4.3.)

Questions of this kind touch upon some basic issues regarding the relationship between language and society. Earlier (in section 3.3.3), I remarked that our language use, and in particular the system of language itself, in both its referential and its syntactic aspects, has a certain affinity with the prevailing social conditions (the example given was the change in gender-based reference and syntactic agreement rules for professional titles in Spanish). While these correspondences are of undoubted empirical value, the other side of the coin has to be examined as well. In fact, the problem is a variant of that other, age-old dilemma: which is first, the chicken or the egg? Transposed to the current context, the question is: does society influence and determine language or does language influence, and maybe determine, society?

The British linguist Dale Spender (1984:195) has remarked that the relationship between language and reality can be summarized in two seemingly contradictory statements: on the one hand, language represents the world in a symbolic fashion: on the other hand, language is also an instrument that we use for organizing the world and 'constructing our culture' (Treichler and Frank 1989:3; see section 11.2.2). How can we reconcile these seemingly incompatible views on the relationships of language and reality?

Taking our cue from the chicken-and-egg problem, the answer could be that for most people living on earth, both chickens and eggs have always been part of their daily lives; we don't have to start from scratch every time like Adam and Eve, who had to make do with whatever they had got from their Creator, whether chicken or egg, and for whom the problem thus probably did not even exist in the first place. Or one could, like a Zen master, turn the question around and tell one's student to stop worrying and either kill the chicken or eat the egg. In a more serious vein, the question is of the ways we think about language in a changing society, and how social changes affect our consciousness and our use of language.

Language, in Marx and Engels's immortal phrase, is our 'practical consciousness' (1974:51). But this consciousness is not an independent entity; as Louis Dupré says, "consciousness is determined by language, and language arises out of social relations, which themselves depend upon the material production" (1966:155) as it is realized through our actions. Language is the practical consciousness of our actions: it tells us what we're doing; but at the same time, it is the conscious instrument of our planning: it tells us what to do (Mey 1985:218–20). Thus, language is both the record-keeper of reality, in that it reflects our actions, and its rule and guideline, in that it, through our actions, continually creates and re-creates reality. Moreover, since our practice of reality (including language) cannot but be social, our linguistic consciousness (being realistic and practical) is by the same token a *social* consciousness. We are born as social humans, long before we realize that we are human individuals.

I conclude that any effort at making things better in society must involve, at some level or other, a consciousness of the conditions that we, along with all the other humans, live under. This consciousness is often dormant, and may have to be awakened (or 'raised': cf. the familiar expression 'consciousness-raising' which gained currency during the seventies and eighties in the wake of the feminist movement). Applying this to the question: 'To what extent can language help us in fighting societal injustice, social inequality and plain oppression?', the answer is: 'To the extent that our language and our "raised" consciousness operate in tandem, reinforcing each other at every twist and turn of the pragmatic circuit.' Only if this condition is met can we think of linguistics as an 'emancipatory' activity.

In order to focus our discussion, let's consider a particular case in order to illustrate the potential of such a pragmatic approach. The next section will deal with the problem of *linguistic sexism*.

11.3.3 Language and gender

For thousands of years, the social formations in which most of our species has lived have been dominated by males. In this oppressive societal condition (Mey 1985:25f), the powerful dominate the powerless, not only in material respects, but also regarding other, less tangible matters, such as the use of language. Becoming aware of this oppression is the first condition for engaging oneself actively on the side of the oppressed, first of all, of the women, for whom the fact that 'man made language' (Spender 1980) is the main condition of linguistic oppression.

Awareness alone, of course, does not make oppression go away. But forcing ourselves to bring the problem out into the open, 'wording it', is one major, if not the only way for us to deal with it in a practical perspective, through the use of language. An 'emancipatory' language, that is, a use of language that does not subscribe to the commonly established prejudices about, and skewed images of, women, will change men's ways of thinking of women, while it makes women conscious of the importance of language in their lives. Every time we force ourselves to use a form like 'she or he', rather than the so-called generic 'he' (supposedly covering both sexes),[131] a little step is taken toward the realization of the fact that 'man-made language' is an historical accident, not a natural condition which cannot be changed. The presence of women in the world can be emphasized and protected through this seemingly insignificant small shift in the language – and therefore, it is not useless or in vain.

The British philosopher and educationalist Trevor Pateman, reflecting on how an outer change can affect an inner attitude, concludes that by changing a practice, we "restructur[e] a social relationship, and [the] experience in the new social relationship thereby created . . . can effect the inner change" (1980:15). In turn, and just as naturally, the inner change will affect the outer world: language is a social activity, and promoting a change in language is a way of telling the world that it has to change as well. Ideally, emancipatory language is the "adequate expression of a true societal consciousness, one which is neither oppressed nor oppressing" (Mey 1985:374).

For some decades now, conscious linguists have waged war on sexism in language use; small but significant victories have been won in this skirmish: witness the growing number of journals that subscribe to the guidelines for the 'non-sexist' use of language adopted and promulgated by various scientific societies, such as the American Psychological Association, the American Anthropological Association, the Modern Language Association of America, the Linguistic Society of America, the International Pragmatics Association, along with their various journals: *American Anthropologist*, *PMLA*, *Language*, *Journal of Pragmatics*, *Pragmatics* and so on.

Of course, the mere substitution of a 'combined' pronoun such as *he/she* for the supposedly 'generic' *he* cannot, of itself, change a society that oppresses and underprivileges its female members. However, to quote Sally McConnell-Ginet, "earlier feminist research has established that *he*, no matter what its user intends, is not unproblematically interpreted as generic, and the consequent shift in the community's beliefs about how *he* is interpreted has influenced what one can intend the pronoun to convey" (1989:49). In other words, the non-generic use of the personal pronoun is one of the areas in which emancipatory linguistics actually has been successful, albeit to a modest degree. A whole new code for the use of pronouns in English has been established (and widely accepted). Their non-gendered use reflects our growing consciousness of women's presence in society; at the same time, and with apparent success, this change of language use changes the ways society's members (both female and male) speak, write and think about women, treat women and interact with women.

Such a change, however, is not something that just happens, once and for all; it has to be continuously negotiated and nurtured, so as to prevent a relapse. Let me once more quote McConnell-Ginet: "[language] matters so much precisely because so little matter is attached to it; meanings are not given but must be produced and reproduced, negotiated in situated contexts of communication" (1989:49). That is, the use of language needs to be negotiated between the users of language themselves in their daily social and communicative relations and linguistic interactions.

Thus, the question I raised in section 1.3.2.1: 'Why do we need pragmatics?' has now (at least partially) been answered: we need pragmatics because it represents the societally necessary and consciously interactive dimension of the study of language.

Moreover, we must extend our theoretical speculations about language into the realm of practice, and show people how pragmatics can assist us, as language users, in our endeavors to realize our personal goals in the social setting we live in. At the same time, we continue to try and improve that setting so that it may become a proper environment for all users of language. Pragmatics is the linguistic side of what the Norwegian philosopher Arne Næss once called 'ecosophy', the reasoned relationship of humans with their world. Pragmatics *is* ecological linguistics.

One particular effort in this direction is associated with the concept of 'critical language awareness'; this will be the subject of the final section of my book.

11.3.4 Critical pragmatics

11.3.4.1 What is 'critical'?

The word 'critical' is often used to indicate a reflective, examining stance toward the phenomena of life. In the tradition of the social sciences, the term was introduced by the Frankfurt School of the thirties (Horkheimer, Adorno, Benjamin) and their post-war heirs, the 'Neo-Frankfurtians', among whom Jürgen Habermas is perhaps the best known. Common to all these thinkers is that they examine social life, and society itself, from the angle of what I would call a 'considered subjectivity'. They do not believe in the 'naked facts' of any science, in particular not when that science deals with humans. The point of view of the observer, and his or her interests in observing, have always to be taken into account.

For many of these original critical philosophers, sociologists, literates and linguists, however, a subjective interest did not suffice as an explanatory ground; it had to be supplemented (or even supplanted) by the objective interests of class, in a Marxist-oriented approach to social science; hence in the past, 'critical' and 'Marxist' (or 'Marxian', as preferred by some) were often considered to be more or less synonymous.

In pragmatics, the origin of the term 'critical' goes perhaps back to an early article which the present author wrote under the title 'Toward a critical theory of language' (Mey 1979). In that article, I tried to formulate some minimal conditions for an activity of 'linguistic emancipation', especially in relation to the media of instruction in the schools. Perhaps because the piece was written in German, but more probably because it appeared at a time when the Marxist inspiration of critical theory was on the wane, the thoughts expressed there went mainly unobserved by the linguistic community.

At about the same time, a group of researchers in England (Roger Fowler and his colleagues at the University of East Anglia; Fowler et al. 1979) developed their notion of 'critical linguistics', in which they put great emphasis on the relationship between social power and language use; they intended to show how the ruling classes of society also determine the ruling language. Due to the subsequent geographical dispersion of the group, this approach too did not have, at the time, the impact it deserved; however, in many ways it was responsible for the subsequent revival and success of the critical tradition in Australia and

England, in the latter country especially as embodied in the ideas propagated by the Lancaster group (on which see below).

In a book I wrote some years later (Mey 1985), I applied the concepts of Marxian dialectics to the problems of social language use, in particular the language of labor disputes and their reflections in the media. Another focus of attention in that work was the linguistic and pedagogical methods used in second language training for adult immigrants. The recurrent themes of the book were the same as those stressed by earlier critical social scientists and linguists; its general tenor can be encapsulated in a rule of thumb as follows: to find out what language is used for, you have to find the user, and determine what makes him or her speak. The employer speaks in a different fashion than does the worker, and this is not so much a matter of the various dialects they use, but of the different ways in which they 'word the world', as I called it (Mey 1985:166).

In the late eighties and early nineties, with the growing impact of pragmatics on the linguistics and language scene, several movements arose, professing a critical approach to matters of language use. Since pragmatics, by its very definition, concerns the users of language, the critical approach in pragmatics had to narrow its focus to those areas where language use was critically determined by the relations of power in society, placing the language users in a 'critical' position. Institutional discourse, in particular, became a focus of attention, as I have shown in section 11.1, with respect to medical, educational and media language. The following sections will broaden the scope of discussion, focusing in particular on the power relations determining these and other societal discourses.

11.3.4.2 'Critical pragmatics': the Lancaster School

Since nobody, to my knowledge, has appropriated the term yet, I suggest letting the approaches mentioned in the preceding sections be suitably captured by the common denominator of 'critical pragmatics'. Here, I'm thinking not only of work done by people such as Teun van Dijk (in a number of articles, and mainly through his influential journal *Discourse and Society*, published since 1990), but also, and mainly, of the so-called 'Lancaster School' of critical language awareness, centered on Norman Fairclough and his co-workers (cf. Fairclough 1989, 1992, 1995).

For Fairclough too, 'critical' has to do with examining the fundamental relations that assign power to various groups in our society; at the same time, however, he insists on having language (the 'text') along, the latter being one particularly important instrument of exercising that power.

In Fairclough's work, the language people speak and write looms large, just as it does in the writings of his collaborators and (former) students (Clark, Talbot, Wallace, to name a few; see the collection edited by Fairclough in 1992). The other aspect, that of power, is emphasized as what one seizes through discourse; power *is* discourse in a power-oriented society (Fairclough 1992:50). That means that we read a text in different ways, depending on whether we as readers construe it in a powerful or in a powerless situation. The following example is due to Janks and Ivanič (1992).

An overseas academic visitor to England found himself enrolled as a student in a graduate course at the hosting university, even though he was a full-time researcher in his home country, and had advised graduate students of his own. The ensuing identity conflict made it difficult for him to critically evaluate his role as a language user, especially when doing the reading assignments for his courses. After many frustrating months, he decided to take the matter up with his supervisor, who realized what the nature of his problem was, and rather than assigning him yet another paper to read for the course, gave him some of her own work to read and discuss. The foreign lecturer/student now started to use language in a totally different way: what had been an instrument of oppression (teaching as imparted by authority) became now an instrument of emancipation (reading as part of a collegial discourse among equals). He found that not only had his reading changed, but his own stance in the reading process had become another: from being the subservient consumer, he became an active co-producer of the text.[132] As Janks and Ivanič succinctly express it: "From the empowered position, failure to comprehend was not assumed to be a weakness in him, the reader, but in the writing. He shifted from asking, as a student, 'Can I understand this?' to asking, as a colleague, 'Is this understandable and useful?'" (1992:310–11).

What this story shows is the significance of societal emancipation for an 'appropriate' (Fairclough 1995) use of language; conversely, it underscores the important role that language plays in emancipating us from the slavery of words. Slavery, both in language and in real life, is essentially lack of power: slaves cannot dispose of their time and labor power, or even of their lives. Similarly, the enslaved language users cannot dispose of their speaking, reading and other uses of language: they must execute their language duties as directed, not as preferred, and their language lives are always at the mercy of some authority, telling them what is appropriate use of language, and what not.

A special case of this power relationship may be observed when the power goes underground, so to speak, being assimilated by the powerless. This process, called 'naturalization', will be the subject of our next section.

11.3.4.3 Power and naturalization

Even though in the eye of the naïve beholder, power and its cruel executors may seem the most obvious element of oppression (the SS guard cracking the whip over a line of camp inmates, Brutus's father swinging the ax that will separate his disobedient son's head from his body,[133] the dictator standing in his open car, acknowledging the devoted salute of the obedient masses), what characterizes power as a *social* factor is not its brute force as such, but rather, its being accepted as a *natural* thing. 'You can't fight City Hall' is the philosophically resigned expression of such a naturalized understanding of the powers that be.

Naturalization is said to happen whenever what should be critically examined and resisted is taken as a natural matter, with the self-evidence of the commonsensical world which "goes without saying because it comes without saying", to vary Bourdieu's elegant quip (1977:167).[134] It is natural for the police to question a prospective detainee, and even if the law tells us that the only information we need to give out is our names and addresses (and perhaps, in certain countries, our social security numbers or equivalents), it is 'natural' for somebody who is pulled over to answer, without protesting, all the police officer's questions, even if they go beyond the limits of the morally and legally permissible.

In the following extract from a taped police interrogation (Fairclough 1995), the legitimacy of the policemen's interventions is never doubted by the detainee, even though, under every aspect proper to normal conversation (cooperation, turn-taking and so on), the police's questioning methods must be characterized as 'out of order':

(*A young woman is brought in to a police station in England, having charged three men with rape. A is the woman, B and C are police officers*)

C: . . . so we can confirm . . . that you've had sex with three men . . . if it does confirm it . . . then I would go so far as to say . . . that you went to that house willingly . . . there's no struggle . . .
. . .
C: . . . so what's to stop you . . . shouting and screaming in the street . . . when you think you're going to get raped . . . you're not frightened at all . . . you walk in there quite blasé you're not frightened at all . . .
A: I was frightened
C: you weren't . . . you're showing no signs of emotion . . .
B: . . . you're female and you've probably got a hell of a temper . . . if you were to go . . .
A: I haven't got a temper
B: I think if things were up against a wall . . . I think you'd fight and fight very hard. (1995:29–30)

The point of this 'conversation' is for the officers to bill the complainant as a person who has no right to complain about being raped: one, she probably was asking for it; two, if she had been attacked, she would have put up a struggle; and three, since she has a violent temper, she would have been able to fight off her aggressors quite easily. All this is expressed in both innuendoes and direct statements, and no matter what the woman says or tries to deny, the policemen do not budge an inch from their preconceived notions about what has happened; they are not going to take this case seriously.

The naturalness of this interview in terms of police officer behavior and client response is attested by the fact that at no point of the interrogation is the legitimacy of the police's interventions questioned, not even when they flatly accuse the woman of lying, of being hysterical, of making things up, and so on. Again, it's a case of 'You can't fight City Hall' (or, for that matter, the Precinct): the harder we try, the more entrapped we get in our own submission and the more vicious the authorities' retributions become for what they consider to be impertinent behavior.

The same 'naturalized' behavior is evident in the following incident, which recounts a personal experience:

(*In late March of 1964, I was travelling through the French city of Auxerre on my way to Troyes, where my daughter was hospitalized. I was in a hurry, trying to make the official visiting hours, and in my confusion misinterpreted a local policeman's manual traffic directions at an intersection. I was pulled over, told to stay put and wait for him to be done with his duties. When the policeman, at the end of fifteen minutes' waiting, ordered me to report to the precinct office to pay my fine, 3,000 (old) francs, I protested, telling him that I was in a hurry, for the reasons given above. His answer was:*)

Vous ne pouvez dire deux mots sans mentir! Lorsque vous aurez payé votre contravention, on vous croira!

('You cannot say two words without lying! When you've paid your fine, we'll believe you!')

Needless to say, having paid the fine, I didn't bother to inquire further about my credibility rating, and left the police station with mixed feelings of impotence, rage and wonder: 'How could a police officer make such a statement about a person he'd never seen in his life, and get away with it?' The answer, again, is: 'naturalization': police power is so ingrained in our everyday representations of normal, civil life that it never occurs to us to even question it.

It is the task of a critical pragmatics to examine the conditions that underlie such naturalized behaviors (which are frequent also in other societal settings; for a medical parallel, cf. Nijhof 1998). As Fairclough remarks, "naturalization gives to particular ideological representations the status of *common sense*, and thereby makes them . . . no longer visible as ideologies" (1995:42; my italics; the expression 'common sense' is borrowed from the work of Gramsci; see Mininni 1990). The ideology of the police as powerful friends of the population ('your friendly local police') masks the reality of police oppression by naturalizing and 'familiarizing' it. When asking for the conditions implicitly determining this situation, we must resort to an analysis of the political power that drives the ideology, as we have seen in section 11.2.

11.4   Conclusion

The social aspects of pragmatics are many, but they all have this in common: they deal with the question of 'whose language' (Mey 1985) we are speaking, and on whose authority we can form our words and utter our sentences, if not 'correctly', at least 'appropriately'. What is important in pragmatics is to critically examine, and try to understand, the social functioning of language and its various manifestations of use. Different language use is not just a matter of linguistic variation, to be described and classified in purely theoretical terms, or to be analyzed with the aid of sociological variables denoting class or other societal parameters. The main impact of pragmatics as a *social* science is in the ways it helps us to recognize social discrimination and motivates us to work toward ending it.

From this perspective, the interesting aspect of, say, *speech acts* is not how they can be categorized, or what felicity and other conditions they should obey (as discussed in sections 5.2 through 5.5): what interests the pragmaticist is what people can do, given those conditions, how they can act pragmatically, obeying those conditions. In this way, every felicity condition becomes "Felicity's condition", as Goffman pointed out in a posthumous article (1983:53).

Likewise, analyzing *conversation* should not be restricted to describing the mechanisms of turn-taking or of the ways people have of announcing and maintaining, say, 'turn-constructional units' and other conversational techniques (as described in section 6.3). From a critically pragmatic perspective, what conversation analysts should primarily worry about is how these mechanisms are related to the powers of society that operate in discourse (including, but not limited to, conversation).

Under the *pragmatic perspective* (cf. section 1.2.2.1), the truly interesting aspects of conversations (as of speech acts) are in the different ways they manifest themselves in different user contexts. Thus, using language in conversation can be many things: from an exchange between equals on the job or in the home, to 'passing the time of day' with total strangers, to specialized types of conversation such as the medical or job interview, or even the 'conversations' with the police or other authorities that we looked at in the preceding section.

The purposes and affordances of conversation, as of any other use of language, are strictly determined by the *social setting* (in particular, the institution) in which it occurs. This setting is responsible for the linguistic interaction's organizational framework; it does not allow too many degrees of freedom or independence for the individual language users, in particular the disempowered ones (Janks and Ivanič 1992:311ff). Pragmatics, especially in its social-critical variety, aims at increasing that freedom and independence by making the users of language conscious of, unveil and (if necessary) oppose, the institutional and linguistic conditions of power that they are living under.

Summing up, using Fairclough's words:

from the critical perspective, a statement of the conditions under which inter-actions of a particular type [including conversation and all sorts of verbal cooperation] may occur is a necessary element of an account of such interac-tions, and such a statement cannot be made without reference to the distrib-ution and exercise [of power] in the institution and ultimately, in the social formation [i.e., the society at large]. (1995:48; glosses added by me)

Review and discussion

1. In section 11.2.1, we have seen how the world is 'worded' mostly through our use of various metaphors (many of which remain below our level of aware-ness; the so-called 'dead' metaphors). Similarly, our maneuvers of linguistic manipulation are largely based on the use of metaphor. It was also remarked that the 'real' content of the metaphor is perhaps not as important as the social and other situations it evokes. Consider, for instance, the press's use of metaphoric expressions to characterize the US military action against Iraq in January of 1993, as illustrated by the following expressions found as newspaper headings in the Chicago area:

(a)

U.S. warplanes punish Iraq

(b)

A slap on the wrist for Saddam Hussein

(c)

Saddam receives spanking

Questions:
The three expressions above have one feature in common; can you identify it? (Hint: look first at (c).)
Can you characterize the metaphoric 'source universe' that these expressions come from?

What are the social implications of using this kind of metaphoric source?
What motivates the journalists to use such expressions?
Do you think their choice of metaphors (as in this case) is always a conscious one? If not, how to explain the amazing convergence of the three expressions, (a), (b) and (c)?

How do these metaphors manipulate the reader? (Hint: refer back to section 11.1.3, where the language of the media was discussed. Compare also section 11.1.4 on the situation of patients in a mental hospital.)

2. The following statement is from an advertisement for a bank, Avondale Federal Savings, 'For Four Generations Of Homeowners' (radio station WBEZ, Chicago, September 23, 1992):

> These are the building blocks from which Avondale has grown, and that will continue to guide it into the future: friendly service, a quality product, and an unrelenting commitment to safety.

Questions:
The above text illustrates what is often called a 'mixing of metaphors'. Can you identify the various 'source domains' that get mixed up here? (The 'source domain' is where the metaphor originally comes from).
Can you provide further examples of this phenomenon?

Compare now the fact that school teachers and journal editors generally frown on metaphor mixing, and do everything they can to eradicate its use.
Why do you think such a use is offensive? (Hint: try to establish what *causes* metaphors to get mixed up; cf. also the 'dead' metaphors mentioned above.)

The amount of energy that people display chasing down undesirable language uses (such as faulty spelling, bad grammar, mixed metaphors and so on) is often astonishing. Do you have any explanation to offer why this is so? (Hint: refer to section 11.1.2, on the role of 'correct' language in an educational setting. As with all uses of language, also 'bad' use is socially conditioned.)

3. This and the following two exercises deal with what is often broadly called 'sexist use of language'. Consider the following case:

> In July [1993], Judge Robert Zack of Broward County, Florida, found topless hot-dog vendor Terri Cortina not guilty of indecent exposure. In court, Zack read aloud a law that stipulated that it is illegal "for any person to expose or exhibit his sexual organs."
> Said Zack, "I don't think this lady has male sexual organs. I [have] no choice but to release her." (*Reader*, Chicago, December 4, 1992, Section 4, p. 25)

Questions:
What was Judge Zack's opinion based on, from a linguistic point of view? (Hint: refer to the discussion in section 11.3.3 of 'generic' pronouns vs. pronouns and other linguistic items that are strictly determined by gender.)
Do you feel that, in the context of the law text, *his* is used as a generic pronoun? Are you familiar with similar uses in other official documents, and can you give some examples?

Was Zack right in acquitting the defendant?

Suppose you, a radical feminist, were present in the Florida courtroom where Judge Zack pronounced his sentence. Would you have objected (if you legally could) to his use of a 'generic loophole' to prevent a female from being punished for transgressing a male-imposed and male-oriented restriction on nudity? (Compare that under Austin, Tex., City Ordinances, it is legal for a woman to appear topless in public, the motivation for this rule being an officially adopted policy of equality between the sexes.)

Would you say that the judge's decision is acceptable from a pragmatic viewpoint? (Motivate your answer.)

4. WBEZ, the Chicago public radio station, had an interview on August 28, 1992, with the (male) director of advertising of a New York firm, which had placed an ad in the *New York Times* for tartan bras (complete with matching boxer shorts) for the astonishing price of $78. The topic of the discussion was: why would women be willing to pay so much for underwear?

The (male) interviewer suggested that it might have something to do with the feeling that underwear was important to women, so important in fact that the girls thought it was normal, if one went out with a man, that he'd pay for the dinner, since they had already paid so much for the underwear! Next, he mentioned the curious fact that, although this was a typically feminine topic, the two people who were discussing it were both male. The interviewer continued:

> [INTERVIEWER:] So here we were discussing this at the office with a group of women, and how come when I call, that I'm talking to a man?
> [DIRECTOR OF ADVERTISING:] Well I'm the director of advertising, and since you inquired about an ad . . .
> [INT.:] Well, Mr O'Brien, I suppose that if it had been a woman who'd called, the interview would have gone better.
> [DIR.:] It went badly??
> (*microphone cut off by interviewer*)

Questions:
Underlying this interview are some assumptions about the relationship between men and women, in particular how they relate to money expenditures individually and vis-à-vis one another. Can you make these assumptions explicit, and say whether they are:
(a) realistic
(b) pragmatically justified
(c) sexist?
Motivate your answers.

Suppose the marketing director and the journalist had been females, how would you suppose the interview would have come off?

How if one of them had been male, the other female? (Hint: there are two possibilities. Consider both.)

What is presupposed in the journalist's assumption that the 'interview would have gone better'? (Hint: what is the necessary presupposition for anything to become 'better'?)

What does the journalist imply by saying this? (Hint: who does he think is to blame?)

And what does the journalist infer from the director's reaction 'It went badly?' (Hint: why do you think he cut the man off?)

(On presuppositions vs. implicatures, see sections 3.2.3 and 7.2.3.2. For an enlightening discussion of the differences between implicatures and inferences, see Thomas (1996:58–9).)

5. In January 1993, the CTA (Chicago Transit Authority) buses and suburban trains carried big outside ads for a device called 'The Club', a means of blocking an automobile's steering wheel, thus protecting the car from being stolen. There was also a picture of an installed 'club', most of all resembling a prehistoric mace inserted into the wheel at an angle. The ad carried the following text:

Beware of imitations!

THE CLUB!

Anti-theft device for cars

POLICE SAY:

"USE IT"

OR LOSE IT

The persuasive force of advertisements usually does not depend on *what* they say (which is most of the time banal, sometimes tautological, occasionally truly inane), but on the *way* they say it, and on the innuendoes and inferences that people are allowed and invited to draw. Thus, we have seen how an ad for Carlsberg beer owes its appeal to the clever way in which a beer truck is maneuvered into an attractive natural scene; the word 'beer' is never even mentioned. (See chapter 8; cf. also exercise 3 in the same chapter, where a cigarette ad gets by without mentioning either 'cigarette' or tobacco', but instead places all its pragmatic weight on the picture of a sexy waitress.) In the current announcement, you should look for similar 'eye-catchers', and read the text in relation to the entire pragmatic act-setting (the 'situated action' of section 8.4.2).

Questions:
What does the 'it' in 'Use it' refer to, as against the 'it' in 'Lose it'? Are they the same, and how do we know which is which?

In what way is this text different from that well-known slogan 'America: Love It or Leave It', and in what sense is it the 'same'? (Hint: is the ad a slogan? Where is the slogan usually observed?)

What is the hidden (subliminal) force of the announcement? (Hint: consider the shape of the device.)

Given that ads for cars mostly are written so as to appeal to the male half of the human population, in what sense could this announcement be called (and shown to be) sexist?

6. Manipulation and conditionals

In section 11.3.1, I talked about the manipulatory power of language. A particular pattern of language use, the so-called conditionals ('if–then' sentences), has been shown to have great manipulatory potential. In order to see this, consider first half-irregular, but quite innocuous uses of the conditional, where the condition seems to be no real condition at all, but something that happens on another level of conceptual linking, as in the following case:

> There's a natural affinity between Swedish *gravlaks* and Russian *blini* and caviar if one thinks about it, and chef Katsuo Nagasawa has . . . (*Gourmet* 52(5), May 1992:46)

In this example, the 'implication' is rather far removed from its standard use, as described in section 3.2.2. The same holds of the following (where even the regular conditional indicators 'if' and 'then' are missing):

> The way times change, it's nice to know that quality like that hasn't changed one bit. Come to think of it, it's that kind of quality that made Uncle Ben's converted Brand Rice more than just a part of American cooking, but part of a legend, as well. (*Bon Appétit* 37(6) June 1992:67)

Even more bizarre is the following 'conditional' (due to Bruce Fraser):

> If you think our waiters are rude, you should see the chef,

where, on one reading, the 'if–then' condition is close to being ludicrous, on another resembles a cautious question.

The Arkansas-based linguist Suzette Haden Elgin has, in a series of books (e.g., 1989), discussed the manipulatory potential of 'if–then' sentences, and comes to the conclusion that many of them really aren't conditionals at all, but rather *indirect verbal attacks*. The basis for this view is the traditional theory of the 'irreal conditional': i.e., a conditional whose first part is assumed to be false, and whose second part, by its negative form, is supposed to confirm the falsity of the first part. For example, if my significant other says to me:

> If you really loved me, you would not screw around like this,

the real message is 'you don't love me' – but the part that attracts my attention is the implicit accusation that I'm entertaining 'inappropriate relationships' with other people. Here is one of Elgin's own examples:

If you really wanted the job, you wouldn't come to the interview in jeans.

In this case, the discussion is bound to be turning around the question of whether or not jeans are appropriate attire for a job interview, while the underlying postulate: 'You are not interested in the job' is quietly and unobtrusively smuggled into its place.

Haden Elgin calls the 'if'-part the 'hook', the 'then'-part the 'bait': one swallows the bait (one starts discussing the 'then'-part: 'are jeans acceptable for a job interview?'), but forgets that doing so, one has automatically and implicitly ingested the hook, that is one has accepted the non-truth of the 'if'-part ('is this person interested in the job?') (Elgin 1989).

Questions:
What is the manipulatory importance of Suzette Haden Elgin's construction?

Illustrate her point by making up your own example in which an 'if'-sentence functions as hook, a 'then'-sentence as bait.

Would Elgin's explanation fit the 'waiter–chef' case quoted above?

Referring back to the discussion of 'naturalization' in section 11.3.4.3, ask yourself whether Elgin's conditionals could be accommodated within this framework. (Hint: recall the definition of naturalization as accepting the 'self-evidence' of things that should properly be resisted.)

7. *On language and social institutions*
Historically, institutionalized language use is heavily represented among the first speech acts discovered by Austin (1962). Even though such acts are relatively rare in everyday speech, the concept of the institution as a macro-social factor has been valuable not only as a classificatory criterion, but also as a way of looking at what speech acts really do, and how they are able to do what they do. In the following, the short story 'The Breakdown'[135] by the Swiss author Friedrich Dürrenmatt provides an illustration of the institutional power that is invested in language, even when the institution as such is a 'fake' one.

In this story, a traveling salesman meets three people in the dining room of a hotel in the small provincial town where he has to spend the night because his car has broken down. For some reason, the three gentlemen seem to be overjoyed to see him, and invite him for a late supper at the home of one of the three. During and after the meal, the conversation becomes more and more focused on the hosts' past occupations, respectively as attorney general, judge and trial lawyer; in the end, the trio enacts a mock 'court' session, in which the traveling salesman (who by now has lost any sense of the dimensions in time and space) is condemned to the severest penalties for his past misdeeds.

What is truly interesting here is the way in which we see a societal institution being (re)instituted through the use of speech. By force of their earlier occupations, the three gentlemen manage to create the illusion of a court session in which the accused ends up confessing his alleged crimes and accepting his sentence. In this mini-scenario, the institution of the judiciary as manifested in a court of law is realistically conjured up through the combined workings of language and institutionalized social relations.

However, this is only one side of the phenomenon. Not only do the institutions allow for, and determine, the language used (in speech act terminology: the illocutionary point of the appropriate speech acts), they are themselves construed through the societally recognized uses of the appropriate language. One of these uses (and probably a primordial one) is that of recording.

Language is used to record what has been going on, and accepted, in the context of society, in particular, of its institutions. For example, the practice of law in Roman society (a practice which survives in segments of modern legalistic thinking, especially in the far northwestern reaches of the northern hemisphere such as England or Scandinavia) was based on cases (hence the use of the term 'casuistry', literally: 'case-based reasoning', for 'finding a good case to argue your point of view'; the negative connotations are of later date). Thus, the discourse of the legal institutions became embedded in cases; and those cases needed to be stabilized in language in order to be useful and legally acceptable. The resulting records may initially have been in oral form, but as soon as writing was invented, bookkeeping and case-recording were among its first practical uses. The elaborate case records of the past have resulted in such egregious collections (called *corpora*) as the famous *Corpus Iustinianum*, or the *Corpus Iuris Canonici*, to name just two of the historical mainstays of legal thinking that were originally descriptions of cases and how they were resolved.

Over time, this preservative role of language in recording cases becomes more and more a prescriptive one. The roles that are prescribed for the exercise of the legal functions are given in terms of words pronounced ('speech acts'), words recorded ('transcripts'), and words handed down in written form to the next generation ('laws'). 'Law' now becomes synonymous with 'written law' – which is why we still talk about a person 'reading law', or 'reading at the bar', when we mean that he or she does studies in the legal domain with the intention of obtaining an authorization to practice as a lawyer.

The significance of Dürrenmatt's little game is that it shows us how the 'law', as embodied in legal cases and roles and their corresponding language, may become semi-independent of its original societal anchoring. For the individual subject, the hapless traveler who fell into the clutches of the (il)legal trio, the administration of the law in its quasi-practice was every bit as damning and condemning as would have been the case had he been summoned by a regular court. And not only that: the court needn't even be there at all; as long as we're aware

it's there, it can stay in the background, as in the case of Josef K in Kafka's
Process. In Berger and Luckmann's words,

> Only through . . . representation in performed roles can the institution mani-
> fest itself in actual experience. The institution, with its assemblage of 'pro-
> grammed' actions, is like the unwritten libretto of a drama. The realization of
> the drama depends upon the reiterated performance of its prescribed roles by
> living actors. (1966:70)

In this pragmatic view of legal practice, the language embodying the law takes
on a life of its own (cf. section 5.4.3): the speech act of sentencing not only creates
a state of affairs (the person sentenced is now going to jail), but it also creates
and re-creates itself (the sentence imposed and pronounced confirms the reality
of the legal system). Conversely, a law that isn't practiced is no law; a judge who
does not sentence is no judge; a district attorney who does not prosecute is not
a proper district attorney; and a chief of police who never makes an arrest is not
a good policeman, as we know from Thorbjørn Egner's well-known portrayal of
Police Chief Bastian among 'people and robbers' in Kardemomme City (1960).
This is the psychological, sociological and pragmatic relevance of the legal 'joke'
perpetrated on the traveler in the Dürrenmatt story.

Questions:
Confronting the above story with the concept of 'naturalization' introduced in
section 11.3.4.3, would you characterize the court institution as a 'natural' thing,
even in the disguise of a play or a game?

Did Dürrenmatt's hero actually receive his punishment? (Hint: check out the
story!) How does this ending compare to what happened to Kafka's Josef K in
the end? (Hint: re-read *The Process*.)

In section 9.5, I talked about the pragmatic act of reading as a process of 'co-
creation', by which the reader takes part in the author's creative process. How
would this fit in with the story as told by Dürrenmatt? (Hint: consider the salesman as one who 'naturalizes' the law, and thus not only confirms its validity but
actively acts out its consequences.)

Can we generalize from this to formulate a general rule of societal discourse, by
which people create and re-create their institutions in their own images?

How would you argue for such a rule from a pragmatic point of view?

What is the principal instrument that people use to obtain this result?

Are they always conscious of doing this?

Epilogue: Of Silence and Comets

(Reflections on a cover picture)

People often ask me what motivated the choice of my cover picture, *Pegwell Bay*, by William Dyce, a relatively unknown Pre-Raphaelite, whose unique masterpiece (properly subtitled: 'A Recollection of October 5th, 1858') is on display in the Tate Gallery, London, where I saw it for the first time on March 20, 1986, a year before I started writing the first, Danish version of my book.

The reason for my original attraction was quite trivial, if anything is trivial in this world. I had been reading Susan Hill's fascinating novel *The Bird of Night* (1976), being the life and memories of the crazed poetic genius Francis Croft ("England's most eminent poet"; Hill 1976:173), as told by his life-long friend and later chronicler Harvey Lawson. Croft is often, when missing from his home in South Terrace, found in front of this picture in the Tate, deeply absorbed in meditation.[136] But what is there to meditate about, I asked myself, on seeing that painting for the first time, a picture that leaves no stone unpainted, where all the minutest details are taken care of in the most realistic way?

The clue is in the date. On that particular day, the comet known as Donati's was visible over large parts of southern England, and the people depicted on the canvas are out at the beach in order to watch the celestial phenomenon, visible even in clear daylight (the reproduction does not do justice to the painting's original color tones, with the people standing about in "the pallid autumn light", corresponding to "the time of day, just before evening" (as the Tate Gallery description has it; Anonymous 1985:54); rather, they suggest the end of a bright summer's day, with the sunlight still in the sky).

The curious thing about this tableau is that almost none of its inhabitants actually look at the comet; they are busy gathering shells, talking to each other, or doing something totally unrelated (like the man with the cart in the background). The first printings of my book did, moreover, not even show the comet itself: it had been cropped off the top of the reproduction, its tail being the only part that was (barely) visible, if one knew where to look. Similarly, the man to the right, the only one who could be seen as paying attention to the comet, having his back toward us, had also been sacrificed to the constraints of the format. So, whenever I was asked to explain my picture, I used to say that unfortunately, some essential clues to its understanding had been cut off, but that the next printing would have a complete, uncut reproduction.

That completeness (at least as far as the content of the painting was concerned; the colors still aren't quite right) came finally into being at the book's fourth printing in 1996, but by that time I had become so accustomed to looking at the picture of people not looking at a non-existent or invisible comet that I had started to wonder if there was perhaps a deeper meaning in all this than just a vicarious cut of the scissors somewhere during the process of reproducing the Dyce painting. Here is how my standard (over time not a little trite) explanation of the cover used to run:

> The picture is an allegory: people are going about their business, not realizing that there is something spectacular going on right above their heads. In the same way, many of today's linguists keep on doing their usual thing, not being interested in the rise of a new star (a comet?), called pragmatics, on the scientific firmament. Only one person, the invisible man at the (cut-off) right edge, is looking, and he, just like the comet itself, has been removed from the picture: a most suitable allegory of what happened to a pragmaticist in those early linguistic milieus!

Since then, two things have happened. I came across an insightful article by Stacie Withers on 'Silence and communication in art' (1997), and a real comet (Hakutake's) introduced itself into my life; my first conscious meeting with a heavenly body of that kind. Of course, one doesn't have to be a magus from the East to cherish a new star and "rejoice with exceeding great joy" (Matthew 2:10), but it helps to be in such good company, and besides, kings seldom come without a present. Also, having become 'comet-conscious' does not mean that I'm looking at our new companion in the skies all the time, or even get my binoculars out every night; it means I'm aware of it, and find a deep satisfaction in realizing my privilege of observing an epi-phenomenon of the kind that at one point of time in our history had such joyful consequences (being a true Epi-phany), as it continues to have even today, wherever the *Reyes* still go about their business of bringing gifts.

But back to those people at Pegwell Bay, for whom business was just as usual, as if nothing of importance was going on in those October skies. To understand them, and grasp the deeper meaning of our picture, we have to consider the *silence* that is evident in Dyce's painting. Stacie Withers, in the article mentioned above, comments on the 'silence of art', as it is manifested in the "intensity of its concentration, the removal of the time element, the appeal to a noetic faculty rather than to our rational faculty, an economy of symbols and a harmony of colour and line" (1997:559). Withers exemplifies her thoughts by discussing a painting by Breughel, *The Fall of Icarus* (around 1555), in which the eponymous figure almost isn't there (recall that in Dyce's picture, the comet isn't even mentioned in the title of the painting):

> The viewer has to look very hard to find the tiny figure of Icarus tumbling into the sea in the background; the whole concentration is on the peasant in the foreground going about his daily work with tremendously calm indifference to the momentous event going on behind him. . . . The intense concentration of the peasant also contributes to the silence of this painting, as he is completely absorbed in his daily task. It is this complete absorption, whether of plowing a field, reading a book, pouring from a jug, making lace or tying a child's bonnet, that gives so much genre painting of artists like Vermeer, De Hooch or Chardin a quality and a depth of *silence*. (Withers 1997:365; my emphasis)

The silence depicted in the painting of Pegwell Bay is not one of 'holding your tongue', but rather one of 'holding your breath' and realizing what you're here in this world for: to go about your business, live the moment and not gab about it, to collect your riches in your hands and head, without squandering them right away through idle words. Our pragmatic justification is not just through our words (cf. Matthew 12:36),[137] but through our acts, not least including a justified, and justifying, *silence*.

Applying these reflections to Dyce's and my own comet, we may be able to avoid a big misunderstanding that is apt to occur; for one doesn't have to *look* at a comet to be comet-wise. In fact, the man in the picture supposedly directing his gaze at the comet probably understands less than those other people paying no obvious heed. Dyce shows us people who have their attention fixed on the daily businesses at hand, but who at the same time, on another level of consciousness, are aware of the fact that these businesses somehow relate to 'higher things': after all, their entire *raison d'être* on Pegwell Beach is the comet. Which is exactly the role that pragmatics plays in relation to our everyday language: it is there, not as an observed phenomenon, but rather as something that we are aware of on another level of consciousness – a passive awareness that of course may be prodded into activity by a proper use of linguistic and pragmatic techniques (as my readers hopefully have learnt from the book they just have perused).

Jan-Ola Östman (1987, 1995b) has coined the beautiful expression 'implicit anchoring' as characteristic of our pragmatic activities: our thoughts and our words are anchored outside of us, *implicated* in society; but we are not explicitly referring to that anchor every time we open our mouths. On the contrary, we never (at least consciously) 'do pragmatics' when we use language: rather, doing pragmatics is 'doing being', more precisely, 'doing being a language user', to vary Manny Schegloff's quasi-immortal phraseology. In this perspective, the man gazing at the comet may be the only person who is explicitly aware that something is going on, but at the same time, he forgets to attend to his regular use of language: he isolates himself from conversation and contact with his fellow beachgoers, that is, from the real business of language. (Maybe he is doing linguistics, but certainly not pragmatics.)

To get the proper, *pragmatic* perspective on language and the ways it is used, one does not have to be familiar with all the technical intricacies that surround its genesis and operation, just as it is not necessary to know all about the physics of sunrise or sundown to experience those phenomena on a higher level of personal experience. Or even more poignantly, one sometimes is only able to get the right perspective on things by considering them metaphorically, rather than in the scientifically correct fashion, as many eminent physicists and biologists repeatedly have told us.[138]

This, of course, is also what painters and other artists have known all the time: perspective, no matter how defined, is what makes proper art, and silence is an integral part of it. Indeed, in the words of a contemporary Danish painter, Per Kirkeby, writing about his nineteenth-century colleague N.A. Abildgaard: "At intervals the earth has to be made flat in order that we may see clearly" (Kirkeby 1993:14).[139]

And for this reason, since it is the *pragmatic* study of language that informs us of the proper ways of speaking, and being silent, about comets and other important events of life, "in order that we may see [them] clearly", I feel that my cover picture, more than ever, is a suitable visual introduction to the study, and above all, the practice of pragmatics.

Notes

1 The allusion is to a well-known series of monographs and books published under the common name of *Pragmatics and Beyond* by John Benjamins, Amsterdam/Philadelphia, since 1978, and now counting more than sixty volumes.

2 Levinson has described this shift from a more technical-linguistic point of view as follows: "as knowledge of the syntax, phonology and semantics of various languages has increased, it has become clear that there are specific phenomena that can only naturally be described by recourse to contextual concepts. On the one hand, various syntactic rules seem to be properly constrained only if one refers to pragmatic conditions; and similarly for matters of stress and intonation. It is possible, in response to these apparent counter-examples to a context-independent notion of linguistic competence, simply to retreat: the rules can be left unconstrained and allowed to generate unacceptable sentences, and a performance theory of pragmatics assigned the job of filtering out the acceptable sentences. Such a move is less than entirely satisfactory because the relationship between the theory of competence and the data on which it is based (ultimately intuitions about acceptability) becomes abstract to a point where counter-examples to the theory may be explained away on an *ad hoc* basis, *unless* a systematic pragmatics has already been developed" (1983:36; emphasis in original).

3 This seems to be Carnap's (1956) stance.

4 Another scholar, the American Ralph Fasold, similarly feels that such a 'Continental' approach "makes any aspect whatsoever of linguistic interaction a legitimate topic for pragmatic research" – which he sees as a return to the view of pragmatics espoused by Morris: that "pragmatics is about everything human in the communication process, psychological, biological, and sociological" (Fasold 1990:176; cf. Verschueren 1987:5).

5 One may want to distinguish between a *societal* context which is primarily determined by society's institutions, and a *social* context which is primarily created in interaction; the conditions referred to in the above definition are properly societal, not social. On the other hand, and all things being equal, a societal environment

can only develop and bloom in a social context; vice versa, the social can only unfold itself in a societal environment. This distinction is akin to one introduced in sociology by Erving Goffman some thirty years ago, between 'systemic' and 'ritual' constraints, and which will be discussed at the end of the present section.

6 Early transformational grammarians (Ross, Lakoff) invented a similar theoretical monster called 'semantax', in order not to disturb the unity and indivisibility of linguistics, viewed as '(deep) syntax'.

7 Depending on whether one prefers to delimit either the semantic field or the pragmatic field most closely, the result of the delimitation and its effect on the practitioners in each field will vary. Typically, one school wants to create a sharp line of demarcation setting semantics off from all the rest by a strict criterion such as the operation of truth conditions. Then, in pragmatics we can be working with as broad a sense of 'meaning' as possible, taking in aspects such as metaphor, irony, implicit communication, and so on. Conversely, we could define a strictly linguistic pragmatics, in the sense discussed above, viz., one that will only recognize pragmatic phenomena to the extent that they are linguistically marked. Here, the pragmatic 'module' becomes a bit neater, and its boundaries with the other disciplines a bit clearer; however, the price we pay is to have to do away with all the interesting fringes.

8 Bühler remarks, somewhat facetiously, that he has chosen the term *Appell* because of a certain current fashion: "today, as everybody knows, we have a sex appeal, and it seems to me that next to that, a *speech appeal* must be just as real a thing" (1934:29).

9 According to Levinson, in the area of conversational analysis, "at least, the would-be functionalist is offered the kind of rich and intricate structure that may match the detailed organization of linguistic structure, and so can be claimed plausibly to stand in a causal relation to it" (1983:47).

10 What the oracle actually said was (Ennius, *Annales* 167; cf. Cicero, *De divinatione* 2:116): *Aio te Aiacida Romanos uincere posse*, which is translated as either: 'I'm telling you, offspring of Aiacus, that you can win over the Romans' or, on an alternative reading: 'I'm telling you, offspring of Aiacus, that the Romans can win over you.' The 'correct' reading of this construction, an *accusativus cum infinitivo*, where either accusative can be interpreted as the subject or the object of the sentence, depends on how we are 'set up' to understand it (and, albeit to a lesser degree, on what we perceive as the 'normal' order of constituents in a sentence: subject first, then object, then verb). On the importance of being 'set up' for a particular understanding, see section 8.3.2.

11 Cf. Jenny Thomas's wry musings: "Years after having heard it, I still long to know what one woman was talking about when she said to her fellow bus passenger: ... And just think, if he hadn't fallen out of bed, I'd never have found out about it!" (Thomas 1996:9). Without the proper context, Thomas remarks, "it is perfectly possible to understand the sense of every word a speaker utters, yet still not understand what the speaker means" (ibid.).

12 This is the familiar problem of 'presuppositions'; see further section 2.5. (Technically, *to regret* is a 'factive' verb, as we also will see there; cf. also n. 19.)

13 'Iconicity' is often understood as a superficial similarity between the conceptual and the linguistic, as when I normally would say:

I inserted my card into the cash machine and withdrew sixty dollars

rather than:

I withdrew sixty dollars and inserted my card into the cash machine.

In the latter case, the order of the two parts of the conjunction runs counter to the order of things, as I conceptualize it in real life. The former sentence is syntactically 'iconic', the latter is not.

14 According to Leech (1983:2), it is more appropriate to consider another, programmatic article by Lakoff as evidence, viz., the one printed in the same volume under the title 'On generative semantics' (Lakoff 1971a).

15 The notion of 'progress' in conversation is discussed extensively in Stalpers 1993.

16 Many languages reflect the fact that not all swimming or other body movements are alike, cross-culturally, by a difference in categorization and/or lexical choice. As to the first, inanimate objects such as logs can 'swim' in German, but not in any other Germanic language, with the possible exception of Early Modern English ("And the man of God said, Where fell it? And he shewed him the place. And he cut down a stick, and cast it in thither; and the iron [i.e., the ax head] did swim"; II Kings 6:6). As to the second, some languages do indeed have categorically different motion verbs where animals are concerned, as opposed to humans (as an example, consider the words for 'running' in West Greenlandic: whereas a human *arpappuq*, an animal *pangalippuq*).

17 A favorite party game among linguists is to discuss whether or not a particular expression is 'correct' or 'grammatical'. Such discussions (which as a rule take place in the immediate vicinity of the refrigerator, to secure a constant supply of cold drinks during the often heated debates) invariably end with one or several of the discussants invoking the authority invested in themselves as native speakers of some dialect of English (or whatever), in which precisely such and such a construction is 'grammatical' or 'ungrammatical', whichever the case may be. Robin Lakoff comments on this curious phenomenon as follows: "So one linguist's intuitive judgment was equal to another's, and there was no way to discriminate. 'That's not in my dialect', you could say to a colleague, but that didn't obligate him to change his mind. Hence Ross's version of the American Linguist's National Anthem: 'Oh, see if you can say . . .'" (1989:960).

18 The technical term for the latter is 'entailment'.

19 This is why *to regret* is called a 'factive' verb, viz., one that entails (presupposes) its complement; see Gazdar 1979:119; Levinson 1983:188; the original reference is Kiparsky and Kiparsky 1971.

20 Incidentally, this example also shows that the logicians' 'principle of compositionality' (by which the truth value of a compound sentence is the conjoined truth value of its components) is not valid in pragmatics. A lot has been written on presuppositions, not all of it relevant to pragmatics. The interested reader is referred to Levinson (1983:175ff) or Seuren (1998) for a complete account. I will deal in more detail with the pragmatics of presuppositions in chapter 7.

21 This example is due to Alvaro G. Meseguer (1988:108).

22 Even fifteen years after the privatization of the Japanese National Railways, the difference is only very slowly disappearing.

23   The exceptions are words that imitate sounds, the so-called *onomatopoietica*. But even here one can be misled: for instance, animal sounds are rendered in vastly different ways across languages, as everybody knows.

24   Cf. also the more technical-philosophical terms 'to implicate' and 'to explicate', which are derived from the same original Latin root and have related meanings. Not all authors distinguish between 'implication' and 'implicature'; for instance, Leech and Thomas (1988:19) call an 'implicature' simply a 'pragmatic implication', following Grice, who wasn't too careful, when he "concocted" his famous "notion of conversational implicature", about telling us how to derive the substantives: from the everyday verb 'to imply' or from its philosophical cousin 'to implicate'. For Grice, implicature is a kind of implication, hence he sometimes uses 'implies' as a non-technical synonym to 'conversationally implicates' (cf. Grice 1981:184–5).

25   One can make these logical equivalencies clear with the aid of so-called 'truth tables' indicating the conditions under which a proposition or a combination of propositions is true or false. Most handbooks of logic will tell you how to construct a truth table; however, this kind of logical push-ups is outside the scope of the present book. A biblical *à propos*: the owner of the vineyard in St Matthew 20:1–16 was logically correct in giving the latecomers the same hire as he had promised those who had borne the "burden and heat of the day". What he had said was: "If you go into my vineyard, I'll give you a penny each" – and so he did at the end of the day. There was no logical injunction against giving the penny also to those who hadn't worked, or not worked enough, and the vineyard owner did what he thought he had to do ("whatsoever [was] right"), in strict conformity with the laws of logic. (The pragmatics of the labor market tell a different story, as we know.)

26   Namely, if the number of raisins is exactly equal to the 'some' that Alex had pinched (cf. Quine 1958:67–71).

27   We are dealing here with a 'scalar' implicature in the sense defined by Gazdar (1979:56). See further section 4.2.

28   Sperber and Wilson call an explicitly communicated assumption an 'explicature' (1986:182).

29   The famous unsuccessful denial of Jesus by St Peter in the high priest's courtyard is a case in point: "Surely thou also art one of them; for thy speech betrayeth thee", said the damsel (Matthew 26:73); and no amount of denying could convince "them that stood by" that the addressed was not a Galilean, hence potentially associated with the 'King of the Jews'.

30   The word 'received' has acquired a certain notoriety as a euphemism for 'higher-class' pronunciation, as in 'RP' (received pronunciation) – the 'public [*sic*] school' variety of spoken English propagated by vast numbers of EFL ('English-as-a-foreign-language') teachers all over the world.

31   In such an automatic conclusion, the first sentence 'entails' the second; however, the converse is not true. (See further the discussion in section 4.4.2.2, and Horn 1984:15.)

32   This kind of 'exploitation' has been called 'flouting' a conversational maxim (of politeness) by Grice (1975; see further section 3.2.4). Thus, I can flout politeness in order to obtain a special effect (e.g., of familiarity), as when I say to a friend, when meeting him on the streets of Bologna: 'Come va, vecchio stronzo?' (literally, 'How's it going, old fart?'; Umberto Eco, pers. comm.).

33   The colon is interesting in that it occupies a place in between 'and' and 'but' – its true sense emerging only in the given context (just as in the case of Hebrew *wa*). In many cases, the connection is kept intentionally vague by the writer.

34   Incidentally, this is why the Russian-American linguist Roman Jakobson (following an earlier suggestion by Otto Jespersen) called such words 'shifters'. (More on this in section 3.3.3; see also section 7.2.3).

35   'Deictic' is the adjective to 'deixis', literally: 'the act of pointing' (from the Greek verb *deíknumi* 'point, show'). It is used to indicate the function that certain words, such as personal and demonstrative pronouns, place and time adverbs like 'here', 'now', and others have in the language. That function is always bound up with the time and place of the utterance, seen in relation to the speaker. Thus, we say 'Come here', but 'Don't stand over there.' A related Latin word is *index* 'pointer', or 'fore-finger'; the English term 'index' is similarly used to denote the body part which serves as the human 'pointer' *par excellence*.

36   Honorifics, or honorific expressions (literally: 'honor makers'), mark the social distance between the speaker and his or her interlocutor(s) by prescribing a particular linguistic expression to be used in particular circumstances. (For a complete, up-to-date account of honorifics see Shibatani 1998.)

37   And on the view that men like *melameds* have of their wives (personal comment by Inger Mey).

38   The same holds, *mutatis mutandis*, for cataphora.

39   Cf. "a grammar is justified to the extent that it is a *principled* descriptively adequate system" (Chomsky 1965:27 italics mine). Since the theory which provides the principles is also the theory according to which the grammar is evaluated, a 'principled' system is necessarily 'justified', and the term 'principled', as used here, is vacuous.

40   These cases will be dealt with later; see especially section 6.3.3.

41   The status of the items 'many', 'few' and 'none' on the scale raises some problems. First of all, the scalar ordering of 'some' vs. 'few' can be discussed; I will leave this problem aside here. More important is the following: 'many' and 'few' are relative concepts, whereas 'none' and 'all' are universal 'quantifiers', as the logicians say. If I say that 'all' of the guests left, I still don't know if there were 'many' or 'few' guests: that depends entirely on other factors, such as what I take to be the relative value of 'many' or 'few'. Here is an example: so far, I have married off four of my five daughters in what I consider as 'big' weddings, that is, parties with 'many' guests. The third was the biggest of them all, with 'very many' (to be exact, eighty-two) guests; yet, in the context in which the wedding happened (Manistee, a small town in Michigan), this was considered a small party, with rather 'few' guests. (A normal wedding would have 200 guests; a big one 350–400, in that context.) In a case like this, saying that 'all' of the guests had left wouldn't in principle entail that there were 'many' who had left; whereas saying 'many had left' would mean that, seen against the background of the total number of guests, a significant portion had taken their leave.

The inclusion of 'none' in the scale (which is my addition) has caused some eyebrow-raising among 'some' of my readers; Ken Turner is one of them. He argues (pers. comm.) that 'few' never subsumes ('entails') 'none' (like 'all' does 'some'); or, in terms of the above discussion, that if I say 'none', I could not also mean 'few' or 'some'. However, in analogy with the 'delegates' example, I could perfectly well say:

"After Swedish tycoon Kroeger's business empire went down in the 1929 crash, he lost his entire holdings in the match industry; only the Uddevalla factory remained in his control." And when as a boy I once asked my father (who was an economist) what all this talk about the 'coffers of the [Dutch] state being empty' was supposed to mean (this also happened around that time), he told me: "Well, what they want to say is that there are only a couple of million [guilders] left." I found this a highly interesting proposition, and it certainly helped me to revise my idea of the relation between 'none' and 'few'.

42   As the title of an early paper by Cutler has it: 'Saying what you mean without meaning what you say' (Cutler 1974). (For more details, see Leech 1983:9, from where the example is originally taken.)

43   This kind of argumentation reminds one of the old, rhetorical *argumentum ex baculo,* that is, the stick-behind-the-door argument. As an example, cf. the following text, often seen on the backs of Norwegian trailer trucks: 'UTEN BILEN GÅR NORGE I STÅ' ('Without the car, Norway stops'). Here, an implicit threat is formulated as a statement. However, the threat has only a limited effect and scope, since the statement itself is ambiguous: 'stop' may either be read as 'normal functions no longer being performed' (such as: getting to the shop or to the doctor's office, carrying goods and mail across the country, and so on), or as 'stop functioning under the currently prevailing conditions', which would imply, among other things, an end to the unlimited proliferation of (especially private) automotive transportation, to the uninhibited construction of new roads (often at the cost of massive destruction of the human habitat), and so on. Clearly, only in the former sense can the threat concealed in the statement above be said to affect (all the inhabitants of) 'Norway'; by contrast, the reading of the statement in the latter sense (that of 'providing a check on the ideology of growth at all cost') has its scope in the limited class of true believers in the blessings of automotive transportation.

44   This issue will be dealt with in depth in chapter 11, where I discuss pragmatics and politics.

45   Hartmut Haberland (pers. comm.) has drawn my attention to the fact that 'face', in its original Chinese context, represents the acquired and ascribed status an individual has in society. In this sense, it cannot be 'lost'. When the Japanese borrowed the concept from the Chinese, it was 'nipponized' to receive a typical Japanese orientation toward 'social relativism', as Kasper has called it. In Kasper's words, "while negative politeness, addressing territorial concerns for autonomy and privacy, derives directly from the high value placed on individualism in Western culture, for Japanese society, by contrast, the overarching principle of societal interaction . . . compris[es] concerns about belongingness, empathy, dependency, proper place occupancy and reciprocity" (1990:195). See further chapter 10, where pragmatics is discussed in a cross-cultural perspective.

46   'Opting out' of a potentially face-threatening situation is the alternative that Brown and Levinson offer to not perform the face-threatening act; see Thomas 1996:175 (with reference to unpublished work by Tanaka 1994).

47   "If you can't say anything nice, don't say anything at all" (American folk maxim).

48   'Bottom-to-top' (or 'bottom-up') and 'top-to-bottom' (or 'top-down') are metaphorical expressions from the area of automated sentence analysis: one can either start

'parsing' a sentence, beginning with the grammatical categories ('top-down'), or with the actual string of words ('bottom-up').

49 Recall Gazdar's warning: "Informal explanations, not based on formal theory, particularly those that trade on words like 'relevant', are always liable to the fallacy of equivocation" (1979:54).

50 An interesting aside is that this implicature would not be possible unless both agents had the information necessary to determine the location of honey, given the usual facts about beehives. We assume this to be a simple inference, but that needn't be the case, as the sad case of Joe Bear shows, in another of his computer-generated pranks: "One day, Joe Bear was hungry. He asked his friend Irving Bird where some honey was. Irving told him there was a beehive in the oak tree. Joe walked to the oak tree. He ate the beehive" (Meehan 1981:218).

51 One is sometimes in doubt whether to speak of 'linguistic philosophy' or 'philosophy of language'; the two are often used indiscriminately. If a distinction is to be made, it should probably follow the lines suggested by John R. Searle: "Linguistic philosophy is the attempt to solve particular philosophical problems by attending to the ordinary use of particular words or other elements in a particular language. The philosophy of language is the attempt to give philosophically illuminating descriptions of certain general features of language, such as reference, truth, meaning and necessity; and it is concerned only incidentally with particular elements in a particular language" (1969:4).

52 This use of 'performative' should be kept apart from what in early, non-aligned transformational grammar started to be called the 'performative hypothesis'. Briefly, this hypothesis assumes that in all utterances, there can be found a hidden, 'performative' verb of 'declaring'. Thus, when I say: 'It's cold in here', what I'm supposed to be really saying is: 'I'm stating the fact that it's cold in here.' Obviously, there is no end to this 'stating'; so why not: 'I state the fact that I state the fact that . . .' and so on *ad infinitum*? (See further section 5.3.2.)

53 Austin and Searle often use 'force' and 'point' interchangeably, especially in their earlier writings. Later on, 'force' is sometimes set aside to denote the intensity of a particular speech act; e.g., 'ask for' and 'demand' both represent a kind of 'requesting', but the latter carries more 'force'; similarly, an 'oath' would be a 'promise' with added 'force'. Jenny Thomas comments on this as follows: "you will find the terms speech act, illocutionary act, illocutionary force, pragmatic force or just force, all used to mean the same thing – although the use of one rather than another may imply different theoretical positions" (1996:51).

54 Cf. Levinson: "If bet you sixpence that I can outrun you, but you fail to hear, I cannot be said truthfully to have betted you sixpence" (1995:377). Famous (or perhaps one should say notorious) cases of (sometimes intentional) misfiring of speech acts are found in connection with the laws governing the Roman Catholic institution of marriage. According to canon law, an intention (whether or not expressed before or during the ceremony) not to consummate the marriage, not to have children, or maybe not even to get married is sufficient to render the marriage null and void. This, clearly, is a most important aspect of the speech act of 'pronouncing' (in this case, marriage vows), as it is almost the only way a Catholic can be released from his or her vows (divorce being not permitted). Historically, the difficulty has of course always been to establish the appropriate (failure of) intention:

here, the mighty of the earth have had the advantage of being able to produce such evidence with the help of underlings who would be willing to testify under oath that the king in fact had said such and such on the eve of his marriage to the queen he now wants to get rid of – irrespective of the truth of the matter. (England's Henry VIII and his Cardinal Wolsey are the classic case.) As Thomas wryly remarks "This escape clause [from marriage] operates mainly for the rich and famous" (1996:53).

55 Similarly in the Bible, where we are admonished by the Apostle St James to abstain from oaths and suchlike forceful speech acts: "Let thy speech be Aye, Aye and No, No, lest thou shalt fall under judgment" (5:12).

56 It goes without saying that not all linguists are overly happy with conditions like this (not to speak of the literary people). Quite another matter is that people in the deaf community would not be very pleased with being referred to as 'handicapped' (Elizabeth Keating, pers. comm.).

57 Is there such a thing as an insincere promise, that is, a promise without the intention to fulfill the act? Searle seems to think so, but it is not quite clear what this kind of promise is worth, pragmatically speaking, especially with regard to the next, 'essential' condition.

58 As Levinson remarks, it would be more appropriate to speak of 'sentence types' "instead of the misleading term *mood*" (1983:243), mood being a strictly verbal inflectional category, only indirectly characterizing a type of sentence. Searle's speech act classification will be discussed later on in this chapter; section 5.5. (See also Lyons 1977:747.)

59 Cf. the following sanguine *rêverie*, found elsewhere in Verschueren's work: "Language is certainly not less complicated than physical or biological reality. Biologists recognize about 30,000 different species of spiders and 250,000 species of beetles. I am convinced that if we kept making distinctions with as much patience as biologists have traditionally done, we would come up with a set of SAs [speech acts] approaching the astronomical number of species in the whole animal kingdom" (1980:4).

60 On the difference between 'constative' or 'descriptive' utterances vs. 'performative' ones, cf. Leech (1983:176). See further section 5.5.2.5.

61 The asterisk denotes a form that is not found in the language.

62 As a schoolboy, when asked how much is three times nine, I was told by the headmaster that my answer: 'I believe it's twenty-seven' was wrong because, as he admonished me: 'Believing is something you do in church – here, you have to know it!'

63 Verschueren (1979:4–5) offers a lengthy list of some 180 such verbs.

64 The latter verb, 'to know', may indeed occur as a performative, as, e.g., in "Know all ye men, women and children by these presents", but only in this and similar kinds of use. The performative use occurs implicitly in official, 'posted' signs: 'No hunting' (meaning: 'Know that hunting here is not allowed'), '55' ('Know that the speed limit here is 55 m.p.h.'), or the all-purpose 'Posted' ('Know that something is not allowed here'); or even explicitly, as in the suggested reading of the following road sign

TEXAS
SPUR
2

as: 'Know that it is two miles to Spur, Tex.' – actually one of the more spurious multiple choices for an answer to a question on a sixties' Texas driver's test.

65 Some of my readers may think that this kind of detailed reasoning is going too far. Let them be assured that, in Searle's own opinion, this treatment has not been detailed enough; in his own words, "I have not, for example, discussed the role of the assumption of sincerity, or the ceteris paribus conditions that attach to various of the steps"! (1975:63). On the other hand, Searle also admits that "in normal conversation, of course, no one would consciously go through the steps involved in this reasoning" (1975:63).

66 Similar observations have been made by Wodak and by O'Barr with regard to courtroom hearings (Wodak-Engel 1984; O'Barr 1982).

67 To quote Levinson: "there are no isolable necessary and sufficient conditions on, for example, question-[or answer-]hood; . . . rather, the nature of the use to which interrogatives are put can vary subtly with the nature of the *language-games* or contexts in which they are used" (1983:275).

68 Incidentally, these 'properties' need not be limited to inner states: in certain cultures, one can congratulate people on the acquisition of material objects such as new cars, snappy clothes etc. In America, it is usual to congratulate people on getting a new job, or achieving a task, or winning the lottery (sometimes even before the act, as in those impossible mail offers: "Congratulations! You may already have won!"). In Denmark, it is quite OK to congratulate people on their new cars or other kinds of pets.

69 In the following, I will use this broader concept of 'context' as the unmarked term (the 'default'), and only talk about 'co-text' whenever I want to restrict its content.

70 Some linguists have called these 'imperatives-in-the-form-of-a-question' (type 'Why don't you get lost?') *whimperatives*. The term is originally due to Jerry Sadock (1974).

71 Actually a quotation: from the novel *Bright Lights, Bright City*, by Ian McInerney (New York: Doubleday, 1984).

72 The term *aizuchi* is said to refer to the striking of the iron by the blacksmith and his helper, operating in tandem: the strikes are timed exactly right so as to avoid clashes and let the work continue without interruption.

73 Good examples are provided by Allwood (1976). Cf. also the literature on 'anarchic' conversation types in the West Indies, as, e.g., described for Antigua by Reisman (1989). Consider also conversational contexts in many linguistic communities, where interruption is not only tolerated, but necessary in order to hold one's own: the cocktail-party small talk, the bar or locker-room conversation, peer banter and so on. (Anybody who has ear-witnessed a flock of Japanese teenage girls 'conversing' in the Tokyo subway will recognize the phenomenon.)

74 The term 'phatic' goes back to the Polish anthropologist and linguist Bronislaw Malinowski. Jakobson, who is usually quoted as the source of this term, uses Malinowski's terminology, 'phatic communion', but interprets it as a 'communicative exchange' which happens mostly for the purposes of contact (e.g., greetings). See Jakobson (1960:357); Lyons (1968:417).

75 To understand to what extent such phenomena are directly dependent on the language used (considered as an expression of the culture), cf. the case of the American student who tried to compliment a Japanese student at Boston University on

her dress, and was rudely turned away. The problem was that he spoke Japanese, and in Japanese, such compliments from a male to a female are infelicitous. A fellow student, who spoke to the girl in English, congratulating her on her good taste in clothes, got the obligatory demure smile as his reward (Bruce Fraser, pers. comm.).

76 Max Silberztein, pers. comm.

77 For complete details on repairs, see Levinson (1983:339–42).

78 Example due to Bruce Fraser (pers. comm.).

79 'Cohesion' is defined by Halliday and Hasan (1976:29–30) as: "the linguistic means by which a text is enabled to function as a single meaningful unit". Note that these authors do not formally distinguish 'coherence' and 'cohesion'; however, one may consider the former to be implicitly presupposed as that which makes a text differ from a non-text (in the same way as sense differs from non-sense), so that it can "function as a single meaningful unit".

80 ELIZA is the brainchild of Joseph Weizenbaum, a well-known (now retired) computer scientist at MIT. Though not initially planned as a serious effort at simulating human cognitive activity, the program (which simulates a therapist–patient interaction) has become extremely popular among the general public. In the artificial intelligence (AI) community, by contrast, it is often gleefully quoted as an example of 'How *not* to do AI'. As any introductory AI text with respect for itself mentions ELIZA, no specific references are given here except to Weizenbaum's original paper (1966).

81 Except in special cases such as answering a summons, or a roll call in the military, as in 'Lieutenant Sparre' – 'Here!' (adjacency pair 'summons–answer').

82 I will disregard the fact that one may get upset for other reasons, e.g., when we think we've got a right to ask the question, and the answer we get is one like (iv).

83 On the notion of 'script', see the standard references (e.g., Minsky 1975; Schank and Abelson 1977; Schank 1981).

84 Even in case the addressee refuses to answer, his or her silence may be a relevant answer, because we're inside a 'pair', and hence interpret the silence as the second half of that pair. (See section 6.3.2.2; on 'silence', cf. section 10.2.4.)

85 Alan Perlis was Professor of Computer Science at Yale University, and author of some important theorems in automata theory. Even though he had to spend the last years of his life in a wheelchair, his spirits, wit and acumen remained unchallenged.

86 Leech means the grammatical, not the semantic or pragmatic subject. This makes his reasoning somewhat dubious, as many languages regularly suppress the (grammatical as well as the semantic) subject without resulting ambiguity. Japanese is a prime example; cf. the following dialogue:

>   (*A young man comes hurriedly to the scene where his date is waiting for him*)
>   MALE: *Sumimasen – machimashita-ka.*
>   ('I'm sorry – have you been waiting?')
>   FEMALE: *E, sanjippun moo machimashita.*
>   ('Yes, I've already waited for half an hour.')

In the above, expressed subjects ('you', 'I') are expected in English, whereas no such need is experienced in Japanese: *machimashita* means simply: 'have waited'; the particle -*ka* expresses the question, and no subject is expressed in either of the utterances. Moreover, the verb forms (apart from the attached particle) do not differ, as grammatical persons are not distinguished in the Japanese verb.

87 Larry Horn, to whom I owe this quotation, establishes an even more original source: George K. Zipf, who introduced the Economy Principle in linguistics in the forties (Horn 1984:11). Elsewhere in the same article, Horn remarks, much to the point, that such general 'least effort' principles simply are too powerful (p. 28).

88 As is done by, e.g., Levinson (1983). For him, discourse analysis is a hybrid, grammar-and-speech-act-oriented analysis of spoken language, and as such "fundamentally misconceived" (1983:88).

89 Since metapragmatic indexicality relies heavily on the context, some authors (e.g., Gumperz 1992) use the term 'contextualization'; others speak of 'entextualization' (e.g., Silverstein 1993:47).

90 Rancière's original wording alludes to a seminal work by the French sociologist Pierre Bourdieu, *Ce que parler veut dire* (1983).

91 See Enfield 1998 for an enlightening discussion of this issue.

92 I have opted for this terminology (pragmeme, pract, allopract) for purely practical reasons, viz., to provide my readers with a familiar, not too overworked framework that would be accessible to anybody with a minimal background in linguistics.

Some might object to my choice on the grounds that it "extend[s] the analysis of language systems to embrace a certain range of related social facts, rather than [does] any rethinking of the basic assumptions underlying the postulation of language systems in the first place", as Roy Harris has remarked (1998:9). While such criticisms may have a point (they have also has been leveled at Kenneth's Pike's terminological neologism 'behavioreme', created to capture the entire context of human behavior), this is not the place to enter into a discussion of foundational issues as they are reflected in terminology.

93 On 'adaptability' (as contrasted to 'adaptivity') in the domain of the interaction between humans and computers, see Mey (1992a, 19934a) and Gorayska and Mey (1996).

94 Computer wizard Simon Cray, inventor and builder of the Cray supercomputer, is said to have been able to reboot his machines directly from the main console, using machine language.

95 An interdict is a legal measure, inflicted by the Holy See on a certain part of its jurisdiction, or on a certain category of persons, and severing the connections between it, or them, and the church. It amounts thus to a 'territorial excommunication', an ecclesiastical state of siege.

96 One may wonder about the appropriateness of the term 'narration' and its cognates to characterize such different text genres as novels, poems, technical prose and so on. However, inasmuch every text bears the imprint of a producer, a 'teller', it seems fair to use the cover-all technical expression for 'telling', namely *to narrate*, in order to characterize all sorts of textual activity. The problem is intimately related with that of the text's 'voices'; see below, section 9.4, for details.

97 Such stories are often, following Genette (1980), called 'intradiegetic' (Toolan 1994:81).

98 In actual life, such protestations are often overheard, and the author is punished for what he or he has allowed her or his narrator to reveal. No amount of

distancing himself from the fictitious worlds he had created in his satirical narratives could prevent Jonathan Swift from being sent in exile to Ireland by his offended king.

99   The fact that Bulgakov prefers the past to a present form (like *uznajem* 'we will learn') may have to do with the fact that he is telling a story in the past, and doesn't want to break its continuity; an English reader would perhaps be happier with a translation like 'as we will learn subsequently'.

100   A more recent English translation of Bulgakov's work fares slightly better: "as was learned subsequently" is how Burgin and O'Connor render the discussed passage (1995:5). Even so, the tense problem remains.

101   For this quotation from Donne I am indebted to A.S. Byatt (1996:43). Incidentally, Donne's text ('Of the progresse of the soule. The second anniversarie'; ll. 244–6) also refers to a dead woman (though not a matriarch: fifteen-year-old Mistress Elizabeth Drury, who died in 1610).

102   The notion of 'point of view' has gained considerable popularity in the Anglo-American world of literary criticism, as Toolan (1994:68) remarks. However, for reasons of the "great and continuing nuisance perpetuated by the term" (p. 68), I prefer to use that of 'voice'. (On the relationship between 'focalization' and 'voice', see Mey 1999:ch. 6.1.)

103   One recent honorable exception is the work of Chafe (1994).

104   The nature of this representation will vary widely, of course, depending on the kind of society we are dealing with: elitist and aristocracy-oriented, or a more democratically organized type of commonwealth. Historically, the different organizations reflect themselves in the way audiences are arranged: compare the egalitarian, more democratic seating in Shakespeare's Globe playhouse with the stiffly hierarchical structure of the Italian-inspired baroque theater (such as the Fenice in Venice): royalty in their separate boxes, the rest of the spectators having their seats assigned in accordance with their societal positions and worldly wealth.

105   The only exception being 'Darl', who possesses two voices, one 'natural', the other 'preternatural', printed in italics, to show that this is the voice of somebody speaking *through* him: an omniscient 'helper', maybe.

106   Among the latter Virginia Woolf, "who probably over-uses the device" (Fludernik 1993:165).

107   A similar reasoning may have prompted the new measures recently announced by the US government to curb tobacco consumption among minors. In future, the use of models, pictures, colors etc. in cigarette advertising will be prohibited and only back-and-white ('tombstone') lettering permitted. In his speech on the lawn of the White House on August 23, 1996, in which he announced the new measures, President Bill Clinton had it right when he said: "I hereby pronounce Joe Camel and the Marlboro Man dead" (National Public Radio News, August 24, 1996, noon). And indeed, since destroying the 'set-up' takes away the necessary presuppositions for a pragmatic act, advertising by speech acts alone (if it were feasible) would be bound to be significantly less effective than our present way of pulling out all the thinkable media stops in order to create an overwhelming advertising set-up, an 'offer we cannot refuse'.

108   Bleikasten refers here to the classic rhetorical technique called *prosopopeia* (literally: 'personification'), i.e., the creation of a mask and a voice for a free-

standing character by the author, in accordance with his or her narrative needs. (1973:154, n. 9)

109 For some amusing and elightening examples, the reader is referred to the 'special encodings' in the futuristic novel *Native Tongue* by the linguist Suzette Haden Elgin (1984:242 and *passim*). For instance, there exists an interesting area of the human body, consisting of the inner surfaces of hand and arm up to the elbow, for which no common denomination ever has been invented in English, but which may be seen, and lexicalized, as an *athad*, and subsequently will be able to start a life of its own, in reality as in language. (See also the review of this book in Mey 1989b.)

110 Like those Hungarian kids that ask every tourist "Sprechen Sie Deutsch?" – whereupon they vanish in thin air as soon as the tourist starts to answer in German!

111 As a comic instance, consider the native 'broken talk' of Triballós, a character introduced by Aristophanes in his *Birds*. The person (supposedly one of the local gods) speaks gibberish (Illyrian?), but even so apparently makes sense in his own crooked idiom, only to be exploited as some kind of external oracular authority in a crucial dispute. ('What do you say, Triballus?'; 'Nabaisatreu'; 'You see? Even he agrees': *Ornithes* 1614–15; or: 'Triballus, what do you think, should we let it ride?'; 'Saunaka baktarikrousa'; 'He says that would be a good idea': *Ornithes* 1627–8 (Aristophanes 1888: II, 65).

112 In certain cultures, such as the Mediterranean, showing a person your open hand is supposed to bring on a curse; which is why people there beckon with their palms down, rather than with outstretched fingers and palms up, like we do.

113 The proper Italian term is *pentito di Camorra*, 'Camorra repentant'.

114 An 'extra indexicality' occurs also in what is called (following Gundel et al. 1993) 'reminder deixis' (see section 3.3.3).

115 But recall what was said earlier on 'pragmatic acts' as contrasted with 'speech acts': the latter depend on the former for their realization, not vice versa. A pract needs no speech.

116 Actually, Peirce first used the term 'pragmatic' in a notebook entry in 1861. The notion then remained dormant until 1898, when he started writing an encyclopedia article on the topic of 'Pragmatic, Pragmatism' (published in 1901) and started out by using his old notes (Fisch 1986:114, 218).

117 Many linguists (and especially, many pragmaticists) do not feel the need to maintain a strict, tripartite division of the linguistic disciplines. In fact, much of traditional syntax and semantics leads us directly to pragmatic issues and problems, as we have seen earlier, sections 2.4 and 2.5. For a review of the syntactic evidence for pragmatics, see Green (1989:128ff).

118 The term 'hegemony' is originally due to the Italian Marxist theoretician and linguist Antonio Gramsci. For a definition, cf. Mininni (1998:337): 'the ability of a group to lead the whole community to accept them freely as the ruling group'.

119 In the early nineties, the yearly tuition fees in US private universities ranged from $14,000 to well over $20,000 a year (*Daily Northwesterner*, January 10, 1991). The costs have since increased by 15–20 percent.

120 What these tests measure is mainly test-taking skills, not verbal comprehension and retention, as a report in *Science News* 137 (1990:199) has shown.

121 See Jourdan (1989) and Keesing (1989) for an enlightening discussion of the pidgin vs. English situation in the Solomons.

122   As the manager expressed it, when asked for a reason: "We want a safe, effectively supervised, one language workplace" (the San Antonio, Tex., monthly *Hispanic*, March 1998:50).

123   The distinction between 'oppression' and 'suppression' is originally due to Pateman (1980).

124   The classical reference to Bernstein is his two-volume work *Class, Codes and Control* (1971–3), later expanded to include two additional volumes (1975 and 1990). Bernstein (1981) attempts to frame the theory more explicitly in terms of social classes. In a work dated 1990, Bernstein answers some of the criticisms that had been raised of his theory, by de-emphasizing 'code' as a particular form of language use. Even so, he cannot entirely escape the ghosts of the past, as when he speaks of "classroom talk" as being "restricted" (1990:107).

125   The party now prefers to call itself, in another interesting semantic development, 'liberal'.

126   Full details on the 1976 labor conflict, one of the biggest in Danish history, can be found in chapter 2 of my 1985 book, where also a number of examples supporting the above assertions can be found. For a complete documentation and a critical discussion of what went on in the media during that week, see also Qvortrup (1979).

127   Gabriel García Márquez, in one of his bittersweet short stories ('La luz es cómo el agua'; 1992a), tells us about two boys who demand that their parents give them the boat they had been promised in return for getting straight As and making the school's honor list. The parents point out that the only available body of water for miles around is the shower in their fifth-floor Madrid apartment. However, the boys insist and in the end, the parents comply. One night, when the parents are away at the movies, the boys get the boat out and flood the apartment with light. When the parents come home, they find the sleepy sailors floating in the living room on a lake of light: their father had once told them how light is like water; you turn it off and on, like tap water; and they had not only believed, but lived out the metaphor.

128   This concept of 'wording' is different from that introduced by Halliday (e.g., 1978:200, 208). For him, 'wording' represents the coding of meaning at the lexico-syntactic level (where the 'words' are). Such a concept of 'wording', however, is too narrow, in that it considers the level of the 'words' as semi-independent of the rest of the language, with contacts mediated only through coding and decoding processes ('meaning' is coded into 'wording', 'wording' into 'sounding' or 'writing', respectively).

129   Cf.: "The landless (*sem-terra*) are the new environmental villains"; by contrast, "the [Company of] Vale do Rio Doce [the biggest developers in the Amazonas region] protects the last continuous wooded segment of the region [namely, the Vale dos Carajás] that is threatened by the invasion of the landless" (*Amazônia, um tesouro ameaçado*, in the review *Veja* (São Paulo), December 1997, p. 22, 50d). Ironically, the Vale dos Carajás was the scene of a massacre perpetrated against the landless in 1996, when over twenty of them were killed by the military police.

130   Cf. the 'Kissinger case', quoted in section 11.1.2.1.

131   "[According to] traditional grammars, the word *man* functions . . . to encompass human beings of both sexes: 'Man stood upright, and a new day dawned'" (Treichler and Frank 1989:3).

132 On the reader as 'co-creator' of the text, see Mey (1999:ch. 8).

133 As depicted on a marble frieze in the Council Room of the Amsterdam Royal Palace.

134 By a felicitous quirk of language homology, the French original is directly transposable into English, while conserving the pun: "Ce qui va sans dire, vient sans dire."

135 The original title of the story is 'Die Panne' (Dürrenmatt 1956).

136 In my 1976 edition, Hill wrongly ascribes the picture to a painter named Boyce. There *is* a (much earlier) painter of that name, and a small oil canvas of his is on display in one of the neighbouring rooms at the Tate. (Later editions of Hill's book have the correct reference.)

137 "But I say unto you, that every idle word that men shall speak, they shall give account thereof in the day of judgment. For by thy words thou shalt be justified, and by thy words thou shalt be condemned" (Matthew 12:36–7, King James version).

138 Thus Berkeley microbiologist Gunther Stent, one of Watson and Crick's collaborators, in a lecture at the Department of Computer Science, Yale University, in the summer of 1982.

139 Compare the use of 'visual silence' in the works of a painter such as Giorgio de Chirico, or that "courage of empty or dead surfaces" which we may experience in Abildgaard's works (Kirkeby 1993:12). As to the role of perspective in literary art, see my book *When Voices Clash* (1999: esp. ch. 6).

References

Allwood, Jens. 1976. 'Linguistic communication as action and cooperation'. Gothenburg: Göteborgs Universitet. (Ph.D. diss.) (= Gothenburg Monographs in Linguistics, 2).

Allwood, Jens, Joakim Nivre and Elisabeth Ahlsén. 1991. 'On the semantics and pragmatics of linguistic feedback'. *Gothenburg Papers in Theoretical Linguistics* 64.

[Anonymous] 1985. *The Tate Gallery: An Illustrated Companion*. London: Tate Gallery Publications Department. (Third, revised edn) [Originally published in 1979].

Ariel, Mira. 1991. *Accessing Noun-Phrase Antecedents*. London and New York: Routledge.

Aristophanes. 1888. *Ornithes*. In: *Comoediae* (Th. Bergk, ed., 2 vols). Lipsiae: Teubner., I:1–70. (186 BC) [The Birds].

Auerbach, Erich. 1998. *Mimesis. Verklighetsframställningen i den västerlandska litteraturen* (trans. Ulrika Wallenström) Stockholm: Bonnier. [Original title: *Mimesis. Dargestellte Wirklichkeit in der abendländischen Literatur*. Tübingen and Basel: Francke. 1946].

Austin, John L. 1962. *How To Do Things With Words*. Oxford: Oxford University Press.

Bakhtin, Mikhail M. 1994. *Speech Genres and Other Late Essays* (trans. Vern W. McGee). Austin, Tex.: University of Texas Press. [1986].

Bar-Hillel, Yehoshua. 1971. 'Out of the pragmatic waste-basket'. *Linguistic Inquiry* 2:401–7.

Barton, Ellen L. 1990. *Nonsentential Constituents. A Theory of Grammatical Structure and Pragmatic Interpretation*. Amsterdam and Philadelphia: John Benjamins. (Pragmatics and Beyond, New Series, 2).

Bauman, Richard and Joel Sherzer, eds. 1974. *Explorations in the Ethnography of Speaking*. Cambridge: Cambridge University Press.

Berger, Peter L. and Thomas Luckmann. 1966. *The Social Construction of Reality*. New York: Doubleday.

Bernstein, Basil. 1971–5. *Class, Codes and Control* (3 vols). London: Routledge and Kegan Paul.

Bernstein, Basil. 1981. 'Codes, modalities, and the process of cultural reproduction: A model'. *Language in Society* 10:327–63.

Bernstein, Basil. 1990. *The Structuring of Pedagogic Discourse* (= *Class, Codes and Control*, vol. 4). London and New York: Routledge.

Bernstein, Carl and Bob Woodward. 1974. *All the President's Men.* New York: Simon and Schuster.

Bickhard, Mark and Robert Campbell. 1992. 'Some foundational questions concerning language studies: with a focus on categorial grammars and model theoretical possible worlds grammars'. *Journal of Pragmatics* 17(5/6):401–33. (Special Issue on 'Foundational questions concerning language studies').

Bilmes, Jack. 1986. *Discourse and Behavior.* New York and London: Plenum.

Blakemore, Diane. 1992. *Understanding Utterances: The Pragmatics of Natural Language.* Oxford: Blackwell.

Bleikasten, André. 1973. *Faulkner's 'As I Lay Dying'.* Bloomington and London: Indiana University Press (trans. Roger Little from the French).

Bloomfield, Leonard. 1950. *Language.* London: George Allen and Unwin. [1933].

Blum-Kulka, Shoshana, Juliane House and Gabriele Kasper (eds). 1989. *Cross-cultural Pragmatics: Requests and Apologies.* Norwood, N.J.: Ablex.

Bolinger, Dwight D. 1980. *Language, the Loaded Weapon: The Use and Abuse of Language.* London: Longman.

Borutti, Silvana. 1984. 'Pragmatics and its discontents'. *Journal of Pragmatics* 8(4):437–47. (Special Issue on 'Metapragmatics', ed. Claudia Caffi).

Bourdieu, Pierre. 1977. *Outline of a Theory of Practice.* Cambridge: Cambridge University Press. [Original title: *Esquisse d'une théorie de la pratique.* 1972].

Bourdieu, Pierre. 1983. *Ce que parler veut dire.* Paris: Fayard. (Engl. trans. *Language and Symbolic Power.* Cambridge: Polity Press. 1991).

Brown, Penelope and Stephen C. Levinson. 1978. 'Universals in language usage: Politeness phenomena'. In: Esther Goody (ed.), *Questions and Politeness: Strategies in Social Interaction.* Cambridge: Cambridge University Press. pp. 56–311. (= Cambridge Papers in Social Anthropology Vol. 8).

Brown, Roger and Albert Gilman. 1961. 'The pronouns of power and solidarity'. In: Thomas A. Sebeok (ed.), *Style in Language.* Cambridge, Mass.: MIT Press. pp. 253–76.

Bühler, Karl. 1934. *Sprachtheorie.* Jena: Fischer.

Bulgakov, Mikhail [A.]. 1969. *Master i Margarita.* Frankfurt: Posev. (trans. Mirra Ginsburg, *The Master and Margarita.* New York: Grove Press. 1967; new trans. Diana Burgin and Katherine Tiernan O'Connor. Dana Point, Calif.: Ardis. 1995). [1940; first Russian edn 1966–7].

Byatt, A.S. 1992. *Angels and Insects.* London: Chatto and Windus.

Byatt, A.S. 1996. *Babel Tower.* New York: Random House.

Caffi, Claudia. 1984a. 'Introduction'. *Journal of Pragmatics* 8(4):433–5. (Special Issue on 'Metapragmatics', ed. Claudia Caffi).

Caffi, Claudia. 1984b. 'Some remarks on illocution and metacommunication'. *Journal of Pragmatics* 8(4):449–67. (Special Issue on 'Metapragmatics', ed. Claudia Caffi).

Caffi, Claudia. 1994a. 'Metapragmatics'. In: *Encyclopedia of Language and Linguistics.* Oxford: Pergamon. pp. 4:2461–5.

Caffi, Claudia. 1994b. 'Pragmatic presupposition'. In: *Encyclopedia of Language and Linguistics.* Oxford: Pergamon. pp. 6:3320–7.

Carberry, Sandra. 1989. 'A pragmatics-based approach to ellipsis resolution'. *Computational Linguistics* 15(2):75–98.

Carnap, Rudolf. 1956. *Meaning and Necessity*. Chicago: University of Chicago Press.

Casares, Julio. 1947. 'Femenismo mal entendido'. In: *Divertimentos filológicos*. Madrid: Calpe. pp. 302–6.

Chafe, Wallace. 1994. *Discourse, Consciousness and Time*. Chicago: University of Chicago Press.

Chomsky, Noam. 1957. *Syntactic Structures*. The Hague: Mouton. (= Janua Linguarum, Series Minor, Vol. 4).

Chomsky, Noam. 1965. *Aspects of the Theory of Syntax*. Cambridge, Mass.: MIT Press.

Cicero, M. Tullius. 1856. *Oratio Philippica in M. Antonium* II, ed. Karl Halm. Berlin: Weidmann. pp. 61–123. [44 BC].

Coetzee, J.M. 1984. *The Life and Times of Michael K*. New York: Viking Press.

Coetzee, J.M. 1988. *White Writing: On the Culture of Letters in South Africa*. Johannesburg: Radix.

Cooper, David. 1971. *The Death of the Family*. London: Pantheon.

Cortázar, Julio. 1982. 'Clone'. In: *Los relatos, 2: Juegos*. Madrid: Alianza Editorial. pp. 242–58.

Cortázar, Julio. 1985. 'Historia con migalas'. In: *Queremos tanto a Glenda y otros relatos*. Madrid: Ediciones Alfaguara. pp. 29–44.

Cutler, Anne. 1974. 'On saying what you mean without meaning what you say'. In: *Papers from the 10th Regional Meeting, Chicago Linguistic Society*. Chicago: Chicago Linguistic Society. pp. 117–27.

Davidson, Brad. 1998. 'Dialog in cross-linguistic medical interviews: the interpretation of interpretive discourse'. Paper presented at SALSA VI, Symposium About Language and Society at Austin, April 24–6. University of Texas at Austin.

Donne, John. 1615. The Second Anniversarie. Elegy on the Passing of Mistress Martha Drury. In: Donne 1958.

Donne, John. 1958. *The Poems of John Donne*, ed. Herbert J.C. Grierson. Oxford: Oxford University Press. Vol. 1. [1912].

Dupré, Louis. 1966. *The Philosophical Foundations of Marxism*. New York: Harcourt, Brace and World.

Duranti, Alessandro. 1996. *Linguistic Anthropology*. Cambridge: Cambridge University Press.

Dürrenmatt, Friedrich. 1956. 'Die Panne' [The Breakdown]. Zurich: Arche (trans. Richard and Clara Winston, *A Dangerous Game*. London: Jonathan Cape, 1960).

Eco, Umberto. 1979. 'Lector in fabula: pragmatic strategy in a metanarrative text'. In: *The Role of the Reader*. Bloomington, Ind.: Indiana University Press. pp. 201–66. [1977].

Egner, Thorbjørn. 1960. *Folk og Røvere i Kardemomme By* [People and Robbers in Cardamom Town]. Oslo: Aschehoug.

Ehrlich, Susan. 1990. *Point of View: A Linguistic Analysis of Literary Style*. London and New York: Routledge.

Elgin, Suzette Haden. 1984. *Native Tongue*. New York: DAW Books.

Elgin, Suzette Haden. 1989. *The Gentle Art of Verbal Self-defense*. Englewood Cliffs, N.J.: Erlbaum.

Enfield, Nick. 1998. 'On the indispensability of semantics: defining the "vacuous"'. In: Andrzej Bogusławski and Jacob L. Mey (eds), *E Pluribus Una: A Festschrift for Anna*

Wierzbicka. Odense: Odense University Press. (= *RASK, Internationalt tidsskrift for sprog og kommunikation*, vol. 9/10).

Enninger, Werner. 1987. 'What interactants do with non-talk across cultures'. In: Karlfried Knapp, Werner Enninger and Annelie Knapp-Potthoff (eds), *Analyzing Intercultural Communication*. Berlin: Mouton de Gruyter. pp. 269–302. (= *Studies in Anthropological Linguistics*, vol. 1).

Fairclough, Norman. 1989. *Language and Power*. London: Longman.

Fairclough, Norman, ed. 1992. *Critical Language Awareness*. London: Longman.

Fairclough, Norman. 1995. *Critical Discourse Analysis*. London: Longman.

Fasold, Ralph. 1990. *The Sociolinguistics of Language*. Oxford: Blackwell.

Faulkner, William. 1964. *As I Lay Dying*. New York: Random House. [1930].

Felman, Shoshana. 1980. *Le Scandale du corps parlant*. Paris: Seuil.

Fillmore, Charles J. 1981. 'Pragmatics and the description of discourse'. In: Peter Cole (ed.), *Radical Pragmatics*. New York: Academic Press. pp. 143–66.

Fisch, Max H. 1986. *Peirce, Semeiotic, and Pragmatism*. eds. Kenneth Laine Ketner and Christian J.W. Kloesel. Bloomington, Ind.: University of Indiana Press.

Flader, Dieter and T. Trotha. 1986. 'Über den geheimen "Positivismus" und andere Eigentümlichkeiten der ethnomethodologischen Konversationsanalyse'. (MS, Vienna University, mimeographed).

Fludernik, Monika. 1993. *The Fiction of Language and the Languages of Fiction*. London: Routledge.

Foucault, Michel. 1972. *The Archeology of Knowledge*. New York: Harper. (trans. A.M. Sheridan) [1969].

Fowler, Roger, Robert Hodge, Gunther Kress and Tony Trew. 1979. *Language and Control*. London: Routledge and Kegan Paul.

Frank, Francine Wattman and Paula A. Treichler (eds). 1989. *Language, Gender, and Professional Writing: Theoretical Approaches and Guidelines for Nonsexist Usage*. New York: Modern Language Association of America, Commission on the Status of Women in the Profession.

Fraser, Bruce. 1975. 'Hedged performatives'. In: Peter Cole and Jerry Morgan (eds), *Syntax and Semantics*, vol. 3: *Speech Acts*. New York: Academic Press. pp. 187–210.

Fraser, Bruce. 1980. 'Conversational mitigation'. *Journal of Pragmatics* 4(4):341–50.

Fraser, Bruce. 1990. 'Perspectives on politeness'. *Journal of Pragmatics* 14:219–36.

Freire, Paulo. 1968. *Pedagogy of the Oppressed*. New York: Seabury.

Freire, Paulo and Donaldo Macedo. 1987. *Literacy: Reading the Word and the World*. South Hadley, Mass.: Bergin and Garvey.

Gazdar, Gerald. 1979. *Pragmatics: Implicature, Presupposition and Logical Form*. New York: Academic Press.

Gazdar, Gerald. 1980. 'Pragmatic constraints and linguistic production'. In: Brian Butterworth (ed.), *Language Production*, vol. 2. New York: Academic Press. pp. 49–68.

Genette, Gérard. 1980. *Narrative Discourse*. Ithaca, N.Y.: Cornell University Press. [French original: *Discours du récit*. Paris: Seuil. 1972].

Gibson, James J. 1979. *The Ecological Approach to Visual Perception*. Boston, Mass.: Houghton Mifflin.

Giddens, Anthony. 1979. *Central Problems in Social Theory: Action, Structure and Contradiction in Social Analysis*. Berkeley, Calif.: University of California Press.

Gill, Satinder, Masahito Kawamori, Yashuhiro Katagiri and Atsushi Shimojima. 2000. 'The role of body moves in dialogue.' Paper presented at the Third International Conference on Cognitive Technology, San Francisco, Calif., August 9–13, 1999. *RASK, International Journal of Language and Communication* 12:89–114.

Goffman, Erving. 1958. *The Presentation of Self in Everyday Life*. New York: Basic Books.

Goffman, Erving. 1961. *Asylums*. New York: Doubleday.

Goffman, Erving. 1967. *Interaction Ritual*. New York: Doubleday Anchor.

Goffman, Erving. 1976. 'Replies and responses'. *Language in Society* 5:257–313.

Goffman, Erving. 1983. 'Felicity's condition'. *American Journal of Sociology* 1:1–53.

Good, David. 1996. 'Pragmatics and presence'. *AI and Society* 10:309–14.

Goodwin, Charles. 2000. 'Action and embodiment within situated human interaction'. *Journal of Pragmatics* 32(10):1489–1522.

Gorayska, Barbara and Jacob L. Mey. 1996. 'Murphy's surfers: where's the green? Lure and lore on the Internet'. *AI and Society* 10:292–308.

Green, Georgia M. 1989. *Pragmatics and Natural Language Understanding*. Hillsdale, N.J.: Erlbaum.

Gregersen, Frans. 1979. 'Social class and language usage'. In: Jacob L. Mey (ed.), *Pragmalinguistics: Theory and Practice*. The Hague: Mouton. (*Rasmus Rask Series in Pragmatic Linguistics*, vol. 1). pp. 171–94.

Grice, H. Paul. 1971. 'Meaning'. In: Danny Steinberg and Leon Jakobovits (eds), *Semantics: An Interdisciplinary Reader in Philosophy, Linguistics, and Psychology*. Cambridge: Cambridge University Press. pp. 53–9. [1958].

Grice, H. Paul. 1975. 'Logic and conversation'. In: Peter Cole and Jerry Morgan (eds), *Syntax and Semantics*, vol. 3: *Speech Acts*. New York: Academic Press. pp. 41–58.

Grice, H. Paul. 1978. 'Further notes on logic and conversation'. In: Peter Cole (ed.), *Syntax and Semantics*, vol. 9: *Pragmatics*. New York: Academic Press. pp. 113–28.

Grice, H. Paul. 1981. 'Presupposition and conversational implicature'. In: Peter Cole (ed.), *Radical Pragmatics*. New York: Academic Press. pp. 183–98.

Grice, H. Paul. 1989. *Studies in the Way of Words (The William James Lectures)*. Cambridge, Mass.: Harvard University Press.

Gu, Yueguo. 1993. 'The impasse of perlocution'. *Journal of Pragmatics* 20:405–32.

Gudykunst, William B. and Stella Ting-Toomey (eds). 1988. *Culture and Interpersonal Communication*. Newbury Park, Calif.: Sage.

Gumperz, John. 1992. 'Contextualization and understanding'. In: Alessandro Duranti and Charles Goodwin (eds), *Rethinking Context: Language as an Interactive Phenomenon*. Cambridge: Cambridge University Press. pp. 229–52.

Gumperz, John. 1998. 'Intercultural communication in a practice perspective'. Plenary Lecture, SALSA VI, Symposium About Language and Society at Austin, April 24–6. University of Texas at Austin.

Gumperz, John and Stephen C. Levinson, eds. 1996. *Rethinking Linguistic Relativity*. Cambridge: Cambridge University Press.

Gundel, Jeanette, Nancy Hedberg and Ron Zacharski. 1993. 'Cognitive status and the form of referring expressions in discourse'. *Language* 69(2):274–307.

Haberland, Hartmut and Jacob L. Mey. 1977. 'Editorial: Pragmatics and linguistics'. *Journal of Pragmatics* 1(1):1–16.

Hajičová, Eva. 1997. *Topic-Focus Articulation of the Sentence and its Impact on the Analysis of Discourse*. Prague: Charles University. (Vilém Mathesius Lectures, Series XI).

Halliday, M.A.K. 1978. *Language as Social Semiotic: The Social Interpretation of Language and Meaning*. London: Edward Arnold.

Halliday, M.A.K. and Ruqaiya Hasan. 1976. *Cohesion in English*. London: Longman.

Hanks, William F. 1992. 'The indexical ground of deictic reference'. In: Alessandro Duranti and Charles Goodwin (eds), *Rethinking Context: Language as an Interactive Phenomenon*. Cambridge: Cambridge University Press. pp. 43–76.

Hanks, William F. 1996. 'Language form and communicative practices'. In: Gumperz and Levinson 1996. pp. 232–70.

Harris, Roy. 1998. 'Language as social interaction: integrationalism versus segregationalism'. In: Roy Harris and George Wolf (eds), *Integrational Linguistics: A First Reader*. Oxford: Elsevier Science. pp. 5–14.

Haugen, Einar. 1972. 'The ecology of language'. In: A.S. Dil (ed.), *The Ecology of Language. Essays by Einar Haugen*. Stanford, Calif.: Stanford University Press. [1971].

Hill, Susan. 1976. *The Bird of Night*. Harmondsworth: Penguin. [Originally published in 1972. London: Hamish Hamilton].

Hindmarsh, Jon and Christian Heath. 2000. 'The interactional practice of reference'. *Journal of Pragmatics* 32(12):1855–78.

Hinkelman, Elizabeth. 1987. 'Relevance: computation and coherence'. *Behavioral and Brain Sciences* 10(4):720–1.

Hjelmslev, Louis. 1929. *Principes de grammaire générale*. Copenhagen: Munksgaard.

Hjelmslev, Louis. 1943. *Omkring sprogteoriens grundlæggelse*. Copenhagen: Munksgaard. (trans. Francis Whitfield, *Prolegomena to a Theory of Language*. Madison, Wis.: University of Wisconsin Press. 1953).

Hockett, Charles F. 1959. *A Course in Modern Linguistics*. New York: Macmillan. [1958].

Holberg, Ludvig. 1914. *Comedies*. (trans. Oscar J. Campbell and Frederic Schenk). New York: American-Scandinavian Foundation. [1722].

Horn, Laurence R. 1984. 'Toward a new taxonomy for pragmatic inference: Q-based and R-based implicative'. In: Deborah Schiffrin (ed.), *Georgetown Round Table on Languages and Linguistics 1984*. Washington, D.C.: Georgetown University Press. pp. 11–42. Reprinted in: Asa Kasher (ed.) (1988), *Pragmatics: Critical Concepts, Volume IV (Part VII: Implicature)* . London: Routledge. pp. 383–418.

Ide, Risako. 1998. 'Sorry for your kindness'. *Journal of Pragmatics* 29(5):509–29.

Iser, Wolfgang. 1976. *Die Art des Lesens*. Munich: Pieper.

Jacobs, Scott and Sally Jackson. 1983a. 'Speech act structure in conversation: rational aspects of pragmatic coherence'. In: Robert T. Craig and Karen Tracy (eds), *Conversational Coherence*. Beverly Hills, Calif., and London: Sage. pp. 47–66.

Jacobs, Scott and Sally Jackson. 1983b. 'Strategy and structure in conversational influence attempts'. *Communication Monographs* 50:285–304.

Jacquemet, Marco. 1994. 'T-offenses and metapragmatic attacks: strategies of interactional dominance'. *Discourse and Society* 5(3):297–319.

Jakobson, Roman. 1960. 'Closing statement: linguistics and poetics'. In: Thomas A. Sebeok (ed.), *Style in Language*. Cambridge, Mass.: MIT Press. pp. 350–77.

Janks, Hilary and Roz Ivanič. 1992. 'Critical language awareness and emancipatory discourse'. In: Fairclough 1992. pp. 305–31.

Janney, Richard W. 1996. 'E-mail and intimacy.' In: Barbara Gorayska and Jacob L. Mey (eds), *Cognitive Technology: In Search of a Humane Interface*. Amsterdam and Oxford: Elsevier Science. (= *Advances in Psychology*, vol. 113). pp. 201–11.

Jaworski, Adam (ed.). 1997. *Silence: Interdisciplinary Perspectives*. Berlin and New York: Mouton de Gruyter. (= *Studies in Anthropological Linguistics*, vol. 10).

Jourdan, Christine. 1989. 'Solomons Pijin: an unrecognized national language'. In: Richard Baldauf and Allan Luke (eds), *Language Planning and Education in Australasia and the South Pacific*. Clevedon: Multilingual Matters. pp. 166–80.

Jucker, Andreas. 1997. Review of Dan Sperber and Deirdre Wilson *Relevance: Communication and Cognition*, second edition (1995). *Journal of Pragmatics* 27:112–19.

Judge, A.J.N. 1988. 'Recording of networks of incommensurable concepts in phased cycles – and their comprehension through metaphor'. Round Table discussion on 'Metaphor', International Symposium on Models of Meaning. Varna, Bulgaria, September 1988.

Judge, A.J.N. 1991. 'Metaphors as transdisciplinary vehicles of the future'. Conference on Science and Tradition: Transdisciplinary perspectives on the way to the 21st century. Paris, December 1991. Paris: Union des Ingénieurs et des Techniciens utilisant la langue française.

Karttunen, Lauri. 1969. 'Pronouns and variables'. In: Robert Binnick et al. (eds), *Papers from the Fifth Regional Meeting, Chicago Linguistic Society*. Chicago: Chicago Linguistic Society. pp. 108–16.

Karttunen, Lauri. 1971. 'Implicative verbs'. *Language* 47:340–58.

Kasher, Asa. 1982. 'Gricean inference reconsidered'. *Philosophia* 29:25–44.

Kasher, Asa, ed. 1998. *Pragmatics: Critical Concepts* (6 vols). London: Routledge.

Kasper, Gabriele. 1990. 'Linguistic politeness: current research issues'. *Journal of Pragmatics* 14:193–218.

Kasper, Gabriele and Shoshana Blum-Kulka (eds). 1993. *Interlanguage Pragmatics*. Oxford and New York: Oxford University Press.

Katz, Jerry J. 1977. *Propositional Structure and Illocutionary Force*. New York: Crowell.

Katz, Jerry J. and Fodor, Jerry A. 1963. 'The structure of a semantic theory'. *Language* 39(2):170–210.

Keating, Elizabeth. 1998. *Power Sharing: Rank, Gender and Social Space in Pohnpei, Micronesia*. Oxford: Oxford University Press.

Keenan, Edward L. 1971. 'Two kinds of presuppositions in natural language'. In: Charles J. Fillmore and D. Terence Langendoen (eds), *Studies in Linguistic Semantics*. New York: Holt. pp. 45–54.

Keenan, Elinor [Ochs]. 1976. 'On the universality of conversational implicatures'. *Language in Society* 5:67–80.

Keesing, Roger. 1989. 'Solomons Pijin: colonial ideologies'. In: Richard Baldauf and Allan Luke (eds), *Language Planning and Education in Australasia and the South Pacific*. Clevedon: Multilingual Matters. pp. 149–65.

Kempson, Ruth. 1977. *Semantic Theory*. Cambridge: Cambridge University Press.

Kiparsky, Paul and Carol Kiparsky. 1971. 'Fact'. In: Danny Steinberg and Leon Jakobovits (eds), *Semantics: An Interdisciplinary Reader in Philosophy, Linguistics, and Psychology*. Cambridge: Cambridge University Press. pp. 345–69.

Kirkeby, Per. 1993. *N.A. Abildgaard*. Hellerup: Editions Bløndal. (trans. Reginald Spink).

Kittay, Eva F. 1987. *Metaphor. Its Cognitive Force and Linguistic Structure*. Oxford: Clarendon Press.

Kjærbeck, Susanne. 1998. 'The organization of discourse units in Mexican and Danish business negotiations'. *Journal of Pragmatics* 30(3):347–62.

Kramarae, Cheris, Muriel Schulz and Wiliam M. O'Barr, eds. 1984. *Language and Power*. Beverly Hills and London: Sage.

Kuhn, Thomas A. 1964. *The Structure of Scientific Revolutions*. Chicago: University of Chicago Press.

Kumatoridani, Tetsuo. 1999. 'Alternation and co-occurrence in Japanese thanks'. *Journal of Pragmatics* 31:623–42.

Kunst-Gnamuš, Olga. 1991. 'Politeness as an effect of the interaction between the form and content of a request and the context of utterance'. In: Igor Z. Žagar (ed.), *Speech Acts: Fiction or Reality?* Proceedings of the International Conference, Ljubljana, Yugoslavia, November 15, 1990. [Ljubljana & Antwerp:] IPrA Distribution Center for Yugoslavia, Institute for Social Sciences. pp. 49–62.

Kurzon, Dennis. 1997. *The Discourse of Silence*. Amsterdam and Philadelphia: Benjamins. (Pragmatics and Beyond, New Series, 49).

Kurzon, Dennis. 1998. 'The speech act of incitement: perlocutionary acts revisited'. *Journal of Pragmatics* 29(5):571–96.

Labov, William. 1966. *The Social Stratification of English in New York City*. Washington, D.C.: Center for Applied Linguistics.

Labov, William. 1972. *Language in the Inner City*. Philadelphia, Pa.: University of Pennsylvania Press.

Lacoste, Michèle. 1981. 'The old lady and the doctor'. *Journal of Pragmatics* 5(2):169–80.

Lakoff, George. 1971a. 'On generative semantics'. In: Danny Steinberg and Leon Jakobovits (eds), *Semantics: An Interdisciplinary Reader in Philosophy, Linguistics, and Psychology*. Cambridge: Cambridge University Press. pp. 232–96.

Lakoff, George. 1971b. 'Presupposition and relative well-formedness'. In: Danny Steinberg and Leon Jakobovits (eds), *Semantics: An Interdisciplinary Reader in Philosophy, Linguistics, and Psychology*. Cambridge: Cambridge University Press. pp. 329–40. [1968].

Lakoff, George and Mark Johnson. 1980. *Metaphors We Live By*. Chicago: University of Chicago Press.

Lakoff, Robin. 1989. 'The way we were; or, the real truth about generative semantics: A memoir'. *Journal of Pragmatics* 13(6):939–88.

Leech, Geoffrey N. 1983. *Principles of Pragmatics*. London: Longman.

Leech, Geoffrey N. and Jennifer Thomas. 1988. *Pragmatics: The State of the Art*. Lancaster University: Lancaster Papers in Linguistics.

Le Page, R.B. and Andrée Tabouret-Keller. 1986. *Acts of Identity*. Cambridge: Cambridge University Press.

Lermontov, Mikhail Ju. 1961. *Geroj našego vremenja* [A Hero of Our Times]. Moscow: Izdatel'stvo Pravda. [1838–40].

Lerner, Gene and Tomoyo Takagi. 1999. 'On the place of linguistic resources in the organization of talk-in-interaction: a co-investigation of English and Japanese grammatical practices'. *Journal of Pragmatics* 31:49–75.

Levinson, Stephen C. 1979. 'Activity types and language'. *Linguistics* 17:365–99.

Levinson, Stephen C. 1981. 'The essential inadequacies of speech act models of dialogue'. In: Herman Parret, Marina Sbisà and Jef Verschueren (eds), *Possibilities and Limitations of Pragmatics*. Amsterdam and Philadelphia: Benjamins (Studies in Language Companion Series, 7). pp. 473–92.

Levinson, Stephen C. 1982. 'Caste rank and verbal interaction in Western Tamilnadu'. In: Dennis B. McGilvray (ed.), *Caste Ideology and Interaction*. Cambridge: Cambridge University Press. pp. 98–203.

Levinson, Stephen C. 1983. *Pragmatics*. Cambridge: Cambridge University Press.

Levinson, Stephen C. 1995. 'Interactional biases in human thinking'. In: Esther Goody (ed.), *Social Intelligence in Interaction*. Cambridge: Cambridge University Press. pp. 221–60.

Lewis, David. 1969. *Convention*. Cambridge, Mass.: Harvard University Press.

Lilli, Laura. 1990. 'Caccia al cammello' [Chasing down the camel]. Interview with Umberto Eco. *La Repubblica*, December 7, 1990.

Lodge, David. 1992. *Paradise News*. Harmondsworth: Penguin.

Lucy, John A., ed. 1993. *Reflexive Language: Reported Speech and Metapragmatics*. Cambridge: Cambridge University Press.

Lyons, John. 1968. *Introduction to Theoretical Linguistics*. Cambridge: Cambridge University Press.

Lyons, John. 1977. *Semantics* (2 vols). Cambridge: Cambridge University Press.

Madvig, Johan Nicolai. 1843. *Indbydelsesskrift til Hs. Majsts. Kongens Fødselsdag* [Invitational Treatise for His Majesty the King's Birthday Celebration [at Copenhagen University]]. Copenhagen: Schultz.

Márquez, Gabriel García. 1992a. 'La luz es como el agua' [Light is like water]. In: *Doce cuentos peregrinos*. Buenos Aires: Edición Sudamericana. pp. 207–13.

Márquez, Gabriel García. 1992b. 'Sólo vine a hablar por teléfono' [I only came by to make a phone call]. In: *Doce cuentos peregrinos*. Buenos Aires: Edición Sudamericana. pp. 103–26.

Martinet, André. 1962. *A Functional View of Language*. Oxford: Oxford University Press.

Marx, Karl and Friedrich Engels. 1974. *The German Ideology* (C.J. Arthur, ed.). New York: International Publishers. [1845–6].

McConnell-Ginet, Sally. 1989. 'The sexual (re)production of meaning: a discourse-based theory'. In: Frank and Treichler, 1989. pp. 35–50.

Meehan, James. 1981. 'Tale spin'. In: Roger C. Schank and Christopher K. Riesbeck (eds), *Inside Computer Understanding*. Hillsdale, N.J.: Erlbaum. pp. 197–226.

Meseguer, Álvaro G. 1988. *Lenguaje y discriminación sexual*. Barcelona: Montesinos. (3rd edn).

Mey, Inger Elise. 1996. *Personvern i elektronisk marked* [Personal Privacy in the Electronic Market]. Oslo: University of Oslo, Institutt for Rettsinformatikk.

Mey, Jacob L. 1979. 'Zur kritischen Sprachtheorie'. In: Jacob L. Mey (ed.), *Pragmalinguistics: Theory and Practice*. The Hague: Mouton. (*Rasmus Rask Series in Pragmatic Linguistics*, vol. 1). pp. 411–34.

Mey, Jacob L. 1981. 'Right or wrong, my native speaker'. In: Florian Coulmas (ed.), *A Festschrift for Native Speaker*. The Hague: Mouton. pp. 69–84.

Mey, Jacob L. 1985. *Whose Language? A Study in Linguistic Pragmatics*. Amsterdam and Philadelphia: Benjamins. (Pragmatics and Beyond Companion Series, 3).

Mey, Jacob L. 1987a. 'The dark horse of linguistics: two recent books on pragmatics'. *Acta Linguistica Hafniensia* 20:157–72.

Mey, Jacob L. 1987b. 'Poet and peasant: a pragmatic comedy in five acts, dedicated to Jens Allwood'. *Journal of Pragmatics* 11(3):281–95.

Mey, Jacob L. 1989a. 'The end of the Copper Age, or: Pragmatics 12½ years after'. *Journal of Pragmatics* 13(6):825–32.

Mey, Jacob L. 1989b. 'Not by the word only'. Review of Suzette Haden Elgin, *Native Tongue*. (New York: DAW, 1984). *Journal of Pragmatics* 13(6):1035–45.

Mey, Jacob L. 1991a. 'Between rules and principles: some thoughts on the notion of "Metapragmatic Constraint"'. Symposium on Metapragmatic Terms, Budapest, July 2–4, 1990. *Acta Linguistica Academiae Scientiarum Hungaricae* 39:1–6.

Mey, Jacob L. 1991b. 'Metaphors and solutions: towards an ecology of metaphor'. International Symposium on Models of Meaning. Varna, Bulgaria, September 1988.

Mey, Jacob L. 1992a. 'A note on adaptability'. *AI and Society* 6:1–23.

Mey, Jacob L. 1992b. 'Pragmatic gardens and their magic'. *Poetics* 20(2):233–45.

Mey, Jacob L. 1994a. 'Adaptability'. In: *Encyclopedia of Language and Linguistics*. Oxford: Pergamon. pp. 1:25–7.

Mey, Jacob L. 1994b. 'Pragmatics'. In: *Encyclopedia of Language and Linguistics*. Oxford: Pergamon. pp. 7:3260–78.

Mey, Jacob L. 1994c. 'Economese'. In: *Encyclopedia of Language and Linguistics*. Oxford: Pergamon. pp. 3:1086–7.

Mey, Jacob L. 1994d. 'Edifying Archie or: How to fool the reader'. In: Herman Parret (ed.), *Pretending to Communicate*. Berlin: Walter de Gruyter. pp. 154–72.

Mey, Jacob L. 1995. 'Pragmatic problems in literary texts'. In: Sharon Millar and Jacob Mey (eds), *Form and Function in Language*. Odense: Odense University Press. pp. 151–70. (= *RASK* Suppl. Vol. 2).

Mey, Jacob L., ed. 1998. *Concise Encyclopedia of Pragmatics*. Oxford: Elsevier Science/Pergamon.

Mey, Jacob L. 1999. *When Voices Clash: A Study in Literary Pragmatics*. Berlin and New York: Mouton de Gruyter.

Mey, Jacob L. 2000. 'The computer as prosthesis'. *Hermes*.

Mey, Jacob L. 2001. (in press). 'Accessibility and activation'. In: Festschrift Eli Fischer-Jørgensen. Copenhagen.

Mey, Jacob L. and Mary Talbot. 1989. 'Computation and the soul'. *Semiotica* 72:291–339.

Mininni, Giuseppe. 1990. ' "Common speech" as a pragmatic form of social reproduction'. *Journal of Pragmatics* 14(1):125–35.

Mininni, Giuseppe. 1998. 'Hegemony'. In: Jacob L. Mey (ed.), *Concise Encyclopedia of Pragmatics*. Oxford: Pergamon. pp. 337–8.

Minsky, Marvin. 1975. 'A framework for representing knowledge'. In: Patrick H. Winston (ed.), *The Psychology of Computer Vision*. New York: McGraw-Hill. pp. 211–77.

Mizutani, Osamu and Nobuko Mizutani. 1986. *An Introduction to Modern Japanese*. Tokyo: Japan Times. [1976] [includes non-transcribed audiotapes of Japanese texts].

Morris, Charles H. 1938. *Foundations of the Theory of Signs*. Chicago: University of Chicago Press. (= Rudolf Carnap et al. (eds), *International Encyclopedia of Unified Science*. vol. 2:1).

Morson, Gary S. and Caryl Emerson. 1990. *Mikhail Bakhtin: The Creation of a Prosaics*. Stanford, Calif.: Stanford University Press.

Mumby, Dennis K. and Cynthia Stohl. 1991. 'Power and discourse in organization studies: absence and the dialectic of control'. *Discourse and Society* 2(3):313–32.

Navarro, Vicente. 1991. 'Class and race: life and death situations'. *Monthly Review* 43(4):1–13.

Nerlich, Brigitte and David D. Clarke. 2000. (in press). 'Ambiguities we live by. Towards a pragmatics of polysemy'. *Journal of Pragmatics*.

Nijhof, Gerard. 1998. 'Naturalizing medical discourse'. *Journal of Pragmatics* 30:735–53.

Nissen, Uwe Kjær. 1990. 'A review of language and sex in the Spanish language'. *Women and Language* 13(2):11–29.

Nunberg, Geoffrey. 1981. 'Validating pragmatic explanations'. In: Peter Cole (ed.), *Radical Pragmatics*. New York: Academic Press. pp. 198–222.

O'Barr, William. 1982. *Linguistic Evidence: Language, Power, and Strategy in the Courtroom*. New York: Academic Press.

Östman, Jan-Ola. 1981. *'You Know': A Discourse-functional Approach*. Amsterdam and Philadelphia: Benjamins. (= *Pragmatics and Beyond*, vol. II:7).

Östman, Jan-Ola. 1987. 'Pragmatics as implicitness'. Berkeley, Calif. (University of California Ph.D. thesis).

Östman, Jan-Ola. 1988a. 'Implicit involvement in interactive writing'. In: Jef Verschueren and Marcella Bertucelli-Papi (eds), *The Pragmatic Perspective: Selected Papers from the 1985 International Pragmatics Conference*. Amsterdam/Philadelphia: Benjamins. pp. 155–78.

Östman, Jan-Ola. 1988b. 'Adaptation, variability and effect: comments on IPrA Working Documents 1 and 2'. In: *Working Document #3*. Antwerp: International Pragmatics Association. pp. 5–39.

Östman, Jan-Ola. 1995a. 'Recasting the deictic foundation, using physics and Finnish'. In: Masayoshi Shibatani and Sandra Thompson (eds), *Essays in Semantics and Pragmatics in Honor of Charles J. Fillmore*. Amsterdam: Benjamins. pp. 246–67.

Östman, Jan-Ola. 1995b. 'Explicating implicitness'. *Pragmatics, Ideology and Contacts Bulletin* 2:4–7.

Partee, Barbara H. 1972. 'Opacity, coreference, and pronouns'. In: Donald Davidson and Gilbert Harman (eds), *Semantics of Natural Language*. Dordrecht: Reidel. pp. 415–41.

Pateman, Trevor. 1980. *Language, Truth and Politics*. Lewes: Stroud. [1975].

Paul, Hermann. 1891. *Prinzipien der Sprachgeschichte*. Halle/Saale: Niemeyer. (5th edn 1920; trans. H.A. Strong, *Introduction to the Study of the History of Language*. London).

Petöfi, János S. 1976. 'Formal pragmatics and a partial theory of texts'. In: Siegfried J. Schmidt (ed.), *Pragmatik/Pragmatics 2*. Munich: Fink. pp. 105–21.

Phillipson, Robert. 1991. *Linguistic Imperialism*. Cambridge: Cambridge University Press.

Piñon, Nélida. 1989. *The Republic of Dreams* (trans. Helen Lane). New York: Knopf. [Original title: *A república dos sonhos*. Rio de Janeiro: Alves. 1984].

Quine, Willard Van Orman. 1958. *Methods of Logic*. London: Routledge and Kegan Paul. [1950].

Qvortrup, Lars. 1979. *Danmarks Radio og arbejdskampen*. [Radio Denmark and the Labor Struggle]. Odense: Odense University Press. (= Bidrags Skriftserie, 2).

Rancière, Jacques. 1995. *La Mésentente*. Paris: Galilée.

Reichenbach, Hans. 1947. *Elements of Symbolic Logic*. New York: Free Press.

Reisman, Karl. 1989. 'Contrapuntal conversations in an Antiguan village'. In: Richard Bauman and Joel Sherzer (eds), *Explorations in the Ethnography of Speaking*. Cambridge: Cambridge University Press. pp. 110–24. [1974].

Reuland, Eric. 1979. *Principles of Subordination and Construal in the Grammar of Dutch*. Groningen: Dijkstra Niemeyer.

Riesbeck, Christopher K. and Roger C. Schank. 1987. *Inside Case-based Reasoning*. Hillsdale, N.J.: Erlbaum.

Riffaterre, Michel. 1960. 'Stylistic context'. *Word* 16:207–18.

Riffaterre, Michel. 1961. 'Vers la définition linguistique du style'. *Word* 17:318–44.

Rosaldo, Michelle. 1980. *Knowledge and Passion: Ilongot Notions of Self and Social Life.* Cambridge: Cambridge University Press.

Rosaldo, Michelle. 1982. 'The ways we do things with words: Ilongot speech acts and speech act theory in philosophy'. *Language in Society* 11:203–37.

Rosenbaum, Bent and Harly Sonne. 1986. *The Language of Psychosis.* New York and London: New York University Press. [Danish original: *Det er et bånd der taler.* Copenhagen: Gyldendal. 1979].

Rosten, Leo. 1968. *The Joys of Yiddish.* New York: Bantam Books.

Roth, Wolff-Michael. 2000. 'From gestures to scientific language'. *Journal of Pragmatics* 32(11):1683–1714.

Ruiz Mayo, Jaime. 1990. 'Rumor's delict (delight?) or: The pragmatics of a civil liberty'. *Journal of Pragmatics* 13(6):1009–12, 1034.

Rundquist, Suellen. 1992. 'Indirectness: a gender study of flouting Grice's maxims'. *Journal of Pragmatics* 18(5):431–49.

Sacks, Harvey. 1995. *Lectures on Conversation.* Vols I–II (Gail Jefferson, ed.). Oxford: Blackwell. [1992].

Sacks, Harvey, Emanuel Schegloff and Gail Jefferson. 1974. 'A simplest systematics for the organization of turn-taking in conversation'. *Language* 50(4):696–735.

Sadock, Jerry M. 1974. *Towards a Linguistic Theory of Speech Acts.* New York: Academic Press.

Sajavaara, Kari and Jaakko Lehtonen. 1996. 'The silent Finn revisited'. In: Jaworski, 1997. pp. 263–83.

Saussure, Ferdinand de. 1916. *Cours de linguistique générale.* Paris: Payot.

Saville-Troike, Muriel. 1982. *The Ethnography of Communication.* Oxford: Blackwell.

Schank, Roger C. 1981. *Dynamic Memory.* Hillsdale, N.J.: Erlbaum.

Schank, Roger C. 1984. *The Cognitive Computer.* Hillsdale, N.J.: Erlbaum.

Schank, Roger C. and Robert P. Abelson. 1977. *Scripts, Plans, Goals and Understanding.* Hillsdale, N.J.: Erlbaum.

Schank, Roger C. and Danny Edelson. 1990. 'A role for AI in education: using technology to reshape education'. *Journal of Artificial Intelligence in Education* 1(2):3–20.

Schegloff, Emanuel A. 1972. 'Sequencing in conversational openings'. In: John Gumperz and Dell Hymes (eds), *Directions in Sociolinguistics.* New York: Holt, Rinehart and Winston. pp. 346–80.

Schegloff, Emanuel A. and Harvey Sacks. 1973. 'Opening up closings'. *Semiotica* 7:289–327.

Schegloff, Emanuel A., Gail Jefferson and Harvey Sacks. 1977. 'The preference for self-correction in the organization of repair in conversation'. *Language* 53:361–82.

Schickel, Richard. 1971. 'The truth which dares not speak its name' (Review of Cooper 1971). *Harper's Magazine*, April. pp. 104–8.

Schiffrin, Deborah. 1988. *Discourse Markers.* Cambridge: Cambridge University Press.

Schön, Donald. 1979. 'Generative metaphor: a perspective on problem-setting in social policy'. In: Andrew Ortony (ed.), *Metaphor and Thought.* Cambridge: Cambridge University Press. pp. 254–83.

Scollon, Ron and Suzie B.K. Scollon. 1981. *Narrative, Literacy and Face in Interethnic Communication.* Norwood, N.J.: Ablex.

Scollon, Ron and Suzanne Wong Scollon. 1995. *Intercultural Communication*. Oxford: Blackwell.

Searle, John R. 1969. *Speech Acts: An Essay in the Philosophy of Language*. Cambridge: Cambridge University Press.

Searle, John R. 1975. 'Indirect speech acts'. In: Peter Cole and Jerry Morgan (eds), *Syntax and Semantics*, vol. 3: *Speech Acts*. New York: Academic Press. pp. 59–82.

Searle, John R. 1977. 'A classification of illocutionary acts'. In: Andy Rogers, Bob Wall and John P. Murphy (eds), *Proceedings of the Texas Conference on Performatives, Presuppositions, and Implicatures*. Washington, D.C.: Center for Applied Linguistics. pp. 27–45.

Searle, John R. 1979. 'The classification of illocutionary acts'. *Language in Society* 8:137–51.

Seuren, Pieter A.M. 1998. 'Presupposition'. In: Jacob L. Mey (ed.), *A Concise Encyclopedia of Pragmatics*. Oxford: Elsevier Science. pp. 740–51.

Shibatani, Masayoshi. 1998. 'Honorifics'. In: Jacob L. Mey (ed.), *A Concise Encyclopedia of Pragmatics*. Oxford: Elsevier Science. pp. 341–50.

Sidnell, Jack. 2000. (in press). 'Interruption and turn-taking in the Caribbean'. *Journal of Pragmatics*.

Silverstein, Michael. 1976. 'Shifters, linguistic categories and cultural description'. In: Keith H. Basso and Henry A. Selby (eds), *Meaning in Anthropology*. Albuquerque, N.M.: University of New Mexico Press. pp. 11–55.

Silverstein, Michael. 1992. 'The uses and utility of ideology: some reflections'. *Pragmatics* 2(3):311–23.

Silverstein, Michael. 1993. 'Metapragmatic discourse and metapragmatic function'. In: Lucy, 1993. pp. 33–57.

Silverstein, Michael. 1996. 'Achieving adequacy and commitment in pragmatics'. *Pragmatics* 7(4):625–33.

Simon, Herbert. 1969. *The Sciences of the Artificial*. (The Compton Lectures.) Cambridge, Mass.: MIT Press.

Skutnabb-Kangas, Tove and Robert Phillipson. 1994. 'Linguicide'. In: *Encyclopedia of Language and Linguistics*. Oxford: Pergamon. pp. 4:2211–12.

Smitherman, Geneva. 1984. 'Black language and power'. In: Cheris Kramarae, Muriel Schulz and William M. O'Barr (eds), *Language and Power*. Beverly Hills and London: Sage. pp. 101–15.

Spender, Dale. 1980. *Man Made Language*. London: Routledge and Kegan Paul.

Spender, Dale. 1984. 'Defining reality: a powerful tool'. In: Cheris Kramarae, Muriel Schulz and William M. O'Barr (eds), *Language and Power*. Beverly Hills and London: Sage. pp. 194–205.

Sperber, Dan and Deirdre Wilson. 1986. *Relevance: Communication and Cognition*. Cambridge, MA: Harvard University Press. [2nd edn 1995].

Stalnaker, R.C. 1977. 'Pragmatic presuppositions'. In: Andy Rogers, Bob Wall and John P. Murphy (eds), *Proceedings of the Texas Conference on Performatives, Presuppositions, and Implicatures*. Washington, D.C.: Center for Applied Linguistics. pp. 135–47. [1974].

Stalpers, Judith. 1993. 'Progress in discourse: The impact of foreign language use on business talk'. (Tilburg University Ph.D. thesis).

Strawson, Peter F. 1950. 'On referring'. *Mind* 59:320–44.

Streeck, Jürgen and Werner Kallmeyer. 2000. (in press). 'Interaction by inscription'. *Journal of Pragmatics*. (Focus-on Issue 'Embodiment').

Stubbs, Michael. 1983. *Discourse Analysis*. Oxford: Blackwell.

Talbot, Mary M. 1987. 'The pragmatic analysis of presuppositional phenomena in Levinson's *Pragmatics*'. *Acta Linguistica Hafniensia* 20:173–87.

Talbot, Mary M. 1994. 'Relevance'. In: *Encyclopedia of Language and Linguistics*. Oxford: Pergamon. pp. 6:3524–7.

Tannen, Deborah. 1984. *Conversational Style: Analyzing Talk among Friends*. Norwood, NJ: Ablex.

Taylor, James R. and François Cooren. 1997. 'What makes communication "organizational"?'. *Journal of Pragmatics* 27:409–38.

Thomas, Jenny. 1996. *Meaning in Interaction: An Introduction to Pragmatics*. London: Longman.

Tolstoy, Lev N. 1962. *Anna Karenina*, vols 1–2. Moskva: Izdatel'stvo Pravda. [1889].

Toolan, Michael. 1994. *Narrative: A Critical Linguistic Introduction*. London: Routledge. [1988].

Treichler, Paula A. 1989. 'From discourse to dictionary: how sexist meanings are authorized'. In: Frank and Treichler 1989. pp. 51–79.

Treichler, Paula A. and Francine Wattman Frank. 1989. 'Introduction: scholarship. feminism, and language change'. In: Frank and Treichler 1989. pp. 1–34.

Treichler, Paula A., Richard M. Frankel, Cheris Kramarae, Kathleen Zoppi and Howard B. Beckman. 1984. 'Problems and *Problems*: power relationships in a medical encounter'. In: Cheris Kramarae, Muriel Schulz and William M. O'Barr (eds), *Language and Power*. Beverly Hills and London: Sage. pp. 62–88.

Tsui, Amy B. 1991. 'Sequencing rules and coherence in discourse'. *Journal of Pragmatics* 15(2):111–29.

Tsur, Reuven. 1992. *Toward a Theory of Cognitive Poetics*. Amsterdam and New York: North Holland/Elsevier.

Tyler, Stephen A. 1967. *The Said and the Unsaid*. Houston, Tex.: Rice University Press.

Van der Auwera, Johan. 1985. *Language and Logic*. Amsterdam and Philadelphia: Benjamins. (= Pragmatics and Beyond Companion Series, vol. 4).

van Dijk, Teun A. 1977. *Text and Context*. London: Longman.

Verschueren, Jef. 1979. 'What people say they do with words'. Berkeley, Calif. (University of California Ph.D. diss.).

Verschueren, Jef. 1980. *On Speech Act Verbs*. Amsterdam and Philadelphia: Benjamins. (Pragmatics and Beyond, vol. I:4).

Verschueren, Jef. 1987. 'Pragmatics as a theory of linguistic adaptation'. In: *Working Document* #1. Antwerp: International Pragmatics Association.

Verschueren, Jef. 1999. *Understanding Pragmatics*. London: Arnold.

Wardhaugh, Ronald. 1986. *How Conversation Works*. Oxford: Blackwell.

Wardhaugh, Ronald. 1998. *An Introduction to Sociolinguistics*. Oxford: Blackwell. (3rd edn) [1992].

Watzlawick, Paul, Janet Helmick Beavin and Don D. Jackson. 1967. *Pragmatics of Human Communication. A Study of Interactional Patterns, Pathologies, and Paradoxes*. New York: Norton.

Weber, Max. 1978. *Economy and Society*. Berkeley, Calif.: University of California Press.

Weizenbaum, Joseph. 1966. 'ELIZA: a computer program for the study of natural language communication between man and machine'. *Communications of the ACM* 9:36–45.

Whorf, Benjamin L. 1969. *Language, Thought, and Reality* (John B. Carroll, ed.). Cambridge, Mass.: MIT Press. [1956].

Withers, Stacie. 1997. 'Silence and communication in art'. In: Jaworski 1997. pp. 351–66.

Wodak, Ruth, Peter Nowak, Johanna Pelikan, Helmut Gruber, Rudolf de Cillia and Richard Mitten. 1990. "*Wir sind alle unschuldige Täter*". *Diskurshistorische Studien zum Nachkriegsantisemitismus*. Frankfurt: Suhrkamp. (STW 881).

Wodak-Engel, Ruth. 1984. 'Determination of guilt: discourse in the courtroom'. In: Cheris Kramarae, Muriel Schulz and William M. O'Barr (eds), *Language and Power*. Beverly Hills and London: Sage. pp. 89–100.

Woolf, Virginia. 1978. *Jacob's Room*. New York: Harvest Books. [1922].

Yamaguchi, Haruhiko. 1997. 'Context and speech representation: towards a unified perspective on the metalinguistic use of language'. Second IALS Conference, Freiburg, Germany, September 1997.

Yngve, Victor. 1970. 'On getting a word in edge-wise'. *Chicago Linguistic Society* 6:567–78.

Subject Index

Name Index

当代国外语言学与应用语言学文库（升级版）
已出版书目

—— **Applied Linguistics 应用语言学**

Qualitative Research in Applied Linguistics: A Practical Introduction
《应用语言学中的质性研究实践导论》
Juanita Heigham & Robert A. Croker

—— **Cognitive Linguistics 认知语言学**

Cognitive Linguistics and Language Teaching
《认知语言学和语言教学》
Randal Holme

An Introduction to Cognitive Linguistics (Second Edition)
《认知语言学入门（第二版）》
F. Ungerer & H.-J. Schmid

Multimodality and Cognitive Linguistics
《多模态与认知语言学》
María Jesús Pinar Sanz

Women, Fire, and Dangerous Things: What Categories Reveal about the Mind
《女人、火与危险事物：范畴所揭示的心智》
George Lakoff

—— **Computational Linguistics 计算语言学**

Natural Language Processing and Computational Linguistics 1: Speech, Morphology and Syntax
《计算语言学概论（第一卷）：语音、词法、句法》
Mohamed Zakaria Kurdi

Natural Language Processing and Computational Linguistics 2: Semantics, Discourse and Applications
《计算语言学概论（第二卷）：语义、篇章、应用》
Mohamed Zakaria Kurdi

General Linguistics (Fourth Edition)
《普通语言学概论（第四版）》
R. H. Robins

An Introduction to Linguistics
《语言学入门》
Stuart C. Poole

Language
《语言论》
L. Bloomfield

Language: An Introduction to the Study of Speech
《语言论：言语研究导论》
Edward Sapir

——History of Linguistics 语言学史

A Short History of Linguistics (Fourth Edition)
《语言学简史（第四版）》
R. H. Robins

——Intercultural Communication 跨文化交际

Intercultural Communication: A Discourse Approach (Third Edition)
《跨文化交际：语篇分析法（第三版）》
Ron Scollon, Suzanne Wong Scollon & Rodney H. Jones

Intercultural Interaction: A Multidisciplinary Approach to Intercultural Communication
《跨文化互动：跨文化交际的多学科研究》
Helen Spencer-Oatey & Peter Franklin

——Language Education 语言教育

Approaches and Methods in Language Teaching (Third Edition)
《语言教学的流派（第三版）》
Jack C. Richards & Theodore S. Rodgers

A Course in English Language Teaching (Second Edition)
《语言教学教程：实践与理论（第二版）》
Penny Ur

Experiences of Second Language Teacher Education
《第二语言教师教育经验》
Tony Wright & Mike Beaumont

Principles of Language Learning and Teaching (Sixth Edition)
《语言学习与语言教学的原则（第六版）》
　　H. Douglas Brown

Teaching by Principles: An Interactive Approach to Language Pedagogy (Fourth Edition)
《根据原理教学：交互式语言教学（第四版）》
　　H. Douglas Brown & Heekyeong Lee

Usage-inspired L2 Instruction: Researched Pedagogy
《使用驱动的二语教学：实证依据》
　　Andrea E. Tyler, Lourdes Ortega, Mariko Uno & Hae In Park

——Neurolinguistics 神经语言学

The Handbook of the Neuropsychology of Language (2 Volume Set)
《语言的神经心理学手册》
　　Miriam Faust

Introduction to Neurolinguistics
《神经语言学导论》
　　Elisabeth Ahlsén

——Philosophy of Language 语言哲学

How to Do Things with Words
《如何以言行事》
　　J. L. Austin

——Phonetics and Phonology 语音学与音系学

English Phonetics and Phonology: A Practical Course (Fourth Edition)
《英语语音学与音系学实用教程（第四版）》
　　Peter Roach

——Pragmatics 语用学

Meaning in Interaction: An Introduction to Pragmatics
《言谈互动中的意义：语用学引论》
　　Jenny Thomas

Pragmatics: An Introduction (Second Edition)
《语用学引论（第二版）》
　　Jacob L. Mey

Relevance: Communication and Cognition (Second Edition)
《关联性：交际与认知（第二版）》
Dan Sperber & Deirdre Wilson

—— **Psycholinguistics 心理语言学**

The Articulate Mammal: An Introduction to Psycholinguistics (Fourth Edition)
《会说话的哺乳动物：心理语言学入门（第四版）》
Jean Aitchison

Research Methods in Psycholinguistics and the Neurobiology of Language: A Practical Guide
《心理语言学及语言的神经生物学研究方法实用指导》
Annette M. B. de Groot & Peter Hagoort

—— **Research Method 研究方法**

Projects in Linguistics and Language Studies: A Practical Guide to Researching Language (Third Edition)
《语言学课题：语言研究实用指导（第三版）》
Alison Wray & Aileen Bloomer

Research Perspectives on English for Academic Purposes
《学术英语的多维研究视角》
John Flowerdew & Matthew Peacock

—— **Second Language Acquisition 第二语言习得**

Fossilization in Adult Second Language Acquisition
《成人二语习得中的僵化现象》
韩照红（Zhaohong Han）

Innovative Research and Practices in Second Language Acquisition and Bilingualism
《二语习得与双语现象的创新研究及实践》
John W. Schwieter

Linguistics and Second Language Acquisition
《语言学和第二语言习得》
Vivian Cook

Second Language Learning and Language Teaching (Fifth Edition)
《第二语言学习与教学（第五版）》
Vivian Cook

Second Language Needs Analysis
《第二语言需求分析》
　　Michael H. Long

Tasks in Second Language Learning
《第二语言学习中的任务》
　　Virginia Samuda & Martin Bygate

Working Memory in Second Language Acquisition and Processing
《工作记忆与二语习得及加工》
　　温植胜（Edward），Mailce Borges Mota & Arthur McNeill

——Semantics 语义学

Analyzing Meaning: An Introduction to Semantics and Pragmatics (Second Edition)
《意义分析：语义学与语用学导论（第二版）》
　　Paul R. Kroeger

Meaning in Language: An Introduction to Semantics and Pragmatics (Third Edition)
《语言的意义：语义学与语用学导论（第三版）》
　　Alan Cruse

Semantics (Fourth Edition)
《语义学（第四版）》
　　John I. Saeed

——Sociolinguistics 社会语言学

The Handbook of Sociolinguistics
《社会语言学通览》
　　Florian Coulmas

An Introduction to Sociolinguistics (Seventh Edition)
《社会语言学引论（第七版）》
　　Ronald Wardhaugh & Janet M. Fuller

——Stylistics 文体学

The Bloomsbury Companion to Stylistics
《布鲁姆斯伯里文体学导论》
　　Violeta Sotirova

A Linguistic Guide to English Poetry
《英诗学习指南：语言学的分析方法》
　　Geoffrey N. Leech

Patterns in Language: Stylistics for Students of Language and Literature
《语言模式：文体学入门》
Joanna Thornborrow & Shân Wareing

Stylistics: A Practical Coursebook
《实用文体学教程》
Laura Wright & Jonathan Hope

——Syntax 句法学

Chomsky's Universal Grammar: An Introduction (Third Edition)
《乔姆斯基的普遍语法教程（第三版）》
V. J. Cook & Mark Newson

Syntax: A Generative Introduction (Fourth Edition)
《句法学：生成语法导论（第四版）》
Andrew Carnie

——Testing 语言测试

Assessing the Language of Young Learners
《少儿和青少年的语言测评》
Angela Hasselgreen & Gwendydd Caudwell

Designing Listening Tests: A Practical Approach
《英语听力测试设计指导》
Rita Green

Language Testing and Validation: An Evidence-Based Approach
《语言测试与效度验证：基于证据的研究方法》
Cyril J. Weir

Second Language Pronunciation Assessment: Interdisciplinary Perspectives
《二语语音评测：跨学科视角》
Talia Isaacs & Pavel Trofimovich

Statistical Analyses for Language Assessment
《语言测评中的统计分析》
Lyle F. Bachman & Antony J. Kunnan

Writing English Language Tests (Second Edition)
《英语测试（第二版）》
J. B. Heaton

——Text Linguistics 语篇语言学

The Language of Evaluation: Appraisal in English
《评估语言：英语评价系统》
J. R. Martin & P. R. R. White